BROADCASTING LAW

BROADCASTING LAW

A COMPARATIVE STUDY

ERIC BARENDT

CLARENDON PRESS · OXFORD

Oxford University Press, Walton Street, Oxford OX2 6DP
Oxford New York
Athens Auckland Bangkok Bombay
Calcutta Cape Town Dar es Salaam Delhi
Florence Hong Kong Istanbul Karachi
Kuala Lumpur Madras Madrid Melbourne
Mexico City Nairobi Paris Singapore
Taipei Tokyo Toronto
and associated companies in
Berlin Ibadan

Oxford is a trade mark of Oxford University Press

Published in the United States
by Oxford University Press Inc., New York

First published 1993
First issued in paperback (with corrections) 1995

British Library Cataloguing in Publication Data
Data available

Library of Congress Cataloging in Publication Data
Barendt, E. M.
Broadcasting law: a comparative study / E. M. Barendt.
p. cm.
Includes bibliographical references and index.
1. Broadcasting—Law and legislation—Great Britain.
2. Broadcasting—Law and legislation—Germany. 3. Broadcasting—Law and legislation—United States. 4. Broadcasting—Law and legislation—European Community countries. I. Title.
K4325.4.B37 1993 343.09'94—dc20 [342.3994] 93-15071

ISBN 0-19-825254-4
ISBN 0-19-826021-0 (pbk)

Printed in Great Britain
on acid-free paper by
Bookcraft Ltd., Midsomer Norton, Bath

Preface

My aim in writing this book has been to explore the regulation of broadcasting in five countries: Britain, France, Germany, Italy, and the United States. Generally it takes as its starting-point the law in the United Kingdom and then looks at the comparable rules in the other legal systems. There are occasional references to the law elsewhere, but no other national system is discussed in detail. Comparative law books should not attempt to be legal encyclopaedias. However, the book does conclude with a chapter on international and European law.

One theme is that there are significant differences in the regulation of broadcasting in European countries on the one hand and in the United States of America on the other. Although the principles of law in the former states are far from uniform, they have more in common with each other than they do with those on the other side of the Atlantic. Historical and cultural factors largely explain the divergence. But the interpretation of constitutional principles also contributes to these differences. The United States courts regard freedom of speech almost entirely as a liberty against the state, while constitutional courts in Europe treat it as a value which may sometimes compel government to act. In the broadcasting context that view justifies the regulation, for example, of programme standards and of advertising in the interests of viewers and listeners. Government must act to promote broadcasting freedom, not merely refrain from interfering with it.

Constitutional considerations have, of course, played no part in the development of British broadcasting law. The fact that in many respects it is similar to that in, say, France or Germany may show the relative unimportance of constitutions and Bills of Rights. But that would be a complacent and erroneous inference. Increasingly, broadcasters in the United Kingdom, particularly but not exclusively the BBC, are vulnerable to political pressure. They cannot rely on the law, as the German public broadcasting corporations have done, to protect their independence. Also the government alone may decide the scope of anti-trust and merger laws, which are necessary if plurality of opinion is to be protected; British courts cannot correct unprincipled measures, as constitutional courts can in other European jurisdictions. Put briefly, broadcasting freedom in Britain only exists under weak conventions, which can easily be disregarded by confident (or arrogant) governments.

This book makes no attempt to deal with every aspect of law concerning radio and television. There is, for example, no discussion of the rules of libel and contempt of court. Only fleeting reference is made to copyright law. Indeed, private law issues are only raised in the chapter on advertising, where there is a discussion of the use of moral rights to control the excessive interruption of films on television. Instead, I have concentrated on the central regulatory questions: the relationship of public and private broadcasting, the scope and enforcement of programme standards, the application of anti-trust laws, and the access of political parties, groups, and individuals to the media. There is, therefore, room for other comparative studies of branches of the law not covered here.

I did much of the research for this book at the European University Institute, Florence, where I spent the academic year 1987–8 as a Jean Monnet Fellow. I am grateful both to the Institute for a very happy year, as well as to St Catherine's College, Oxford, which granted me extended study leave for that period. I would also like to thank the Max-Planck Institute for International and Comparative Public Law, Heidelberg, and the Department of Public Law of the University of Rome for their hospitality. Conversations in Rome with Professor Alessandro Pace were particularly valuable in enriching my knowledge of Italian law. I owe an enormous debt to colleagues and students at University College London for their thoughts and support during the last two years when this book has been completed.

Sandra Coliver and Monroe Price both read several chapters and made valuable suggestions on points of substance and style. Others helped by drawing my attention to literature I would otherwise not have read or by commenting on particular chapters: Sabine Astheimer, Walter Berka, Alan Boyle, Sabino Cassese, Giuseppe Corasaniti, Bruno De Witte, Marc Franklin, Dieter Grimm, James Michael, Giuseppe Rao, Martin Schellenberg, Didier Truchet, Ad van Loon, and Richard Whish. I am very grateful to all of them, and take responsibility for the errors which remain. Finally, I should like to thank Sylvia Lough and Jevon White, who have tutored me in the still exciting art of word-processing.

Broadcasting law in any one country changes so rapidly that it is difficult to be up to date. With five countries to consider, the enterprise is doomed to failure. Nevertheless, I have attempted to take developments up to October 1992 into account.

ERIC BARENDT

November 1992

Preface to the Paperback Edition

I have been able in this paperback edition to correct some errors in the original text, revise the bibliography, and add a short postscript. This final chapter concentrates on developments in the last two years in the United Kingdom, in particular the proposals in the 1994 White Paper for the future of the BBC. I would have liked to have covered as comprehensively recent events in other European countries. But it is difficult to do justice to such a rapidly changing subject in one country, let alone three or four; it seemed, therefore, sensible to be selective in the discussion of continental European material. I am grateful to Dieter Grimm, Albrecht Hesse, and Alessandro Pace for their assistance in this respect.

ERIC BARENDT

October 1994

Contents

A Note on Abbreviations

Some of the abbreviations used in the notes in this book will be unfamiliar. References to French, German, and Italian periodical literature may need some explanation, so a short list of abbreviations is appended.

FRENCH ABBREVIATIONS

AJDA	*L'Actualité Juridique—Droit Administratif*
Rev. fr. droit adm.	*Revue française de droit administratif*
RIDA	*Revue internationale du droit d'auteur*

GERMAN ABBREVIATIONS

AöR	*Archiv des Öffentlichen Rechts*
DÖV	*Die Öffentliche Verwaltung*
DVBl.	*Deutsches Verwaltungsblatt*
EuGRZ	*Europäische Grundrechtezeitschrift*
NJW	*Neue Juristische Wochenschrift*
JZ	*Juristenzeitung*
ZUM	*Zeitschrift für Urheber- und Medienrecht*

ITALIAN ABBREVIATIONS

Giur. cost.	*Giurisprudenza costituzionale*
Giur. it.	*Giurisprudenza italiana*
Foro amm.	*Foro amministrativo*
Riv. trim. di diritt. pubb.	*Rivista trimestrale di diritto pubblico*

Secondly, a number of works are referred to frequently, so that in their case for reasons of space reference in the footnotes is given only to the author or a short-title. These works are:

Debbasch	C. Debbasch, *Les Grand Arrêts du droit de l'audiovisuel* (Paris, 1991).
Franklin and Anderson	M. A. Franklin and D. A. Anderson, *Mass Media Law*, 4th edn. (New York, 1990).
Humphreys	P. J. Humphreys, *Media and Media Policy in West Germany* (Oxford, 1990).
Pace	A. Pace, *Stampa, giornalismo, radiotelevisione* (Padua, 1983).

Powe	L. A. Powe, *American Broadcasting and the First Amendment* (Berkeley, Calif., 1987).
Il sistema radiotelevisivo	E. Roppo and R. Zaccaria (eds.), *Il sistema radiotelevisivo pubblico e privato* (Milan, 1991).

Table of British Statutes

Table of Cases

TABLE OF BRITISH CASES

TABLE OF FRENCH CASES

TABLE OF GERMAN CASES

TABLE OF ITALIAN CASES

TABLE OF UNITED STATES CASES

Island Trees School District *v.* Pico 457 US 853 (1982) 38

Johnson & Walton *v.* FCC 829 F.2d. 157 (DC Cir. 1987) 173, 187

Kennedy for President Committee *v.* FCC (Kennedy I) 636 F.2d. 417
(DC Cir. 1980) 172, 187

Kennedy for President Committee *v.* FCC (Kennedy II) 636 F.2d. 432
(DC Cir. 1980) 175

KFKB Broadcasting Association *v.* Federal Radio Commission, 47 F.2d. 670
(DC Cir. 1931) 29

Meredith Corp. *v.* FCC 809 F.2d. 863 (DC Cir. 1987)........................161

Midwest Video Corp. *v.* FCC 571 F.2d. 1025 (8th Cir. 1978)........... 165, 166

Morrisson *v.* Mt. Mansfield Television 580 F.Supp. 512 (DC Vt. 1974) 175

Muir *v.* Alabama Educational Television Commission 656 F.2d. 1012
(5th Cir. 1981) 38, 49

National Broadcasting Co. *v.* FCC 516 F.2d. 1101 (DC Cir. 1975) 160

National Broadcasting Co. *v.* United States 319 US 190 (1943) 29, 30, 125

National Citizens' Committee for Broadcasting & Friends of the Earth
v. FCC 567 F.2d. 1095 (DC Cir. 1977) 160

Neckritz *v.* FCC 502 F.2d. 411 (DC Cir. 1974) 160

(The) Network Project *v.* CPB 561 F.2d. 963 (DC Cir. 1977) 49

Office of Communication of United Church of Christ *v.* FCC 359 F.2d. 994
(DC Cir. 1966) 49, 94, 116, 119

Ohralik *v.* Ohio State Bar 436 US 447 (1978) 192

Preferred Communications *v.* City of Los Angeles 754 F.2d. 1396
(9th Cir. 1985), 476 US 488 (1986) 7, 165

Public Media Center *v.* FCC 587 F.2d. 1322 (DC Cir. 1978) 104, 159

Quincy Cable TV Inc. *v.* FCC 768 F.2d. 1434 (DC Cir. 1985) 110, 165

Red Lion Broadcasting Co. *v.* FCC 395 US 367 (1969) 5, 30, 47, 147,
158–9, 161, 162, 187, 244

Retail Store Employees Union Local 880 *v.* FCC 436 F.2d. 248
(DC Cir. 1970) 160

Syracuse Peace Council *v.* FCC 867 F.2d. 654 (DC Cir. 1989), cert. denied,
110 S. Ct. 717 (1990) 33, 106, 161

Telecommunications Research and Action Center *v.* FCC, 801 F.2d. 501
(DC Cir. 1986) 161

Trinity Methodist Church *v.* Federal Radio Commission, 62 F.2d. 850
(DC Cir. 1932) 29

Turner Broadcasting System *v.* FCC 129 L. Ed. 2d. 497 (1994) 244, 252

Table of Decisions of the European Court of Justice

Table of Decisions of the European Commission and Court of Human Rights

I
The Historical and Constitutional Background

I. INTRODUCTION

Broadcasting is an activity of enormous political and social significance. For many people it constitutes their principal source of information and entertainment. Politicians believe that elections are won and lost on the nation's television sets. The broadcasting media are also of economic importance, both as service industries in themselves and in providing outlets for advertising. It is therefore hardly surprising that there have been sharp disputes about the appropriateness and character of broadcasting regulation, and further that in many countries there is a constitutional dimension to these disputes. In Britain arguments about the structure and control of radio and television are resolved politically rather than by the courts. But parliamentary debate on these questions is vigorous and may touch points of principle which in other countries would probably be brought before constitutional tribunals.[1]

Broadcasting law is a well-developed subject in many continental European jurisdictions and in the United States. Recourse to the courts is relatively common in these countries (compared to Britain) because broadcasting law is subject to constitutional constraints. In Germany broadcasting freedom (*Rundfunkfreiheit*) is specifically protected by the Basic Law, whereas elsewhere courts have applied the constitutional guarantee of freedom of speech (and of the press) to the newer media. (The relationship between broadcasting freedom and the underlying freedom of speech is considered in the second chapter of this book.) The contributions of the German and Italian Constitutional Courts to the development of their broadcasting systems have been particularly striking.[2] Among the issues they have determined have been the legitimacy of the public broadcasting monopoly and the permissible scope of pro-

[1] This is illustrated by the debates in both Houses of Parliament on the Broadcasting Bill 1990, e.g. concerning the requirement of 'due impartiality' and the restrictions on cross-media ownership (that is, the ownership by one person or group of interests in both press and broadcasting).

[2] See E. M. Barendt, 'The Influence of the German and Italian Constitutional Courts on their National Broadcasting Systems' [1991] *Pub. Law* 93.

gramme standards. Another major question addressed by many constitutional tribunals is the application of anti-trust law to the media.[3] In all these cases the constitutional question is how far the particular type of broadcasting regulation is compatible with, or alternatively required by, the freedom of speech (or broadcasting) clause. Of course broadcasting cases may involve issues of administrative, competition, or election law, or indeed questions of private law, but even they often have a constitutional dimension.

A fundamental assumption underpins broadcasting law, or at least that central part of it which is the concern of constitutional courts. It is that broadcasting, unlike the press, should be subject to a degree of special regulation beyond the general law of libel, confidentiality, obscenity, and so on. The assumption has existed since the inception of radio in the 1920s. At first, it was used to justify the public broadcasting monopoly, at any rate when that was called into question. Later it was invoked in support of restrictions on the freedom of private commercial broadcasters to devise their programme schedules—restrictions which, imposed on newspaper editors, would have been regarded as intolerable interferences with press freedom. In the last decade, however, the assumption has been widely challenged, particularly in American academic writing. Further, technical developments, such as the advent of cable and satellite, have made it harder to defend a pattern of regulation, which perhaps made more sense when there was only a handful of terrestrial channels.

The justifications for subjecting radio and television to a special degree of regulation are fully considered in the next section of this chapter. In fact the controls on broadcasting are now being reduced. This is most clearly the case in the United States, where in the last few years the Federal Communications Commission (FCC) has repealed most of the restrictions previously imposed on licensees. Similar developments have occurred in Britain and France, though deregulation in European jurisdictions has not gone nearly so far. Arguably, even in Europe, the regulation which remains in force is increasingly of a cosmetic character. Regulatory authorities may not really intend to enforce certain rules, such as those requiring channels to show a number of serious programmes, or these requirements may in practice be unenforceable. Other rules, such as those restricting advertising to 20 per cent of transmission time, may be so generous as only to have symbolic value.[4] While there may be some truth in these observations, it remains the case that broadcasters are generally subject to constraints which are not imposed on their colleagues in the press. For example, broadcasting laws frequently impose duties on

[3] These rules are discussed in Ch. VI below.

[4] See W. Hoffman-Riem, 'Law, Politics and the New Media: Trends in Broadcasting Regulation' (1986) 9 *West European Politics* 125, 134–44.

licensees to be impartial and not to take an editorial line; there is also a standard requirement in European jurisdictions that broadcasters show a certain proportion of material produced in those countries.[5] Whatever the position may be in the United States, the age of broadcasting deregulation can hardly be said to have arrived in Europe.

Indeed, in one respect there is now more European broadcasting law than there used to be. Both the European Community (EC) and the Council of Europe have recently introduced measures designed to facilitate the transmission of television broadcasts across their member states' frontiers. States must not prevent the reception in their territories of programmes from other states which satisfy the standards laid down in these instruments. Underlying the measures is the desire to ease the provision of commercial services across national borders as well as the wish to realize the dream of greater cultural unity. Further, it is no longer practicable with the arrival of satellite and cable to regulate broadcasting purely at a national level. It is likely that EC law will continue to develop, particularly in the area of competition and mergers regulation.

The two European measures, fully discussed in Chapter X, apply only to television and not to radio. An explanation is that there has been no interference since the last world war with the transmission of radio programmes across boundaries in Western Europe. But their scope also reflects the diminished importance these days of the older broadcasting medium. This is a far cry from attitudes in the immediate post-war period, when radio was regarded as the more significant cultural force. Indeed, it was for that reason that in Britain the BBC monopoly of radio was sustained long after the introduction of commercial television.[6] Most of the interesting law, statutory and constitutional, discussed in this book concerns television rather than radio. The latter is discussed separately only when the relevant rules are in important respects different from those applicable to television. This does not imply that radio is of little significance, but only that more controversies, including those taken to court, concern the other medium.

2. WHY REGULATE BROADCASTING?

The justifications for the legal regulation of broadcasting have been vigorously contested in academic literature, most particularly in the United States of America, and to some extent now in public and political

[5] For detailed discussion, see Ch. V (impartiality rule and other programme standards) and Ch. X (European quota rules).

[6] See the discussion in B. Sendall, *Independent Television in Britain*, i: *Origin and Foundation, 1946–62* (London, 1982), 10–14.

debate.[7] In countries other than Britain the arguments have a constitutional dimension. Some of the points discussed here have been made in judgments of the courts, albeit in an abbreviated form. The central question is: Why should radio and television be subject to a significantly greater degree of regulation than that applied to newspapers and other media, for example, the theatre and (in some countries) the cinema? Broadcasters must be impartial and must show news and (usually) some other serious programmes, whereas the press is free to publish what it wants, subject only to the constraints of the criminal and civil law.

A number of rationales have been put forward to justify broadcasting regulation. Four will be discussed here in detail, though the exposition is far from exhaustive.[8] The first is that, because the airwaves are a public resource, the government (or some agency on its behalf) is entitled to license their use for broadcasting on the terms it sees fit. A similar argument can now be deployed in respect of cable broadcasting, where an authority must give permission before roads can be dug up for laying cable. The case is unconvincing, for it infers that it is right for government to regulate broadcasting from the fact that it has the opportunity to do this. It would be perfectly possible for government (or a licensing authority) to allocate frequencies or cable franchises without programme conditions on the basis of a competitive tender and allow their resale by the purchaser. Indeed, such schemes have been advocated by free-market liberals.[9] The first argument therefore does not work. It does not begin to justify broadcasting regulation, but at most explains how it is feasible. (It has also been objected that governments act improperly if they use their licensing powers to purchase broadcasters' constitutional rights of free speech.[10] That argument is less persuasive, as it assumes that broadcasters do enjoy the same (constitutional) rights of free speech as individuals talking in a bar or leafleting in a high street.)

The second rationale, the scarcity argument, has almost certainly been the most widely deployed. The frequencies for broadcasting, it is said, are very limited. It is impossible for everyone to acquire a licence to broadcast or to enjoy access to air his or her views on radio or television (whether public or private). Therefore, government may reason-

[7] In Britain the classic discussion is to be found in the Peacock Committee Report on Financing the BBC (1986) Cmnd. 9824.

[8] For some of the rich USA literature, see H. Kalven, 'Broadcasting, Public Policy and the First Amendment' (1967) 10 *Jo. of Law and Economics* 15; L. C. Bollinger, 'Freedom of the Press and Public Access' (1976) 75 *Mich. L. Rev.* 1; I. de Sola Pool, *Technologies of Freedom* (Cambridge, Mass., 1983), *passim*, but esp. ch. 6; S. L. Carter, 'Technology, Democracy and the Manipulation of Consent' (1984) 93 *Yale L. Rev.* 581; Powe, ch. 11.

[9] See R. Coase, 'The Federal Communications Commission' (1959) 2 *Jo. of Law and Economics* 1.

[10] Powe, 199.

ably require licensees to share their privilege with other representative members of the public, and may compel them to present a balanced range of programmes in the interests of listeners and viewers. In short broadcasters' rights may properly be regulated. The classic judicial expression of this view is to be found in the famous Supreme Court decision in *Red Lion Broadcasting Co.* v. *FCC*:[11] 'When there are substantially more individuals who want to broadcast than frequencies to allocate, it is idle to posit an unabridgeable First Amendment right comparable to the right of every individual to speak, write, or publish.' The limited number of frequencies has also been used by the Constitutional Courts in Germany and Italy to justify a public broadcasting monopoly.[12]

The argument is, however, less clear than appears at first sight. Does, for example, the scarcity of frequencies refer to the limited number *allocated* by the government as available for broadcasting or to the actual *numerical shortage* of broadcasting stations?[13] If the former, it can be argued that the scarcity is an artificial creation of the government (rather than a natural phenomenon) since it reserves a number of frequencies for the use of the army, police, and other public services; government is then not in a good position to argue for restrictions on broadcasters' freedom. Further, economic liberals contend that if broadcasting licences were sold to the highest bidders (as happened in Britain in 1991), and they were then free to sell them, there would probably not be an excess of those wishing to broadcast over the supply of frequencies. That problem arises when a government chooses to award licences for nothing (or at below market price). On the alternative formulation of actual scarcity, it has been pointed out that in the United States there has been an increase in the number of broadcasting stations during the last twenty years, while there are fewer newspapers than there used to be.[14] Comparable developments have occurred in European countries in the same period, especially since the advent of cable and satellite.

The scarcity argument cannot easily be divorced from economic considerations. The German Constitutional Court, for instance, coupled them when it held positive regulation of the broadcasting media constitutionally necessary. The shortage of frequencies and the high costs of starting up broadcasting channels explained their dearth in comparison with the numbers (in 1961) of newspapers and magazines.[15] However, it

[11] 395 US 367, 388 (1969).
[12] See the *First Television* case, 12 BVerfGE 205, 262 (1961), and Decision 59/1960 of the Italian Constitutional Court [1960] *Giur. cost.* 759.
[13] See the judgment of Starr J. in the Court of Appeals in *Syracuse Peace Council* v. *FCC* 867 F. 2d. 654 (1990).
[14] See Powe, 204–8.
[15] See 12 BVerfGE 205, 262 (1961).

is now probably as difficult to finance a new newspaper as it is a private television channel, if not more so. Certainly that is true if a comparison is made between the costs of setting up a national newspaper and a local community radio station. Yet anybody rich enough to afford the former is free to publish what he wants, while there are (in most countries) limits on what the latter may broadcast. If, on the other hand, it is relatively easy to enter the press market, it may be hard to see why policy-makers should be so concerned about the prohibitive costs of instituting a broadcasting station: those unable to afford that would be able to communicate effectively in other ways.[16]

Finally the scarcity argument is much less tenable now than it used to be. Cable and satellite have significantly increased the number of available or potentially available channels, so that there are more broadcasting outlets than there are daily newspapers (national and local), though it is harder to calculate the respective numbers of television or radio stations and specialist magazines. Whether an unregulated broadcasting market would offer the variety of choice afforded by the print media is another matter. The point is only that the scarcity argument hardly works to justify the different legal regimes applicable to the two media.

The third major argument for the differential treatment emphasizes the character of the broadcasting media. Television and radio, it is said, are more influential on public opinion than the press, or at least are widely thought to be. In the *Pacifica* case the United States Supreme Court majority said that they intrude into the home, are more pervasive, and are more difficult to control than the print media.[17] In particular, it is hard to prevent children from being exposed to broadcasts, while it is relatively easy to stop them looking at magazines and papers (which in any case they may not be able to read or purchase). These claims underpin the extension of legal control in Britain over violent and sexually explicit programmes (through the establishment of the Broadcasting Standards Council) and the strengthening of the impartiality rules.[18]

A somewhat different version of this argument has been formulated by the German Constitutional Court in the *Third Television* case:[19] regulation is necessary to guarantee pluralism and programme variety, whether or not there is now a shortage of frequencies and other broadcasting outlets. The free market will not provide for broadcasting the

[16] See Bollinger, 'Freedom of the Press and Public Access', 11.

[17] *FCC* v. *Pacifica Foundation* 438 US 726 (1978): see Ch. V, S. 4 below. Also see the reasoning of the German Constitutional Court in the *Lebach* case, 35 BVerfGE 202 (1973), where it was held that a television programme is more damaging to privacy rights than a comparable press report.

[18] For a full discussion of these changes, see Ch. V below.

[19] 57 BVerfGE 295, 322–3 (1981).

same variety found in the range of press and magazine titles. It follows that programme content should be regulated and that media monopolies should be cut down by the application of anti-trust laws. The implications of these propositions may differ from those which flow from the *Pacifica* rationale; but both the United States and German arguments lay stress on the power of television and its unique capacity to influence the public.

The arguments are difficult to assess. Broadcasting does not intrude into the home unless listeners and viewers want it to. From the point of view of constitutional principle, it is not easy to justify the imposition of greater limits on the medium on the ground that it is more influential than the written word. It cannot be right to subject more persuasive types of speech to greater restraints than those imposed on less effective varieties. On the other hand, the Court majority in the *Pacifica* case was probably right to regard broadcasting (particularly television) as a 'uniquely pervasive presence' in the lives of most people. Regrettable though it may be, much more time is spent watching television than reading; further, the presence of sound and picture in the home makes it an exceptionally potent medium. It may also be harder to stop children having access to 'adult material' on television than to pornographic magazines. This may not apply to subscription channels, enjoyment of which is dependent on a special decoder, and there may therefore be more tolerance of explicit films on these channels.[20] Finally, experience in the United States (and more recently in Italy) suggests that a free broadcasting market does not produce the same variety as the press and book publishing markets do.

These first three justifications for broadcasting regulation are inconclusive. There may still be something to the scarcity rationale, and it is probably true that broadcasting is the most influential medium of communication. But it is doubtful whether the case is powerful enough to justify the radically different legal treatment of the press and broadcasting media. A separate question is whether it is appropriate to continue to treat radio in the same way as television. There is generally a large choice of local, if not national, radio programmes, and it is hard to believe that they exercise a dominating influence on the formation of public attitudes.[21] A similar question arises for cable television.[22] Although a permit must be obtained from a licensing authority, several franchises

[20] The Broadcasting Standards Council considered applying different standards to subscription channels, but rejected this, largely because it felt that uniform standards would be more acceptable.

[21] Perhaps for these reasons the strict 'due impartiality' constraint is not applicable to local radio in Britain: see Ch. V, S. 2 below for further discussion.

[22] The United States courts have been unsure whether to treat cable as similar to the press or to terrestrial broadcasting when ruling on the constitutionality of its regulation: see P. Parsons, *Cable Television and the First Amendment* (Lexington, Mass., 1987). Among the leading cases are: *Berkshire Cablevision* v. *Burke* 571 F. Supp. 976 (D. R.I. 1983) and *Preferred Communications* v. *City of Los Angeles* 754 F. 2d. 1396 (9th Cir. 1985), 476 US 488 (1986).

may be physically accommodated and a wideband cable system may be able to carry up to thirty or forty or even more channels. The scarcity rationale therefore seems inapplicable to cable, and, further, it is hard to believe that this mode of broadcasting exercises such a strong influence that stringent programme regulation is justifiable.[23]

The last argument for the divergent treatment of the press and broadcasting media has been made by a leading American scholar, Lee Bollinger.[24] He admits that there is no fundamental difference in the character of the two mass media. But they have been perceived as different, a phenomenon to be explained in terms of their history. Broadcasting is still a relatively new means of mass communication, and it is understandable that society has wanted to regulate it, just as it has treated the cinema with more caution than it has the theatre.[25] Bollinger's case is, however, not based solely on tradition. He justifies the divergent treatment of the two media on the ground that society is entitled to remedy the deficiencies of an unregulated press with a regulated broadcasting system. That may be preferable to attempting to regulate both sectors. Regulation poses the danger of government control, a risk which is reduced if one branch of the media is left free.

This seems an unsatisfactory compromise. It does not appeal to the advocates of broadcasting deregulation.[26] If regulation of the press is always wrong (and perhaps unconstitutional) and if there is no significant difference between its position and that of the broadcasting media, it follows that the latter should also be wholly unregulated. On those assumptions, Bollinger's case would appear to lack coherence.[27] For it attempts to justify the unequal treatment of the liberties of broadcasters and newspaper proprietors and editors, when in all material respects their position is identical.

The argument is also unconvincing from the opposite perspective that regulation of the broadcasting media compensates for the weaknesses of an unregulated press. Suppose one shares Bollinger's view that there are powerful arguments for regulating the press, for example, by mandating in some circumstances rights of reply or access to it. His argument is that

[23] The obligations imposed on the providers of cable programmes by the British Broadcasting Act 1990 are lighter than those imposed on Channel 3 licensees: see Ch. V below.

[24] See his article 'Freedom of the Press and Public Access' and his essay 'The Rationale of Public Regulation of the Media', in J. Lichtenberg (ed.), *Democracy and the Mass Media*, (Cambridge, 1990), 355.

[25] In Britain the cinema is still subject to pre-distribution censorship, abolished for the theatre in 1968.

[26] Powe's book *American Broadcasting and the First Amendment* was written in response to Bollinger's thesis.

[27] For the requirement of coherence and integrity in law, see R. M. Dworkin, *Law's Empire* (London, 1986), ch. 6.

we have become used to an unregulated press and that there are good reasons for only regulating one part of the mass media. The question is then whether it makes sense to correct the (alleged) shortcomings of the press by regulating the broadcasting media to ensure that they are not repeated there. This is doubtful. In Britain, for instance, the press is overwhelmingly sympathetic to the Conservative Party, while broadcasters must not express their views and their programmes must be impartial. These latter restraints will only remedy a lack of balance in the newspaper industry on the assumption that otherwise broadcasters would also present predominantly Conservative programmes. However, the government imposed a tougher impartiality requirement in the Broadcasting Act 1990, because (some of) its supporters felt television and radio programmes were too left-wing![28]

In short the partial remedy of regulating one sector of the media to correct market defects in the other is clumsy. Indeed, in some circumstances it makes the situation worse. Nevertheless, Bollinger is surely right to see in history and tradition rather than in abstract reason the explanation for the divergent treatment of the two media. It is hard to imagine that, if the press and broadcasting media had evolved at the same time, one would have been regulated and the other not. This insight, however, does not answer the question what should be done now, during a period when the character of both media is changing and in particular when there is a radical expansion in the number and modes of broadcasting outlets. The usual view is that, in the absence of convincing arguments for any difference between the press and broadcasting, the latter should be deregulated. The alternative, less often considered, is that some regulation of the press could be contemplated, for example, through the application of stronger competition and merger controls and the provision of legally enforceable rights of reply.[29]

There is therefore no convincing explanation for the regulation of the broadcasting media in contrast to the liberal regime enjoyed by the press. Nevertheless, constitutional courts in Germany and Italy, as well as at times the United States Supreme Court, have accepted that free speech principles should be applied differently to the two media. While newspaper proprietors and editors enjoy the same rights of freedom of speech as individuals speaking in their homes and gardens, the freedom of broadcasters to speak and to draw up their own programme schedules may legitimately be limited. Indeed the legislatures in Germany and Italy have been required to draw up positive rules to ensure that listeners and

[28] For further discussion, see Ch. V below.

[29] For the view that structural regulation of the press is not contrary to freedom of speech and of the press, see J. Lichtenberg, 'Foundations and Limits of Freedom of the Press', in *Democracy and the Mass Media*, 102.

viewers enjoy access to a wide range of programmes and opinions on radio and television. This theme is developed in the next chapter.

3. FIVE LEGAL SYSTEMS

This final section describes the principal constitutional provisions and statutes regulating broadcasting in five legal systems. As many of the more important substantive rules are discussed at length in later chapters, the principal concern of these pages is to highlight the main characteristics of the different regimes. The position in Britain is striking because of the complete absence of constitutional principles and the relative dearth of case-law. In contrast there is a great deal of constitutional law in Germany and Italy, while recently the Conseil constitutionnel has significantly influenced French broadcasting legislation. The First Amendment has also played an important role in the history of broadcasting regulation in the United States, though relatively few cases have been taken as far as the Supreme Court. Further, the courts in that country have not been required to say anything about the relationship of public and private broadcasting, since the former is of relatively little importance. In contrast the Constitutional Courts in Germany and Italy have often ruled on this question, in some respects the most fundamental contemporary issue in broadcasting regulation.

(i) Great Britain

The legal history of broadcasting in Britain goes back to 1922, when the first licence was granted to the British Broadcasting Company to operate eight stations. The Company was originally a commercial enterprise manufacturing wireless sets, but after the appointment of John Reith as its General Manager at the end of 1922 it gradually became more imbued with the public service approach to broadcasting. (Reith subsequently became the first and very powerful Director-General of the Corporation.) The Company's position was twice reviewed by government committees in the 1920s. The Sykes Committee considered that overall state control of radio was essential in view of its influence on public opinion, but rejected operation of the medium by the state.[30] It was equally opposed to censorship and even contemplated that at some stage the Postmaster-General (then the responsible minister) might permit the establishment of private radio stations. While it was hostile to

[30] Sykes Committee on Broadcasting (1923) Cmd. 1951. For a history of public broadcasting in Britain, see the magisterial four-volume work by A. Briggs, *The History of Broadcasting in the United Kingdom* (Oxford, 1961–79), and R. H. Coase, *British Broadcasting: A Study in Monopoly* (London, 1950).

advertising, the Committee was relatively well disposed to the financing of programmes by sponsorship. It envisaged, however, a licence fee, levied on persons possessing a radio set, as the principal source of broadcasting finance.

The short report of the Crawford Committee in 1925 was more influential in shaping the legal development of British broadcasting.[31] It considered that radio should remain a public monopoly, in contradistinction to the United States system of 'free and uncontrolled transmission'.[32] But the Company should be reorganized as a Commission, either under a special statute or as a public company limited by guarantee. The government instead opted for the establishment of the British Broadcasting Corporation by Royal Charter, a decision which was designed to reflect the special status of the BBC and its independence from day-to-day scrutiny by the House of Commons. The first Charter was granted to run for ten years from 1 January 1927.

The Charter has been renewed periodically at intervals since that date. It is the primary constituent instrument, setting out the responsibilities of the BBC and its Governors and arranging for the appointment of Advisory Committees. But it is the Licence and Agreement made between the BBC and the responsible minister (now the National Heritage Secretary) which is of greater legal interest: it prohibits the BBC from expressing its own opinion on current political and social issues and from receiving revenue from advertising or commercial sponsorship. Further, it is under the Licence that a direction may be given not to broadcast a particular matter, a power exercised recently to ban interviews with supporters of Irish terrorist organizations.[33] It was at first used to stop the BBC broadcasting on any matter of controversy, but this restriction was lifted in March 1928.

The BBC monopoly continued until 1954. It was scarcely challenged before the Second World War,[34] but afterwards there were voices advocating its reconsideration.[35] The post-war Labour government favoured its retention, as did the majority of the Beveridge Committee, which examined broadcasting policy from 1949 to 1951.[36] But for the first time there was a note of official dissent. The minority report of Selwyn Lloyd, MP, favoured the introduction of commercial broadcasting. In his view a

[31] Crawford Committee on Broadcasting (1925) Cmd. 2599.

[32] Ibid., para. 4. This view of the American position was not exactly fair, and further the choice the Committee posed between chaos on the airwaves and a public monopoly was a false one.

[33] Cl. 13(4): see Ch. II, S. 2 below.

[34] The Ullswater Committee on Broadcasting (1936) Cmd. 5091 did not think this was an issue worthy of mention.

[35] See Coase, *British Broadcasting*, chs. 7 and 8.

[36] Beveridge Committee on Broadcasting (1951) Cmd. 8116.

monopoly, whether public or private, was dangerous; the position of the BBC was as anomalous as would be that of a British Press or Publishing Corporation. He rejected the argument that the monopoly was necessary to preserve programme standards. The Conservative government which took office in 1951 decided to introduce commercial television, but not radio. It was in the latter area that the BBC had established its reputation, and there was a greater willingness to countenance an experiment with the newer medium.[37]

The Television Act 1954 established the Independent Television Authority (ITA), the function of which was to enter into contracts with programme companies for the broadcast of commercial programmes. The service was organized on a regional basis, eventually licences being issued for fifteen separate areas. These ranged in size from the larger, more populated areas such as London, the Midlands, and Yorkshire to small regions like the Borders and the Channel Islands. In law the ITA was the broadcaster; therefore it had authority to censor a programme which a programme contractor proposed to put in the schedule. Indeed, it had reserve powers to make programmes itself, if that proved necessary to achieve a balanced range of material. Following the recommendations of yet another committee, the ITA's regulatory powers were increased to ensure improvements in programme quality.[38] From 1963 the same duty to provide television broadcasting 'as a public service for disseminating education, information and entertainment' was imposed on the commercial sector as it has been on the BBC.[39]

This broadly remained the position for the next twenty-five years. After the Pilkington Committee's highly critical assessment of the first years of commercial television, the BBC was given the third television channel (BBC2), when it became available. Another development was the arrival of local commercial radio in 1973, regulated by the same Authority, then renamed the Independent Broadcasting Authority (IBA). A second national commercial channel, Channel 4, was instituted by the Broadcasting Act 1980. Its schedule has to contain a number of programmes of appeal to tastes and interests not catered for on the other commercial channel. Innovation and experiment in the choice of programmes is to be encouraged; Channel 4 has in effect acted as a publisher rather than a maker of programmes.[40]

[37] For the history of independent broadcasting, see the four-volume history by B. Sendall and J. Potter, *Independent Television in Britain* (London, 1982–90). The background to the 1954 Act is discussed in the first volume, chs. 1–8.

[38] Pilkington Committee Report (1962) Cmnd. 1753. This led to further legislation, the Television Act 1963, consolidated with the earlier Act of 1954, in the Television Act 1964.

[39] Television Act 1963, s. 2(1)(a).

[40] The institution of Channel 4 followed the recommendation of the Annan Committee on the Future of Broadcasting (1977) Cmnd. 6753, for the establishment of a fourth channel

The original impetus for the recent major reform of broadcasting law came from the report of the Peacock Committee, established primarily to examine the question whether the BBC should be compelled to take advertising.[41] It rejected that idea, much to the disappointment of Mrs Thatcher, but advocated deregulation of radio and television. One important suggestion was that franchises for commercial television should be put out to competitive tender. The government accepted this proposal, making it a corner-stone of the Bill introduced at the end of 1989.[42]

The Broadcasting Act 1990 is primarily concerned with the reorganization of private broadcasting, and only affects the BBC in minor respects. It replaces the IBA with a new regulatory body, the Independent Television Commission (ITC). Unlike its predecessor it does not have power to preview and censor licensees' programmes. Its role is principally to award licences for television services, including a new national Channel 5 service, and apply in appropriate cases sanctions for breach of their conditions. The ITC also exercises these powers over cable and satellite services; the former had been regulated by a Cable Authority.[43] The legislation further sets up a Radio Authority to exercise comparable powers over radio services, including the licensing for the first time of national commercial stations. The measure was significantly amended during its passage through Parliament. Among the changes made were the imposition of more onerous programme requirements on applicants for the Channel 3 television licences before their cash bids could be considered, and a tightening of the 'due impartiality' standard. The Act of 1990, intended to apply a lighter touch to programme control, in the end imposed as many new restraints on broadcasters' freedom as it lifted. New Channel 3 television licences were awarded in October 1991 (see Chapter IV, Section 4), but the ITC decided in 1992 not to make any award for the Channel 5 service, as it was unsure of the (sole) applicant's ability to sustain its financial plans.

(ii) France

Constitutional principles exercise some influence on French broadcasting law, but this has only become significant in the last decade. Paramount among these principles is Article 11 of the Declaration of the Rights of Man of 1789, affirmed in the Preamble to the Constitution of the Fifth Republic (1958) and treated as binding on all branches of government.

to be controlled by an Open Broadcasting Authority. Channel 4 was regulated by the IBA (and now the Independent Television Commission).

[41] Peacock Committee on Financing the BBC (1986) Cmnd. 9824.

[42] See the White Paper *Broadcasting in the '90s: Competition, Choice and Quality* (1988) Cm. 517.

[43] Instituted by the repealed Cable Broadcasting Act 1984.

The Article formulates the freedom of dissemination of thought and opinion. All citizens may exercise the right freely, but are answerable for abuse of it in the circumstances determined by the law (*la loi*). In its jurisprudence, as will be explained later, the Conseil constitutionnel has given precise content to this fundamental freedom, deriving from it other principles which must be reflected in statutes regulating radio and television.

None of this was of relevance in the early days of broadcasting.[44] At first licences were granted to private radio stations to function alongside the public network. Through the Ministry of Posts, Telegraph, and Telephones the state kept ultimate control. At the outbreak of war the private stations were closed, and after it their licences were formally revoked. From 1945 to 1982 broadcasting was a state monopoly. The government kept firm control, particularly over the broadcasting of news.[45] Radiodiffusion télévision française (RTF) was placed under the supervision of the Ministry of Information, and was not given a formal legal structure until 1959. An ordinance of 4 February 1959 legalized government control; there was no administrative council for RTF, let alone an independent Director-General.

The first important post-war reform came in 1964, when the law of 27 June changed the state organization into the Office de la radiodiffusion-télévision française (ORTF). The public monopoly was affirmed, but the institution was now directed by an Administrative Council and a Director-General. The latter and his deputies were appointed by the government, while half of the Council members represented it. In practice, therefore, ORTF enjoyed little autonomy, although there was some liberalization under the premiership of Chaban-Delmas from 1969 to 1972.[46] Further legislation of 3 July 1972 restated the monopoly of public broadcasting, while reorganizing the Office into eight separate establishments (*régies*), a step towards the breakup of ORTF two years later. The *loi* of 1972 introduced the right of reply to broadcasting and also regulated advertising, which had been permitted four years earlier. More controversially it restricted the right of journalists and other employees to strike, in order to ensure the continuity of a minimum service during such periods.[47]

The government of Giscard d'Estaing brought about a more substantial reform. The main effect of the law of 7 August 1974 was the dissolution of ORTF into seven separate institutions, each with its own administrative

[44] See C. Debbasch, *Droit de l'audiovisuel*, 2nd edn. (Paris, 1991), 98–130, and G. Drouot, *Le Nouveau Droit de l'audiovisuel* (Paris, 1988), 3–21. Also see R. Thomas, *Broadcasting and Democracy in France* (Bradford, 1976) for the period until 1974.

[45] See Thomas, *Broadcasting and Democracy in France*, 126–35.

[46] Ibid. 30–2.

[47] See Ch. II, S. 4 below.

structure.[48] There were four national programme companies (one for radio and three for separate television channels), a company for television programme production, another for transmission and the expansion of networks, and the Institut national de l'audiovisuel for the provision of some common services, such as film archives and training. The purpose was to introduce competition between the three public television channels, Télévision française 1 (TF1), Antenne 2 (A2), and FR3. The production company competed with private producers to supply programmes to the three channels. The government retained a significant degree of control through its appointment of the company presidents and its issue of the *cahiers des charges*, the documents imposing programme obligations on the television and radio channels. The government also determined the licence fee (*redevance*). Parliament could veto its collection, but otherwise had no influence on the amount of the fee or how it was distributed among the companies. After these reforms the government apparently exercised less control over the content of news bulletins, but there was still pressure on broadcasters to support the government at election times.[49]

There were various attempts throughout the late 1960s and 1970s to introduce private broadcasting, opposed by both Gaullists and Socialists. In fact a number of peripheral private radio stations, as well as one or two television stations, broadcast from just outside the frontiers, for example, from Monaco and Andorra, with the approval and indeed the financial involvement of the French government.[50] With the new technical possibilities for private broadcasting and an appreciation of its success in other countries, the pressure for abandoning the monopoly became irresistible. The courts played little part in this development. In 1948 the Conseil d'État held that the government was entitled to withdraw a private licence which had not been exploited for a number of years.[51] Broadcasting services were regarded as essentially public. Further, the Conseil constitutionnel rejected a challenge to the constitutionality of the monopoly in 1978 when a Bill making it a criminal offence to broadcast from an unlicensed radio or television station was referred to it.[52] As the monopoly had been established by earlier legislation of 1972 and 1974, it was too late to challenge it; the Conseil is only

[48] See R. Kuhn, 'Government and Broadcasting in France: The Resumption of Normal Service' (1980) 3 *West Europ. Pol.* 203, and Thomas, *Broadcasting and Democracy in France*, ch. 2.

[49] See Kuhn, 'Government and Broadcasting in France', 213–15.

[50] See Thomas, *Broadcasting and Democracy in France*, 101–7. The programmes and advertising of these stations were subject to French law: see the decision of the Conseil d'État in *Société des Laboratoires Ciba*, 1957 Rec. 637, Debbasch, 62.

[51] *Société française radio-atlantique*, 1948 Rec. 65, Debbasch, 40.

[52] Decision 78–96 of 27 Aug. 1978, Debbasch, 154.

able to consider the constitutionality of legislation before it is formally promulgated.[53]

Perhaps surprisingly the broadcasting regime was liberalized by the Socialist government which took office after the election of Mitterrand in 1981. The statute of 29 July 1982 is really the starting-point of modern broadcasting law in France.[54] Its fundamental principles were stated at the outset. Article 1 provided: 'La communication audiovisuelle est libre.' Article 2 added that citizens have a right to a free and pluralist broadcasting system. Nevertheless, permission to institute a private broadcasting station was dependent on prior authorization from the government, or in the case of a national television service on the grant of a contractual concession.[55] The Conseil constitutionnel had upheld these provisions as compatible with Article 11 of the Declaration of the Rights of Man.[56] It was for the legislature in the light of prevailing technical constraints (presumably, a reference to the shortage of frequencies) to balance the right to freedom of speech with other constitutional values. These include public order and respect for the rights of others, and also, most pertinently, the preservation of pluralism in the expression of opinion. Another major change was the institution of a High Authority, the first of three supervisory bodies which have regulated French broadcasting in the last decade. Its principal duty was to guarantee the independence of the public broadcasting system, in particular to ensure that the values of pluralism and balance were respected. It appointed the presidents of the public programme channels and had the responsibility for granting licences for local broadcasting services.[57] There were nine members, three chosen each by the President of the Republic, the President of the Assembly, and the President of the Senate. (The same composition and method of selection applies to the Conseil supérieur de l'audiovisuel (CSA), the body which now supervises broadcasting.)

There was no immediate decision to authorize the national private broadcasting channels contemplated by the 1982 law. On the other hand, more than 1,500 local radio stations were established. After 1984 these could be financed by advertising. Canal Plus was then established as a subscription channel, largely for showing films. It is in effect the fourth national channel. It was only at the end of 1985 that amending legislation was passed to make more specific provision for the institution of private

[53] A. Stone, *The Birth of Judicial Politics in France* (New York, 1991), esp. ch. 9, emphasizes this unusual feature of constitutional review in France.

[54] For a legal analysis, see J. Chevallier, 'Le Statut de la communication audiovisuelle' (1982) *AJDA* 555. A vivid account of the background to the law is provided by M. Cotta, *Les Miroirs de Jupiter* (Paris, 1986).

[55] Law of 29 July 1982, Arts. 78 and 79.

[56] Decision 82–141 of 27 July 1982, Debbasch, 198.

[57] Law of 29 July 1982, Arts. 12–26.

television at both the national and the local levels.[58] Following the recommendations of the Bredin Report, two national channels were authorized; they opened in February 1986.[59]

The Chirac government, elected in the spring of 1986, was determined to bring about a more radical liberalization of broadcasting law. Its most controversial decision was to privatize TF1, a move which provoked a general strike of broadcasting personnel and public demonstrations. The new law of September 1986 also replaced the High Authority with a Commission nationale de la communication et des libertés (CNCL), a body with a larger composition (thirteen members) and with wide powers over both broadcasting and telecommunications.[60] It assumed responsibility for licensing radio and television channels, terrestrial and satellite, and (at the suggestions of a commune or groups of them) cable networks. The CNCL had substantial discretion to lay down licensees' programme obligations.

The opposition referred the Bill to the Conseil constitutionnel, which found a number of its provisions unconstitutional.[61] Most strikingly the tribunal stated that the principle of pluralism of sources of opinion was one of constitutional significance, against which the concrete provisions of the Bill must be assessed. Access to a variety of views was necessary for the effective guarantee of the freedom of speech protected by the Declaration of the Rights of Man. The Conseil held the anti-concentration provisions of the Chirac Bill deficient because they failed to honour the requirements of effective pluralism.[62] On the other hand, it saw nothing wrong with the fundamental decision to favour private television. It was for Parliament to determine the appropriate structure for broadcasting in the light of the freedom of communication and other pertinent constitutional values: public order, the rights of others, and the pluralism of opinion. These values were indeed given explicit recognition in Article 1 of the 1986 statute.

The concessions for the fifth and sixth television channels were reallocated by the CNCL after public hearings.[63] The fifth channel (La Cinq) was awarded to a consortium dominated by Robert Hersant, a French press lord, and Silvio Berlusconi, the Italian media magnate. (Subsequently control changed to an alliance of Berlusconi and the leading

[58] Law of 13 Dec. 1985.

[59] Bredin Report, *Les Nouvelles Télévisions herziennes* (Paris, 1985).

[60] See J. Chevallier, 'Le Nouveau Statut de la liberté de la communication' (1987) *AJDA* 59, and J. Morange, 'La Commission nationale de la communication et des libertés et le droit de la communication audiovisuelle' (1987) *Rev. fr. droit adm.* 372.

[61] Decision 86–217 of 18 Sept. 1986, Debbasch, 245.

[62] For detailed discussion of this topic, see Ch. VI below.

[63] For the revocation of the concessions granted by the Socialist government and their reallocation by the CNCL, see Drouot, *Le Nouveau Droit de l'audiovisuel*, 53–8.

French publishing group Hachette, but La Cinq became bankrupt at the end of 1991.) The sixth channel, known now as M6, is largely given over to popular music and programmes for youth. The privatized TF1 has remained the leading channel, its success clearly contributing to the demise of La Cinq. Its programmes are regulated, like those of the two surviving public television channels, by *cahiers des charges*, which impose somewhat more stringent obligations than those imposed on the other private channels by their permit conditions. Antenne 2 is now the principal public channel. It must transmit parliamentary debates and allow time for political broadcasts, and uniquely is bound to transmit religious services on Sundays. FR3 is the more highbrow of the two public channels and also shows a range of programmes of interest to viewers in particular regions. The two public channels, recently renamed France 2 and France 3, are financed by a licence fee and advertising revenue. Finally, a publicly financed satellite channel, La Sept, with a cultural and European programme remit, has recently been allocated a terrestrial frequency.

The recent reform of the Rocard Socialist government does not materially affect this landscape.[64] The most significant change is the replacement of the CNCL by the Conseil supérieur de l'audiovisuel. The former body had, perhaps unfairly, attracted a great deal of criticism for the way in which it had awarded licences.[65] The CSA is chosen in the same way as the old High Authority. It enjoys slightly less regulatory power than its immediate predecessor. On the other hand the CSA is able to apply a wider range of sanctions for breach by licensees of the conditions on which they were permitted to broadcast.[66] One interesting point is that private broadcasting authorizations under the 1989 law, as under the 1982 statute, are granted by a contract between the administrative authority and the applicant. It is surprising that Socialist governments have preferred this technique, while the right-wing Chirac regime was content to require the issue of a simple permit by the CNCL.

The minor character of the amendments made in 1989 justify hopes that at last the rules of the French broadcasting system have been settled. Perhaps more than in any other jurisdiction discussed in this book broadcasting has been a political football kicked around by governments of different political persuasions. To some extent this may be a legacy of the tradition of government control, particularly of news and current affairs

[64] Law of 17 Jan. 1989. The Conseil constitutionnel was as usual asked to rule on the constitutionality of the Bill, and had held some provisions invalid: Decision 88–248 of 17 Jan. 1989, Debbasch, 319. See Ch. III, S. 3 and Ch. IV, S. 3.

[65] See J. Morange, 'Le Conseil supérieur de l'audiovisuel' [1989] *Rev. fr. droit adm.* 235, 240–1.

[66] The Conseil upheld the constitutionality of these provisions, in particular ruling that they did not infringe Art. 11 of the Declaration of the Rights of Man: Decision 88–248 of 17 Jan. 1989, paras. 25–8.

programmes, which had prevailed for thirty years after the Second World War. Of more concern now is the ability of the public channels to compete effectively without too great a decline in the quality of their programmes. Equally the fall of La Cinq indicates that it may be difficult for private channels to survive if their programmes are tightly regulated.[67]

(iii) Germany[68]

The principal characteristic of the West German broadcasting system has been its federal organization. This has been extended to the united Germany by the State Treaty of September 1990 between the Federal Republic and the former GDR. Since the last world war radio and television have been controlled by the *Länder* (states) and not by the Bund (federal) government. This is an understandable reaction to the exploitation of radio by the Nazis. In 1945 the Allies delegated broadcasting powers to the zone commanders, so that to some extent the pattern of broadcasting in each area reflected the ideas of the British, French, and American authorities.[69] For example, in the north the British set up a large centralized system, the North-West German Broadcasting Service, to some extent modelled on the BBC, while the Americans preferred smaller stations, generally based in individual *Länder*, where the broadcasting councils were chosen from socially representative groups.

The pattern which emerged in the 1950s was one of nine regional public broadcasting organizations. Some of these covered one state only, such as Bayerischer Rundfunk or Radio Bremen, while others straddled state boundaries. Examples of the latter are Sudwestfunk, which covers part of Baden-Württemberg and Rhineland-Pfalz, and Norddeutscher Rundfunk (NDR) instituted by the *Land* governments of Lower Saxony, Schleswig-Holstein, and Hamburg.[70] Broadly there have been two types of broadcasting organization within these nine systems: the majority of them follow the 'corporate' model, while the NDR and the Westdeutscher Rundfunk Köln (WDR) have adopted a 'parliamentary' model. In the former, the organization is governed by a broadcasting council (Rundfunkrat), composed of representatives of important social groups, such as the churches, womens' organizations, unions, and chambers of commerce, as well as the government and the political parties. This system, designed

[67] For further discussion of this topic, see Ch. V, S. 1 below.

[68] The historical account is confined to the former West German state, the Basic Law of which applies to the united country of Germany.

[69] See Humphreys, ch. 3, to which this account is much indebted. Also see A. Williams, *Broadcasting and Democracy in Germany* (Bradford, 1976). The leading German historical work is H. Bausch, *Rundfunk in Deutschland* (Munich, 1980).

[70] The NDR was instituted by a state treaty (*Staatsvertrag*) in 1955. It was the final step in the breakup of the giant broadcasting service established in the British zone, from which North Rhine–Westphalia had already detached itself.

to strengthen the independence of broadcasters from party dominance, is one of the leading characteristics of the German system; it is discussed in more detail in Chapter III. In the other model, members of the authorities have been chosen by the state Parliaments, largely from their members; parties are represented according to their strength. Politicians and parties have often attempted to control broadcasting, irrespective of its mode of organization. Parties may influence the selection of members of the broadcasting councils or the appointment of the Director-General (Intendant).[71]

In 1950 the state broadcasting corporations formed an association, the Arbeitsgemeinschaft der öffentlich-rechtlichen Rundfunkanstalten der Bundesrepublik Deutschland (ARD). It is under this association that the television network now constituting the first public channel was formed. By agreement the state broadcasters contribute programmes for common distribution, the larger bodies, such as WDR, NDR, and Bayerischer Rundfunk naturally providing the majority. In this way a *de facto* national news service, for example, is broadcast each evening from Hamburg. However, programmes between 6.00 and 8.00 p.m. are provided by each regional organization for their own area. This is in effect a system of voluntary co-operation, from which the regional organizations are free to withdraw at any time. It is in no sense a federal channel.

During the late 1950s there were attempts to set up a national commercial channel under the control of the Bund government. Both Konrad Adenauer, the Federal Chancellor, and business interests favoured this.[72] But the Basic Law of 1949 seemed to exclude the possibility. A key provision is Article 30, which states: 'The exercise of governmental powers and the discharge of government functions shall be incumbent on the *Länder*, in so far as this Basic Law does not otherwise prescribe or permit.' The result is that the states have legislative authority over a subject, unless there is a specific provision in the Basic Law conferring exclusive or concurrent authority on the Bund. The latter has authority to legislate for postal and telecommunications services, but this has never been understood to include power to regulate broadcast programmes. (It does, however, authorize the laying of cable lines, an activity much encouraged by the federal government in the 1980s.) Another crucial provision is Article 5, the first clause of which provides:

Everyone shall have the right freely to express and disseminate his opinion by speech, writing, and pictures and freely to inform himself from generally acces-

[71] See A. Grosser, 'Federal Republic of Germany: From Democratic Showcase to Party Domination', in A. Smith, *Television and Political Life* (London, 1979), 114, and Williams, *Broadcasting and Democracy in Germany*, 120–37.

[72] G. Braunthal, 'Federalism in Germany: The Broadcasting Controversy' (1962) 24 *Journal of Politics* 545.

sible sources. Freedom of the press and freedom of reporting by means of broadcasts and films are guaranteed. There shall be no censorship.

German law therefore explicitly protects broadcasting freedom (*Rundfunkfreiheit*); in that respect it is unique among the systems considered in this book. The text does not give any indication whether broadcasting freedom has the same meaning as press freedom, or for that matter freedom of expression.

This is the constitutional background to the first of the many broadcasting cases which have come before the Federal Constitutional Court (Bundesverfassungsgericht). The establishment of a national commercial television channel by the Adenauer Christian Democrat government was challenged by four states controlled by the opposition SPD. The Court upheld the challenge, first, because there was a violation of Article 30 of the Basic Law, and secondly, because the articles of association establishing the channel violated Article 5.[73] The Court's ruling on this second point was particularly significant, articulating principles which apply today. Unlike the press, the broadcasting media should be regulated. While there was a shortage of frequencies and it was costly to establish a television station, the public broadcasting monopoly could be justified, although it was not constitutionally mandatory. What was crucial in the Court's view was that broadcasting, whether public or private, should not be dominated by the state or by commercial forces, and should be open for the transmission of a wide variety of opinion.

After this there were no further attempts to set up a federal channel.[74] Instead the states under treaty (*Staatsvertrag*) instituted at the end of 1961 the second public television channel, Zweites Deutsches Fernsehen (ZDF). Unlike the ARD channel, this is a genuinely national service, broadcast from Mainz. It only provides a television (and not a radio) service; the programmes are co-ordinated with those of ARD. Its administrative structure is similar to the regional broadcasting corporations organized on the 'corporate' model. The party political element is stronger than it is generally in the regional broadcasting organizations: Kohl and Genscher have been members of the broadcasting council.[75] The third public channel was introduced at various stages in different parts of West Germany during the 1960s. It is organized by the regional broadcasting bodies, either individually or in co-operation between neighbouring institutions, to show programmes of regional interest and appealing to highbrow and other minority tastes.

[73] 12 BVerfGE 205 (1961). For a fuller discussion of the ruling, see Barendt, 'The Influence of the German and Italian Constitutional Courts', 98–100.

[74] But there are two federal radio stations, Deutsche Welle and Deutschlandfunk, for broadcasting world-wide and to the former East Germany and Europe respectively.

[75] See Humphreys, 166–8, for political influence over ZDF.

The primary source of finance for public broadcasting is the licence fee (*Gebühr*). This is a charge on the possession of a radio or a television set, a higher supplementary fee being paid for the latter. One important feature of the system is the institution of an equalization fund by the ARD, by means of which the larger wealthier stations support the smaller ones, so that they are able to carry on an adequate service.[76] Advertising provides a subordinate source of revenue. There are more significant restrictions on the times at which advertisements may be shown than in France and Italy—in particular, they must be shown in blocks before 8.00 p.m. and are forbidden on Sundays and holidays—and they are also completely banned on the third channel.[77]

As in France there was a long battle before private commercial broadcasting was introduced. Its establishment was made more difficult by the federal system. The SPD-controlled states were largely hostile to the development, while it was naturally favoured by the advertising lobby and the CDU and CSU parties, whose members often thought that programmes on the public systems were biased towards the SPD.[78] The first laws permitted private broadcasting on an experimental basis for a limited period. One of these, a Saarland law, was referred to the Constitutional Court.[79] It ruled that private broadcasting is compatible with Article 5 of the Basic Law, provided it is properly regulated. Unlike the press, it should not be left to market forces to ensure that a wide variety of voices enjoy access to it. But the Court accepted that the regulations applied to public broadcasting were not always appropriate for its commercial competitors, a perspective elaborated in later decisions.[80]

With the change in government in 1982 from the SPD–FDP coalition to one dominated by the Christian Democrats came a significant increase in federal support for private broadcasting. The new government encouraged the CDU *Länder* to introduce private broadcasting statutes, while it financed cabling for the distribution of satellite and terrestrial programmes. Most of the states enacted laws in the mid-1980s. The SPD generally resisted the development, some of its members in the Bundestag challenging the constitutionality of the lower Saxony law of 1986. The Bundesverfassungsgericht took the opportunity to pronounce on the relationship of public and private broadcasting.[81] The main points of the ruling, discussed in detail in later chapters, are that in the present circumstances the principal public service functions of broadcasting are

[76] Humphreys, 175–6.

[77] For restrictions on advertising, see Ch. IX, S. 4 below.

[78] See Humphreys, 190–229, for a full account of the political controversy and the early cable projects which pioneered private broadcasting.

[79] The *Third Television* case, 57 BVerfGE 295 (1981).

[80] See Barendt, 'The Influence of the German and Italian Constitutional Courts', 100–1.

[81] *Fourth Television* case, 73 BVerfGE 118 (1986).

the responsibility of the public institutions. Private broadcasters may be subject to less onerous programme restrictions, for otherwise their survival might be endangered.

This view of the complementary role of public and private broadcasting has been subsequently refined.[82] In the *Sixth Television* case the Court emphasized that the Basic Law does not prescribe any particular method of organizing broadcasting. A law may provide, as does that of North Rhine–Westphalia, for co-operation between the public and private broadcasters as a means of providing finance for the former. What is important is that the public broadcasters are able to discharge their fundamental responsibility (*Grundversorgung*) of providing the community with a wide range of programmes. Further, state Parliaments may, but are not obliged to, impose lower standards of comprehensiveness and impartiality on private broadcasting companies than those required of the public institutions.[83]

Initially private television in Germany was largely transmitted by cable. However, after its legitimacy was conclusively established in the *Fourth Television* case and the agreement of the *Staatsvertrag* of 1987, the state licensing authorities allocated new terrestrial frequencies both to local companies and to large private consortia. The latter, in particular SAT 1 and RTL Plus, have established a national service through cable retransmissions of their satellite programmes.[84] Although the public channels still enjoy a large share of the audience, they must increasingly compete with their well-financed competitors for the purchase of films and for the acquisition of rights to cover sports events.[85] ARD and ZDF have pressed unsuccessfully for removal of the limits on showing advertisements in peak viewing hours. Instead they have won a significant increase in the licence fee under the state treaties agreed towards the end of 1991.

Under the treaty of unification between West and East Germany, broadcasting in the eastern part of the united country is to be instituted on the same legal principles which have governed its organization in the western *Länder*. By the end of 1991 two new broadcasting institutions were established: Mitteldeutscher Rundfunk for the states of Saxony, Saxony-Anhalt, and Thüringen, and Rundfunk Brandenburg for that state. The *Land* of Mecklenburg-Vorpommern has joined the NDR.

[82] *Fifth Television* case, 74 BVerfGE 297 (1987), and *Sixth Television* case, 83 BVerfGE 238 (1991). Also see the partly successful challenge to the Bavarian private broadcasting law of 1984 under its constitution, which provides in Art. 111a(2) that broadcasting is to be conducted with a sense of public responsibility: [1987] *NJW* 251.

[83] See Ch. V, Ss. 1 and 2, for further consideration of this topic.

[84] Humphreys, 280–92 and 310–12.

[85] This topic is discussed in Ch. VI, S. 5 below.

Private broadcasting has also been authorized, though the frequencies hitherto allocated to it are limited.[86]

The German Constitutional Court has exercised an enormous influence on shaping the contours of broadcasting law. We will see in the next chapter how it has developed a view of broadcasting freedom which contrasts sharply with that generally held in the United States and to some extent supported by the British Conservative Party. Moreover, the German courts have developed sophisticated concepts with regard to broadcasting standards and the organization of public broadcasting which make their contribution to a comparative study particularly rich. Whether it makes much difference to the overall quality of radio and television is another matter. What perhaps can be said is that the public service tradition of broadcasting has survived more vigorously in Germany than in France or Italy, and for that reason alone its structure should be of interest to British readers.

(iv) Italy

As in other European countries radio at its inception was under state control.[87] In 1924 the Fascist government gave a private company an exclusive licence for broadcasting; its programmes were tightly controlled. From 1944 this monopoly was vested in Radio audizioni Italia (RAI). Renamed in 1952 RAI-Radiotelevisione italiana this company still holds the concession for public radio and television broadcasting. In law it is a private company, the vast majority of its shares being owned by a state holding company (recently privatized) and the remaining 1 per cent by the Italian authors' and editors' society.

After the war broadcasting was regulated by a statute of 1947, which established a Parliamentary Commission to ensure RAI's political independence. However, it lacked executive powers and was regarded as an ineffective guarantor of broadcasting freedom. Radio (and subsequently television) were in effect controlled by the Christian Democrats, who have dominated governments since the war. The Minister for Posts and Telecommunications refused to grant licences to private groups. Eventually this was challenged in the courts and a reference was made to the Constitutional Court in Rome.

The post-war Italian Constitution promulgated at the end of 1947 makes no specific reference to broadcasting. However, a number of

[86] There is a brief outline of the system in the eastern states by W. Kleinwachter (1991) 8 *Media Bulletin* (European Institute for the Media), no. 4, 11.

[87] This short account owes much to G. Rao, *The Italian Broadcasting System: Legal (and Political) Aspects*, European University Institute Working Paper 88/369. Also see D. Giacalone, *Antenna libera: La RAI, i privati, i partiti* (Milan, 1990).

provisions are relevant to its legal regulation.[88] Article 21(1) provides: 'Everyone has the right to express himself freely verbally, in writing, and by any other means.' Potential private broadcasters have used that provision to support their claim that there is a right to set up commercial stations, but they have also relied on Article 41. That provision formulates a freedom of private economic enterprise to be conducted in conformity with social utility and in such a way as not to damage security, liberty, and human dignity. Equally RAI used to rely on Article 43 to defend the monopoly: it enables legislation to reserve (or expropriate subject to compensation) for the state businesses which are concerned with vital public service or are natural monopolies, and which are of pre-eminent public interest.

In its first broadcasting ruling the Constitutional Court upheld RAI's monopoly under Article 43, and denied the existence of rights under Articles 21 and 41 to institute private radio or television stations.[89] In view of the shortage of frequencies broadcasting was a natural monopoly. In addition the public system was the best method to secure the access of all important political and social groups to the airwaves. Private broadcasting would inevitably be dominated by a few corporations. When the Court considered the question again in 1974, it put more emphasis on these latter points.[90] Broadcasting provided an essential service in a democratic society. It could legitimately be reserved for a public institution, provided certain conditions were met. In particular radio and television should be put under parliamentary, and not executive, control to ensure their independence, and rules should be drawn up to guarantee the access of significant political and social groups. In so far as they did not meet these conditions, the laws were declared invalid.

Parliament immediately enacted the *legge* of April 1975 which still provides the legal basis for public broadcasting.[91] The powers of the Parliamentary Commission were strengthened. It exercises a general supervisory role, laying down guide-lines concerning the objectivity of programmes, and it appoints the members of the RAI's Administrative Council. Another of its functions is to determine which applications to make access programmes should be granted. These access provisions are unique to the Italian system, but have not proved particularly successful.[92]

[88] For a fuller exposition, see Barendt, 'The Influence of the German and Italian Constitutional Courts', 107–8.

[89] Decision 59/1960 [1960] *Giur. cost.* 759.

[90] Decision 225/1974 [1974] *Giur. cost.* 1775. In a companion case, Decision 226/1974, ibid. 1791, the Court rejected the public monopoly of local cable broadcasting. Cable in its view was not a natural monopoly and there was no danger that private oligopolies would replace the public monopoly.

[91] Law 103 of 14 Apr. 1975.

[92] See the discussion in Ch. VII, S. 3 below.

The 1975 statute also contains provisions for the financing of public broadcasting by a compulsory licence fee (*canone*) and by advertising revenue as a subsidiary source. But strict limits are imposed on the proportion of broadcasting time which may be devoted to commercials. Until recently private broadcasting channels have not been limited in this respect, and have, therefore, been in receipt of much greater advertising revenue.

Contemporaneously with the introduction of this law the principal parties in the governing coalition, the Christian Democrats and the Socialists (PSI), agreed privately on the allocation (*lottizzazione*) of the television and radio channels: the Christian Democrats were to control RAI-1, the premier television channel, and one radio channel, while the Socialists took RAI-2 and two radio channels.[93] By convention the political parties appoint the directors of the channel they control and influence other appointments. Party bias is clearly reflected in the presentation of news programmes. The third television channel, instituted in 1977, has been to some extent under the control of what used to the Communist Party (now the Party of the Democratic Left). It shows more regional and cultural programmes, a characteristic, it seems, of continental third channels, and is therefore less popular.

The Constitutional Court made its most significant contribution in 1976, the year after the reform of RAI and the 'secret' agreement between the parties. References were made to it when criminal proceedings were launched against local television stations for operating without a licence. While upholding the position of RAI at the national level, the Court ruled the monopoly unconstitutional as far as local broadcasting was concerned.[94] In that context there was no danger of private monopolies or oligopolies, as more frequencies were available and the costs of starting up a station were relatively low. The ambiguities of this crucial decision are explored later in Chapter IV. What is clear is that the Court ruled that the law must allow private broadcasting, albeit only at the local level. In Germany and France the constitutional courts have ruled only that private broadcasting is permissible.

The immediate consequence was the emergence of a large number of local stations. Unfortunately frequencies had not been allocated to avoid interference between these stations or with RAI and other public non-broadcasting use of the airwaves. Chaos resulted. Despite various attempts at legislation the governing parties could not agree on a measure.[95] Gradually national networks developed, though they had not

[93] See D. Sassoon, 'Italy: The Advent of Private Broadcasting', in R. Kuhn (ed.), *The Politics of Broadcasting* (London, 1985), 122, 126–32.

[94] Decision 202/1976 [1976] *Giur. cost.* 1267.

[95] For the history of the period 1976–85, see Giacalone, *Antenna libera*, chs. II and III.

been legitimized by the 1976 ruling. In 1981 the Court reaffirmed the constitutionality of RAI's national monopoly, at least until the enactment of adequate anti-trust laws to avert the danger of private oligopolies.[96] That case involved a *de facto* chain set up by the Rizzoli group, but a more serious problem was posed by the development in the 1980s of the Berlusconi networks. Silvio Berlusconi founded Canale 5 in 1980. Two years later he acquired another network, Italia 1, and then in 1984 he bought Retequattro from the Mondadori publishing group. His activity led to a wave of litigation between the private broadcasting companies and between them and RAI.[97] In 1984 magistrates ordered the closure of some private stations, because they infringed RAI's lawful monopoly.

The government should have reacted with a comprehensive statute to regulate private broadcasting, but all it could produce was a temporary law.[98] Designed initially to hold the position for six months, it was subsequently renewed for further periods. All private stations and *de facto* networks existing on 1 October 1984 were legalized. Since the largest networks were controlled by Berlusconi's Fininvest company, the law was blatantly framed to ensure their survival. Craxi, the Socialist Prime Minister at the time, was a close friend of Berlusconi. Indeed the PSI, rather strangely for a socialist party, blocked all attempts to regulate the growth of the private networks and ensured that the law, eventually introduced in 1990, was extremely favourable to Berlusconi.

In the hope of further legislation the Constitutional Court delayed hearing a number of references from magistrates concerning the constitutionality of the public monopoly and the legality of the 'temporary' law of 1985. Eventually in 1988 it called again for prompt and comprehensive regulation of private broadcasting; the new law should contain adequate anti-trust and other rules to safeguard pluralism. In the meantime the 1985 law could continue in force. In language echoing that of the Bundesverfassungsgericht, the Italian Constitutional Court emphasized the different roles of public and private broadcasting and called for the former to be adequately financed.

After further delays the coalition presided over by Andreotti enacted a comprehensive measure in 1990.[99] The *legge Mammì*, named after the responsible Minister of Posts, set up a system for licensing private radio and television. The Act contains some complex advertising rules and imposes some (very limited) programme obligations. The anti-trust and cross-media ownership provisions are particularly controversial. A

[96] Decision 148/81 [1981] *Giur. cost.* 1379.

[97] The cases are discussed by A. Pace, 'La Radiotelevisione in Italia con particolare riguardo alla emittenza privata' [1987] *Riv. trim. di diritt. pubb.* 615, 624–7.

[98] Law 10 of 4 Feb. 1985.

[99] Law 223 of 6 Aug. 1990. *Il sistema radiotelevisivo* provides a comprehensive commentary.

company may own three national television networks or three local stations, provided the latter are in different areas. But an owner of three national networks must surrender control of all his press interests.[100] Therefore, the 1990 statute allows Berlusconi to keep his networks, a result which led to the resignation from the government of a number of Christian Democrat ministers. His Fininvest group was duly awarded three national licences in the summer of 1992.

It would not be surprising if there is a challenge to the adequacy of these rules. The 1990 statute is a political compromise, reached only because of the demands of the Constitutional Court. In Italy, as in France and Germany, broadcasting has been a matter of intense political controversy. The inability of the partners in coalition governments to agree on any coherent principles has been a recipe first for legislative inertia and then for an inadequate law. The picture is therefore very different from that found in France, where the scene has changed rapidly, as governments of different political colour have replaced one another.

(v) *United States of America*

Radio was not comprehensively regulated in the United States until 1927. Broadcasting had developed in the 1920s in an anarchic way, the stations competing with each other for the use of available frequencies.[101] For the most part they provided light entertainment and increasingly were financed by advertising revenue. The Radio Act 1927 established the Federal Radio Commission, with authority to grant three-year licences to operate a radio station on an assigned frequency. There was, however, little regulation of advertising or programme content, and an amendment to impose 'common carrier' status on broadcasters was rejected, as it was in 1934 when the Federal Communications Bill passed through Congress. Under the 'common carrier' model, broadcasters, like telephone companies, would have been compelled to make their channels available to groups and individuals who wished to make programmes or address the community served by the station. But it was considered this would be an interference with the licensees' freedom.[102]

Licences have been issued only to local stations. But national networks were already developing. In 1926 the Radio Corporation of American (RCA) launched the National Broadcasting Company (NBC), which soon controlled two networks, while a third, now the Columbia Broadcasting System (CBS), was formed in the following year. Increasingly local

[100] These rules are considered in Ch. VI below.

[101] For the early history, see R. B. Horwitz, *The Irony of Regulatory Reform* (New York, 1989), 112–25, and D. Kellner, *Television and the Crisis of Legitimacy* (Boulder, Colo., 1990), 26–41.

[102] Pool, *Technologies of Freedom*, 136–8.

stations affiliated to a network; the former agreed to transmit the network's programmes, often supplied without cost in exchange for a commitment to schedule them at particular times. In 1941 the Federal Communications Commission (FCC) issued Chain Broadcasting Rules to prohibit exclusive ties between broadcasting stations and a network; the Supreme Court held the regulations did not interfere with licensees' freedom to draw up their own programme schedules and were, therefore, compatible with the First Amendment.[103] The rules had been addressed to the local stations. In contrast control over the national networks has only been indirect and perhaps less effective for that reason. Nevertheless, one result of the Chain Rules was that RCA divested itself of one of its networks, which from then on was controlled by the American Broadcasting Company (ABC).

The purpose of the Communications Act 1934 was to put the control of telephone and wireless communications into the hands of one body, the Federal Communications Commission. But its broadcasting functions were essentially those conferred on its predecessor. The FCC has authority to assign frequencies for particular areas, to prescribe the nature of the service to be provided by different types of station, and to rule on licence applications. The only standard to guide them in the exercise of these wide powers is that of 'the public interest, convenience and necessity'. On the basis of this vacuous formula the FCC has at various times laid down general rules regarding programme contents, limits on the accumulation of licences and the combination of press and broadcasting interests, and advertising regulations. Perhaps the best-known rules are those of the Fairness Doctrine, promulgated in 1949.[104] While permitting licensees to editorialize, it required them to devote some time to the discussion of important issues and to present contrasting views on controversial topics. The requirements inhibited their freedom to use broadcasting privileges as they liked.

At the time of its introduction there were relatively few doubts about the Doctrine's constitutionality. The First Amendment to the United States Constitution does indeed state: 'Congress shall make no law . . . abridging the freedom of speech, or of the press'. But no inference was drawn that broadcasting regulation was unconstitutional. Federal courts had upheld the non-renewal of a licence on the ground that the station owner had exploited it for the purpose of self-advertising or to make intemperate religious and political speech.[105] Freedom of speech did not

[103] *NBC* v. *US* 319 US 190 (1943): see Ch. VI, S. 2 below.

[104] *Report on Editorializing by Broadcast Licensees* 13 FCC 1246 (1949). For a detailed examination of the Doctrine and its repeal, see Ch. VII, S. 4 below.

[105] *KFKB Broadcasting Association* v. *Federal Radio Commission*, 47 F. 2d. 670 (DC Cir. 1931); *Trinity Methodist Church* v. *Federal Radio Commission*, 62 F. 2d. 850 (DC Cir. 1932).

entail a right to broadcast without a licence or unconditionally with one.[106] The Fairness Doctrine itself received the approval of the Supreme Court in the *Red Lion* ruling.[107] The Court reasoned (in terms familiar in European discourse) that broadcasters, unlike newspaper editors, enjoyed a privilege which they should exercise in the interests of the public.

The FCC was, however, reluctant to impose precise programme standards. Moreover, it refused generally to treat violations of the Fairness Doctrine or other programme requirements as a justification for non-renewal of a licence.[108] As a result there was little inducement for stations to show serious programmes to counter the advertisers' pressure to schedule popular fare. One important development occurred before the era of broadcasting deregulation. In 1967–70 public broadcasting was established on a national basis, through the institution of the Corporation for Public Broadcasting (CPB), the Public Broadcasting Service for television, and a national radio service.[109] The CPB, the funding organization, is financed by annual appropriations from Congress, a system which makes public broadcasting vulnerable to political pressures. Local public broadcasting stations also rely heavily on corporate sponsorship of programmes. But there is no spot advertising. Public broadcasters are now as free as private stations to editorialize,[110] a freedom denied in European legal systems.

Attitudes to broadcasting regulation changed radically towards the end of the 1970s. It was argued that programming restraints were contrary to the First Amendment as well as unproductive, and that broadcasting licensees should enjoy the same rights as newspaper editors and owners.[111] While previously the FCC had considered how to enforce its rules more effectively, now under the chairmanship of Mark Fowler (appointed by President Reagan) it moved to deregulate broadcasting. Requirements to show news and current affairs programmes and advertising restrictions were scrapped. Most controversially the Fairness Doctrine was repealed in 1987. Reagan vetoed a Bill to put it on a firm legislative basis.[112] For a

[106] *NBC* v. *US* 319 US 190 (1943).

[107] *Red Lion Broadcasting Co.* v. *FCC* 395 US 367 (1969).

[108] See R. L. Barrow, 'The Attainment of Balanced Program Service in Television' (1966) 52 *Va. L. Rev.* 633, and B. F. Chamberlain, 'Lessons in Regulating Information Flow: The FCC's Weak Track Record in Interpreting the Public Interest Standard' (1982) 60 *N. Carolina L. Rev.* 1057.

[109] See Kellner, *Television and the Crisis of Democracy*, 201–7.

[110] *FCC* v. *League of Women Voters of California* 468 US 384 (1984): see Ch. V, S. 2 below.

[111] M. S. Fowler (later chairman of the FCC) and D. L. Brenner, 'A Marketplace Approach to Broadcast Regulation' (1981) 60 *Texas L. Rev.* 207. Also see the literature referred to in n. 8 above.

[112] See Ch. VII, S. 4 below.

time there were not even controls on advertising during children's programmes.[113]

These developments illustrate the widely divergent approaches to broadcasting regulation in the United States and (for the most part) in Europe. This is partly an aspect of the more sceptical attitude to government and to administrative regulation which has prevailed in the USA, at any rate in the last twenty years. The First Amendment has been interpreted as conferring on broadcasters rights, which have not been derived from the comparable provisions in continental countries. Another explanation is that in the USA private commercial broadcasting enjoyed for a long time a *de facto* monopoly, while in Britain, France, Germany, and Italy there was a public monopoly. It is interesting that there has been a continuity to US broadcasting law, which (perhaps sadly) is not found in these European jurisdictions. The Federal Communications Act has remained in force since its passage in 1934, though it has been amended on a handful of occasions. These fundamental differences are reflected in many of the details of broadcasting law discussed in later chapters of this book.

[113] See p. 195 below.

II
Broadcasting Freedom

1. BROADCASTING AND FREEDOM OF SPEECH

In liberal societies broadcasting freedom is now considered to be as important a value as freedom of the press has been for the last two or three centuries. But it is rare for the freedom of the broadcasting media to be stated explicitly in the text of a constitution. The German Basic Law is unusual in its reference to this freedom (*Rundfunkfreiheit*). In contrast Italy and the United States cover press freedom expressly, but make no mention of the newer media. However, this disparate treatment has not proved particularly important. Courts regard broadcasting as covered by freedom of speech or expression clauses. This is not only the case with national constitutional courts. The European Court of Human Rights has held that broadcasting, like the press, is covered by Article 10 of the Convention guaranteeing the right to freedom of expression.[1]

But the application of freedom of speech principles to the broadcasting media is far from straightforward.[2] As the discussion in the first chapter of this book showed, radio and television are much more tightly regulated than the press and other publishers. The justifications for the difference may be based on outmoded ideas, but constitutional courts in Europe and until recently the US Supreme Court have accepted it. Further, the difference is reflected in legislation and regulations, even in the United States, where deregulation has gone much further than in Europe. Broadcasters are not always free to schedule what programmes they like or (except in the USA) to take their own editorial line on matters of current political and social controversy. It follows that broadcasting freedom cannot simply be regarded as freedom of expression applied without modification to the broadcasting media.

Another difficulty is revealed when we ask the question: Who exercises rights to freedom of speech within the context of broadcasting? To what extent, for example, may a reporter, programme producer, or editor

[1] *Groppera* v. *Switzerland* (1990) 12 EHRR 321 and *Autronic* v. *Switzerland* (1990) 12 EHRR 485. The ECHR had earlier ruled that newspapers enjoyed the protection of Art. 10 in *Sunday Times* v. *UK* (1979) 2 EHRR 245.

[2] For a further discussion of these points, see E. M. Barendt, 'Press and Broadcasting Freedom: Does Anyone have Any Rights to Free Speech?' (1991) 44 *CLP* 63, 64–7.

claim these rights, or are they only enjoyed by the broadcasting institution or the owner of the channel? (There are similar questions in the case of the press, where there are frequently arguments about whether the proprietor of a newspaper is entitled to 'interfere' with the editor's freedom to determine its contents and overall political line.[3]) The interests of programme producers, editors, and channel owners (whether public or private) frequently conflict. It is hard to see how they can all assert *individual* free speech rights. Another difficulty is that viewers and listeners may also claim rights to hear a balanced range of programmes or to have a particular programme kept on the air, even though the broadcaster wishes to remove it from the schedule. There is additionally the issue whether individuals or groups enjoy free speech rights of access to the media to present their particular views on current topics or whether the recognition of such rights would compromise the free speech interests of broadcasters. This final topic is fully considered in Chapter VII.

One approach is of course simply to ignore these difficulties and assert that broadcasting freedom means simply the right of the broadcasting companies (whether public or private) to show exactly what they want, subject only to the general laws of libel, obscenity, and so on. This seems to have been the approach of the Federal Communications Commission when it removed virtually all programme standards in the 1980s. The FCC and some judges in the United States have taken the view that this course is required by the First Amendment.[4] This assumes that only the licensee (the channel owner) may successfully assert free speech rights in the broadcasting context. It is surely, however, unacceptable to leave the free speech interests of viewers and listeners entirely out of account. An unfettered freedom for licensees to select which programmes appear on their schedules to the complete disregard of the interests of the public appears more like a property right than an attribute of freedom of speech. This seems particularly clear when the programmes chosen are not in any sense an expression of the licensee's own beliefs, but a mixture of films, quiz shows, and other light entertainment. Moreover, the FCC approach, not in any case universally shared by commentators in the United States, sheds little light on the concept of broadcasting freedom in Europe. In all European jurisdictions, programme standards are imposed in the interest of the public, yet few argue that broadcasting freedom is, therefore, a meaningless concept or that freedom of speech does not exist on radio and television.

The different European perspective on the relationship of broadcasting

[3] See T. Gibbons, 'Freedom of the Press: Ownership and Editorial Values' [1992] *Pub. Law* 279.

[4] See e.g. *CBS* v. *FCC* 453 US 367, 395 (1981) and *Syracuse Peace Council* v. *FCC* 867 F. 2d. 654 (DC Cir. 1989).

freedom to freedom of speech has been most fully articulated in Germany. *Rundfunkfreiheit* is regarded by the Constitutional Court as an instrumental freedom (*dienende Freiheit*), serving the more fundamental freedom of speech in the interests of both broadcasters and the public.[5] Broadcasting freedom in other words is to be protected in so far as its exercise promotes the goals of free speech: an informed democracy and the lively discussion of a variety of views. It is not enough to regard the freedom primarily as an immunity from government intervention, as it is treated in the USA. Instead the constitutional guarantee of freedom of expression requires the enactment of legislation to safeguard free speech in the context of broadcasting to ensure, for example, that it is dominated neither by the state nor by any commercial group. On this approach programme standards promote, rather than run counter to, broadcasting freedom. They protect the interests of audiences in a wide range of programmes and give access to minority views. Further, it is less material from this perspective to determine who exercises individual free speech rights than it is to ensure that broadcasting institutions are so composed and regulated that they promote the exercise of free speech.

A similar approach is to be found in the jurisprudence of the Italian Constitutional Court and in some decisions of the Conseil constitutionnel in France.[6] Although not articulated at a constitutional level it also underlies broadcasting regulation in Britain. Whether this perspective is correct depends to some extent on the acceptability of the arguments for the regulation of the broadcasting media discussed in the previous chapter. If regulation is justified, the law must take account of the interests of listeners and viewers; it cannot then be correct to understand broadcasting freedom as the freedom only of broadcasters. What is clear is that some coherent content can be given to this notion of broadcasting freedom. A crucial element is the freedom of broadcasters from state control. A second dimension is that broadcasting freedom should primarily be regarded as a set of institutional rather than of individual rights. An important question discussed in the final section of the chapter is how far listeners and viewers enjoy rights as an aspect of broadcasting freedom.

2. FREEDOM FROM STATE CONTROL

Whatever else it means, broadcasting freedom surely entails freedom from state or government control. In particular the censorship by government of programmes would appear incompatible with it. As the Peacock

[5] 57 BVerfGE 295, 320 (1981) and 73 BVerfGE 118, 152 (1986).

[6] In particular see Decision 225/1974 of the Italian Constitutional Court [1974] *Giur. cost.* 1775, and Decision 86–217 of the Conseil constitutionnel, Rec. 1986, 141, Debbasch, 245.

Committee (set up to investigate methods of financing the BBC) put it, pre-publication censorship has no place in a free society, whether it is applied to books, films, plays, or broadcasting.[7] It is constitutionally proscribed in Germany by Article 5 of the Basic Law, while in the United States the Federal Communications Act does not allow censorship of broadcasting.[8] The principle applies as strongly to public as it does to independent private broadcasting. For public broadcasting is not to be equated with state broadcasting, any more than public education in a free society means the indoctrination of the government's values. It is arguable, however, that the principles of freedom from state control embrace more than the absence of programme censorship, and that they require the broadcasting authorities (whether public or private) to be genuinely independent of government. This would have consequences for the overall composition of these bodies, the methods by which their members are chosen, and their security of tenure.

The legal consequences of freedom from state control (*Staatsfreiheit*) have been explored at length in Germany. In its first decision on the structure of broadcasting,[9] the Constitutional Court emphasized the importance of freedom from state control when it held the foundation by the federal government of the Deutschland-Fernsehen-GmbH contrary both to the Basic Law's distribution of powers between federal and state government and to the fundamental principle of broadcasting freedom guaranteed by Article 5. That principle prohibits state control, direct or indirect, of broadcasting authorities or companies (though not some state representation on these bodies). The Court found that the new broadcasting institution was to be entirely under federal government control; the guide-lines which provided for editorial independence could easily be amended, since they had not been incorporated in a Parliamentary statute. Its establishment would, therefore, be incompatible with Article 5.

In subsequent cases the Bundesverfassungsgericht has emphasized that freedom from state control requires the legislature to frame some basic rules. These should ensure that the government is unable to exercise any influence over the selection, content, or scheduling of programmes. Both in the *Fourth* and in the *Sixth Television* cases provisions in state laws were found unconstitutional for permitting the *Land* government or licensing authority unlimited discretion in the allocation of permits and frequencies.[10] What is objectionable, the Court stressed in the later case, is that the executive could choose between particular applicants (in particular between the public broadcaster and a private competitor) on the basis of its

[7] (1986) Cmnd. 9824, para. 696.
[8] S. 326.
[9] *First Television* case, 12 BVerfGE 205 (1961).
[10] 73 BVerfGE 118 (1986) and 83 BVerfGE 238 (1991).

programming. Parliament should formulate in primary legislation general criteria on the basis of which these choices could be made by an independent authority. The Court has also laid down the fundamental rules for the composition and selection of the independent broadcasting authorities, an integral aspect of freedom from government control. These guide-lines are considered in the next chapter.

The constitutional position of the BBC would appear incompatible with the fundamental principles of broadcasting freedom formulated by the German Constitutional Court in these cases. The Corporation is constituted by Charter under the Royal Prerogative, rather than by statute.[11] That in itself violates the requirement that public broadcasting should be regulated by law, and not by government order or decree. More seriously, the Charter may be revoked at any time if the government considers that the BBC has failed to perform its terms or those in its accompanying Licence and Agreement.[12] A decision to revoke the Charter would of course not be lightly taken. But it is not clear that such a decision could be challenged in the courts, since they are traditionally reluctant to interfere with the exercise by the government of its Royal Prerogative powers.[13] Moreover, in principle it is wrong for the public broadcasting system to be dependent on the goodwill of government for its continued existence. In comparison the licence of private broadcasters may only be withdrawn by a decision of the Independent Television Commission, an independent regulatory body.

As already stated, broadcasting freedom would appear to preclude the banning of particular programmes or types of programme on the basis of their contents. Most obviously it is incompatible with censorship by government itself. Yet in Britain the government enjoys wide powers to direct the broadcasting authorities not to include 'any matter or classes of matter' in their programme.[14] Before 1988 the powers had only been exercised five times and then in general terms, for example, to direct the BBC not to express its own opinion on political topics.[15] However, towards the end of that year it was exercised in a more controversial manner, which raises fundamental issues of broadcasting freedom. The Home Secretary prohibited the broadcasting authorities, both BBC and IBA (then responsible for private commercial broadcasting), from broadcasting directly any words spoken by representatives of prescribed organ-

[11] For detailed discussion, see Ch. III, S. 3 below.

[12] Charter, Art. 20(2).

[13] *Council of Civil Service Unions* v. *Minister for the Civil Service* [1985] AC 374 is the leading authority on this topic.

[14] The powers are now found in Broadcasting Act 1990, s. 10 (with regard to the independent sector) and in cl. 13(4) of the Licence and Agreement between the government and the BBC.

[15] Annan Committee Report (1977) Cmnd. 6753, para. 5. 10.

izations (for example, Sinn Fein and the Ulster Defence Association) or their supporters. The object was to prevent terrorists and their sympathizers from securing publicity. The ban was less complete, and arguably less coherent, for allowing broadcasters to show film of terrorists being interviewed with a voice-over and to show speeches and interviews during electoral campaigns. Challenges to the ban brought by members of the National Union of Journalists (though not by the broadcasting authorities themselves) proved unsuccessful.[16] Both the lower courts and the House of Lords rejected arguments that it was an unreasonable (or disproportionate) exercise of the Home Secretary's statutory powers or that he had failed to take proper account of Article 10 of the European Convention, protecting freedom of expression. (On the latter point, of fundamental constitutional importance, the English judges took the view that it would be wrong to require government ministers to have regard to the Convention when exercising statutory powers which on their face gave them unlimited powers. That course would have been in their view to incorporate the Convention into English law.)

It is less clear whether previewing and censorship by an independent regulatory authority is incompatible with broadcasting freedom. In fact regulatory authorities rarely, if ever, exercise such powers, and as already mentioned the Federal Communications Commission is expressly denied any censorship power by its constituent legislation. The Independent Television Commission set up by the Broadcasting Act 1990 does not enjoy any previewing powers, but its predecessor, the IBA, did have them. It was itself in law the broadcaster, and was under a statutory duty to satisfy itself that as far as possible its programmes did not offend against taste or decency, etc. The scope of its powers was considered by the Court of Appeal in two cases. In the first, *A.-G.* v. *IBA ex rel. McWhirter*, an attempt was made to prevent the showing of a programme about the pop artist Andy Warhol.[17] An interim injunction was granted to stop the broadcast, pending examination of the programme by members of the IBA themselves, but when they gave permission for it to be transmitted, it was discharged. The Court of Appeal refused to question the IBA decision, for '[t]hey are the censors'.[18] In normal circumstances it was appropriate for the Authority to rely on the judgement of its staff, as it would be quite impracticable for it to preview more than a tiny fraction of the companies' programmes. But it should be prepared itself to examine them when, as in this case, it was clear that they might be offensive to public feeling. In the second case the Court of Appeal again

[16] *R.* v. *Home Secretary, ex parte Brind* [1991] 1 AC 696.
[17] [1973] 1 QB 629.
[18] Ibid. 652 per Lord Denning MR.

refused to interfere.[19] It held acceptable an arrangement whereby it was for the Director-General (the senior officer of the Authority) to decide whether to refer a programme to the members of the Authority, though they could also preview on the basis of their own viewing and newspaper and audience reactions.

In view of the IBA's position as the broadcaster, this control does not seem to have amounted to impermissible censorship power, incompatible with broadcasting freedom. The position was similar to the control exercised within a broadcasting institution by senior producers or programme controllers. Their powers could hardly be regarded as raising censorship issues. Even in the United States the power of broadcasters and broadcasting authorities to regulate their programme schedules has been upheld against First Amendment challenge. There is generally no objection to previewing by the licensee or its staff.[20] Further, in *Muir* v. *Alabama Educational Television Commission*[21] residents of the state challenged the withdrawal of a controversial film, which had been scheduled for broadcast on non-commercial educational television. In two decisions the Court of Appeals for the Fifth Circuit held that the withdrawal did not amount to unconstitutional censorship: the Commission was not part of the state, but even if it were so regarded, there was a difference in the Court's view between censorship by the state of other people's speech and its own editorial discretion to broadcast what it thought appropriate. One merit of this decision is that it avoids the troublesome distinction between the withdrawal of an already scheduled programme on the one hand, and on the other the decision not to schedule it in the first place. The latter clearly does not constitute censorship, and it would be odd to treat withdrawal differently.[22] In Germany too there is probably no constitutional objection to previewing by a broadcasting authority (Rundfunkrat), though in practice this never happens; programme control is exercised by the Intendant (Director-General).[23]

Other types of state regulation might conceivably interfere with broadcasting freedom. In particular there is often controversy about the scope of police powers to search for and seize material in the possession of broadcasters on the ground that it might be material evidence in a criminal

[19] *R.* v. *IBA, ex parte Whitehouse*, *The Times*, 4 Apr. 1985.

[20] See *Yale Broadcasting Co.* v. *FCC*, 478 F. 2d. 594 (DC Cir. 1973), holding that there is no First Amendment objection to FCC Notice and Order reminding licensees that they should take steps to determine before transmission the meaning of drug-oriented lyrics.

[21] 656 F. 2d. 1012 (1981), reviewed and confirmed *en banc*, 688 F. 2d. 1033 (5th Cir. 1982).

[22] The Court of Appeals distinguished *Island Trees School District* v. *Pico* 457 US 853 (1982), where the Court had upheld a challenge to the withdrawal of books from a school library.

[23] See S. 3 below, and the note by C. Starck [1979] *JZ* 305.

prosecution.[24] Wide powers of this character, it is argued, may inhibit the preparation of programmes dealing with controversial subjects, for example, terrorism, espionage, or criminal activity. Broadcasters fear that the police might raid their premises to search for photographs, scripts, tapes, or other potential evidence. In the British Broadcasting Bill introduced in 1989 the government included a wide power exercisable by any police officer of or above the rank of superintendent to make an order requiring the person named in it to produce any script or visual or sound recording to enable the police to make a copy; this power was to be exercisable whenever the officer had reasonable grounds for suspecting that certain offences under the public order or obscene publications legislation had been committed or were likely to be committed in respect of a programme. After vigorous criticism, the scope of the power was significantly cut down.[25] In particular an order may only be made by a magistrate and it can only be made in respect of a sound or visual recording (and not a script) where there is reasonable ground to suspect that a particular offence has previously been committed. There is no power to anticipate a likely offence.

Broad police powers of this kind may affect people other than broadcasters. Both press and broadcasting institutions claim to be inhibited when their journalists are ordered to disclose their sources of information.[26] In principle unlimited or even very wide search and copying powers, or judicial powers to order the disclosure of sources, imperil media freedom. But generally statutory provisions take some account of the interests of the media by imposing restrictions on the relevant powers or by conferring on journalists some procedural privileges or limited immunities.[27] Courts are reluctant to regard these privileges and immunities as constitutionally mandated.[28] The German Constitutional Court has held that in principle broadcasting freedom covers the preparation of programmes through the collection of documents and the taking of film.[29] This must be balanced

[24] Witness the controversy over the confiscation under warrant of documents and film from the offices of BBC Scotland discussed in K. D. Ewing and C. Gearty, *Freedom under Thatcher* (Oxford, 1990), 150–2, and over the contempt order made in July 1992 against Channel 4 for refusing to disclose the identity of its source for a programme alleging collusion between the security forces and terrorist organizations in Northern Ireland.

[25] Broadcasting Act 1990, s. 167.

[26] For a discussion of this problem, see E. M. Barendt, *Freedom of Speech* (Oxford, 1987), 73–7.

[27] e.g. Contempt of Court Act 1981, s. 10, and Police and Criminal Evidence Act 1984, ss. 11 and 13–14.

[28] *Branzburg* v. *Hayes* 408 US 665 (1982) (no First Amendment privilege not to disclose sources of information), *Zurcher* v. *Stanford Daily* 436 US 547 (1978) (no immunity of newspaper officers from search under warrant), and *Spiegel* case, 20 BVerfGE 162 (1966) (Court holds press freedom includes a degree of immunity from searches, without upholding one in the case itself).

[29] 77 BVerfGE 65 (1988).

against the obligation of everyone, including journalists, to assist in the investigation of crime. The Court, therefore, held that the seizure from ZDF offices of unpublished film taken at a demonstration was compatible with *Rundfunkfreiheit*. It also said that self-researched material was not entitled to the same degree of protection as information given in confidence to the press and broadcasting media. In short, broadcasting freedom might be infringed by draconian police powers framed or exercised without regard to that freedom. That will not be the case if such powers are exercised for proper purposes and with due regard for the interests of the broadcasting company and the public.

3. INDIVIDUAL AND INSTITUTIONAL FREEDOM

(i) Who exercises broadcasting freedom?

As discussed in Section 1 above, one view of broadcasting freedom is that it is simply the exercise of the rights of individuals to speak on radio and television. According to this approach broadcasting journalists, programme producers, and controllers, as well as contributors to discussion programmes and interviewees, would all be entitled to claim freedom of speech on radio and television. In one respect this is a plausible view. All these individuals should be entitled to claim broadcasting freedom against the state, that is, they should be entitled to express their views on the media free from government censorship and the constraints discussed in the previous section of this chapter. To that extent the same freedom may be claimed both by the broadcasting institutions and by their employees and contributors. Apart from this point, however, the perspective is (as already intimated) an incoherent one. For it is quite impossible for invited speakers, broadcasting journalists, programme producers, and controllers all to claim the same rights of free speech on the media as they exercise elsewhere. That would inevitably lead to conflict.[30] A journalist cannot claim a right to say what he wants to in a documentary or current affairs programme when the producer favours a programme with a different slant or balance. Further, the latter is not entitled to have the programme transmitted on the date and time he wishes, if the channel controller decides that for some reason it should not be shown at all, or at that particular time because another programme has higher priority. Finally all broadcasting employees are subject to the overall control of the Director-General (or other administrative head), who may himself on rare occasions be instructed not to show a particular programme by the governing authority, such as the BBC Governors or a German Rundfunkrat.

[30] Royal Commission on the Press (1977) Cmnd. 6810, para. 2.2.

Quite apart from these conflicts, there is the point that broa
bodies are, as already mentioned, subject to substantial restric
their freedom of speech. For example, they are not entitled
countries to express their views on current political or industrial controversies. (The position in the United States is significantly different in this respect: both public and private broadcasters are permitted to editorialize.)[31] Public and to a lesser extent private broadcasters are required to show a balanced and comprehensive range of programmes, a significant restraint on their freedom to draw up their own schedules. Neither of these restraints applies to newspapers. From the perspective of the broadcasting institutions and their employees, freedom of expression is limited and indeed amounts to the freedom from government censorship of the type described in the previous section.

We have seen that the special restraints on the freedom of broadcasters which exist in all European countries can be justified on free speech grounds. Freedom of expression includes the right to receive information and ideas, as well as the freedom to impart them.[32] The free speech interests of viewers and listeners in exposure to a wide variety of material can best be safeguarded by the imposition of programme standards, limiting the freedom of radio and television companies. What is important according to this perspective is that the broadcasting institutions are free to discharge their responsibilities of providing the public with a balanced range of programmes and a variety of views. These free speech goals require positive legislative provision to prevent the domination of the broadcasting authorities by the government or by private corporations and advertisers, and perhaps for securing impartiality. It is crucial that the institutions are free; it is much less important which individuals within them exercise free speech rights. Broadcasting freedom is therefore primarily an institutional freedom of the broadcasting corporation.[33] That is why there has been in many countries so much anxiety about the mode of selection, composition, and powers of the broadcasting or regulatory bodies. Broadcasting freedom is certainly endangered if there are no legal limits on the ability of government to pack television authorities with its supporters. It is less obvious that it is violated when the freedom of individual journalists is limited, as it must be from time to time, by programme controllers or the Director-General.

Broadcasting freedom, therefore, refers to an institutional autonomy rather than a set of individual rights to speak freely on radio and television. The broadcasting corporation through its responsible officer, for example, the Director-General of the BBC or the German Intendant, has (or

[31] For further discussion, see Ch. V, S. 2 below.

[32] Art. 10(1) of the European Convention on Human Rights.

[33] See the German *First Television* case, 12 BVerfGE 205, 261 (1961).

should have) a right to draw up a schedule of programmes and to transmit them free from government censorship. The right is, however, limited by legislatively imposed obligations to show a balanced range of programmes and to be impartial. This account of broadcasting freedom is particularly pertinent for public broadcasters, though it also applies to a considerable extent to private broadcasting, where the quality controls are generally a little weaker than those imposed on the former.[34] Although the freedom of broadcasters is restricted in the interests of viewers and listeners, the latter do not have rights to determine what is contained in the broadcasting schedules (as discussed in Section 4). Broadcasters are, therefore, free from legal challenges by individual viewers and listeners (or their associations) to dictate what they watch and hear. This programme freedom is far from negligible. But it is more circumscribed than press freedom or the freedom of speech normally recognized outside the context of broadcasting.

In many continental European countries broadcasting freedom is a constitutional value, which influences the development of the law, both public and private. In other words its significance is not exhausted by the rights of individuals and institutions. In Germany the Constitutional Court has interpreted *Rundfunkfreiheit* to justify the imposition of special responsibilities, particularly on the public broadcasting institutions.[35] Secondly, all branches of the law must be interpreted in the light of the freedom, a principle which has been applied to allow public broadcasting companies some limited immunity from the normal constraints of labour law.[36] In these situations it is idle to speculate which individual broadcasters exercise fundamental rights.

(ii) Programme rights and internal broadcasting freedom

If broadcasting freedom is primarily regarded as an *institutional* freedom, questions arise who is entitled to claim that freedom on behalf of the institution and how disputes between senior officials and the governing body of the broadcasting corporation should be resolved. How far may individual journalists claim rights against the authority, the problem referred to in German law as internal broadcasting freedom (*innere Rundfunkfreiheit*)? Sometimes responsibility for drawing up programme schedules is vested by law with a Director-General or the Intendant. For example, under the State Treaty constituting the second public television channel in Germany, Zweites Deutsches Fernsehen (ZDF), the Intendant

[34] See Ch. V, S. 1 below.

[35] For the concept of *Grundversorgung* in German law, see Ch. III, S. 2 below.

[36] 59 BVerfGE 231 (1982). The general principle that the basic rights in the *Grundgesetz* influence the interpretation of all areas of law was formulated in the *Numerus Clausus* case, 33 BVerfGE 303, 330 (1972).

is responsible for programme planning and content, as well as for the appointment of the Programme Director and Chief Editor in agreement with the Administrative Board.[37] On the other hand, the Television Board (Fernsehrat) has the responsibility for drawing up programme guide-lines and advising the Intendant on their planning and preparation. It must also oversee compliance with these guide-lines and the rules set out in the State Treaty.[38] These are limited supervisory powers; in particular they do not confer authority to preview programmes or stop their showing.[39] That would undermine the primary responsibility of the Intendant. The Administrative Court of Hamburg has indeed suggested that the Administrative Board might have exceeded its powers in holding NDR's programming unbalanced.[40] The Director-General's standing to challenge the decision was upheld, although the application succeeded on the ground that the Board was improperly composed.

In Italy the responsibilities of both the Director-General of RAI and the directors of each radio and television channel are briefly set out in the 1975 statute. Subject to the guide-lines established by the Parliamentary Commission, the Administrative Council approves on a three-monthly basis RAI's programme plans and exercises supervisory control, making periodic reports to the Commission.[41] The directors of each channel are statutorily responsible to the Director-General for its political direction, indicating how relatively formal is the distribution of the channels between the parties.[42]

In contrast there is little law in Britain about the respective functions of the Governors of the BBC and the Director-General. Instead there have been conventions and changing practice. While the Charter indicates that the Governors are responsible for all activities of the Corporation,[43] they have in fact almost always left programming entirely to the Director-General and the staff. Indeed the so-called 'Whitley document', named after the Chairman of the Governors at that time, explicitly conferred all executive powers on the Director-General.[44] The Governors regarded themselves as representatives of the public, able at the most to lay down very general guide-lines and to discuss listeners' complaints. However,

[37] ZDF *Staatsvertrag* of 31 Aug. 1991, Art. 27.

[38] Ibid., Art. 20.

[39] See E. W. Fuhr, *ZDF-Staatsvertrag*, 2nd edn. (Mainz, 1985), 270–1.

[40] [1980] *DVBl.* 491.

[41] Law 103 of 14 Apr. 1975, Art. 8.

[42] Ibid., Art. 13, para. 7. See E. Santoro, 'Il giornalista nel servizio pubblico radiotelevisivo', in E. Roppo (ed.), *Il diritto delle communicazioni di massa: problemi e tendenze* (Padua, 1985), 193, 197–8.

[43] BBC Charter, Arts. 5–7. Art. 12 enables the Governors to appoint staff for the discharge of their responsibilities.

[44] T. Burns, *The BBC: Public Institution and Private World* (London, 1977), 21–2.

in the 1960s under the chairmanship of Lord Hill they began to assert a more active executive role. The Annan Committee considered this should not extend other than exceptionally to the previewing of particular programmes.[45] Programme control should be exercised only after transmission. That remains the general practice. But in 1985 the Governors, acting under pressure from the Home Secretary, Leon Brittan, forbade the transmission of a documentary on the Northern Ireland troubles, featuring an interview with a prominent member of the IRA. The decision created outrage among the staff and some public criticism, but there is little doubt that the Governors were acting legally, albeit contrary to previous practice.[46] The BBC Governors may preview programmes without infringing broadcasting freedom, since they stand, as the IBA did, at the apex of the institution's structure.[47] For that freedom is not a right of the Director-General, let alone his staff, but of the Corporation as an institution.

There is a relatively clear answer to the question who is entitled to assert broadcasting freedom on behalf of the company. It depends on how the legislation (or other rules) allocate responsibility for drawing up the programme. In Germany and Italy primary responsibilities are given by law to the Director-General, so it is this figure who is entitled to protect freedom against state infringement. In contrast the BBC Director-General has enjoyed power only as a result of personality (as with Lord Reith) or under a general practice, at most amounting to a weak convention. In the case of private radio and television, the broadcasters, rather than the regulatory authorities, enjoy the freedom; the position of the IBA as broadcaster was anomalous.

The institutional character of broadcasting freedom is also shown when the position of individual producers and journalists is considered. The Administrative Appeal Court of Münster has held that a producer had no constitutional right to challenge the decision of the WDR Administrative Council, which had banned his programme because of its violent and extremist content.[48] The complainant could only rely on *Rundfunkfreiheit* in conjunction with, or as a representative, of the organization. He could not assert an individual right of broadcasting freedom against it. Moreover, the Council decision was not addressed to him, but to the Intendant. In effect the complainant only enjoyed contractual and labour law rights.

Although surely correct in principle, this position has understandably

[45] (1977) Cmnd. 6753, para. 9.69.

[46] For a naturally partial account of the episode, see A. Milne, *DG: The Memoirs of a British Broadcaster* (London, 1988), ch. 12.

[47] For the exercise by the IBA of its previewing powers, see S. 2 above.

[48] [1981] *DVBl.* 1012. See H. Bethge, 'Zum Rechtschutz des Redakteurs einer Rundfunkanstalt gegen Entscheidungen eines Rundfunkorgans' (1981) 12 *Archiv für Presserecht* 386.

been challenged by associations of producers, editors, and other workers in the broadcasting (and press) media. This challenge poses questions of *innere Rundfunkfreiheit* (internal broadcasting freedom), that is, the extent to which employees may enjoy some rights within the broadcasting system.[49] Although they do not usually enjoy a freedom to assert their own views over the wavelengths, they are surely at least entitled not to participate in programmes which violate their own beliefs and not to be presented in programme descriptions as sharing views they do not hold. These rights are aspects of an individual's own negative freedom of speech.[50] Further, any employee is entitled to say and write what he likes outside the broadcasting context, though there could be nice constitutional questions whether this freedom may be limited by provisions in his contract of employment with the authority. There is much to be said for publishing these rights in staff codes. The sensitive position of broadcasting employees can also be safeguarded to some extent by representation on relevant administrative bodies. Thus, in Bremen and Hesse they are entitled to nominate some members of the Verwaltungsrat (Administrative Board).[51] The exact content of such provisions is a matter for legislative discretion; but employee representatives should not be so numerous as to interfere with the overall authority of the executive head or to imperil the principle of broadcasting freedom which precludes domination of the media by particular groups.

In the *Sixth Television* case the Bundesverfassungsgericht held it constitutional for the authorities to treat the degree of editors' involvement in preparing programme schedules as a material factor in licence allocation.[52] Their participation could be regarded as relevant to the guarantee of plurality of opinion. The Court emphasized, however, that this factor would not permit editors to broadcast their own opinions. In practice, of course, producers, particularly those of some seniority, will have considerable freedom to make the programmes they want. Broadcasting which is preoccupied with the constraints of the public service tradition may become dull. It is important that there should be some scope for the individual voice on the broadcasting staff. But that is not a matter of legal, let alone constitutional, right.

(iii) Broadcasting freedom and labour law

Broadcasting freedom as a constitutional value may limit employees' rights in at least two respects. This perhaps only applies in the context of

[49] For discussion of the vigorous campaign in Germany to secure rights for broadcasting journalists, see H. Bausch, *Rundfunk in Deutschland: Rundfunkpolitik nach 1945* (Munich, 1980), 817–29.

[50] See Barendt, *Freedom of Speech*, 63–5.

[51] Hesse law of 2 Oct. 1948, Art. 11(1); Bremen law of 18 June 1979, Art. 9(1).

[52] 83 BVerfGE 238 (1991).

public broadcasting corporations, which have significant constitutional responsibilities. First, they should be free on occasion to replace key personnel such as the Director-General, heads of particular channels, programme controllers, perhaps even producers, when this is necessary to discharge their responsibilities. A programme controller, for example, might be found to have arranged too frequently an unbalanced schedule, and it might be desirable to replace him with someone more reliable. Constitutions may, therefore, impose constraints on the security of tenure which senior employees would otherwise enjoy under labour law. An issue of this character has arisen in Germany. The Constitutional Court held that broadcasting freedom justified the prerogative of the corporation to employ *freie Mitarbeiter* (freelance workers) to discharge key programme work, free from the constraints of labour law.[53] The Federal Labour Law Court had misapplied the Basic Law when it had conferred on these workers the security from dismissal enjoyed by other employees engaged in technical and administrative work. It had thought this would give the freelance workers more independence in discharging their editorial responsibilities. But in the Constitutional Court's view the engagement of permanent staff would put at risk the values of balance and variety, which were crucial to broadcasting freedom. This decision incidentally supports the view that the freedom confers institutional rights, rather than individual rights for employees.

Secondly, broadcasting freedom may have some impact on the right to strike of television and radio staff. Even if the right to strike is covered by a freedom of association clause (such as Article 9 of the German *Grundgesetz*), its exercise may be limited by the requirements of specific laws or other constitutional rights. A labour law court in Munich issued an injunction to restrain a planned political strike by employees of the NDR; a strike would have imperilled broadcasting freedom and the freedom of the public to be informed (also protected by Article 5).[54] It is possible that the same order would have been made if the object of the strike had been purely economic.[55] In these circumstances *Rundfunkfreiheit* is used as a factor in justifying limitations on the (constitutional) rights of workers, rather than recognized as conferring an absolute right for employers. The particular circumstances of each case must be taken into account, when one constitutional right is weighed against another. A total black-out of all news programmes on radio and television would clearly have more impact on broadcasting freedom than would a series of sporadic strikes which prevented the live broadcasting, say, of certain sports events.

[53] 59 BVerfGE 231 (1982), followed in 64 BVerfGE 256 (1963). For commentary, see R. Bietmann, 'Rundfunkfreiheit und Arbeitnehmer Begriff' [1983] *NJW* 200.

[54] [1990] *NJW* 957.

[55] R. Ricker, 'Die Zulässigkeit des Streiks in Presse und Rundfunk' [1980] *NJW* 157.

Under French law a minimum service, which presumably includes national and regional news programmes, weather and traffic forecasts, etc., must be provided during strikes on the public broadcasting channels.[56] However, a Bill in 1979 which attempted to ensure the provision of normal services during these periods was held an unconstitutional interference with the right to strike.[57] In its more recent ruling on the 1986 statute, the Conseil affirmed this distinction between a normal and an essential minimum service; limits on the right to strike may only be imposed to ensure the continuity of those aspects of public services, such as broadcasting, which are essential to the country's needs.[58] This formulation may give too much weight to the right to strike and too little to freedom of broadcasting and the citizens' right to be informed. But some balancing of interests is essential. It is doubtful whether it is possible to formulate a precise rule which works satisfactorily in all circumstances.

4. THE RIGHTS OF VIEWERS AND LISTENERS

In a famous passage in his judgment for the Supreme Court in the *Red Lion* case White J. wrote:[59]

> But the people as a whole retain their interest in free speech by radio and their collective right to have the medium function consistently with the ends and purposes of the First Amendment. It is the right of viewers and listeners, not the right of the broadcasters, which is paramount.

This argument justified the limits imposed by the FCC on broadcasters through the Fairness Doctrine, in particular the rule requiring stations to afford free rights of reply to personal attacks; these constraints protected the interests of listeners in access to a balanced range of opinions.[60] Indeed, courts frequently refer to this audience interest as a justification for restrictions on broadcasters' freedom. But they are reluctant to recognize that listeners have rights they can assert in legal proceedings.

In Britain there are, of course, no constitutional rights for either broadcasters or viewers and listeners. But the latter may have standing to challenge decisions of the broadcasting authorities. In the *McWhirter* case (discussed in Section 2) two members of the Court of Appeal said that a member of the public with sufficient interest could apply to the courts for an injunction against a broadcasting authority (in the case the IBA),

[56] Law of 30 Sept. 1986, Art. 57(II).
[57] Decision 79-105, Rec. 1979, 33, Debbasch, 159.
[58] Decision 86–217, Rec. 1986, 141, Debbasch, 245, 261–2.
[59] *Red Lion Broadcasting* v. *FCC* 395 US 367, 390 (1969).
[60] For the Doctrine, see Ch. VII, S. 4.

where the Attorney-General had improperly refused to take proceedings in his own name or had been dilatory in granting consent. A Scottish case has recognized the standing of voters to compel the IBA to secure a proper balance of viewpoints in the political broadcasts transmitted before the Devolution Referendum.[61] The courts are in effect giving some protection to the interest of the public, and, therefore, viewers and listeners, in fair and decent broadcasting. But that stops well short of a right to view a particular programme or to limit directly the programming freedom of broadcasters. At most the result of the intervention is that the court compels the regulatory authority to reconsider its initial decision.

Members of the public have, however, fared no better in countries where freedom of broadcasting is constitutionally protected. For example, the Administrative Appeal Court for Hamburg has denied television viewers a right to have a particular sports programme transmitted, even when the item had already been announced in the schedule.[62] The Court reserved the question whether such a right might be upheld in the case of programmes of exceptional importance; sports programmes did not in its view fall into that category. The decision is in line with the view that the freedom of information (*Informationsfreiheit*) guaranteed by Article 5 of the Basic Law does not confer positive rights, but only entails a liberty to receive information against state interference.[63] Further, recognition of such a right would almost certainly conflict with the freedom of television and radio controllers to draw up their own schedules. This second point is admittedly not decisive in itself, as the law substantially restricts their programming freedom. There is a difference, however, between statutory regulation in the interest of viewers as a whole, and allowing individuals rights which they can assert by legal action.

The Italian courts have also consistently refused to uphold individual legal rights. The Pretura di Roma held that a viewer had no right to enforce RAI's obligation to provide a balanced and comprehensive coverage; in the particular case the complaint concerned the inadequate treatment of some left-wing parties and pressure groups.[64] In another case viewers in the Rome area complained that they had been unable to watch television coverage of an Italy–England football match. Under agreement with the national football association, internationals played in Rome were not broadcast live in that area. The court held that the duty of the public broadcasting company to provide comprehensive and objective news and information was safeguarded by the Parliamentary Commission, rather than by the recognition of individual viewers' rights.[65] Decisions

[61] *Wilson* v. *IBA* 1979 SLT 279, discussed further in Ch. VIII, S. 2.
[62] [1978] *DVBl.* 640
[63] See Barendt, *Freedom of Speech*, 111–12, for discussion of this point.
[64] Decision of 3 Sept. 1974, republished in Pace, 260.
[65] Decision of 12 Nov. 1976, republished in Pace, 278.

about particular programmes were a matter for RAI, subject only to the Commission's control. (The court also denied RAI had an absolute right to show all football matches under Article 21 of the Constitution; rights to broadcast matters of national interest could be limited, when otherwise the interests of others, here the football association, would be damaged.) Viewers' interests are, therefore, institutionally, rather than legally, protected through the Parliamentary Commission and the political process. The Italian courts incidentally take the same view of complaints concerning denial of access opportunities (considered in Chapter VII) and of complaints by political groups that they have not received adequate coverage on television.

The United States courts have granted viewers' associations standing to challenge licence renewals.[66] But they have denied them a First Amendment right to compel the FCC to review changes in a programme schedule on the transfer of a licence.[67] The Supreme Court held that the FCC was entitled to rely on market forces to achieve diversity of programming. Nor do viewers have a right to challenge the decisions of the Corporation for Public Broadcasting or of public broadcasting stations; Congress, and not the courts, exercise oversight over public broadcasting.[68] It was mentioned in Section 2 of this chapter that a federal Court of Appeals refused to intervene when a public broadcasting station at the last minute withdrew a programme from its schedule:[69] to have allowed the viewers' action to succeed would have removed the editorial freedom of the broadcasting authority.

These cases from a variety of jurisdictions show that the broadcaster's programme freedom (when exercised within the constraints imposed by the regulatory authority) has priority over the rights claimed by viewers to see a particular programme or to retain a particular series in the schedule. On the other hand, the interests of viewers and listeners justify the imposition of programme standards, which would not be countenanced for the press or publishing. This factor has a constitutional dimension in European countries, including France, Germany, and Italy. Constitutional courts recognize that viewers and listeners have interests and that they should be taken into account in the interpretation of broadcasting freedom. But the balancing of the (sometimes conflicting) interests of broadcasters and viewers is best discharged by regulatory authorities. Courts are understandably reluctant to contemplate the interference with administrative discretion which would result from their recognition of individual rights.

[66] *Office of Communication of United Church of Christ* v. *FCC* 359 F. 2d. 994 (DC Cir. 1966).

[67] *FCC* v. *Listeners Guild* 450 US 582 (1981).

[68] *The Network Project* v. *CPB* 561 F. 2d. 963 (1977).

[69] *Muir* v. *Alabama Educational Television Commission* 656 F. 2d. 1012 (1981).

III
Public Broadcasting

1. INTRODUCTION

Initially broadcasting in virtually every country was a state or public monopoly. This is true of all the jurisdictions considered in this book, with the exception of the United States, where from the outset radio and television were operated by private undertakings. Moreover, the values of public broadcasting prevailed for some considerable time after the introduction of commercial channels in Europe. This has been particularly evident in Britain. Until the Broadcasting Act 1990 independent channels were under the same duty as the BBC to provide television 'as a public service for disseminating information, education and entertainment'.[1] Lighter programme standards in contrast have been imposed on commercial broadcasters in other countries, where private broadcasting was introduced long after its establishment in Britain.

It is now rare to regard public broadcasting as the norm, from which commercial radio and television provide an aberrant departure. Instead doubts have arisen about the survival of the older system. Governments in recent years have been hostile to the performance by public bodies of services that can in their opinion be carried out more efficiently by private corporations. In addition they do not like the unpopularity which, they suppose, occurs after an increase in the licence fee (or other charge imposed to finance public broadcasting). Further, with the advent of cable and satellite, the BBC and other European public channels may find it hard to sustain their share of the national audience. If it were to drop below, say, 30 per cent over a long period, it would be difficult to justify the maintenance of charges to finance a system appreciated by only a minority.

Nevertheless, the survival of public broadcasting is generally regarded as a cultural imperative. It is argued that only institutions independent of both the state and commercial pressures can discharge the fundamental public service obligations of broadcasters. In Britain this is solely a matter of political rhetoric. But in other countries, particularly Germany and Italy, the debate has a constitutional dimension. The German Consti-

[1] See Broadcasting Act 1981, s. 2(2)(a).

tutional Court has developed a doctrine of the basic broadcasting service (*Grundversorgung*).[2] Under this principle public broadcasters have the responsibility of ensuring that viewers and listeners receive a wide range of programmes. Indeed, it is the discharge of that responsibility which justifies their existence and their support by a licence fee. The first two sections of this chapter, therefore, examine the principles of public service broadcasting and their treatment by constitutional courts. The third section discusses the composition and powers of public broadcasting bodies, while the fourth is concerned with some legal questions connected with their financing.

The public service broadcasting principles are, of course, not sacrosanct. It can be said that to refer to 'public service broadcasting' makes no more sense than to talk of 'public service newspapers'. Broadcasting might be regarded as essentially a private service, such as hairdressing or hotel-keeping. Much of the discussion in the earlier chapters is relevant to this question.[3] There are good, if not overwhelming, arguments for the regulation of broadcasting in order to ensure widespread access to the media and to control its unique power. Moreover, the interests of viewers and listeners justify limits on the freedom of broadcasters. If these arguments are acceptable, it follows that broadcasting should be treated to some extent as a public service. All that need be added here is that many advocates of deregulation envisage, nevertheless, some role for public service broadcasting. Even in the United States where broadcasting is dominated by the private networks and local stations, there is a system of publicly financed radio and television, which adheres to some of the principles discussed in the next section.

2. THE CONCEPT OF PUBLIC SERVICE BROADCASTING

There is no precise definition of the concept of 'public service broadcasting'. On a sceptical view it might be little more than a summary of the principles underlying public systems, although it should be added that private commercial broadcasting in Britain used to be subject to them. But there do seem to be some features which are not only common to most non-commercial systems, but which also explain and justify many of their characteristics and the rules governing them.[4] 'Public service broad-

[2] *Fourth Television* case, 73 BVerfGE 118, 153 (1986). The concept has been refined in two later cases, the *Fifth Television* case, 74 BVerfGE 297, 325–31 (1987), and the *Sixth Television* case, 83 BVerfGE 238, 297–8 (1991).

[3] See Ch. I, S. 2 and Ch. II, S. 1 above.

[4] For discussion of the concept, see the Peacock Committee Report (1986) Cmnd. 9824, paras. 28–35, and J. G. Blumler (ed.), *Television and the Public Interest* (London, 1992), esp. chs. 2 and 12.

casting' is in other words a normative, as well as a descriptive, concept. Its principal features can be identified as the following:

1. general geographical availability;
2. concern for national identity and culture;
3. independence from both the state and commercial interests;
4. impartiality of programmes;
5. range and variety of programmes;
6. substantial financing by a general charge on users.

To some extent these principles overlap. For example, there is an obvious link between the first two, although they are clearly not identical. Impartiality is in part a consequence of broadcasters' independence from political and commercial pressure, but separate rules are necessary to ensure that the broadcasters' own political views are not transmitted. Some of these principles are discussed at length elsewhere in this book, and in those cases only a few remarks are made here.

The first principle of public service broadcasting is that the service should be available to everyone throughout the country. Public service radio and television is a national service, though it may also provide programmes of regional and local interest for smaller areas. But it would not normally be acceptable for a public authority only to provide broadcasting services, say, to 60–70 per cent of a country, as is envisaged for the private Channel 5 television service in Britain. This does not mean that everyone in the country should always receive the identical programme. In Germany, for example, where the state broadcasting authorities control the first public television channel (ARD), the programmes shown between 6.00 and 8.00 p.m. vary between the different *Länder*. Independent television in Britain has until recently been regarded as a public service channel, although it has always been organized on a regional basis. The fact that sometimes a region opted to show its own programme, rather than that scheduled for the rest of the network, did not really affect this position, though it might have done so if the practice had been widespread.

This aspect of the public service tradition has probably been less controversial than most of the others, because unlike them it does not raise freedom of expression problems. Nevertheless, it is significant. In the German Constitutional Court's view the national coverage of public broadcasters is one reason for imposing on them the duty to provide the basic service of a balanced range of information and entertainment programmes.[5] It would be harder to justify its imposition on private channels, which may cover a smaller geographical area. The principle

[5] *Fourth Television* case, 73 BVerfGE 118, 153 (1986).

of national coverage does not, however, justify a public broadcasting monopoly; all it requires is that such a service shows some of its programmes, in particular news and current affairs programmes, to all the country.

The principle can itself be justified by reference to the underlying principles of broadcasting freedom and of equality. All citizens, whether they live in the capital city or in an outlying region, have an equal right to receive news, information, and other essential broadcasting services. A state which did not require the authority to provide such a universal service would, therefore, be discriminating in the allocation of a fundamental freedom. One consequence of this argument is that it might be constitutionally suspect for a country to provide basic broadcasting services on a subscription system, which would effectively discriminate against poorer people, unable to enjoy a fundamental right. The Peacock Committee accepted the principle of universal access, recognizing that a move to a subscription system might undermine this. With that in mind, it urged that at least four channels should continue to be transmitted by terrestrial means until cable and satellite is universally available.[6] However, it thought that the availability of subscription broadcasting to the poorer sections of society should be ensured by changes in the income tax and benefits systems. In its view universal access did not require the continued existence of a licence fee.

The second public service principle is more controversial: broadcasting should aim to promote national identity. General geographical availability is of course necessary for the achievement of this goal, but it does not entail the latter. The fostering of national unity was one of the original aims of the BBC in the 1920s and 1930s.[7] Although that goal now seems outdated, it has left a legacy. At times of national crisis or celebration, viewers still instinctively turn to the BBC for a reflection of the country's mood. National unity was also stated as one of the purposes of public broadcasting in the 1968 Canadian Broadcasting Act. The difficulty is that it can easily be seen as chauvinistic, and might conceivably be exploited by an interfering government to require the showing of programmes sympathetic to its policies. So it may run counter to the third public service principle, that broadcasting should be immune from control by the government or vested commercial interests. It also seems incompatible with the requirement that there should be a range of viewpoints expressed in the programmes as a whole, a principle which requires the presentation from time to time of minority positions strongly opposed to the prevailing mood.

[6] Peacock Committee Report, paras. 567–70 and 699.

[7] See T. Burns, *The BBC: Public Institution and Private World* (London, 1977), ch. 1.

Partly for these reasons the Canadian Task Force on Broadcasting Policy recommended the removal of the 'national unity' provision, as a fetter on the broader Canadian cultural mission of broadcasting.[8] Under the 1991 statute the Canadian system must now provide a service 'essential to the maintenance and enhancement of national identity and cultural sovereignty', presumably against the dangers posed by United States quiz shows and soaps.[9] The idea that public service broadcasting should reflect that country's culture to itself is acceptable. This broad policy constitutes a justification for the requirements that a certain proportion of programmes should be made in the country's language, a common rule in France.[10] (It is also a general requirement in EC states under the Broadcasting Directive 1989 that a proportion of the programmes are European in origin.) However, extreme steps to exclude or severely ration the number of foreign programmes may create problems in international and European law.[11]

The other four principles raise issues more fully treated elsewhere in this book. Independence from state control is a crucial aspect of broadcasting freedom discussed in the previous chapter. This part of the third principle applies equally to public and to private broadcasting. For the former, it emphasizes that public broadcasting is not the same as state broadcasting, and it has some significance for the composition and functions of its governing bodies (see Section 3). The second part, independence from particular commercial pressures, is really only relevant to private broadcasting. In contrast the fourth principle, that programmes should be impartial, is a requirement of both public and (to a lesser extent) private channels. No equivalent restraint is imposed on newspapers and magazines, and indeed an impartiality rule would be regarded as contrary to press freedom.

Whatever the merits of the general arguments for limits on programming freedom, there is an overwhelming case for regarding the impartiality rule as integral to public broadcasting. Listeners and viewers expect the BBC and other comparable bodies to be dispassionate in their presentation of information and even-handed in the time allocated for the airing of opinion. This is a legitimate expectation. It would be wrong for public channels, financed by all television viewers, to take sides on political and social controversies. In this context, it is interesting to note that in the United States public broadcasters (unlike their European equivalents) are free to editorialize.[12] But public broadcasting in that country attracts only

[8] Report of the Task Force on Broadcasting Policy (Ottawa, 1986), 283–4.

[9] S. 3(1)(d).

[10] For this requirement, see Ch. V, S. 4.

[11] See Ch. X, S. 2, for a discussion of this question.

[12] *FCC* v. *League of Women Voters of California* 468 US 364 (1984): see Ch. V, S. 2 below.

a relatively small minority of viewers and is largely financed by sponsors and subscribers, able to withdraw their support if a station takes a line they dislike. In addition to the argument of principle, there is the practical point that a public broadcasting company consistently biased in favour of opposition parties would be unlikely to survive, while one with the opposite prejudice would in effect have become a vehicle for state propaganda.

Impartiality rules should be distinguished from those concerned with the range and variety of programmes. The fifth requirement of public service broadcasting is that it provides a varied diet, that is, that it offers news bulletins and documentaries, light entertainment, films, drama, and sports and other live events. Public service broadcasting, as exemplified by the BBC channels or German public television, contrasts with many commercial stations, most particularly in Italy, which show nothing apart from films and quiz shows. It also contrasts with specialist educational or community channels which are, for example, frequently provided by cable networks in the United States. The idea underlying this principle is that sometimes viewers will be tempted to look at programmes they would not watch if they were only available on a specialist channel. The classic formula is that described in the Preamble to the BBC Charter that broadcasting services are 'means of disseminating information, education and entertainment'. The same words were used to impose public service obligations on the terrestrial commercial channels in Britain before the Broadcasting Act 1990 came into force. With the lightening of their programme standards, it has become clearer that the duty to provide a comprehensive service is really a characteristic of public broadcasting, a point also emphasized in the jurisprudence of the German Constitutional Court.[13] Recent suggestions that the BBC abandon its popular music radio channels indicate a move away from this aspect of public service broadcasting.[14] That would certainly occur if public broadcasting were confined, say, to one radio and one television channel for the transmission of programmes which could not find a place in commercial schedules.

The sixth public service principle is that broadcasting should be financed by a licence fee or other charge imposed on all members of the public who possess a receiving set. The principle reinforces the third principle that broadcasting should not be dominated by commercial interests. Advertising is the principal alternative means of finance. But that carries the risk that programme companies will be influenced by their paymasters, the advertising agencies, in drawing up programme schedules. Another possible source is subscription income, but (as already argued)

[13] See S. 3 of this chapter below.

[14] The Peacock Committee Report, paras. 637–44, first made this suggestion, which has often been repeated in subsequent discussion.

reliance on it might infringe the equal right of citizens to enjoy access to broadcasting. It is, therefore, often said that the imposition of a public charge, whether collected by the tax system or by a special levy, is integral to the concept of public service broadcasting. Indeed, the German Constitutional Court has recently held its imposition justified on the ground that it ensures the performance by public broadcasters of their fundamental responsibilities.[15]

On the other hand a public broadcasting system will come to rely on the decision of a government minister to increase the licence fee (or equivalent charge) in line with inflation. In extreme cases that might call into question its independence from government influence. A flat-rate licence fee, or equivalent charge, is also regressive; in theory one would expect it to attract the same odium as the poll-tax, though that has not been the case. Moreover, the assessment of a high licence fee would attract the objection made to the introduction of subscription charges, that it would be beyond the means of low-income groups.

In practice in most European countries public broadcasting is financed by a mixture of a general charge and advertising revenue. That is true of France, Germany, and Italy. Only in Britain is advertising on the public channels totally prohibited. The merit of mixed financing is perhaps that it reduces the risk of dependence on any particular source. On the other hand, it cannot be said that its introduction in other European countries has improved the quality of their programmes.

3. THE CONSTITUTIONAL POSITION

Until recently the major constitutional question concerning public broadcasting companies was whether they were entitled to provide a monopoly service. Clearly the question did not arise in the United States, and in Britain in the absence of any written constitution there was no avenue for legal challenge to the BBC's position. But there were constitutional disputes in Germany, Italy, and France, particularly in the 1970s and 1980s. In the overwhelming majority of these cases the public monopoly was upheld. However, the courts did not hold that the monopoly was required by the constitution, only that it was permitted. It was for the legislature to decide the structure of the broadcasting system, provided its statutes satisfied certain constitutional requirements, in particular the principle of freedom of expression. Only in Italy has the Constitutional Court ruled that the monopoly could not be sustained in some contexts, the most important of these being local (as opposed to national) terrestrial and cable broadcasting.

[15] 87 BVerfGE 181 (1992).

Private commercial broadcasting has been gradually introduced in most European countries in the last two decades, while in Britain it has existed since the Television Act 1954. Consequently the constitutional issues with regard to public broadcasting have changed. The most important one, addressed in Germany and to a lesser extent Italy, concerns the relationship between public and private broadcasting, and in particular whether the former has a distinctive role after the introduction and development of its junior competitor. But the courts' approach to these questions has been significantly influenced by the earlier case-law in which it had considered the monopoly position of public broadcasting.[16]

In Germany the Bundesverfassungsgericht has from the beginning ruled that a public monopoly was lawful.[17] In the absence of sufficient frequencies to accommodate everyone who might wish to operate a service, the monopoly was a reasonable method of securing equal access to the media. But the legislature could alternatively opt to permit private broadcasting as long as it was regulated to bring about equality of access and to prevent its domination by interest groups.[18] A similar approach was taken by the Italian Constitutional Court. Initially it held on the basis of the scarcity argument that broadcasting was a natural monopoly, so that RAI's position could be justified under Article 43 of the Constitution.[19] Subsequently, most particularly in the landmark ruling of 1974,[20] the Court also based this conclusion on the vital service provided by broadcasting in a modern democracy. The medium was uniquely able to reach all citizens in a direct and immediate way, informing them of the conflicting currents of opinion. However, neither this nor the scarcity argument applied so convincingly in the case of local broadcasting, whether distributed by cable or by conventional terrestrial means, so it followed that the public monopoly could not be upheld in those contexts.[21]

The French Conseil constitutionnel was also invited to consider the constitutionality of the ORTF monopoly. In 1978 a Bill creating criminal penalties for the violation by pirate radio stations of the public broadcasting monopoly was sent to the Council for consideration. It was argued that the measure was contrary to Article 11 of the Declaration of the Rights of Man, guaranteeing liberty of communication of thoughts and opinions. The application was rejected, because the Conseil does not have power to review laws which have already been enacted; the measures

[16] For a general discussion of these questions, see E. M. Barendt, 'The Influence of the German and Italian Constitutional Courts on their National Broadcasting Systems' [1991] *Pub. Law* 93.

[17] *First Television* case, 12 BVerfGE 205 (1961).

[18] *Third Television* case, 57 BVerfGE 295 (1981).

[19] Decision 59/1960 [1960] *Giur. cost.* 759.

[20] Decision 225/1974 [1974] *Giur. cost.* 1775.

[21] See Decision 202/1976 [1976] *Giur. cost.* 1267.

establishing the monopoly time had been passed in 1972 and 1974.[22] With the introduction of private broadcasting under the laws of 1982 and 1986 the monopoly issue, as in Germany and Italy, has become dead.

The pertinent question for the 1990s is whether the existence of public broadcasting is constitutionally guaranteed. That would become particularly significant if the public institutions were to find it difficult to compete with their less regulated private competitors. The formers' financial position might become so acute that their very survival would be endangered. Might it then be held that the state had a constitutional duty to ensure their existence? An affirmative answer to these questions is suggested by rulings of the German and Italian Constitutional Courts. In the *Fourth Television* case the German Constitutional Court formulated the *Grundversorgung* doctrine.[23] Previously it had held that broadcasting freedom must be protected by legislation, to ensure, for example, that viewers and listeners received a comprehensive range of unbiased programmes. Now it ruled that programme restraints could be relaxed a little for the private channels, because the essential basic provision (*unerlässliche Grundversorgung*) of public service broadcasting was the responsibility of the public channels. This obligation was imposed on them because their programmes reached the whole public and they were not subject to the commercial pressure of advertisers. It was the duty of the public channels, ARD and ZDF, to provide the public with a wide range of informative and cultural programmes, as well as entertainment. Further, it was necessary to ensure that these institutions were organized and financed so that they are able to discharge this responsibility.

The *Grundversorgung* doctrine has been clarified in later decisions.[24] Some of these developments concern the position of private broadcasters and programme standards; they are discussed in later chapters.[25] As far as public broadcasting is concerned, the doctrine guarantees its existence and development, at least while private channels are unable to fulfil the demands imposed on public service broadcasters. In the *Sixth Television* case the Court upheld a number of provisions in the North Rhine–Westphalia law of January 1988. One of them was Article 3, which allowed Westdeutscher Rundfunk (WDR), the public broadcasting company, to develop transmission by cable and satellite and to exploit other commercial possibilities relevant to broadcasting, for example, the publishing of programme magazines. The provision was intended to protect the existence and development of WDR (*Bestands- und*

[22] Decision 78-96 of 27 Aug. 1978, Debbasch, 154.

[23] 73 BVerfGE 118 (1986).

[24] *Fifth Television* case, 74 BVerfGE 297, 325–31 (1987); *Sixth Television* case, 83 BVerfGE 238, 298–310 (1991); 87 BVerfGE 181 (1992).

[25] See Ch. IV, S. 2 and Ch. V, Ss. 3–4.

Entwicklungsgarantie). It was held constitutional in so far as it enabled the company to discharge its responsibilities under the *Grundversorgung* doctrine. The Court made the further point that the public broadcasting companies should not be limited to the existing means of transmission by terrestrial airwaves. On the other hand their position was only protected within the confines of the *Grundversorgung* principle.

An echo of this approach can be heard in the 1988 ruling of the Italian Constitutional Court.[26] Among the references made to it was one from the Pretore di Roma, who had considered the monopoly position of RAI unconstitutional on the ground that the Berlusconi networks provided sufficient competition to allow for the variety of opinion required by Article 21 of the Constitution. The Court did not share this perspective, as it ignored the different roles of public and private broadcasting. The former's distinctive function is to disseminate a wide range of opinions on political and social issues. The Court was repeating an argument it had deployed in earlier cases before the creation of the Berlusconi networks.[27] What was new was the point that Parliament must provide adequate frequencies and financial resources to enable the public channels to discharge this responsibility. In Italy, too, public service broadcasting, therefore, appears to enjoy a measure of constitutional protection.

It would be wrong to infer from these decisions that in Italy and Germany public broadcasting is constitutionally guaranteed in perpetuity. These decisions were taken in the context of a mixed system, where private broadcasters operate under fewer restrictions than their public competitors. Indeed, in Italy at the time of the 1988 ruling the Berlusconi networks were subject only to skeletal temporary regulation.[28] If, however, the full public service obligations were imposed on (some of) the private channels (as used to be the case in Britain), there would be much less need for the continued existence of public broadcasters. It is also unclear how effectively constitutional courts can protect the latter, if the legislature (in effect the government) starves them of finance through freezing the licence fee. Courts could scarcely enforce a constitutional duty on governments to increase it in line with inflation. One possible solution (available at least in Germany and Italy) would be for the courts in these circumstances to hold private broadcasting statutes unconstitutional until they were revised to impose full public service obligations on the commercial channels. Then the legislation would ensure that the basic service (*Grundversorgung*) was provided, albeit by private bodies.

[26] Decision 826/1988 [1988] *Giur. cost.* 3893.

[27] See the cases referred to in nn. 19 and 20 above.

[28] See Ch. I, S. 3 above.

4. PUBLIC BROADCASTING AUTHORITIES

One way in which the values of public service broadcasting can be safeguarded is by ensuring that the controlling bodies of broadcasting authorities have a balanced composition. Statutes may require, for example, that their members represent a wide variety of interest groups or at least that they are not chosen solely by one individual, such as the Prime Minister. Organizational rules of this character help to avert the danger of domination of the media by the governing political party or by particular commercial interests. Otherwise there is a risk that government will nominate its supporters to administer the authority, while private radio and television will be used to promote their owners' commercial and ideological interests. These concerns have been most strongly felt in Germany, almost certainly because of memories of Nazi use of radio for propaganda. In a number of cases the Court in Karlsruhe has emphasized the constitutional necessity for appropriate organizational rules for the composition and powers of the broadcasting authorities. The German principles apply both to the public and to the private sectors. This chapter is only concerned with the former; the equivalent rules for the bodies regulating private broadcasting are discussed in Chapter IV. But in France, unlike the other European jurisdictions discussed in this book, one supreme authority, now the Conseil supérieur de l'audiovisuel (CSA), regulates both public and private broadcasting. Its role with regard to the former is discussed in this section.

German law is particularly striking. In the *First Television* case the Bundesverfassungsgericht emphasized the need for adequate rules to ensure that all significant social forces are able to exercise influence on the administration of the public broadcasting authorities.[29] They must be set out in parliamentary laws and not left to the discretion of the executive. The Court did not exclude some state representation on the controlling bodies, but in its view Article 5 of the Basic Law precluded state control, whether direct or indirect. In fact from the outset the *Länder* statutes have generally provided for the proportionate representation on the Rundfunkrat (Broadcasting Council) of all significant political, cultural, and industrial groups in order to ensure the provision of a comprehensive range of impartial programmes.

The constitutional principles have been most fully stated in the *Sixth Television* case, where there were challenges, *inter alia*, to the composition of both the WDR Rundfunkrat and the regulatory authority for the private broadcasting companies. The Court affirmed its earlier pronouncement that members of the broadcasting councils are not appointed to protect the interests of the groups they represent, but to serve the common

[29] 12 BVerfGE 205, 261–2 (1961).

interest.[30] Broadcasting laws should incorporate this principle, though the Court recognized it was impracticable to enforce total disinterestedness on the part of council members. Parliaments had wide discretion in deciding which groups should be represented; only in extreme cases would the over- or under-representation of any group be incompatible with the guarantee of *Rundfunkfreiheit*. There was no constitutional objection to the omission of certain groups, in this case, newspaper publishers, refugees, and women's organizations. On this point the Court followed an earlier case, where it had rejected the claim of the FDP that it had a constitutional right to be represented on the NDR Rundfunkrat.[31]

It has been argued that there is a constitutional right to membership of a broadcasting council, as it compensates for the denial of any entitlement to set up a private broadcasting station.[32] (A similar argument has been used to justify the recognition of rights of access to speak on the media.[33]) But quite apart from doubts (discussed in the next chapter) about the existence of any right to institute private broadcasting channels, the claim ignores the point that members of the supervisory governing councils are not appointed to protect the interests of their groups. What is important is that the councils are composed of a sufficiently wide range of members from different organizations to guarantee a variety of impartial programmes. It is not important, and quite impracticable, for every influential interest group to be represented on a governing body. On the other hand, in some circumstances an excluded group, say, a prominent church, might claim a right to be represented because it is peculiarly qualified to act dispassionately in the public interest.[34] The Administrative Court of Luneberg has recognized the standing of the north German Protestant churches to challenge the composition of the NDR broadcasting council on the ground that there was (then) an over-representation of political parties and that other groups were not free to choose their own members.[35] But the Court denied that the churches themselves had a *constitutional* right to be represented, while indicating that on the relevant statutory criteria they should be able to nominate representatives.

The composition of the public broadcasting Rundfunkräte is set out in the state laws. A Council generally has at least 30–40 members. (The national ZDF Board now has as many as 77 members.[36]) Typically it is composed of, say, one member of the government, a member of each

[30] 83 BVerfGE 238, 333–4 (1991), developing 60 BVerfGE 53 (1982).
[31] 60 BVerfGE 53 (1982).
[32] C. Starck, 'Teilhabeansprüche auf Rundfunkkontrolle und ihre gerechtliche Durchsetzung—ein Pladoyer', in *Presserecht und Pressefreiheit—Festschrift für Martin Löffler* (Munich, 1980), 375, esp. 381–4.
[33] See Ch. VII, S. 1.
[34] M. Stock, 'Neues über Verbände und Rundfunkkontrolle' (1979) 104 *AöR* 1.
[35] [1979] *DÖV* 170.
[36] ZDF *Staatsvertrag* of 31 Aug. 1991, s. 21.

political party represented in the legislature, a representative of the Catholic and Evangelical Churches, the Jewish community, trade union councils, employers' associations, sports, women's and youth associations, teaching, farming, and music bodies, and so on.[37] Where the body is composed in this way, sometimes known as the 'corporate model', the political party representatives form only a small proportion of its members. This is now the standard model. Politicians used to be more significantly represented in the Councils of the NDR and WDR (the 'parliamentary model'). Moreover, all their members were chosen by the *Länder* parliaments, the political parties having the right to nominate on the basis of their strength.[38]

Major modifications were made to this second structure in 1980. First, the number of political appointees was limited to one-third. This is probably not required by the Basic Law, although the Bavarian Constitution contains such a limit after an amendment approved by referendum in 1972.[39] Secondly, the constitution of the NDR Council was changed to give effect to an administrative court ruling in 1979.[40] This had established that it is for the non-political associations themselves to nominate members, though there would be nothing wrong in the *Landtag* (state Parliament) making the final choice from among the nominees. In fact in most *Länder* associations choose their own members, though there may be complicated procedural rules for selection where there is no clearly defined constituency. It may, for example, be unclear which nature and environmental organizations collectively have the right to appoint one member to the Rundfunkrat; in that event the choice of their representative is left to a committee of the *Landtag* (or, if it fails to elect, a special electoral college of twenty-five experts).[41]

The Rundfunkrat shares responsibility for the control of the broadcasting institution with two other organs, the Verwaltungsrat (Administrative Board) and the Intendant (Director-General).[42] The former is a much smaller body, composed typically of seven to nine members. They are generally chosen by the Broadcasting Council, though one member is sometimes selected by the *Land* government. The Board is responsible for the administration of the broadcasting institution, for its financial plans and budget (subject to the consent of the Council) and the preparation of the annual report and accounts. It is not involved generally with programme matters, which are the responsibility of the Intendant.

[37] See e.g. the Saarland law of 11 Aug. 1987, s. 16.

[38] For a comparison of the two models, see C. Starck, 'Rundfunkräte und Rundfunkfreiheit' [1970] *Zeitschrift für Rechtspolitik* 217. Also see Humphreys, 142–7.

[39] Humphreys, 177–80.

[40] Administrative Appeal Court of Luneberg [1979] *DÖV* 170.

[41] Saarland law of 11 Aug. 1987, s. 16(3).

[42] Humphreys, 142–4.

This officer is appointed (typically for five years) by the Broadcasting Council, which may also decide to revoke the appointment in certain circumstances. He represents the institution legally, appoints its principal officers (sometimes with the consent of the Administrative Board), and prepares the programme schedules and financial plans.[43] In practice the Intendant takes the most important decisions, while the Rundfunkrat performs a largely supervisory role. The observations in Chapter II with regard to the responsibilities of the ZDF Fernsehrat apply equally to the state councils.[44] They issue guide-lines about programme content and supervise their enforcement; above all they represent, as do the Governors of the BBC, the public, providing a forum for general discussion of viewers' complaints and overall broadcasting policy.

Quite apart from the minor legal difficulties described above, there are some reservations of principle about the Broadcasting Councils' composition. Established interests, such as the political parties, employers' organizations, trade unions, and the churches, are well represented. On the other hand, ordinary individuals and less powerful pressure groups are unrepresented, except through the political parties. (There is though a provision in the Bremen law which allows five members to be chosen to represent unorganized interests or viewers' associations.[45]) Moreover, the Councils are large bodies, which are not required to meet more than a few times a year, and for this reason they may not in practice exercise a significant degree of control. Experience has also shown that their members are not immune to party political and interest group influence, despite the constitutional requirement that they should act in the public interest rather than as delegates of the nominating group. At all events, the Annan Committee thought that the members of the equivalent British bodies, the BBC and (then) the IBA, should continue to be nominated by the government, rather than chosen by representative organizations.[46]

Whatever the drawbacks of the German system, it compares favourably in principle with the Italian model. Under the law of 1975, the supreme administrative and regulatory body for public broadcasting is a joint committee of the two chambers of Parliament, the Commissione parlamentare per l'indirizzo generale e la vigilanza dei servizi televisivi.[47] The previous Parliamentary Commission had only enjoyed advisory powers and was widely regarded as ineffective.[48] RAI was in practice organized for the

[43] For legal provisions setting out the responsibilities of the Intendant, see e.g. ZDF *Staatsvertrag* of 31 Aug. 1991, ss. 27–8, and Saarland law of 11 Aug. 1987, s. 27.

[44] Ch. II, S. 3(ii).

[45] Bremen law of 18 June 1979, s. 6(2).

[46] Annan Committee Report (1977) Cmnd. 6753, paras. 5.17–5.28.

[47] Law 103 of 14 Apr. 1975, Art. 1.

[48] S. Fois, 'RAI-TV: "Governo" del monopolo pubblico, o "governo" di un servizio pubblico?' in *Il servizio pubblico radiotelevisivo* (Naples, 1983), 15.

benefit of the ruling Christian Democrats. This was one of the respects in which the Constitutional Court found the legal basis for the public monopoly unsatisfactory. In 1974 it required Parliament, as representative of the national community, to assume responsibility for the service, in particular to ensure its comprehensiveness and impartiality.[49] Government control was incompatible with the freedom of expression guaranteed by Article 21 of the Constitution. The Commission is now composed of forty members, chosen by the Presidents of the two chambers, from all the Parliamentary groups. Thus, there is some safeguard against domination by one party, if not necessarily against rule by the governing coalition parties.

The Parliamentary Commission has a variety of functions. One of these, deciding which groups are entitled to exercise rights of access, may be classified as quasi-judicial.[50] Secondly, it lays down general guide-lines for the achievement of objectivity and impartiality. It may also formulate rules supplementary to those in the statute with regard to advertising control, though apparently it has not exercised this power. Thirdly, it appoints the members of the Administrative Council. Under the 1985 law (still in force in this respect) the majority of the Commission appoints twelve members of the Council, the minority (or opposition party members) the other four.[51] The Council is responsible for the financial management and planning of RAI and supervises compliance with the Commission's programme guide-lines. But after 1985 it lost the power to nominate the Director-General. He is now appointed by the shareholders of RAI. Since the overwhelming majority of shares are held by IRI (Istituto per la ricostruzione industriale, a government controlled agency), in effect the government chooses the Director-General. Like the Intendant in Germany, he is the most important single figure in the Italian public broadcasting system. Under Article 11 of the 1975 law, he is responsible to the Administrative Council for the broadcasting services, with supervisory powers over the directors of each channel.

As already mentioned, the control of RAI was transferred to a committee of Parliament, because the Constitutional Court had ruled government supervision incompatible with freedom of expression. It is now a nice question whether the present arrangements satisfy the Court's requirements. It is surely unsatisfactory to entrust the guarantee of objectivity, balance, and diversity, to a Parliamentary Commission composed entirely of politicians, with a majority of government members. Further, this majority now appoints the Administrative Council, while the government indirectly chooses the Director-General through its control of IRI.

[49] Decision 225/1974 [1974] *Giur. cost.* 1775.
[50] Law 103 of 14 Apr. 1975, Art. 4. See Ch. VII, S. 3 for further discussion.
[51] Law 10 of 4 Feb. 1985, Art. 6.

Under this system the views of the political opposition may be inadequately represented, while the voice of minority social and cultural groups are excluded altogether. This appears to have happened in the context of access programmes, a matter fully discussed later in this book (see Chapter VII).

The French Commission nationale de la communication et des libertés (CNCL), instituted to replace the former High Authority by the law of 30 September 1986, represented in a sense a compromise between the German and Italian provisions. It was composed of thirteen members: the President of the Republic, the Senate President, and the Assembly President each appointed two members, and the Conseil d'État, Cour de cassation, Cour des comptes, and the Académie française each appointed one of their number to be a member. The other three members, chosen from those with experience respectively in the fields of television, telecommunications, and the press, were co-opted by the first ten. The Commission itself elected its own President, who had a casting vote when it was equally divided.[52] Its functions were to ensure that radio and television, both public and private, presented a range of opinions and treated each interest group fairly.[53] It was with this in mind that the Conseil constitutionnel insisted that only the working members of the Conseil d'État and the two courts participated in the election of their representatives; otherwise government officials seconded to these bodies could have influenced the choice.[54]

In theory the composition of the Commission should have been sufficiently balanced to preclude government or political control. In fact it was frequently criticized for undue sympathy to the broadcasting policies of the Chirac government, which had instituted it. Perhaps it was inevitable that a broadcasting authority which enjoyed such wide powers over both the public and private sectors and which presided over the privatization of TF1 should have attracted controversy.[55] Moreover, it was thought to have too many members, though it was in fact little larger than the BBC Board of Governors or the ITC. It was a considerably smaller body than the German Broadcasting Councils. At all events the Rocard Socialist government replaced it in 1989 with the Conseil supérieur de l'audiovisuel (CSA). Mitterrand had even advocated giving the regulatory body constitutional status, with a membership drawn from

[52] Law of 30 Sept. 1986, Art. 4.
[53] Ibid., Arts. 3 and 13.
[54] Decision 86–217 of 18 Sept. 1986, Debbasch, 245.
[55] For discussion of the Commission and the reasons for its replacement by the CSA, see J. Morange, 'Le Conseil supérieur de l'audiovisuel' (1989) 5 *Rev. fr. droit adm.* 235, 238–41.

professional organizations. The idea was not pursued. The body instituted by the law of 17 January 1989 is composed of nine members, nominated in the same way as the Conseil constitutionnel: one-third by the President of the Republic, one-third by the President of the Assembly, and one-third by the President of the Senate.[56] The Council president is chosen by the President of the Republic, a move away from the autonomy enjoyed in this respect by the CNCL.

Broadly the CSA enjoys much the same administrative powers over public broadcasting as its predecessor.[57] Under Article 13 of the 1986 law (as amended in 1989) it is responsible for the guarantee of plurality of opinion on these channels, particularly in the case of news and current affairs programmes. Unlike the CNCL, it cannot enforce this by the issue of binding general recommendations. But the CSA has power to require the head of a public programme company to remedy a serious breach of its programme obligations within a fixed time. It is required to give published advice to the government on the public programme companies' *cahiers des charges*:[58] these are the documents laying down their programme standards. However, an attempt to give the CSA regulatory power over all channels (both public and private) with respect to advertising and sponsorship was held unconstitutional. The Conseil constitutionnel ruled that such a grant would exceed the limited powers of executive law-making permitted by Article 21 of the Constitution.[59] In this respect the new regulatory body enjoys less power than its predecessor, which was competent to lay down general rules with regard to programmes and their production. The CSA must instead be consulted by the government before the latter issues decrees in the Conseil d'État. It appoints (as did the CNCL) the head of the public programme channels, but otherwise it is not concerned with their management. Nor does it have any responsibility with regard to the raising or allocation of proceeds from the *redevance* (licence fee). Financial matters are determined by Parliament.[60]

The CSA, therefore, has less regulatory power than its predecessor, partly because Parliament decided to reduce it and partly because the Conseil constitutionnel has curtailed the scope of the law-making powers delegated to administrative agencies. General rules may now only be issued by the CSA in the context of election broadcasts, the right of reply

[56] Law of 17 Jan. 1989, Art. 4, replacing Art. 4 of the law of 30 Sept. 1986.
[57] Morange, 'Le Conseil supérieur de l'audiovisuel', 242–7.
[58] Law of 30 Sept. 1986, Art. 48, as amended by the law of 17 Jan. 1989.
[59] Decision 88-248 of 17 Jan. 1989, Debbasch, 319.
[60] For the *redevance*, see S. 5 below. The Council may, however, make recommendations about the distribution of licence fee and advertising revenue between the public channels in its annual report: see amended Art. 18 of law of 30 Sept. 1986.

to government announcements, and access rights.[61] In all other circumstances rule-making power has passed back to the government. It remains to be seen whether this transfer proves significant in practice. In principle it can be justified on the argument that it is important for general rules to be laid down by a politically accountable body rather than by an independent agency. On the other hand there may be a risk that the government will exploit its regulatory power to the advantage of one political party or interest.

Discussion of the administration of the BBC has been left to the end because it is so peculiar in comparison with every other system. An initial point is that the Corporation is constituted by Royal Charter rather than by statute. This was a deliberate decision. It was felt at the time of the BBC's foundation that a statutory framework would be too inflexible and would encourage Parliament to intervene in its regulation.[62] The institution of the Corporation, however, under the Crown's prerogative powers removes any opportunity for Parliamentary scrutiny of its constitutive documents: the Charter and the Licence and Agreement regulating its programmes and financing.[63] Another drawback is that the Charter is only granted for a limited period. At first the period was only ten years, but it has been extended to twelve and in 1981 fifteen years. In theory this means that the BBC is less secure than continental public broadcasting systems; the terms of their existence may only be altered by legislative amendment, while periodic review of the BBC is automatic. Finally, the government may revoke the Charter if the Corporation breaks its terms or those of the Licence and Agreement, a power which it does not enjoy over private broadcasting.[64]

The BBC is controlled by its Governors, of whom there are normally twelve, though recently there have been fewer. One is nominated as Chairman, another as Vice-Chairman, and of the others one is designated as the National Governor for Scotland, a second as Governor for Wales, and a third as Governor for Northern Ireland.[65] All are appointed under the Royal Prerogative, which means that they are in effect chosen by the Prime Minister. Not surprisingly some Prime Ministers have taken personal interest in these appointments, particularly of the Chairman.[66]

Another oddity of the BBC legal structure is the complete absence

[61] Law of 30 Sept. 1986, Arts. 16, 54, and 55 (in these respects unamended in 1989).

[62] Burns, *The BBC*, 15–16. The Crawford Committee on Broadcasting (1925, Cmd. 2599) had contemplated its institution by statute or as a company limited by guarantee under the Companies Acts.

[63] The fact that the BBC is constituted by Crown prerogative does not entail prerogative immunity from taxation: *BBC* v. *Johns* [1965] Ch. 32.

[64] Charter, Art. 20; Licence and Agreement, Art. 23.

[65] Charter, Art. 5.

[66] See M. Cockerell, *Live from Number 10* (London, 1988), 134–6 and 311–12.

of any rules setting out the Governors' powers with regard to programmes or defining their relationship with the Director-General and the Corporation's staff. The Director-General indeed has no legal status at all; the position is not mentioned in any of the BBC's legal documents.[67] He may be summarily dismissed as Alasdair Milne found in January 1987.[68] In the Annex to the Licence and Agreement the Governors assume responsibility for the range and impartiality of programmes on the ground that governments of all political parties have recognized that it belongs to them.[69] In practice it is delegated to the Director-General and his staff, and, as Chapter II explained, the Governors intervene only in exceptional circumstances to preview and ban the showing of a programme. But in law there is no doubt of their entitlement to do so.

Two major and (to some extent) related criticisms can be made of these arrangements. First, the government in the person of the Prime Minister enjoys a monopoly of the power of appointment to the controlling body unparalleled in the continental countries discussed in this book. This carries risks for the impartiality of the BBC. The suggestion that other organizations should have nominating powers was rejected by the Annan Committee on the ground that it was imperative to retain the accountability of Ministers to Parliament with regard to the appointment and dismissal of Governors.[70] Few outside the House of Commons now take this argument seriously. Secondly, in other countries the governing institutions have clearly defined responsibilities. The German Rundfunkräte and the Italian Parliamentary Commission have broad supervisory powers, while the Intendant and Director-General in those countries have responsibility for the planning of programmes. In Germany the latter may have legal rights to attend meetings of the supervisory board. The legal powers of the CSA in France are limited: it cannot ban particular programmes and has no control over the financing of the public companies. Clearly these arrangements vary substantially, but in all the other European countries there is a balance of power within the public broadcasting organization, which is recognized by law. In contrast in Britain legal power is concentrated in the Board of Governors and only dispersed by weak conventions which are easily broken. There are, therefore, no legal, let alone constitutional, guarantees for the BBC's independence. Its freedom from state control is dependent purely on the benevolence of Ministers and the reluctance (or incapacity) of the Governors to interfere with programme schedules.

[67] Art. 12 of the Charter requires the Corporation, in effect the Governors, to appoint officers and staff and to fix their rates of pay and conditions of service.

[68] A. Milne, *DG: The Memoirs of a British Broadcaster* (London, 1988), esp. ch. 16.

[69] See the first paragraph of the Governors' Resolution of 8 Jan. 1981.

[70] Annan Committee on the Future of Broadcasting (1977) Cmnd. 6753, para. 5.22.

5. THE FINANCING OF PUBLIC BROADCASTING

Public broadcasting on the mainland of Europe is generally financed by a mixture of licence fee and advertising revenue. The BBC is unusual in its virtually total dependence on the former. It is not clear how long that will continue to be the case. Although the Peacock Committee opposed the introduction of advertising on the BBC and recommended the retention of the licence fee for a period, it urged moves towards its financing by subscription, both on a pay-per-channel and on a pay-per-view basis.[71] It contemplated that eventually subscription income would replace the licence fee completely, as the best way to establish a market in which consumer choices could prevail.[72] With the government's encouragement the BBC has started to develop subscription services in the hitherto silent night hours. The licence fee will be continued at least until the expiry of the present Charter in 1996 and is generally increased in line with inflation.[73] In its 1988 White Paper the government looked forward to its replacement by subscription,[74] and it is possible that steps will be made in that direction when the Charter is renewed in 1996.

Broadcasting finances raise a number of complex issues of economic and social policy.[75] There are also a number of constitutional and legal questions related to topics already discussed in this chapter. One is whether public broadcasting is entitled to any particular form or level of financial support. Both the German and Italian Constitutional Courts have ruled that it must be adequately financed to enable it to discharge its particular responsibilities.[76] But neither has indicated that the finance must come from any particular source. In the *Fifth Television* case the Court upheld bans imposed by the Baden-Württemberg *Landesmediengesetz* of 1985 on advertising on the public regional and local channels, and also on their financing by subscription or other individual charges until this was allowed by statute or state treaty.[77] These restrictions were constitutional, since Article 5 of the Basic Law does not require public broadcasters to be financed by advertising or indeed in any particular way. It is for each state Parliament to decide how adequate support is provided.

[71] Peacock Committee Report, paras. 615–25 (advertising and licence fee), 668, and *passim* (subscription).

[72] Ibid. 671–81. For commentary, see S. Brittan, 'Toward a Broadcasting Market: Recommendations of the British Peacock Committee', in J. G. Blumler and T. J. Nossiter (eds.), *Broadcasting Finance in Transition* (Oxford, 1991), 335.

[73] In 1991 an increase of 3 per cent below the annual rate of inflation was allowed.

[74] *Broadcasting in the '90s: Competition, Choice and Quality* (1988) Cm. 517, para. 3.10.

[75] See *Broadcasting Finance in Transition* for a study of these issues in a number of countries.

[76] *Fourth Television* case, 73 BVerfGE 118 (1986); Decision 826/1988 [1988] *Giur. cost.* 3893.

[77] 74 BVerfGE 297 (1987), upholding law of 16 Dec. 1985, ss. 13(2) and (3).

The law has been developed by the Constitutional Court in the *Sixth Television* case.[78] It upheld the mixed system of financing by the *Gebühren* (licence fees) and advertising. Reliance on advertising revenue as the predominant source of finance for public broadcasting would imperil its capacity to discharge its responsibility to provide a wide range of programmes. But partial dependence on this revenue did not imperil the survival of either the press or private broadcasting channels, and, therefore, was not constitutionally suspect. Indeed mixed financing was preferable to total reliance on either the licence fee or advertising revenue, as it reduced the danger of dependence on government or commercial organizations. In a recent case, affirming the constitutionality of the ban on advertising on the Hesse third public channel, the Court stressed the necessity for the licence fee. It enables the public channels to discharge their basic broadcasting responsibilities under the *Grundversorgung* doctrine.[79] In fact the larger state broadcasting institutions and ZDF draw between 60 and 70 per cent of their revenue from the licence fee. RAI also receives about two-thirds of its income from the fee. In contrast the principal French public channel, Antenne 2, receives only about 35 per cent of its income from the *redevance*, the larger part of it coming from advertising and sales.

Another set of questions concerns the character (in German *Rechtsnatur*) of the licence fee: is it a tax, a special fee or duty, or a charge for services rendered by the broadcasting company? In a number of countries it has been argued that only viewers who actually view (or are able to view) the public channels should be liable to pay it. Its characterization as a tax or a charge for (contractual) services rendered will affect resolution of this issue. It is also relevant to the question, recently raised in Germany, whether the fee should be assessed and periodically reviewed by the government or by the broadcasting authority itself. The dependence of a broadcasting body on a government decision to review the level of the licence fee may compromise its autonomy, while there are at the same time obvious objections to leaving assessment to the discretion of the broadcasting body itself.

The British licence fee is imposed by the Wireless Telegraphy Act 1949. It is an offence to install or use any apparatus for wireless telegraphy except under licence (now granted by the Secretary of State for National Heritage). Regulations may exempt certain types of apparatus from the need for a licence; radio sets have been exempt since 1971. The annual fee for a colour television licence from April 1993 is £83, and for a black-and-white set £27.50. French law also discriminates between the liability

[78] 83 BVerfGE 238 (1991).
[79] 87 BVerfGE 181 (1992).

for possession of a monochrome and a colour television set and (since 1977) has not imposed any fee for use of a radio set. On the other hand in Germany there is a basic fee (*Grundgebühr*) imposed for possession of a radio, and a higher fee (about twice as high) for possession of a television set. There is no distinction, however, between the charges imposed for different types of television. Italy does impose a higher fee for possession of a colour set, but sensibly does not charge for possession solely of a radio. In many countries evasion of licence fee payment is widespread, so it makes no sense to impose a charge in respect of a domestic (as opposed perhaps to a car) radio.

A number of administrative and legal questions have arisen in Britain. First, collection of the fee is now the responsibility of the BBC itself.[80] The Corporation obviously has more incentive than the Post Office or any government department to collect it efficiently. Secondly, it seems that on at least one occasion a magistrates court has acquitted a defendant on a charge of non-payment of the fee, because it accepted his argument that he used his set only to receive satellite programmes. The decision has been criticized on the ground that the 1949 legislation prohibits the installation (or use) of apparatus capable of receiving terrestrial broadcasts, whether it is in fact used for that purpose or not.[81]

Although not directly concerned with it, some administrative law decisions may shed light on the question whether the licence fee should be regarded as a tax. In *Congreve* v. *Home Office*[82] the Court of Appeal held it was unlawful for the Home Secretary to threaten to revoke an overlapping television licence unless the plaintiff paid £6. The plaintiff had acquired this licence perfectly properly before his current one had expired, so he could avoid paying the extra £6 for a new annual licence. The Court of Appeal considered that in these circumstances the Home Secretary was demanding money for the use of the Crown without authority of Parliament, contrary to the rule in the Bill of Rights 1689. The Wireless Telegraphy Act 1949 does authorize the charge of fees on the issue or renewal of a licence,[83] but that did not cover these facts, where the Minister was in effect imposing a supplementary duty. One possible implication, therefore, of the case is that (aside from the exceptional circumstances which obtained there) the licence fee should not be regarded as a tax, but as a charge for the licence. The Court of Appeal had held in an earlier case that the Corporation is not an agent of the Crown for the

[80] It is given necessary enforcement powers by the Broadcasting Act 1990, s. 173(3), amending the Wireless Telegraphy Act 1949.

[81] See the note in [1990] *Justice of the Peace* 432. Also compare the Italian cases discussed below.

[82] [1976] QB 629 (CA).

[83] S. 2(1).

purposes of immunity from taxation.[84] That also suggests that the Bill of Rights rule (prohibiting the levying of money for or to the use of the Crown without Parliamentary authority) does not normally apply to the licence fee; it is not money for the use of the Crown. But it may be wrong to derive so much from these cases.

There are more direct rulings of the French and Italian tribunals on the characterization of these fees. The Conseil constitutionnel has held that the *redevance* should be regarded as a parafiscal duty, rather than a tax or a charge for services.[85] The significance of the decision, the first ever given by the Conseil on the constitutionality of a Parliamentary law, was that it was for the executive, and not Parliament, to determine the level of the fee.[86] The decision has been criticized, and the general view, adopted in the law of 30 September 1986, is that the *redevance* is a tax which can be levied by Parliament.[87] The Conseil d'État has less controversially denied that it is a contractual charge for broadcasting services, when it refused to hold a wife liable for her husband's non-payment; if it were a contractual debt, she would have been liable under the Civil Code.[88]

Italian courts and commentators have for long debated the appropriate characterization of the fee (*canone*) paid for public broadcasting.[89] The Constitutional Court regards it as a duty (*imposta*) which the legislature may constitutionally impose on anyone possessing a radio or television set capable of picking up broadcasting signals.[90] It is not a charge for services, so it is no defence to a prosecution for failure to pay it that the defendant was unable to receive RAI programmes. He is liable to pay even if the apparatus could only pick up private terrestrial or cable programmes. The Court has similarly rejected arguments that the duty violates Articles 3 (equality) and 53 (everyone is bound to contribute to public expenditure on the basis of their capacity to pay). There was no violation of equality in view of the small amount of the licence fee. On the other hand, the Court has intimated that it might refuse to require payment if the administration had made no effort to make television services available in the area.

The German Constitutional Court in the *Second Television* case ruled that the *Gebühren* were not charges for services, and hence that the

[84] *BBC* v. *Johns* [1965] Ch. 32 (CA).

[85] Decision 60–8 of 11 Aug. 1960, Debbasch, 71.

[86] For commentary, see C. Debbasch, *Droit de l'audiovisuel*, 2nd edn. (Paris, 1991), 385–8.

[87] Art. 53 of this law refers to the fee as a tax.

[88] *Dame Delaby*, CE Decision of 6 July 1983, Debbasch, 217.

[89] See R. Esposito, in *Il sistema radiotelevisivo*, 465–72.

[90] Decision 81/1963 [1963] *Giur. cost.* 680; Decision 535/1988 [1988] *Giur. cost.* 2528; Decision 219/1989 [1989] *Giur. cost.* 956.

public broadcasting revenue derived from them were not liable to federal turnover tax.[91] But it did not answer the question whether they should be regarded as a type of taxation or instead as a compulsory contribution to the cost of the broadcasting service. The issue has been much discussed in German literature.[92] The fees were generally regarded as duties, rather than taxation (*nichtsteurliche Abgabe*), or as contributions payable to meet the costs of the public broadcasting service. But this view may be less tenable after the development of the mixed broadcasting system. The Constitutional Court said that the licence fees were a means to support the broadcasting system as a whole.[93] For a few years a small part of the fees were used to finance the experimental cable projects, and since 1988 2 per cent of their total income has been allocated as a contribution to the costs of the private broadcasting regulatory bodies.[94] It may be preferable to treat the *Gebühren* as a regulatory tax (*Zwecksteuer*).

The characterization of the fees is relevant to the question who is entitled to assess them. Traditionally this function in Germany has been discharged by the Minister-Presidents of the *Länder* and the level of the fees is stated in a state treaty. It has often proved extremely difficult to secure agreement among the states to increases. Since 1975 a mixed commission of broadcasting experts and state appointees has reviewed the financial needs of the public corporations every two years and made proposals for increases, but the final decision remains with the states. In 1989 the Bavarian Administrative Court ruled it was contrary to broadcasting freedom for the states to enjoy this power.[95] It enabled them to influence the conduct of the public broadcasting corporations and was, therefore, contrary to the Basic Law. The fees should instead be determined by the broadcasting bodies themselves. The decision has attracted a number of critics.[96] Broadcasters might be tempted to assess too high a fee, and in any case it would probably be unacceptable to the public to give them this prerogative, particularly when it now enjoys the alternative of private television. Moreover, in principle it is wrong for a taxing power to be transferred from the states to other bodies (though

[91] 31 BVerfGE 314 (1971), discussed by P. M. Blair, *Federalism and Judicial Review in Germany* (Oxford, 1981), 188–92. In 87 BVerfGE 181 (1992) the Court regarded the fees as payable for the possession, not the use, of radio and television sets.

[92] See in particular K. Hümmerich and K. Beucher, 'Rundfunkfinanzierung auf dem Prüfstand' (1989) 20 *Archiv für Presserecht* 708, 713–15; M. Libertus, 'Verfassungsrechtliche Determinanten des gegenwärtigen und eines zukünftigen Verfahrens der Rundfunkgebührenfestsetzung' (1990) 43 *DÖV* 635, 636.

[93] *Second Television* case, 31 BVerfGE 314, 329 (1971).

[94] See now *Rundfunkfinanzierungsstaatsvertrag* of 31 Aug. 1991, ss. 4 and 5.

[95] [1989] *JZ* 242, following the dissent of three judges in the *Second Television* case, 31 BVerfGE 314, 345 (1971).

[96] In addition to the articles mentioned in n. 92 above, see the commentary of W. Hoffman-Riem [1989] *JZ* 247 and H. Bethge (1990) 45 *NJW* 2451.

obviously this objection would not apply if the fees had a contractual basis). Finally, there are better alternatives to the present arrangements: indexation of the *Gebühren* and giving the mixed commission greater powers.

The German Constitutional Court has not yet decided the Bavarian licence fee case. But in its recent decision on the Hesse advertising ban,[97] it laid down a number of pertinent principles. The discretion of state Parliaments should not be unlimited; the level of finance must be that required (*erforderlich*) to enable public broadcasters to perform their functions properly. This went beyond the support necessary to facilitate the discharge of the *Grundversorgung*, but encompassed the whole range of their programmes. In view of the imprecision of these substantive standards, it was important that the procedure for assessing the fee should encourage a satisfactory compromise to be struck between the interests of broadcasters and viewers. It seems likely the Court will approve the present arrangements for fixing the *Gebühren*, albeit with some modifications.

All European systems seem to have experienced difficulties in this context. Governments do not like to increase the licence fee, because they think this course will be unpopular with the electorate. It has, moreover, become harder to defend the principle of what is in effect a regressive broadcasting tax, particularly when many viewers watch almost exclusively commercial television. Indexation of the fee, or its determination by an independent commission, would meet the former difficulty, but not the latter. Indeed, many would consider it wrong in principle for the government to abdicate political responsibility for taxation decisions. But in practice the result of the reluctance to increase fees has been the greater reliance of public broadcasters on advertising and perhaps a decline in the quality of their programmes. No better alternative to the licence fee has been found.

[97] 87 BVerfGE 181 (1992).

IV
Private Broadcasting

I. INTRODUCTION

Almost all European countries now permit private broadcasting.[1] Britain has enjoyed commercial television since 1955 and local commercial radio since 1973. The introduction of these alternatives to public broadcasting occurred much later in the other European jurisdictions considered in this book.[2] In France the state broadcasting monopoly was not abolished until 1982, though the first private television franchises were only issued four years later. The Chirac government then took the further step of privatizing TF1, so that now the whole balance between public and private television has been radically altered. There had been earlier developments in Italy, where the Constitutional Court has played a large part in breaking down the monopoly enjoyed by RAI. In 1976 it was ruled unconstitutional so far as local broadcasting was concerned. As a result a number of local radio and television stations were instituted. Later a large number of them became part of *de facto* national networks controlled by the Milanese property magnate Silvio Berlusconi. These were strictly illegal, but have now been put on a proper footing by the Italian law of August 1990. Germany too has legalized private television and radio in the 1980s. There was significant opposition to the development, particularly in the *Länder* controlled by the SPD, but now all states permit it.

The expansion of private commercial broadcasting has to some extent been driven by technical developments, in particular the foundation of cable networks and the arrival of satellite television. Governments, for example, the CDU–CSU–FDP coalition in Germany, have encouraged the expansion of cable and satellite for economic reasons. Advertising agents also create pressure for liberalization of the airwaves, first to establish the legitimacy of private broadcasting as an alternative outlet for commercials, and secondly to relax programming constraints. With more popular fare, such as films and soaps, commercial television channels can deliver large audiences to advertisers.

[1] One notable exception is Austria. The European Commission of Human Rights has ruled admissible a challenge to the compatibility of the public monopoly with the Human Rights Convention.

[2] For a fuller discussion of these developments, see Ch. I, S. 3 above.

Generally, public and private broadcasters are regarded as competitors, albeit in a regulated market. The former enjoy the advantage of the financial support provided by the licence fee and its equivalents in continental European jurisdictions.[3] Further, as long-established national channels they may attract a larger number of viewers on certain occasions, such as general elections or major sporting events. On the other hand, private broadcasters are not normally required to provide the same balanced diet as the public channels, which must inform and educate their viewers, as well as entertain them.[4] With the advent of cable and satellite, sometimes offering specialist sports and film channels, there is a real prospect that private broadcasting will become dominant. The public channels may be reduced to a cultural ghetto, mainly providing programmes of minority interest for tastes not otherwise catered for.[5]

However, there is another perspective which sees the roles of public and private broadcasting as essentially *complementary* rather than *competitive*. Each is entitled to flourish. This is the view of the Constitutional Courts of both Germany and Italy.[6] Public broadcasters are required to provide the basic broadcasting service, in Germany termed the *Grundversorgung*. They must show a comprehensive range of programmes, presenting the views of all important political and social groups. In contrast private broadcasters are free to offer specialist channels, while the degree of fairness required of each station may be lower than that expected of public broadcasters. But, as the German Constitutional Court has emphasized, the lower standards required of private broadcasters are only permissible because public broadcasters provide the basic service. Further, a state is free to impose the same standards on both public and private broadcasting companies, at any rate if that course does not endanger the survival of the latter.[7] (The prosperity of private broadcasting cannot be taken for granted, as the collapse of the private French channel La Cinq at the end of 1991 shows.)

In practice the relationship in European countries between public and private broadcasting remains an uneasy one. To some extent they compete with each other to attract mass audiences, while retaining somewhat different conceptions of their roles. The further proliferation of private

[3] See Ch. III, S. 5 above.

[4] For the 'public service' mission of public broadcasters, see Ch. III, S. 2 above and Ch. V, S. 1 below.

[5] See Ch. V, S. 1 above.

[6] See in particular the *Fourth Television* case, 73 BVerfGE 118 (1986) and the article by M. Stock, 'Das vierte Rundfunkurteil des Bundesverfassungsgerichts: Kontinuität oder Wendel?' (1987) *NJW* 217, and the decision of the Italian Constitutional Court 826/1988 [1988] *Giur. cost.* 3893, 3934.

[7] See the *Sixth Television* case, 83 BVerfGE 238 (1991), discussed in this context in Ch. V, S. 1 below.

cable and satellite channels will not necessarily alter this balance. What might change it would be a sharp decline in financial support for the public broadcasting system, which would compel it to compete with its private competitors without regard for its distinctive functions. As we have seen in the previous chapter, such a development would raise constitutional questions in Germany and Italy.[8] The relationship between the private and public sectors is of course quite different in the United States. There the private networks and local stations are longer-established dominant partners, while public broadcasting was only instituted in 1967 and caters largely for minority interests.

The differences in the programme standards imposed on the two systems are explored in the next chapter. The financing of private broadcasting by advertising and sponsorship is discussed in Chapter IX. This one is concerned with the character and composition of the authorities which regulate private television and radio and with the process by which licences are awarded. One important question must, however, be addressed at the outset. Now that the public broadcasting monopoly is no longer sustained, can it be said that there is a *right* to institute a private broadcasting station? Or are regulatory authorities entitled to control the number of licences allocated for broadcasting and to determine the conditions on which they are granted? If there are no rights to obtain a licence, what legal (or constitutional) rights, if any, do private broadcasters have?

2. THE RIGHTS OF PRIVATE BROADCASTERS

The French broadcasting laws of 1982 and 1989 (the latter amending the Chirac statute of 1986 in this respect) begin: 'La communication audiovisuelle est libre.' The exercise of this freedom may be limited to the extent necessary to respect individual rights, to safeguard pluralism of opinion, and to protect public interests, such as national security and public order.[9] Under the 1989 law the freedom is also limited by the inherent technical constraints on broadcasting—namely, that not everyone is able to set up a radio, let alone a television, station, in view of the limits on the number of available frequencies.[10] In fact the ability to operate a radio or television channel in France is dependent on prior authorization from the regulatory body, now the Conseil supérieur de l'audiovisuel. The same is true in Britain, where the Independent Television Commission (ITC) and the

[8] See Ch. III, S. 3 above.

[9] Law of 17 Jan. 1989, Art. 1 (amending the law of 30 Sept. 1986, which had established a wider freedom to set up and exploit telecommunications installations).

[10] See the discussion in Ch. I, S. 2.

Radio Authority (RA) must grant a licence (national, regional, or local) before broadcasting can start.

In France, Britain, and many other European countries, as well as the United States, there is, therefore, at most a statutory right to a licence for those applicants who satisfy the requirements laid down by statute or by the regulatory authority. Sometimes that authority has fairly wide discretion, as used to be the case in Britain under the system which existed from 1954 to 1991. Now the discretion of the ITC, and to a lesser extent the RA, is more circumscribed. The former must award Channel 3, Channel 5, domestic satellite, and local cable licences to the highest bidder, provided it meets certain conditions (discussed below). (The same rule applies to the award of national radio licences by the RA, though that body has rather wider discretion with regard to the allocation of local licences.[11]) Moreover, the ITC must award non-domestic satellite licences and licences to provide cable programmes, unless it is satisfied that the applicant is unable to meet the general programme conditions (as to impartiality and decency, etc.) set out in section 6 of the Act. In all these circumstances it is possible to speak of a conditional statutory right to broadcast. But in others it is less plausible. The United States Federal Communications Act 1934 requires the FCC to grant broadcasting licences, if it finds that the public interest, convenience, and necessity will be served in that way.[12] Such open-textured language suggests at most that an established licensee with a good programme record has a strong expectation that a licence will be renewed.[13] There is clearly no legal right to its issue.

The argument has a significant constitutional dimension in Italy and Germany. This is particularly true in the former country, where some provisions of the Constitution might appear to point to fundamental private rights to broadcast. Article 21 guarantees everyone the right to express himself in speech, writing, and 'by any other means', while Article 41 proclaims a freedom of private economic enterprise. Further, it has been argued that, as Article 33 provides for a right of private bodies to establish schools and institutes, an analogous right to private broadcasting should be recognized.[14] However, the Constitutional Court continued to hold the public monopoly of broadcasting justified, at least at the national level and until adequate anti-trust laws were enacted to prevent the development of private media oligopolies.[15]

[11] Compare Broadcasting Act 1990, s. 100 (national licences) and s. 105 (local licences).

[12] S. 307(a).

[13] Renewal is determined on the same vague criteria as initial licence grants: s. 307(c).

[14] See the reference by the Pretore di Roma on 4 May 1982 to the Constitutional Court, reprinted in Pace, 551. The argument was rejected, however, by the Constitutional Court in Decision 826/1988 [1988] *Giur. cost.* 3893, 3932.

[15] See, *inter alia*, Decision 59/1960 [1960] *Giur. cost.* 759, Decision 225/1974 [1974] *Giur. cost.* 1775, Decision 148/81 [1981] *Giur. cost.* 1379.

Even in the context of local broadcasting, where the Court in its landmark decision of 1976 refused to sustain the public monopoly, it was far from clear whether it was prepared to recognize an individual *right* to establish a broadcasting station.[16] The Court held in that case that criminal proceedings could not be brought against companies operating local stations without permission from the Minister of Posts. They had been brought to protect RAI's monopoly and that could no longer be justified in view of the large number of local frequencies. The monopoly conflicted with the rights to freedom of expression and economic initiative. The companies did, therefore, enjoy an immunity from prosecution, and that is perhaps what was meant by the references in the judgment to a real right (*un vero e proprio diritto*) to broadcast locally. But the Constitutional Court made it plain that legislation was necessary to lay down rules for the assignment of frequencies, to define a 'locality' for broadcasting purposes and to impose advertising limits.[17]

There was some dispute among both courts and commentators concerning the significance of the 1976 ruling. While some understood it to provide a full legal right to establish a broadcasting station at the local level, the majority rejected that interpretation.[18] The Constitutional Court has now resolved the question in favour of the latter view in a 1990 decision.[19] It refused to entertain a challenge to the constitutionality of the administrative steps which had been taken to close down unauthorized private broadcasting stations. The Court held that their owners had no legal rights which could be asserted before the ordinary courts. There could be no right to exploit a public good, the airwaves, which were limited and could not be enjoyed by all. Private broadcasters did, however, have a legitimate interest (*interesse legittimo*) which could be protected by the administrative courts.[20]

Quite apart from the judicial precedents there are overwhelming arguments of principle against the recognition in Italy (or elsewhere) of a constitutional right to establish a private broadcasting channel. Article 21 confers a right to speak freely, using means already at one's disposal, not a right to use public property, such as the airwaves.[21] The analogy with

[16] Decision 202/1976 [1976] *Giur. cost.* 1267.

[17] Ibid., para. 8.

[18] For example, in favour of the 'full right' interpretation were the Pretore di Lucca in Decision of 8 Feb. 1980, reprinted in Pace, 601, and the Tuscany Regional Administrative Tribunal [1981] *Foro amm.* 919. But these decisions were overruled respectively by the Corte di cassazione (the highest civil court) in Decision of 3 Dec. 1984 [1985] *Giur. cost.* 765 and by the Consiglio di stato (the highest administrative court) in Decision of 14 July 1982 [1983] *Giur. cost.* 546. For a review of the authorities and an exposition of the case against the 'full right' interpretation, see A. Pace, 'La radiotelevisione in Italia con particolare riguardo alla emittenze privata' [1987] *Riv. trim. di diritt. pubb.* 615, 623–7.

[19] Decision 102/1990 [1990] *Giur. cost.* 610.

[20] For this concept, see S. Cassese, *Le basi del diritto amministrativo* (Turin, 1989), 333–7.

[21] Pace, 385–90.

the right to establish private schools is weak and has been rejected by the Constitutional Court.[22] That right is explicitly stated in the Constitution, while there is no mention of a right to broadcast. The freedom of private economic initiative recognized by Article 41 expressly requires legislative guide-lines to co-ordinate public and private business. Most fundamentally it is impossible to justify recognition of a right which only a handful of individuals and media companies can enjoy in practice.

It is even clearer that there is no constitutional right of this kind in German law. There is some academic support for its recognition,[23] but none in decisions of the Constitutional Court. In the *Third Television* case it expressly refrained from deciding whether there is a right under the Basic Law to establish a private channel. It was possible to rule on the constitutionality of specific provisions of the experimental Saarland private broadcasting statute without pronouncing on the question.[24] All *Länder* enacted laws permitting private broadcasting in the 1980s, so the issue has become moot. But even in the recent *Sixth Television* case the Court adhered to its position: it is for the state legislature to decide whether to introduce private broadcasting and what was the most appropriate model for its institution.[25] However, if it does introduce private broadcasting, it must not impose on it such onerous programme and advertising restrictions as to imperil its existence.[26] Private broadcasters, therefore, enjoy a right to survive, once their existence is tolerated.

Actual and prospective licensees may enjoy other rights. First, there may, as already mentioned, be limited or conditional statutory rights to acquire a licence. This is not only the position in Britain, but also in some German *Länder*, where the private broadcasting laws provide for such a right when applicants satisfy the conditions of eligibility. But these laws also make provision for the discretionary allocation of permits when there are not enough channels available for broadcasting to satisfy everyone's demand.[27] Secondly, in some countries established private broadcasters enjoy *constitutional* rights to put programmes on their channel free from government restrictions. Broadcasting freedom in this respect confers the same free speech rights on private broadcasters as it does on the public channels.[28] Finally, prospective private broadcasters may have standing

[22] Decision 826/1988 [1988] *Giur. cost.* 3893.

[23] H. H. Klein, 'Rundfunkrecht and Rundfunkfreiheit' (1981) 20 *Der Staat* 174, 189, and H. D. Jarass (1986) 56 *Deutscher Juristentag*, 27–9.

[24] 57 BVerfGE 295, 318–19 (1981).

[25] 83 BVerfGE 238, 296–7 (1991), and see M. Stock, 'Das Nordrhein-Westfalen-Urteil des Bundesverfassungsgerichts' (1991) *Medien Perspektiven* 133, 135.

[26] *Fourth Television* case, 73 BVerfGE 118, 157 (1986).

[27] See e.g. the Baden-Württemberg law of 16 Dec. 1985, ss. 16(2) and 18, and the Rhineland-Pfalz law of 24 June 1986, ss. 5(1) and 7.

[28] See Ch. II, S. 2 for broadcasting freedom and censorship.

to challenge a public monopoly. Whether they are in a position to do this depends on the national rules of standing to bring actions for administrative or constitutional review. They may certainly have standing as 'victims' of a violation of human rights under Article 25 of the European Convention.[29] But an ability or right to challenge a public broadcasting monopoly is not identical to an alleged right to establish a private channel.

The fact remains that in Italy, if not in Germany, the Constitutional Court did rule the public monopoly incompatible with freedom of speech (and of economic initiative), at least at the local level. This result can be explained, however, without recourse to individual rights to institute a broadcasting channel. We saw in Chapter II that the concept of broadcasting freedom should not be reduced to a set of individual rights; it is also a fundamental value which must be taken into account in a variety of contexts.[30] Now that the scarcity argument is no longer wholly convincing,[31] the case for allowing some private broadcasting seems overwhelming. Its introduction can be justified constitutionally on freedom of speech and of broadcasting grounds. But it is for the legislature to decide how this should be done, and in particular how licences should be allocated.

3. LICENSING AND REGULATORY AUTHORITIES

In all the legal systems considered in this book a licence to broadcast must be obtained from an administrative authority. Normally this is an independent body, combining the licensing function with supervisory and regulatory powers over programme standards and compliance with permit conditions. The position in Italy is unusual, in that licences are issued by the Minister of Posts and Telecommunications, while supervision of broadcasters' obligations is principally the responsibility of the Garante per la radiodiffusione e l'editoria (Guarantor of Broadcasting and Publishing).[32] Typically these authorities enjoy considerable discretion in taking licensing decisions and in the formulation and enforcement of programme standards. They may also have some responsibility for enforcing anti-trust rules in the interests of media pluralism, though this is often shared with other competition authorities. For example, in Britain the ITC is required 'to ensure fair and effective competition in the provision' of private broadcasting services,[33] but the Director-General of Fair Trading and the Monopolies and Mergers Commission must determine whether networking

[29] See the decision in Jan. 1992 by the European Commission of Human Rights on the admissibility of the application to challenge the Austrian public broadcasting monopoly.

[30] See Ch. II, Ss. 2–4.

[31] See Ch. I, S. 2 above.

[32] See law 223 of 6 Aug. 1990, Art. 16(19) (issue of licences) and Art. 6 (institution and powers of the Garante).

[33] Broadcasting Act 1990, s. 2(2)(ii).

arrangements satisfy competition law. (The former is responsible for reporting whether the BBC have made enough programme time available to independent producers.[34])

The British Independent Broadcasting Authority (IBA) was unique in that it was the broadcaster responsible for the transmission of independent television, with reserve power to make programmes itself if there was a serious imbalance in a programme contractor's schedule.[35] It also had powers to preview programmes and control the companies' schedules. In contrast the ITC, instituted by the Broadcasting Act 1990, only has supervisory powers, though these are exercisable over cable and all satellite broadcasting as well as programmes distributed terrestrially. The French Conseil supérieur de l'audiovisuel (CSA) is also unusual in that it enjoys supervisory and some administrative powers with regard to both public and private broadcasting.[36] Its powers of programme control are much wider in the private sector, where it determines the terms of the licensees' contracts. These terms impose programme standards and advertising and sponsorship limits under the various heads set out in the statute (as amended in 1989).[37] The Italian Garante also has supervisory and enforcement powers over both public and private broadcasting, though these are relatively minor compared to the broad licensing and disciplinary functions of the CSA. His powers over RAI also seem to be shared with the Parliamentary Commission and nothing is said in the new statute about how these relate to each other.[38]

In principle there seems something to be said for combining the supervisory and other powers over public and private broadcasters in one body. It enables that authority to see the role of both systems in relation to each other. It could take account, for example, of the impact on the public broadcasting system of slack compliance by commercial broadcasters with programme standards. A licensing decision might also in some circumstances be appropriately influenced by experience of the rival public broadcasting system's programme output in that area. The institution of a single authority recognizes that the role of public and private broadcasters is to some extent to complement each other. Their relationship is not purely competitive.

If a regulated private broadcasting system is to be independent of state control (as required by the principles of broadcasting freedom), the licensing and regulatory authority must itself be autonomous. This may

[34] Ibid., s. 39 and Sch. 4, and ss. 186–7.

[35] Broadcasting Act 1981, s. 2(3).

[36] For its composition and powers with regard to public broadcasting, see Ch. III, S. 3 above.

[37] Law of 17 Jan. 1989, amending Art. 28 of the law of 30 Sept. 1986.

[38] See the discussion by G. Corasaniti of the Guarantor's powers in *Il sistema radiotelevisivo*, 97.

be provided for explicitly, as in the laws of some German *Länder*.[39] Attempts by a state or the federal government to give instructions to private broadcasters would be incompatible with the principle of *Staatsfreiheit* guaranteed under Article 5 of the Basic Law.[40] But the authorities' independence is primarily assured by rules concerning their composition and appointment. There is a variety of patterns. A typical structure provides for a state broadcasting commission (Landesrundfunkauschuss) and a smaller directorate (Vorstand).[41] Major decisions, such as those concerning the allocation and withdrawal of permits and compliance with statutory programme standards, are taken by the former body, while the directorate is concerned with financial and daily administrative matters. The state laws set out the division of responsibility in relatively precise terms. What is most interesting from a comparative perspective is the commissions' representative character. They are often composed of forty or more members, chosen by specified organizations, such as the Churches, trade unions, chambers of commerce and employers' bodies, sports, educational, cultural, and women's associations. Political parties may nominate a member, but often members of the state or federal government are ineligible.[42]

The British and French regulatory authorities lack this character. That is inevitable in view of their smaller size. The IBA had a Chairman, Vice-Chairman, and ten other members, and its replacement, the ITC, must have the same officers and eight to ten other members. Amendments to institute a slightly larger body of twelve to fifteen members and to empower the Commission to choose its own Chairman and Vice-Chairman were rejected. The Home Secretary appointed its officers and members. The government rejected an amendment to make appointments subject to approval by the House of Commons, while conceding the point that one member should represent Scotland, another Wales, and a third Northern Ireland.[43] The monopoly selection power (now exercisable by the Secretary of State for National Heritage) inevitably gives rise to the suspicion that members, like the BBC Governors, might have uniform political attitudes.[44] Another weakness is that there are no longer any

[39] See e.g. the Lower Saxony law of 16 Mar. 1987, s. 27 and Saarland law of 11 Aug. 1887, s. 53.

[40] *First Television* case, 12 BVerfGE 205, 252–4 (1961), and *Fourth Television* case, 73 BVerfGE 118, 182–90 (1986).

[41] Lower Saxony law, ss. 27 and 37; Saarland law, ss. 53 and 56. In other states private broadcasting is governed by a commission and a Director: see North Rhine–Westphalia law of 11 Jan. 1988, s. 51.

[42] North Rhine–Westphalia law of 11 Jan. 1988, s. 53; Lower Saxony law, s. 31.

[43] Broadcasting Act 1990, s. 1 and Sch. 1.

[44] For the Crown's power to nominate the BBC Governors, see Ch. III, S. 3 above. There were relatively few overtly political appointments in the period 1968–80: J. Potter, *Independent Television in Britain*, ii (London, 1989), 88–94.

statutory advisory councils or committees to represent the views of important business and social groups or the general public.[45] There might admittedly be little work for them to do with the removal of the regulatory authority's powers to preview and schedule programmes; but they could provide an element of genuine independence to balance an unrepresentative ITC.

As stated in the previous chapter, the CSA is a smaller body than its predecessor, the Commission nationale de la communication et des libertés, with few regulatory powers.[46] There are only nine members. Its independence was not, however, in the view of the Conseil constitutionnel compromised by its dependence every year for funding by the government. The CSA was itself able to make formal proposals for its funding, and that was enough to avoid any infringement of the freedom of speech guaranteed by Article 11 of the Declaration of the Rights of Man.[47] What is important is that it should enjoy a degree of permanence that has eluded its two predecessors.

In contrast the Federal Communications Commission (FCC) has been a model of stability. The same body has regulated radio and later television, including cable, in the United States, since 1934. One of the many independent administrative agencies characteristic of American government, it has recently been the most political of the broadcasting regulatory bodies treated in this book.[48] One reason for this is that the Commissioners, of whom there are now only five, are appointed by the President, admittedly with the consent of the Senate. Under the Federal Communications Act as amended in 1982, a majority of them may be drawn from the same political party.[49] Their period of office is five years (as it is for ITC members), so a US President who serves for two terms may easily be able to appoint the whole Commission. Its recent political stance was shown by its enthusiasm for deregulation under the chairmanship of Mark Fowler, appointed by President Reagan in May 1981; Fowler was an advocate of this process, as shown in a prominent law review article he co-authored at the time of his appointment.[50] It should be added that on previous occasions a majority of the FCC have been Democrats, and their political attitudes probably influenced decisions, particularly in the area of political broadcasting.[51] But quite apart from their bias, concern has

[45] Compare Broadcasting Act 1981, ss. 16–18.
[46] See Ch. III, S. 4 above.
[47] Decision 88–248 of 17 Jan. 1989, Debbasch, 319.
[48] See H. J. Friendly, *Federal Administrative Agencies* (Cambridge, Mass., 1962), 53–4, and G. O. Robinson, 'FCC: An Essay on Regulatory Watchdogs' (1978) 64 *Va. L. Rev.* 169.
[49] 47 USC, s. 154(b).
[50] M. S. Fowler and D. L. Brenner, 'A Marketplace Approach to Broadcast Regulation' (1981) 60 *Texas Law Rev.* 207.
[51] Powe, 160–1.

been expressed about the overall quality of the Commissioners, who enjoy extensive adjudicatory and rule-making powers.[52] These are exercised on the basis of the broad legislative standards of 'public interest, convenience, and necessity'.[53] In theory then the FCC has more discretionary power than any of the other regulatory bodies considered in this book. However, in practice it is significantly constrained by constant pressure from both politicians and the communications industry, while the level of public participation by pressure groups in the licensing process may be higher than in other countries.

It was from an anxiety to get away from the standard collegiate body dominated by political parties that the new Italian law entrusts regulatory powers to one senior officer, the Garante per la radiodiffusione e l'editoria. He is appointed for three years, a term renewable only once, by the state President on a joint nomination by the Presidents of the Chamber of Deputies and the Senate; he must be chosen from former judges of the Constitutional Court, presiding judges of sections of the Court of Cassation, or equivalent figures from the universities or from the mass communications industries. His principal functions, set out in Article 6 of the broadcasting law, are to keep a national register of broadcasting companies (and the press), to examine the accounts of broadcasting companies and (where necessary) of programme producers, distributors, and advertising agents, to monitor the ratings systems, and to apply a range of administrative sanctions for breach by the broadcasters of their programme duties. Together with the ordinary courts he also has power to enforce rights of reply.[54] He decides which programmes should not be interrupted by advertisements and appoints a consultative body of listeners and viewers.[55] His responsibilities, therefore, extend well beyond the primary one of guaranteeing the pluralism of the media, but are not as comprehensive as those of such bodies as the FCC, the ITC, or the CSA.[56]

4. THE LICENSING PROCESS

(i) Applicants

Systems commonly have rules about eligibility to apply for a broadcasting licence and disqualifying certain types of prospective applicant. To some extent they overlap with the rules considered in Chapter VI limiting the

[52] Robinson, 'FCC: An Essay on Regulatory Watchdogs', 187.

[53] 47 USC, ss. 307, 309.

[54] Art. 10 of law 223 of 6 Aug. 1990: for rights of reply, see Ch. VII, S. 4 below.

[55] Broadcasting law of 6 Aug. 1990, Arts. 8(4) and 28.

[56] See the commentary of G. Corasaniti in *Il sistema radiotelevisivo*, 95, 137–41.

accumulation of licences and restricting cross-media ownership. The eligibility rules discussed here exclude unsuitable persons and corporations, whether or not they already have a radio or television permit. Their scope has rarely given rise to legal or constitutional argument. In the *Fourth Television* case the German Constitutional Court upheld the constitutionality of the Lower Saxony law's disqualification of political parties, public employees, and public law organizations (apart from religious associations). Their exclusion was justified on the *Staatsfreiheit* principle, for their control of a channel would mean that it was not truly independent of the state. On the other hand, there was no objection to a newspaper publisher applying for a licence, though equally the press should not enjoy any privileged access.[57]

The British rules are set out in the Broadcasting Act 1990. The ITC or Radio Authority has a general duty not to award a licence to any applicant unless it is satisfied that 'he is a fit and proper person to hold it',[58] while more specific disqualifications are set out in Part II of Schedule 2. Among those disqualified are: individuals who are neither nationals of EC states ordinarily resident in the Community nor ordinarily resident in the UK, corporate bodies not formed under the law of an EC state with a registered or head office or principal place of business within the Community, local authorities, political parties and associated bodies, other broadcasting bodies (the BBC and the Welsh Authority), and advertising agencies. The disqualification of non-EC nationals and corporate bodies does not apply, however, to licences for cable delivery systems, for the supply of programmes for such systems, and for non-domestic satellite services. A number of United States companies have, therefore, been able to enter the British cable market, and indeed they have considerably expanded its coverage in the last few years. Churches and other religious bodies are disqualified from holding most types of licence, but they may be awarded a non-domestic satellite licence, a licence to provide cable programmes, or a licence for a local radio service, provided the ITC or RA (as the case may be) is satisfied it is appropriate for such a body to hold that particular kind of licence. A publicly funded body (principally one which has received more than half its income from public funds) may not be awarded a local radio licence other than one for a restricted service,[59] and a person who has been convicted of illegal broadcasting within the previous five years is disqualified from holding any radio permit.[60] Other rules are designed to prevent evasion of the primary prohibitions; for instance, individuals who are officers of disqualified corporate bodies, associated

[57] 73 BVerfGE 118, 175, 182–90 (1986).
[58] Ss. 3(3)(a) and 86(4)(a).
[59] Broadcasting Act 1990, Sch. 2, Part II, para. 3.
[60] Ibid., s. 89.

bodies, and corporate bodies in which disqualified bodies are participants with more than a 5 per cent interest are also excluded.

The disqualifications in the German statutes are in some ways similar to the British rules, albeit not so detailed. Public law bodies, political parties and dependent associations and persons, and members of the public broadcasting councils and of the state legislative bodies and governments are ineligible. One striking feature of the German laws is that they insist an applicant company must have its headquarters or domicile in Germany.[61] This is conceivably incompatible with the principle of freedom of establishment guaranteed by Article 52 of the Treaty of Rome, conferring on any company formed in one member state a right to set up an undertaking in another member state of the Community under the same conditions as those applicable to that state's nationals. Discrimination on the basis of a company's residence or the place of its headquarters is a disguised form of discrimination on grounds of nationality prohibited by the Treaty, justifiable only if there is a rational justification for the rule or practice.[62] Arguably, however, the German rules can be justified as necessary for the effective enforcement of programme standards and other requirements.

Article 16 of the new Italian statute sets out the threshold conditions for award of a broadcasting licence, whether national or local, television or radio. Both Italian and Community corporations may be granted national licences, while they, and individual citizens of any Community country, are eligible to apply for local licences. Applicants must have a minimum capital holding, for example, 3 billion lire for a national television channel or 500 million for national radio. These requirements ensure a degree of financial stability and continuity in service provision, a matter assessed in Britain by the ITC when considering competing applications.[63] Further, licences can only be granted to companies which are dedicated to broadcasting, publishing, or entertainment. They cannot be granted to companies primarily or significantly interested in other services or to public enterprises,[64] nor to companies which have been engaged in illegal broadcasting.[65] In contrast the French requirements are minimal. The law of 1986 allows applications for radio licences by companies, foundations, and associations, whether commercial or non-profit, while only companies can make applications for terrestrial television licences.[66]

[61] See e.g. Baden-Württemberg law of 12 Dec. 1985, s. 23(1), 5, Hamburg law of 3 Dec. 1985, s. 17(2), and Saarland law of 11 Aug. 1987, s. 40(1), 2.

[62] Also see Art. 58 of the Treaty of Rome, applying freedom of establishment to companies. For commentary, see D. A. Wyatt and A. Dashwood, *The Substantive Law of the EEC*, 2nd edn. (London, 1987), 213–17.

[63] See p. 89 below.

[64] Broadcasting law of 6 Aug. 1990, Art. 16(11) and (12).

[65] Ibid., Art. 16(13).

[66] Law of 30 Sept. 1986, Arts. 29 and 30.

The latter restriction also applies to satellite and cable broadcasting.[67] On the other hand, there are strict limits (considered in Chapter VI) on the amount of capital which individuals may hold in broadcasting companies.[68]

(ii) How licences are awarded

The licensing process involves linked substantive and procedural issues. On what grounds are licences awarded and how much, if any, discretion does the licensing authority enjoy? How open are the procedures by which applications are considered and the final decisions taken? The vaguer the criteria on the basis of which licences are awarded, the stronger may be the case for allowing the public an opportunity to participate in the process. Otherwise it will appear that the licensing authority has unfettered discretion to issue permits to whomsoever it wishes. If, on the other hand, licences are awarded by lottery or by auction, the case for public participation is much weaker. The decision in those circumstances would be taken on objective grounds. Whatever the procedure may be, there are few constitutional constraints in this context, apart perhaps from due process and natural justice requirements compelling the licensing authority to act fairly to applicants. In the *Third Television* case the German Constitutional Court emphasized that the licensing criteria should be set out in a statute and not left to the allocating authority. Every applicant must be given an equal chance to acquire a licence in conformity with the constitutional principle *Gleichheitsatz*.[69]

The IBA was at one stage criticized for allocating franchises entirely in private.[70] A measure of public consultation was introduced when they were reawarded in 1981, meetings being held to receive comments on the partly published applications. But these were not formal hearings and the final decisions were necessarily taken in private, because sensitive financial and personal information was discussed at that stage.[71] The procedure was entirely altered by the Broadcasting Act 1990. The key change is that licences for Channel 3 and Channel 5, local cable delivery systems, domestic satellite broadcasting, and national radio are to be awarded on the basis of the applicant's cash bid, provided it has passed the 'quality threshold' with regard to programme standards and established that it is

[67] Ibid., Arts. 31 (satellite) and 34 (cable).

[68] Ch. VI, S. 3 below.

[69] 57 BVerfGE 295, 327–9 (1981). For a discussion of the licensing criteria in Germany, see V. Porter and S. Hasselbach, *Pluralism, Politics and the Marketplace* (London, 1991), 87–93.

[70] See the Report of the Select Committee on Nationalized Industries (1971–2) HC 465, paras. 95–8, and N. Lewis, 'IBA Programme Contract Awards' [1975] *Pub. Law* 317, 320–6.

[71] See the Report of the Annan Committee on the Future of Broadcasting (1977) Cmnd. 6753, paras. 13.22–13.24.

financially able to maintain the service throughout the licence period.[72] The cash bid is to be paid annually and is to be revised in line with inflation.[73] This is, therefore, a mixed procedure, containing elements of discretion exercisable by the ITC or Radio Authority, and then finally allocation on the objective ground of the size of the bid. There is, however, an important discretionary power not to award the licence to the highest bidder in exceptional circumstances.

The process for allocating Channel 3 regional television licences can now be outlined in detail. The ITC issued (in February 1991) a formal invitation to apply. The document contained, among other things, information on the types of programme which had to be included in the applicant's proposals to meet the 'quality threshold' standards set out in section 16 of the Act. The invitation also specified the application fee and the percentage of the 'qualifying revenue' which each successful bidder is required to pay annually to the Commission. 'Qualifying revenue' is in effect revenue derived from advertising, sponsorship, and subscription.[74] Holders of licences for the larger regions (London, the Midlands, the North-West, and South and South-East England) are naturally required to pay more (11 per cent) than holders in the smaller regions, and indeed five very small ones are not required to pay anything at all under this heading.[75] Applications had to give details of programming proposals, information about the bidder's financial position, proposals for, *inter alia*, training and for promoting the understanding of programmes by deaf, blind, and partially sighted persons, and of course the cash bid.[76] It was after this stage that there was a measure of consultation, as the Commission invited representations on the applicants' published programme schemes.[77]

The ITC was not free to award licences on the basis of the cash bids, until it was satisfied the applicant's programme proposals complied with the requirements set out in section 16 (discussed in Chapter V) and that 'he would be able to maintain that service throughout the period for which the licence would be in force'.[78] The latter requirement is known as the 'sustainability' test. The ITC also had to take account of the representations made to it by members of the public about each applicant's

[72] Broadcasting Act 1990, ss. 16–17 (Channel 3), s. 44 (domestic satellites), ss. 75–6 (local delivery licences), ss. 99–100 (national radio): for programme standards, see Ch. V below. However, the ITC must award an applicant a licence for a non-domestic satellite service, unless it appears that the service would not comply with general programme standards: see s. 45.

[73] Ibid., s. 15(7).

[74] Ibid., s. 19(3).

[75] For details, see the ITC *Invitation to Apply for Regional Channel 3 Licences*, para. 161.

[76] Broadcasting Act 1990, s. 15(3).

[77] Ibid., s. 15(6).

[78] Ibid., s. 16(1).

programme plans.[79] It seems the Commission staff assessed the merits of these plans and the financial position of each applicant separately before concluding whether the threshold requirements had been satisfied; further, it is clear that some attention was paid by its finance officers to the size of cash bids in determining whether the 'sustainability' test had been satisfied.[80]

The duty to award the licence to the highest cash bidder (assuming it passed the two threshold tests) is qualified by a discretionary power on the part of the ITC to award it to a lower bidder in 'exceptional circumstances'. These cover the case where the quality of the service proposed by the lower bidder is 'exceptionally high' and it is 'substantially higher' than that put forward by the highest bidder.[81] This non-exhaustive definition was included in the Bill as a government amendment at Report stage.[82] The 'exceptional circumstances', moreover, need not be unique, so it was open for the ITC to have exercised its discretion in a number of the cases it considered. In fact it did not exercise the power at all when the licences were awarded in October 1991, though apparently it did consider doing so in at least one case. The reason for this reluctance was probably that the Commission was under an obligation to give reasons for exercising this discretion,[83] and that would almost certainly have exposed it to an application for judicial review from a frustrated highest bidder.

Where licences were awarded to the highest bidder (which had satisfied the threshold tests), there was only a statutory duty to state the name of the successful applicant and its cash bid, and to name every other applicant which had satisfied the tests. The intention was presumably to insulate the ITC from applications for judicial review by unsuccessful bidders. If that was the idea, it did not entirely work. TSW, which had held the licence for the South-West region since 1981, challenged the ITC ruling that it was unable to meet the 'sustainability' condition and the consequent award of the licence to its rival, West Country, which had bid substantially less. The Court of Appeal held that in these circumstances, where at first glance something might seem to have gone wrong with the ITC decision, it was appropriate to ask it to explain its decision.[84] When this was done, the Court granted leave to apply for judicial review, but the substantive application was rejected by a majority (Lord Donaldson MR dissenting). The House of Lords unanimously affirmed that decision.

[79] Ibid., s. 16(4).
[80] See the decision of the Court of Appeal in *R.* v. *ITC, ex parte TSW Broadcasting Ltd.* (unreported).
[81] Broadcasting Act 1990, s. 17(3)–(4).
[82] 172 HC Deb. (6th ser.), col. 277.
[83] Ibid., s. 17(12)(c).
[84] If the ITC had refused to explain its decision at all, an adverse inference could be inferred from that silence: see *Padfield* v. *Minister of Agriculture* [1988] AC 997, 1061–2 (HL).

The TSW application had been fairly considered and it had not been misled about the criteria taken into account.[85]

The auction procedure for the allocation of Channel 3 licences was widely criticized, particularly when it became clear that two incumbents (Central and Scottish) had retained their franchises for a cash bid of only £2,000 each, while other successful applicants (Carlton and Yorkshire) made bids of £37–43,000,000. The imposition of a reserve price would have averted these bizarre results. Further, it is arguable that the 'exceptional circumstances' discretion should have been drafted in terms which would have entitled the ITC to take account of an incumbent's proven record and contribution to the ITV system. That might have enabled Thames to keep its London weekday franchise. But the principle of allocation by competitive tender is defensible. Television licences are scarce resources, the possession of which has often been extremely profitable. Their award should so far as possible depend on objective criteria, rather than administrative discretion. Allocation by tender was suggested by members of the Public Accounts Committee in 1959,[86] so it would be wrong to dismiss the procedure solely as an aberration, attributable to the free market ideology which characterized the 1980s.

The British statute contains more detailed provisions, particularly with regard to procedure, than any of the comparable broadcasting laws. For example, the French statute requires the CSA when awarding radio and television licences to take account of a number of factors: the constitutional requirement of pluralism, the need to have a variety of station owners, and the need to avoid abuses of a dominant position and other anti-competitive practices. Subject to these considerations, the experience of the applicant in the media field may be taken into account, as may its financial resources and the consequences of an award to the applicant on the distribution of advertising revenue.[87] Candidates for television licences are entitled to a public hearing of their case,[88] a procedure introduced by the CNCL when it granted the authorizations for the fifth and sixth channels in 1987. This procedure was modelled on the public hearing procedure used in the United States for the award of licences by the FCC, though it was much less formal.[89] The CNCL published accounts of these hearings, a valuable step inasmuch as they gave an indication of its reasoning.[90]

[85] *R.* v. *ITC, ex parte TSW*, unreported (see note by T. H. Jones, [1992] *Pub. Law* 372).

[86] See B. Sendall, *Independent Television in Britain*, i: *Origin and Foundation, 1946–62* (London, 1982), 293–4.

[87] Law of 30 Sept. 1986, Arts. 29(8)–(9) and 30(4)–(5), as amended by law of 17 Jan. 1989.

[88] Ibid., Art. 30(4).

[89] G. Drouot, *Le Nouveau Droit de l'audiovisuel* (Paris, 1988), 57.

[90] *Auditions des candidats à l'exploitation des cinquième et sixième chaînes de television, 18 et 19 fev. 1987* (Paris, 1987).

The new Italian statute lists a number of relatively objective criteria to be taken into account by the Minister of Posts when awarding licences: the applicants' financial resources and their programming and technical plans. For existing licensees, their presence in the market, the quality of their programmes, the proportion of self-produced entertainment and information material in their schedules, and levels of viewership are also relevant.[91] But these considerations are rather theoretical. The statute also makes it clear that for the first licence allocation, where other things are equal, existing broadcasters (that is, in effect the Berlusconi networks) enjoy preference, at least if they satisfy the conditions set out in the law. To mitigate the possible consequences of this provision, the transfer of a preferred licensee's company, or the controlling shares in it, is forbidden for four years from the grant of the licence, on penalty of loss of the broadcasting concession.[92]

(iii) Licence grants

Permits are typically given for a limited period rather than indefinitely. Towards the end of the period, the authority may review such matters as the appropriate size and shape of the regions for which licences are granted and general programme requirements, as well as how satisfactorily the incumbent has discharged its obligations. But the grant period should be long enough to enable the broadcaster to realize its investment and programme plans. The IBA was only permitted to grant franchises for eight years.[93] Now the term is ten years, which may be renewed on one or more occasions for further terms.[94] This is now also the maximum period for private television permits in France, while it had been twelve years under the 1986 statute.[95] Five years is the maximum period for radio licences in that country. In Germany the standard maximum period is ten years, with frequently a minimum period of four to five years prescribed in the law;[96] Baden-Württemberg, however, lays down a short maximum period of five years and a minimum of only one.[97] In other countries the licence term is relatively short: five years in the United States for a first television broadcasting licence and seven years for a first radio licence, while in Italy the term is six years for any category of permit.[98]

[91] Law 223 of 6 Aug. 1990, Art. 16(17).
[92] Ibid., Art. 34(3).
[93] Broadcasting Act 1981, s. 19.
[94] Broadcasting Act 1990, s. 20.
[95] Law of 17 Jan. 1989, Art. 13, amending Art. 28 of the law of 30 Sept. 1986.
[96] For a table setting out the licence periods, see Porter and Hasselbach, *Pluralism, Politics and the Marketplace*, 74–5.
[97] Law of 16 Dec. 1985, s. 26(1).
[98] See the Federal Communications Act 1934, s. 307(c) and the Italian law of 6 Aug. 1990, Art. 16(2). However, in the USA television broadcasting licences may be renewed for a maximum of 10 years: 1934 Act, s. 307(c).

A standard provision in *Länder* statutes is that licences are not assignable.[99] Sometimes this rule is supported by provisions requiring notification to the state regulatory authority of, and its permission for, changes in the composition of the broadcasting corporation.[100] In Britain the ITC must impose conditions requiring licensees to give notice of proposals concerning the shareholdings in, and directors of, the licensee company. Conditions must also be imposed enabling the Commission to revoke a licence, when there is a change in the licensee's structure or in the persons controlling it such that no licence would have been granted to the body in its changed condition.[101] On the other hand, the ITC, unlike its predecessor, has no automatic power to stop take-overs of licensees; but there is a moratorium of one year, during which the Commission must still give its approval to such changes.[102] The new company must, of course, observe the programme proposals submitted by the original licensee, and its entry into the market may be inhibited by the competition rules against an accumulation of licences (Chapter VI). Subject to these points, the government took the view that take-overs may encourage efficiency.[103] They may certainly be anticipated in the new regime, for some of the companies granted franchises at the end of 1991 will struggle to keep their programme promises in the context of their large cash bids and perhaps (relatively) declining advertising revenue.

One final general point concerns the legal form of the franchises or authorizations. In Britain they used to be awarded by contract; the regional companies were strictly programme contractors. The same legal technique has been used in France, both under the 1982 law and now under the 1989 amendments to the 1986 statute.[104] A public law contract is made between the CSA and the successful bidder, which must by law include a number of specific terms concerning programme and advertising standards. Breach of these terms may be sanctioned by contractual remedies, as well as the statutory penalties provided by the statute itself.[105] The advantage of licensing by contract, therefore, is to strengthen the

[99] Baden-Württemberg law of 16 Dec. 1985, s. 26(2); Lower Saxony law of 16 Mar. 1987, s. 7(3); Saarland law of 11 Aug. 1987, s. 39(4); North Rhine–Westphalia law of 11 Jan. 1988, s. 8(1).

[100] Ibid., s. 8(4). For discussion of the complex rules, see B. Holznagel, 'Konzentrationsbekampfung im privaten Rundfunk' [1991] *ZUM* 263, 268–70. There are also strict rules in Italy to prevent transfers of interests in broadcasting companies. Where there is a transfer of any significant shareholding (defined as 2 per cent of any quoted company) the licensee must apply for a confirmation of the permit: law of 6 Aug. 1990, Arts. 16(2) and 17(5).

[101] Broadcasting Act 1990, s. 5(2)(d) and (5).

[102] Ibid., s. 21. For the earlier law, see Broadcasting Act 1981, s. 20(4)–(5).

[103] See the White Paper *Broadcasting in the '90s: Competition, Choice and Quality* (1988) Cm. 517, para. 6.18.

[104] Law of 17 Jan. 1989, Art. 13, amending Art. 28 of law of 30 Sept. 1986.

[105] For the statutory remedies for breach of programme conditions, see Ch. V, S. 5 below.

licensee's commitment to honour its obligations and to provide additional remedies for their breach. In practice the statutory remedies are now sufficiently varied to render these advantages somewhat theoretical.

5. RENEWAL AND WITHDRAWAL OF LICENCES

Some broadcasting laws make explicit provision for the renewal of broadcasting licences, though many of them merely mention the possibility or are silent on the point.[106] Provision seems unnecessary, unless applications for renewal are governed by special rules, or as in the United States the term of a renewal is longer than that of an original licence (ten years for a renewed as compared with five years for a first television permit). The British Broadcasting Act 1990 gives the ITC only a limited discretion *not to renew* a Channel 3 licence.[107] It can refuse renewal if it is not satisfied that the applicant will comply with the programme promises it made on its first application and with the general programme standards imposed on Channel 3 licensees under section 16. Alternatively the application for a second (or further) licence can be turned down, if the ITC proposes to make changes in the areas or times for which the regional services are provided. The original licensees, therefore, have a strong expectation of renewal; certainly there will be no comparison of their performance over the initial eight or nine years and the programme promises of any challengers for the franchise.

In comparison licence renewal has at times been a serious business in the United States. The 1934 legislation requires applicants for renewal to provide the same information about staff, finance, and programmes as they supplied on their initial request; the FCC determines such applications on the same criteria of the 'public interest, convenience, and necessity'.[108] In practice it was impossible for the FCC to investigate the record of every licensee requesting renewal, but it became common for listeners' and viewers' associations to make representations at renewal proceedings after the decision of the DC Circuit Court of Appeals in the *United Church of Christ* case.[109] Burger CJ stressed the importance of hearing their views to bring home to the FCC any deficiencies in licensees' performances. For some time this led to deeper scrutiny of a franchise-holder's record and there have been some cases where its licence was not

[106] The Italian law of 6 Aug. 1990, Art. 16(2) provides that licences are renewable, without further provision.

[107] Broadcasting Act 1990, s. 20(4).

[108] S. 307(d).

[109] *Office of Communication of the United Church of Christ* v. *FCC* 359 F. 2d. 994 (1966).

renewed because its performance did not match its promises or because of a failure to comply with the Fairness Doctrine.[110] But this was relatively rare. With the FCC's removal of virtually all programme standards, non-renewal on these substantive grounds cannot occur; but an application for a second permit may be denied for other reasons, such as dishonesty or the criminal record of a licensee.

Naturally a licensee which has become insolvent, or whose directors have been convicted of a serious offence relevant to acquisition of the licence or to the conduct of the company's business, is likely to have its licence withdrawn before expiry of the normal term. Provision for this step is made in all broadcasting laws. For example, the Italian legislation lists four sets of circumstances in which licences lapse, including insolvency, death, and legal incapacity of the holder.[111] There is a wide provision in the French statute enabling licence withdrawal without preliminary summons where there has been a substantial change in the circumstances on the basis of which it was awarded.[112] This would include alterations to the financial structure or organization of the broadcasting company. Withdrawal of a licence is also the most serious sanction for a failure to satisfy programme standards, a topic considered in the next chapter.

[110] For the former, see *West Coast Media* v. *FCC* 695 F. 2d. 617 (DC Cir. 1982), and for the latter, *Brandywine Main Line Radio* v. *FCC* 473 F. 2d. 16 (DC Cir. 1972).

[111] Law of 6 Aug. 1990, Art. 16(21).

[112] Law of 17 Jan. 1989, Art. 19, inserting new Art. 42-3 in the law of 30 Sept. 1986.

V
Programme Standards

1. INTRODUCTION

The imposition of programme standards lies at the heart of broadcasting law. It distinguishes the legal regulation of radio and television from the less stringent regime governing newspapers and books. While the press is only subject to the general law, for example, the laws of libel, obscenity, and contempt of court, the broadcasting media are controlled by a variety of statutory and other rules. These prohibit, for instance, broadcasters from expressing their views on the media and require them to present a balanced schedule including, say, children's and religious programmes and other serious matter.

These standards were of course originally, at least in Europe, only applicable to the monopoly public broadcasting companies. They were considered necessary to give listeners (and subsequently viewers) access to a wide range of programmes and points of view. Further, it was rightly felt inappropriate for journalists and producers employed by the public company to exploit its monopoly position to put across their own political opinions. Media freedom, as we saw in Chapter II, does not mean that broadcasters have unlimited rights to speak as they wish. Instead, public channels must each present a balanced variety of programmes and views, in Germany termed the *binnenpluralistisch* (internal pluralist) model of broadcasting.[1]

With the number of private commercial channels now available, particularly since the advent of cable and satellite, the case for rigorous programme standards is much weaker. To some extent, it can be argued, a free market should ensure there is a reasonable range of programmes for viewers and listeners to choose from. Specialist channels, generally transmitted by cable, might be able to meet minority tastes, while others may be catered for by channels devoted largely to news, films, or the coverage of sports events. Even some degree of political partisanship might be tolerated on one commercial channel, provided it is compensated by the different range of views expressed on others. While it is clearly wrong for, say, the BBC to show bias in view of its unique position, it is

[1] See in particular the *Third Television* case, 57 BVerfGE 295, 326 (1981).

less obvious that a local commercial radio station should never take a political stance. In short, private broadcasters, particularly at the local level, might be afforded almost as much freedom of speech as the press. This alternative structure has been characterized as providing external pluralism (in German *aussenpluralismus*, in Italian *pluralismo esterno*) in contrast to the internal pluralism required of public (and some private) broadcasting institutions.[2]

None of the European jurisdictions considered in this book has wholly abrogated the standards of comprehensiveness and impartiality. This radical position is found to some extent in the idiosyncratic Dutch system, where a large amount of broadcasting time is allocated to denominational and political associations in proportion to the number of their members.[3] Their programmes are expected to represent particular political and religious views. In the United States, too, private broadcasting has had most programme constraints removed from it. (Indeed in that country even public broadcasters are free to editorialize.[4]) But in Britain, France, and Germany the standards imposed on private broadcasters are similar to those imposed on the public companies, although they are often rather lighter. In Italy relatively few precise standards have been imposed on either sector. Under the secret agreement of 1975[5] the RAI channels each came under the control of one of the major political parties; their influence is often apparent in the presentation of news and other programmes. The private channels and networks were not regulated at all until 1990, an omission attributable to the inertia of the legislature, rather than to any deliberate decision to treat the two branches of the media differently.

The German Constitutional Court has often considered whether it is appropriate to exact lower standards of private broadcasters. In the *Third Television* case it indicated that the private channels, unlike public broadcasters, need not each be required to show a balanced range of programmes.[6] Their schedules could be assessed together in determining whether overall adequate balance had been achieved. But every licensee was expected to show comprehensive and accurate news programmes and to give some time to the presentation of conflicting opinions. The standards

[2] See the judgments of the German Constitutional Court in the *Third Television* case, ibid., and of the Italian Constitutional Court in Decision 826/1988 [1988] *Giur. cost.* 3893, 3934.

[3] For a brief description of the Dutch system, see D. McQuail, 'The Netherlands: Freedom and Diversity under Multichannel Conditions', in J. G. Blumler (ed.), *Television and the Public Interest* (London, 1992), 96. Even in that system, however, the news must be impartial and there are some general programme standards.

[4] See *FCC* v. *League of Women Voters of California* 468 US 364 (1984), discussed further in S. 2 below.

[5] See Ch. I, S. 3 above.

[6] 57 BVerfGE 295, 325–6 (1981).

were further lowered in the *Fourth Television* case.[7] It was unrealistic, in the Court's view, to require each licensee to provide a comprehensive service. Cultural programmes and documentaries might be too expensive for the commercial channels, which must provide fare with mass appeal if they are to survive. It would be wrong to impose programming constraints which endangered their existence. Further, it was not necessary to apply the requirement of impartiality (*gleichgewichtige Vielfalt*) too strictly. The Court, however, made it clear that private broadcasters must still meet a minimum basic standard of fairness. All views, even those of minorities, should be presented on the private channels, as they are on the public.

But it was not clear whether these rulings required the *Länder* to impose lighter standards on private broadcasters than on the public channels, or whether they merely permitted that course. The question was answered in the *Sixth Television* case, when a challenge was made to the legality of the North Rhine–Westphalia statute imposing strict standards (relative to other state broadcasting laws) on the commercial channels.[8] State Parliaments may, but need not, impose somewhat lower programme constraints on private broadcasters. Additionally the basic standard (*Grundstandard*) of fairness, formulated by the Court in the previous case, applied only to the continuing monitoring of programme standards by the *Land* regulatory authority. It was proper for it to exact a higher standard when it allocated licenses. State laws could, moreover, forbid their grant to applicants proposing to show only popular entertainment programmes.

In all three of these cases the Court has been aware of the potential consequences for public broadcasting of the imposition of lower standards on its private competitors. It would make nonsense, for example, of the impartiality rule imposed on the public channels, if there were no restraints at all (or only nominal ones) on the commercial ones. Then the overall balance of views presented on German television would be uneven. Equally the ARD and ZDF channels might feel compelled to show more mass entertainment programmes to compete with an unregulated private sector. Another possibility would be to confine the public channels to the provision of news, current affairs, and cultural programmes, leaving popular entertainment to their commercial rivals. The Court has dismissed this option as unconstitutional.[9] Public broadcasters have rights and responsibilities under the Basic Law to transmit a wide range of programmes which inform, instruct, and entertain.[10]

[7] 73 BVerfGE 118, 157 (1986). For criticism, see W. S. Glaeser, 'Die Rundfunkfreiheit in der Rechtsprechung des Bundesverfassungsgerichts' (1987) 112 *AöR* 215, 249–50.

[8] 83 BVerfGE 238 (1991).

[9] Ibid. 300–1.

[10] This principle was established by the Constitutional Court in its first pronouncement on broadcasting law, 12 BVerfGE 205, 261–2 (1961).

These questions have been discussed in Britain, without of course reference to constitutional considerations. A majority of the Peacock Committee recommended that the BBC's popular music stations, Radios 1 and 2, should be privatized.[11] It envisaged eventually a slimmed-down BBC which would show a narrow range of 'public service' programmes, financed by subscription and grants from a Public Service Broadcasting Council, analogous perhaps to the Arts Council. It is likely that these ideas will be considered when the BBC's Charter comes up for renewal in 1996. Yet, as commentators have pointed out,[12] this development would confine public broadcasting to a cultural ghetto. Such a diminished role would be incompatible with the traditional concept of 'public service broadcasting', outlined in Chapter III. It would also be difficult to justify retention of the licence fee for the support purely of minority programmes.

The maintenance of some programme standards is, therefore, necessary, if public and private broadcasting are to continue to discharge their complementary roles.[13] The former should be allowed (or required) to provide a comprehensive service, at least on its principal channels, while commercial licensees should be compelled to show some serious material of high quality. The standards, however, imposed on the latter may be lighter. It is relatively easy to formulate these principles in legislation, but much harder to enforce them in practice. As the German Constitutional Court has recognized, the concept of balance is really a target (*Zielwert*) which can only be reached approximately.[14] It cannot be reduced to precise rules. The Court explained that a number of satellite and cable channels transmitted from other states and abroad are now receivable in each *Land*, although they are not subject to its jurisdiction. It is, therefore, no longer possible for states strictly to enforce their own impartiality (or other) standards. Similar scepticism was expressed in the USA concerning the practicality of enforcing those programme standards which imposed obligations on broadcasters to present a balanced coverage of important controversial issues.[15]

On the basis of these reflections some commentators have concluded

[11] Peacock Committee on Financing the BBC (1986) Cmnd. 9824, paras. 637–44.

[12] See in particular the essays in Blumler (ed.), *Television and the Public Interest*, esp. J. G. Blumler and W. Hoffman-Riem, 'New Roles for Public Service Television', 202.

[13] For the view that public and private television provide complementary, and not only competitive, services, see Ch. IV, S. 1 above.

[14] *Fourth Television* case, 73 BVerfGE 118, 157 (1986).

[15] In *Accuracy in Media* v. *FCC* 521 F. 2d. 288 (DC Cir. 1975), it was held that the statutory obligation imposed on public broadcasters to adhere strictly to balance in its presentation of controversial issues was not enforceable by the FCC or the courts. See H. Geller, 'Mass Communications Policy: Where We Are and Where We Should Be Going', in J. Lichtenberg (ed.), *Democracy and the Mass Media* (Cambridge, 1990), 290, 297–303.

that programme standards are symbolic rather than effective.[16] They state aspirations, but are not designed to lay down firm rules which broadcasters must meet on pain of licence forfeiture or other penalty. Obviously standards would be quite useless if the regulatory authority, say, the ITC or the Conseil supérieur de l'audiovisuel, were reluctant to punish their breach.[17] There is something to this view, but it seems too gloomy. Where it is plain that a channel has fallen short of the required standards, the regulatory authority will come under substantial pressure to act. Often it will be political. But legal pressure can also be brought if the rules of standing allow citizens' groups to apply for judicial review.[18]

Quality and impartiality may to some extent be safeguarded by means other than the imposition of detailed programme standards. Limits on the frequency of advertisements and sponsorship restrictions, for example, ensure that there are relatively few interruptions to programmes and that their contents are not determined by commercial interests. In some countries, especially Germany, the composition of regulatory bodies is balanced in order to reduce the risk of political bias and to encourage indirectly the access of significant social groups.[19] Anti-trust rules, in particular restrictions on the accumulation of licences, also reduce the risk that the media will be dominated by one or two voices. These rules are discussed elsewhere in this book. In this chapter I outline the various types of programme standard, leaving to its final section a discussion of their enforcement.

2. IMPARTIALITY

The most striking restriction of broadcasters' freedom of speech is the impartiality requirement. In Britain this is coupled with a specific prohibition of 'all expressions of the views and opinions of the person providing the service on matters . . . which are of political or industrial controversy or relate to current public policy'.[20] 'Editorializing', to use the American term, is in effect banned. It is unusual to spell this out explicitly in a broadcasting statute; in continental legal systems it is understood as an aspect of the general duty to be impartial and objective in the presentation of news and current affairs.

The requirements of impartiality and no-editorializing should, however,

[16] See in particular W. Hoffman-Riem, 'Defending Vulnerable Values: Regulatory Measures and Enforcement Dilemmas', in Blumler (ed.), *Television and the Public Interest*, 173, 198–9.

[17] For enforcement of programme standards, see S. 5 below.

[18] See p. 119 below.

[19] See Ch. III, S. 3 and Ch. IV, S. 3 above.

[20] Broadcasting Act 1990, s. 6(4); BBC Licence and Agreement, cl. 13(7).

be treated as distinct. A channel could be permitted to adopt a partisan line and at the same be under a legal duty to present balancing opinions. This was indeed the position in the United States from 1949 until the repeal of the Fairness Doctrine in 1987. The FCC Report *Editorializing by Broadcast Licensees* allowed station owners to use their channels to broadcast their opinions on controversial questions.[21] But it affirmed their duty to make facilities available for the presentation of a balanced range of views on such issues. Even more surprising from a British perspective is the freedom of public broadcasters to take an editorial line. This was established by the Supreme Court in *FCC* v. *League of Women Voters of California*.[22] A bare majority of the Court ruled contrary to the First Amendment a provision in the Public Broadcasting Act 1967, which banned editorializing by non-commercial educational stations in receipt of public grants. Brennan J. considered the ban discriminated between permissible speech (station announcements about their programmes or solicitations for funds) and editorializing; it was a discrimination based on the contents of speech, which American courts are reluctant to countenance.[23] He was not persuaded that the rule was necessary to prevent public stations from becoming vehicles for government propaganda or from becoming spokesmen for particular pressure groups.

This argument would be unlikely to convince European commentators. People expect broadcasters, particularly on the public channels, to be impartial and not to intrude their own personal opinions. Removal of the editorializing ban would allow them to exercise enormous influence, at least until the public learnt to treat opinion on radio and television with the caution with which it regards press leaders. The United States tradition is quite different. Public broadcasting was established more recently and is less widely patronized than commercial radio and television. What is said on the public stations matters much less than it does in European countries.

Broadcasters, of course, may indirectly express their opinions by the way in which programmes schedules are devised, the selection of guests for interview, the arrangement of the news, and so on. Impartiality rules are designed to control these exercises of editorial discretion. They vary considerably in their precision and strictness. At one extreme are the detailed provisions of the ITC Code issued under the Broadcasting Act 1990, which bizarrely for a deregulatory measure tightened up the im-

[21] 13 FCC 1246 (1949). For the early history of this aspect of US law, see S. J. Simmons, *The Fairness Doctrine and the Media* (Berkeley, Calif., 1978), ch. 2.

[22] 468 US 364 (1984).

[23] US courts have traditionally been reluctant to uphold rules which permit the expression of some views or types of speech but ban others: see E. M. Barendt, *Freedom of Speech* (Oxford, 1987), 18 and 96–7.

partiality rules. On the other hand, Article 1 of the Italian law of 1990 simply refers to the fundamental principles of pluralism, objectivity, comprehensiveness, and impartiality as governing the broadcasting system, whether public or private. Similar principles are stated in very general terms in the *cahiers des charges* of the French public programme companies and TF1 and in the contractual conditions of the other private broadcasting channels. The *cahiers* of TF1, for example, require programmes to be made in a spirit of rigorous impartiality and strict objectivity.[24]

An important question is whether impartiality principles should be applied to each channel individually or to the range of programmes shown on all channels available in a particular country or region. Now that there is a (relatively) large number of stations, a lack of balance on the programmes offered by one may be compensated by the different opinions provided by another. The German Constitutional Court has drawn a distinction between the position of public and private broadcasters.[25] Each of the former's channels must be balanced. But in the case of private broadcasting balance may be assessed over its programmes as a whole. A number of the state statutes provide that overall balance (*die Ausgewogenheit der Gesamtheit der Programme*) is assumed to have been reached when at least three (or in some cases four) commercial channels are available. If that is not the case, or the state regulatory authority determines that overall balance has not been attained, then each channel must satisfy the requirement.[26] There are equivalent provisions for nationally available private channels in the 1991 *Rundfunkstaatsvertrag*; a three-quarters majority of the state regulatory bodies may determine that overall the radio or television programmes do not meet the requirements of impartiality, in which case the requirement is exacted of each channel.[27] But no individual channel may be totally biased.[28]

The presumption in many *Länder* statutes that three channels are enough to provide overall balance and impartiality is perhaps rather artificial. On the other hand, it is surely right to treat private broadcasting more leniently than the public channels. Commentators insist that the Constitutional Court has not significantly diluted the impartiality rule. Sanctions can only be applied when there is a serious breach, but the

[24] Decree 87-43 of 30 Jan. 1987, Art. 10. The recruitment and terms of journalists' employment must not depend on their opinions or political associations, a rule designed to exclude government influence on broadcasting.

[25] *Third Television* case, 57 BVerfGE 295, 325–6 (1981), and *Fourth Television* case, 73 BVerfGE 118, 157–9 (1986).

[26] See e.g. the Lower Saxony law of 16 Mar. 1987, Art. 15(2), revised to meet the requirements of the Court in the *Fourth Television* case, and the Baden-Württemberg law of 16 Dec. 1985, Art. 20(1).

[27] *Rundfunkstaatsvertrag*, s. 20.

[28] Ibid., s. 20(4).

level of fairness expected in practice is considerably higher than the basic standard formulated by the Court.[29]

In Britain the same impartiality obligation is imposed on public and private broadcasters. The BBC accepts it as a self-binding rule, recognized by Resolutions of the Governors. The independent sector has a statutory duty to preserve 'due impartiality' with regard to 'matters of political or industrial controversy or relating to public policy'.[30] Outside the context of election broadcasts,[31] the formula has not given rise to litigation or until recently any controversy. Two further provisions are relevant. News, whether given in news bulletins or other forms, must be 'presented with due accuracy and impartiality'.[32] But the general impartiality requirement may be applied over a series of programmes.[33] In other words, an individual programme may in some circumstances express a definite view on a controversial issue, provided it is balanced by another programme in the series. The IBA naturally had considerable discretion in applying these rules. It permitted 'personal view' and access programmes, provided they were clearly indicated as having a special character and they were balanced by other contributions over a reasonable period.[34] Broadcasters were encouraged to consult the IBA before programmes were transmitted.

In its original version the Broadcasting Bill made only one change. The ITC would be required to draw up a Code. However, in the House of Lords maverick Conservative peers, angry with what they considered to be slack enforcement of the rules, persuaded the government to tighten the law.[35] The ITC Code must now ensure that broadcasters are impartial with regard to 'major matters' as well as controversial questions generally and it must specify what constitutes a 'series of programmes'. Other rules must indicate, to the extent the ITC considers appropriate, the period within which a balancing programme is to be included in a series and how the showing of such balancing items is to be announced in advance. It is added, perhaps helpfully, that impartiality does not always require absolute neutrality or 'detachment from fundamental democratic principles'.[36]

[29] F. Ossenbühl, 'Rundfunkprogramm-Leistung in treuhänderischer Freiheit' [1977] *DÖV* 381, 386–7; R. Gross, 'Zum Verfassungsrecht der Programmvielfalt in Rundfunk' [1982] *DVBl.* 118.

[30] See now Broadcasting Act 1990, s. 6(1)(c). The formula existed in the Television Act 1954, s. 3(1)(f).

[31] See Ch. VIII, S. 2 below.

[32] Broadcasting Act 1990, s. 6(1)(b).

[33] Ibid., s. 6(2).

[34] See the IBA Television Programme Guidelines, ch. 6, and C. R. Munro, *Television, Censorship and the Law* (Farnborough, 1979), 36–7.

[35] For the government's attempts to revise the Bill, see L. P. Hitchens, 'Impartiality and the Broadcasting Act: Riding the Wrong Horse' (1991) 12 *Jo. of Media Law and Practice* 48.

[36] Broadcasting Act 1990, s. 6(6).

The ITC responded with a very detailed Code. Its rules constitute licence conditions enforceable by fine or other penalty.[37] Other principles provide guidance on how the impartiality duty should be discharged. The Code, like the provisions under which it was introduced, is hard to interpret. It is unclear, for example, what should be regarded as a 'major matter', which must itself be treated with impartiality, or when a particular programme is to be regarded as one of a series or a discrete item. One or two things, however, are free from doubt. The argument that balance can be assessed with regard to other television or radio channels (as the case may be) is not acceptable. (The ITC Code is in this way stricter than some of the private broadcasting statutes in Germany.) Where appropriate, a right of reply or a discussion programme should follow a personal view programme. (But it is not clear whether it must take place immediately after the latter.) The ITC requires licensees to show that a sufficiently broad range of views has been presented in documentaries and other series at the end of each year or is planned for the following year.

In contrast the ITC may impose a lower duty on the providers of cable programmes.[38] They may be required to demonstrate only that they do not give 'undue prominence' to the views of particular persons, instead of satisfying the impartiality test. In short, on the former alternative the programme provider need not ensure a balanced presentation of conflicting views. The new law appears to take account of the variety of outlets provided by cable, as it also does with local radio.[39]

While a broad impartiality principle can be justified, particularly in the case of public broadcasters, there are dangers to broadcasting freedom in attempts to formulate precise standards. Editors may be reluctant to present challenging documentaries or to show personal view programmes, if they fear the regulatory authority will monitor these items closely and require the transmission of a balancing programme. The United States Fairness Doctrine (comparable to the impartiality rule) fell into disrepute when the FCC took out a stop-watch to determine whether balance had been achieved. Courts began to cast doubt on its constitutionality.[40] Over-rigorous enforcement of its Code by the ITC would give rise to one of two dangers: commercial channels might abandon controversial programmes or the impartiality provisions might be repealed.

[37] The sanctions for breach of programme conditions are discussed in S. 5 below.

[38] Broadcasting Act 1990, s. 47(4)–(5).

[39] Ibid., s. 90(3)(b). However, for national commercial radio the 'due impartiality' rule applies: ibid., s. 90(3)(a).

[40] See *Public Media Center* v. *FCC* 587 F. 2d. 1322 (DC Cir. 1978) and *American Security Council Educational Foundation* v. *FCC* 607 F. 2d. 438 (DC Cir. 1979).

3. THE RANGE AND VARIETY OF PROGRAMMES

Broadcasting laws typically require radio and television channels to show a range of programmes. The requirements, however, vary considerably. Sometimes they are couched in general terms, as for instance in the guide-lines provided by the recent German *Rundfunkstaatsvertrag*:[41] programmes transmitted throughout the country must respect human dignity and moral, religious, and cultural values, and should promote unity in Germany and international understanding. While specialist channels are allowed, general channels must provide a comprehensive service with appropriate proportions of news, cultural, and entertainment material. (The *Länder* may supplement these rules.) But elsewhere there are more specific obligations as, for example, in the French channels' *cahiers des charges*, which prescribe a certain minimum number of hours of original French works and of concerts performed by national orchestras.[42]

Although there is considerable variation in these requirements, one or two general observations can be made. First, all channels, whether public or private, are typically subject to broad *negative* standards, that is, their programmes must not promote violence or race hatred, nor should they be offensive or indecent. (These standards are discussed in the next section.) Secondly, there is a great variety of *positive* programme obligations. In particular, public broadcasters are usually required to show a range of news, current affairs, religious, and children's programmes, as well as some original drama, films, and popular entertainment material. This is an important characteristic of public service broadcasting, reflected for instance in the BBC's Charter obligation to disseminate 'information, education and entertainment'. Sometimes similar duties are imposed on private radio and television, though they are less onerous. In contrast other commercial channels, especially satellite and cable services, are free to show what they like, or have only minimal positive obligations, such as a duty to broadcast news bulletins.

Programme requirements, whether positive or negative, inhibit the broadcasters' freedom to draw up their own schedule. But they have generally been accepted in Europe, because, as we have seen, broadcasting freedom is not regarded solely as a right of the licensee or the programme-maker. Some regulation of the range of programmes is considered necessary in the interests of viewers and listeners.[43] This perspective is not shared in the United States, where in the last few years the FCC has withdrawn

[41] *Staatsvertrag* of 31 Aug. 1991, s. 23.

[42] See, e.g. the obligations imposed by Decree 87-17 OF 28 Aug. 1987 on the two public channels, A2 and FR3.

[43] See Ch. II, S. 1 above.

most of the positive obligations previously imposed on licensees. When the Fairness Doctrine was repealed in 1987, the Commission also removed the duty to produce programmes dealing with important controversial issues of interest to the local community. The majority of the DC Circuit Court of Appeals accepted its conclusion that, with the increasing number of television channels and other outlets for expression, the requirement amounted to an unjustifiable interference with broadcasters' editorial freedom.[44] In their view the market would ensure the transmission of these programmes. A similar argument had prevailed in another case, when the FCC successfully defended its decision no longer to require the networks to show children's programmes.[45] Their needs could be met by non-commercial or cable channels.

The American approach is unattractive. Positive programme obligations do admittedly limit broadcasters' freedom to draw up their own schedules. They may, therefore, constitute a significant restriction on commercial liberty. But they do not really amount to an interference with freedom of speech. As we have seen, in most countries licensees must use their channels with due regard for the free speech interests of others as well as their own freedom of expression.[46] Moreover, requirements, say, to show some serious programmes or to transmit news bulletins hardly interfere with the freedom of broadcasters to use the wavelengths to put across their own views or to show (for most of the time) the programmes they want. Positive standards pose much less danger to broadcasting freedom than the strict impartiality requirements considered in the previous section. They are not designed to deter the making of controversial and challenging programmes, but rather are intended to encourage or compel their inclusion in the schedules.

Before 1993 terrestrial commercial television in Britain was required to inform, educate, and entertain.[47] The IBA (formerly the ITA) required regional contractors to schedule serious programmes in 30 per cent of 'peak-time' (6.30–10.30 p.m.). Certain programmes, such as *News at Ten* and two half-hour current affairs programmes a week, were 'mandated', that is, they had to be shown unless a regional company made a powerful case for transmitting another item of equivalent quality.[48] The IBA was able to enforce these obligations relatively easily since it could refuse to approve a contractor's schedule.

[44] *Syracuse Peace Council* v. *FCC* 867 F. 2d. 654 (1989), cert. denied, 110 S. Ct. 717 (1990): see Ch. VII, S. 4 below.
[45] *Action for Children's Television* v. *FCC* 756 F. 2d. 899 (1985).
[46] See the argument in Ch. II, S. 1 above.
[47] Broadcasting Act 1981, s. 2.
[48] See the Second Report of the Select Committee on Nationalized Industries for 1971–2, HC 465, paras. 55–6, 67–73, and Annex F of the IBA Memorandum to the Committee.

The position is now quite different. The government stressed the importance of viewer choice,[49] and envisaged the imposition of lighter standards on the commercial channels. The Broadcasting Act 1990 requires applicants for the Channel 3 television licences to satisfy the ITC that they will be able to meet specified programme standards before their cash bid is considered. In the original Bill these threshold requirements referred only to news and current affairs, regional and European programmes, and 'programmes (other than news and current affairs programmes) which are of high quality', and which '(taken as a whole) . . . are calculated to appeal to a wide variety of tastes and interests' (the diversity requirement).[50] The government accepted amendments to compel the ITC also to be satisfied that a sufficient amount of time is devoted to religious and children's programmes, while it rejected the imposition of similar obligations to show drama and arts programmes.[51]

The invitation to apply for the Channel 3 licences issued by the ITC in February 1991 made the statutory requirements much more specific. For example, the Commission regards three news programmes a day with a total transmission time of one hour and five minutes as the minimum to satisfy the statutory formula 'a sufficient amount of time'. There must be ten hours a week of children's programmes and two hours of religious broadcasts, including acts of worship. There must be some programmes within each of nine identified strands (for example, drama, factual programmes, education, and arts) to meet the general diversity requirement.[52] Applicants whose proposals did not satisfy these requirements were excluded from further consideration, while the successful bidders are bound by their programme proposals as a condition of their licence.[53]

The provisions in the 1990 legislation with regard to radio are strikingly different. The Radio Authority must do what it can to secure 'a diversity of national services each catering for tastes and interests different from those catered for by the others'. One of the three must be devoted largely to spoken material and another to music which in the Authority's view is not 'pop music'.[54] There must be a range and diversity of local services.[55]

[49] See the White Paper *Broadcasting in the '90s: Competition, Choice and Quality* (1987) Cm. 517, para. 2.5.

[50] These requirements are incorporated in the Broadcasting Act 1990, s. 16(2).

[51] Standing Committee Debates on the Broadcasting Bill, cols. 587–653.

[52] All these requirements were set out in the *Invitation to Apply for Channel 3 Licences* issued by the ITC in 1991, 23–32.

[53] Broadcasting Act 1990, s. 33.

[54] Ibid., s. 85(2)(a). 'Pop music' is defined to include rock and other kinds of popular music characterized by a strong rhythmic element and reliance on electronic amplification: ibid., s. 85(6).

[55] Ibid., s. 85(2).

Diversity in radio, unlike television, is not achieved by requiring each channel to provide a wide range of programmes, but by requiring the services to complement each other. There is perhaps something similar in the mandate given Channel 4, the programmes of which 'must contain a suitable proportion of matter calculated to appeal to tastes and interests not generally catered for by Channel 3'.[56]

The requirement that a 'proper proportion' of matter broadcast on commercial television is of European origin replaces a much older rule (incorporated in the 1954 and later legislation) mandating an appropriate proportion of British programmes.[57] Attempts to prescribe a statutory quota of foreign programmes were rejected.[58] The IBA generally required 86 per cent of programming to be of European Community origin; a different treatment of British and other Community programmes would probably violate the principle of non-discrimination in the provision of services under the Treaty of Rome, although French and Italian law both contain national quotas. The ITC requirement repeats the rule now set out in the Broadcasting Directive of 1989: a majority of programming (apart from prescribed exceptions) must be of European origin. It is open to member states to prescribe stricter quotas.[59]

The imposition of quotas and other rules designed to protect national language and culture have been an important feature of programme regulation in France. The *cahiers des charges* of the two public channels and the authorizations of the private channels prescribe that a minimum number of hours of original French language programming be broadcast annually.[60] These requirements are in addition to the European Community quotas. Another important provision, common to all channels, prohibits the showing of films on television on certain evenings of the week or before particular times, or their transmission until three years from their release in the cinema.[61] Among the other detailed rules are those obliging TF1 to show twelve theatrical works (drama, opera, or ballet) and ten hours of concerts performed by French orchestras annually. Unlike the other private television channels, it must broadcast two news bulletins daily and regular current affairs documentaries. In addition to obligations similar to those imposed on the private channels, A2 and FR3

[56] Ibid., s. 25.

[57] See Television Act 1954, s. 3(1)(d).

[58] B. Sendall, *Independent Television in Britain*, i (London, 1982), 50–1.

[59] For further discussion of the Broadcasting Directive, see Ch. X, S. 4 below.

[60] The Conseil d'État has held the French language quotas compatible with the Treaty of Rome, Art. 7 prohibition of discrimination against nationality: Decision 97-234 of 21 June 1988. But see the doubts expressed below about the Italian rule.

[61] For the enforcement of these rules, see decision of Paris Court of Appeal of 19 Oct. 1988 prohibiting La Cinq from showing a film on a Wednesday evening in breach of Decree 87-36 of 26 Jan. 1987: Debbasch, 305.

have public service duties, for example, to transmit government announcements, road safety messages, and weather forecasts. They must also show documentaries on economic, social, scientific and cultural problems, as well as children's, consumer information, and sports programmes.[62]

In comparison with the British and French requirements, the positive programme obligations of German broadcasters (apart from the duty to be fair and impartial) are relatively slight. Sometimes the law provides that on the allocation of private broadcasting licences preference should be given to the company offering the most comprehensive treatment of local and regional issues.[63] Provisions such as that in the North Rhine–Westphalia law of 1988 requiring each comprehensive service to provide an appropriate time for the treatment of controversial questions of general importance are rare.[64] Perhaps the public authorities and private regulatory bodies can secure the showing of a wide range of programmes by informal methods, as the IBA was able to do before the Broadcasting Act 1990 removed its scheduling powers.

In Italy too there are few positive programme requirements. Aside from the broad principles of objectivity and comprehensiveness,[65] the only significant duties relate to the broadcast of news bulletins, programmes of local news and interest, and European and Italian works. National commercial networks are now obliged to transmit daily news bulletins, but the law is silent about how many there should be or how long they should last.[66] Holders of local licences must devote 20 per cent of their total weekly broadcasting time to local news and non-commercial programmes of interest to that community. Local community (non-commercial) radio stations must devote half the time between 7.00 a.m. and 9.00 p.m. to original self-made programmes concerning their particular character (cultural, political, or religious).[67]

The quota rules raise some problems. Article 26 obliges both public and private broadcasters to reserve for the first three years of their licences at least 40 per cent of the total time allocated to cinema films to European works, a percentage rising to 51 per cent after three years. Further, at least 50 per cent of the time for European works should be reserved for Italian productions. Doubts have been expessed whether these rules are in conformity with European law. First, it seems wrong to confine the European quota to a proportion of the time allocated to

[62] For detailed information on French programme obligations, see C. Debbasch, *Droit de l'audiovisuel*, 2nd edn. (Paris, 1991), 430–45.

[63] See e.g. the Lower Saxony law of 16 Mar. 1987, s. 6(2) and the Hamburg law of 3 Dec. 1985, s. 21.

[64] Law of 11 Jan. 1988, s. 12(3).

[65] Law 223 of 6 Aug. 1990, Art. 1.

[66] Ibid., Art. 20, para. 6.

[67] Ibid., Art. 16, paras. 5 and 18.

cinema films, rather than of the total transmission time (with stated exceptions) as required by the Broadcasting Directive. Secondly, the reservation of 50 per cent of 'European time' for Italian works is arguably in breach of the non-discrimination rule in the Treaty of Rome.[68]

Cable and satellite broadcasting are often wholly immune from positive programme standards, although they may be subject to the same restrictions on the portrayal of violent and sexually explicit behaviour as terrestrial channels. In the *Fourth Television* case the German Constitutional Court ruled that the programme requirements for cable retransmission of foreign broadcasts should not be as strict as those imposed on terrestrial commercial channels.[69] One reason was that such broadcasts exercise relatively little influence on the public. Also it is impracticable to require the observance of impartiality or positive programme requirements. The second point does not, however, justify any immunity for internal cable and satellite services. In Britain all licensed services (terrestrial, cable, and satellite) are subject to the same negative rules regarding indecent and offensive programmes, though the impartiality rule may be replaced for cable programmes by the lighter 'undue prominence' test.[70] On the other hand neither cable nor satellite channels are under any obligation to show any particular types of programme, save for a duty imposed on domestic satellite licensees to show the 'proper proportion' of European programmes.[71] Thus cable programme services and the BSkyB non-domestic satellite service are not required to provide news bulletins, current affairs programmes, or indeed any matter of high quality. Incredibly BSkyB does not fall under any obligation to observe the European quota, although under the EC Directive the UK is required to see that it is met. Nor are cable services now under any obligation to carry the terrestrial programmes available in the area.[72]

The obligation of cable to carry conventional broadcasting programmes has also been removed in the United States. The 'must carry' rule was unpopular with the smaller systems, which had found they had few channels left for their own distinctive programmes. In two cases the DC Circuit Court of Appeals held the regulations incompatible with the First Amendment, since they curtailed the cable operators' editorial freedom to choose which programmes to transmit.[73] The FCC did not prove they

[68] P. Caretti, in *Il sistema radiotelevisivo*, 458–9.

[69] 73 BVerfGE 118, 196–7 (1986).

[70] Broadcasting Act 1990, s. 6, and see S. 2 above for the 'undue prominence' rule.

[71] Broadcasting Act 1990, s. 44(4)(b). At the time of writing there are no domestic satellite services after the merger of BSB with Sky. BSkyB is a non-domestic satellite service.

[72] Cf. Cable and Broadcasting Act 1984, s. 13.

[73] *Quincy Cable TV Inc.* v. *FCC* 768 F. 2d. 1434 (DC Cir. 1985) and *Century Communications Corp.* v. *FCC* 835 F. 2d. 292 (DC Cir. 1987).

were necessary to protect free local broadcasting; further, they were too wide in that they indiscriminately protected all local broadcasters regardless of the circumstances. In an earlier case the Circuit Court had held invalid FCC regulations limiting the number of films and sports events which could be shown on cable subscription channels.[74] Some rules, in particular one restricting films and the coverage of sports to 90 per cent of total transmission time, were held contrary to the free speech rights of the cable operators.

These decisions were influenced by the courts' refusal to assimilate the position of cable operators to that of terrestrial licensees. At that time some regulation of terrestrial programmes (such as the Fairness Doctrine) was considered compatible with the First Amendment. But the scarcity argument for broadcasting regulation hardly applies to cable services.[75] Their position was, in the courts' view, more akin to that of the press. The judges stopped short of attributing to cable operators the same First Amendment rights as those enjoyed by newspaper proprietors, but were prepared to grant them much the same editorial freedom. There is something to be said for this as a practical conclusion. Cable offers scope for specialist channels exclusively devoted to, say, sports, films, music of all kinds, and continuous coverage of Parliament or local authority meetings. It would be absurd to require each channel to provide a comprehensive range of programmes. On the other hand, there is a case for mandating the allocation of some channels for, say, education or local news coverage, and also for access to interested groups and individuals.[76]

4. INDECENCY AND VIOLENCE

Legal systems generally control violent, indecent, and offensive radio and television programmes. In addition to the criminal law, special measures are employed to deal with the broadcasting media on the ground of their pervasiveness and unique influence.[77] Unlike the controls discussed in the previous section, they consist of simple legislative prohibitions, supplemented sometimes by the codes published by the regulatory bodies. The rules typically apply equally to public and private, terrestrial, cable, and satellite broadcasting. In the United States, for instance, the criminal law outlaws indecent or obscene language on the media. Administrative control is also exercised by the FCC, either by the issue of formal

[74] *Home Box Office* v. *FCC* 567 F. 2d. 9 (DC Cir. 1971).

[75] See the discussion in Ch. I, S. 2.

[76] For access to cable, see Ch. VII, S. 5 below.

[77] See Ch. 1, S. 2 above.

warnings to a station or at licence renewal (when repeated violations will be taken into account).[78]

The British Broadcasting Act 1990 requires the ITC to do all it can to secure that 'nothing is included [in programmes] which offends against good taste or decency or is likely to encourage or incite to crime or to lead to disorder or to be offensive to public feeling'.[79] The provision dates back to the original legislation of 1954. Before the recent reform it was relatively easy to enforce; the IBA was the broadcaster with powers to preview and control the scheduling of programmes. Normally it could discharge its responsibility through its staff, although members of the Authority were under a duty to look at a programme themselves in exceptional circumstances, for example, if the press or the public put them on notice that a programme's contents might violate the statutory standards.[80] Lord Denning MR in the *McWhirter* case stressed that the IBA had to see that programmes contained no indecent or offensive matter, not just that they were not in their entirety indecent or offensive.[81]

The special control exercised over sexually explicit programmes is stricter in two respects than the obscenity law (principally the Obscene Publications Act 1959) applicable in England and Wales to books and the press. First, the criterion for the former is whether the material is 'indecent' or 'offensive', rather than 'obscene' (which means that it has a tendency to deprave and corrupt), and secondly, under the English obscenity statute a book or magazine article is to be looked at as a whole. It is not legitimate to condemn a book (unlike a television programme) on the ground that it contains purple passages. The Broadcasting Act 1990, however, also extends the Obscene Publications Act 1959 (and the comparable Scottish law) to radio and television.[82] The result is that, if the ITC is unable to control the showing of sexually explicit programmes, the broadcaster, and the company providing the programme (an independent producer), might be criminally liable.[83]

The British anxiety about sexually explicit and violent programmes is also highlighted by the institution of the Broadcasting Standards Council (BSC), at first informally and then by statute.[84] One of its principal functions is to draw up a Code concerning the portrayal of violence and

[78] See *FCC* v. *Pacifica Foundation* 438 US 726 (1978): control over 'indecent' radio broadcasts compatible with the First Amendment (see Ch. I, S. 2 above); *Action for Children's Television* v. *FCC* 852 F. 2d. 1332 (DC Cir. 1988): regulation of broadcasting after midnight lawful.

[79] S. 6(1)(a).

[80] *Attorney-General ex rel. McWhirter* v. *IBA* [1973] 1 QB 629 (CA), and *R.* v. *IBA, ex parte Whitehouse*, *The Times*, 4 Apr. 1985 (CA).

[81] [1973] 1 QB 629, 650.

[82] Ss. 162–3.

[83] See Broadcasting Act 1990, Sch. 15, para. 2 for the persons criminally liable.

[84] Ibid., ss. 151–61.

sexual conduct and general standards of taste and decency on radio and television. Another is to consider complaints on such matters, either from members of the public or initiated by itself. The BSC may direct the broadcast of its findings, and a requirement to comply with these directions is incorporated in licensees' conditions. The BSC also monitors programme standards and commissions research. One difficulty faced by private broadcasters is that they operate under two Codes, one of the ITC and the other of the BSC. (The BBC is subject to both the BSC and its own guide-lines.) Viewers may complain to one or other or both bodies. Occasionally programmes cleared by the ITC have been the subject of successful complaint to the BSC.[85] It is not that the Codes differ in substance. The ITC Code is considerably shorter and was drafted with regard to the Broadcasting Standards Council's more detailed rules.[86] What creates uncertainty is that broadcasters have to predict the reactions of two different bodies to viewers' complaints.

Information about the regulatory bodies is given in their annual reports and regular bulletins. In its last *Programme Complaints and Interventions Report* in 1991 the ITC reported that the total number of complaints about programmes had declined in recent years from 2,000–2,500 to about 1,500 in both 1990 and 1991. (Perhaps the volume will increase now that the ITC is no longer able to control the scheduling and quality of programmes before transmission.) The BSC with narrower terms of reference receives about the same number of complaints. One or two important points emerge from the Council's lengthy Code of Practice. It approves the BBC and independent channels' 'watershed policy', under which programmes transmitted before 9.00 p.m. must be suitable for family audiences. More adult fare may be shown after that time, though it is wrong to schedule very explicit or violent material immediately after 9.00 p.m. The BSC has also rejected the argument that greater latitude should be afforded subscription channels because it might be easier to prevent children from having access to them.

In contrast to the position in Britain, the law in other European countries is concerned primarily to protect children and adolescents. There is less concern about the transmission of erotic films and other programmes which might offend or disturb adults. The French law of September 1986 requires the CSA to watch over the protection of children and adolescents in broadcast programmes.[87] More specific rules have been issued under this principle; the CSA Directive of May 1989 obliges programme companies (whether public or private) to refrain from showing

[85] This problem does not arise after 1 Jan. 1993, since the ITC is no longer itself the broadcaster and does not give guidance on specific scripts.
[86] Ibid., s. 152(3).
[87] Law of 30 Sept. 1986, Art. 15.

erotic or violent programmes (including films) before 10.30 p.m., and from advertising such programmes before 8.30 p.m. Sadly, erotic films attract large audiences and therefore advertisers, and it seems to have been quite common for private companies to violate these principles for financial gain. In one notorious case the CNCL secured an injunction from the Conseil d'État to prohibit the showing by La Cinq of a pornographic film, *Joy et Joan*, at 8.30 in the evening; it rejected the arguments that it was for parents to stop their children looking at such films and that their transmission at this time had become standard practice.[88]

The German *Staatsverträge* and state broadcasting laws (closely modelled on the former) contain two categories of prohibition. The first forbids the showing of programmes which promote racial hatred or portray acts of violence, which glorify war, which are pornographic, or which are clearly likely significantly to endanger children and adolescents morally.[89] Broadcasts are only to be treated as 'pornographic', if they would be so regarded in a criminal law prosecution. The laws, secondly, contain more detailed provisions to protect children and adolescents. The state treaties provide that programmes capable of interfering with their well-being must not be shown, unless the broadcaster can take steps to ensure that they are unlikely to be watched by children or adolescents of the pertinent age-groups. This can be assumed for programmes scheduled between 11.00 p.m. and 6.00 a.m. Films which may not be seen in cinemas by children under 18 may only be shown on television during these night hours, while films prohibited for children under 16 may only be shown after 10.00 p.m. The public broadcasting authorities and (if permitted by state law) private regulatory bodies may modify these latter rules in particular cases.[90]

The new Italian broadcasting statute has introduced strict rules.[91] Broadcasters may not put on programmes which harm the psychological or moral development of children, which contain gratuitous violence or pornography, or which induce racial, sexual, religious, or national intolerance. It is also forbidden to show cinema films which have not received a certificate from the licensing Ministry or from which children under 18 are excluded.[92] A station violating this rule will be closed. Finally cinema films forbidden to children under 14 may only be shown on television after 10.30 p.m. These rules appear incoherent.[93] It is not

[88] Decision of 20 Oct. 1988, Debbasch, 314.

[89] See, e.g. *Rundfunkstaatsvertrag* of 31 Aug. 1991, s. 3(1) and ZDF *Staatsvertrag* of 31 Aug. 1991, s. 8(1); Baden-Württemberg law of 16 Dec. 1985, s. 49(1); and Saarland law of 11 Aug. 1987, s. 3(3).

[90] *Rundfunkstaatsvertrag*, ss. 3(2)–(4), and ZDF *Staatsvertrag*, ss. 8(2)–(4).

[91] Law 223 of 6 Aug. 1990, Art. 15(10)–(13).

[92] For film censorship in Italian law, see A. Pace, *Problematica delle libertà costituzionali, parte speciale*, 2nd edn. (Padua, 1992), 409–10.

[93] For a critical comment by a leading Italian scholar, see R. Zaccaria, in *Il sistema radiotelevisivo*, 344–50.

clear why the transmission of cinema films on television should be subject to greater restrictions than films made for television or dramatic performances. (The latter are of course subject to the general prohibition of gratuitous violence or pornography.) Secondly, the Italian rule totally forbidding the showing of adult cinema films on television, even during night hours, seems excessive and an unjustifiable discrimination between the two modes of transmission. Adult films can be shown in the cinema, because it is practicable to prevent children having access to them, and the same argument should apply to home viewing.

These national rules implement Article 22 of the EC Directive, and indeed in the case of Italy they seem to have been framed for this purpose. It requires member states to take appropriate measures to ensure that television channels do not put on programmes (particularly involving violence or pornography) which might seriously impair the mental or moral development of minors. Also broadcasts must not incite hatred on grounds of race, sex, religion, or nationality. Provided the programmes of another EC state comply with these standards, member states must allow their retransmission within their jurisdiction, even if they do not comply with their own stricter rules. But they are entitled to suspend transmission where there is a manifest and serious infringement of Article 22 and if there have been two such violations in the previous year.[94] There is therefore a rudimentary set of minimum European programme standards, largely geared to the protection of minors. States are free to impose stricter programme standards on their national companies, but cannot require other EC channels to meet them.

5. ENFORCEMENT OF PROGRAMME STANDARDS

It is virtually useless to lay down programme standards, unless there is some mechanism for their enforcement. Otherwise they are merely aspirations. Consistent failure to meet the standards would be at most a matter for political debate, while generally broadcasters would be expected to regulate their behaviour themselves. In fact statutes do provide penalties for such failures. These take a variety of forms, ranging from administrative warnings at one end of the scale to the ultimate sanction of licence withdrawal at the other. In between these extremes, financial penalties and shortening of licence periods are now popular remedies.

However, there remain doubts about the efficacy of these measures.[95] The uncertainty inherent in many rules, particularly those imposing positive

[94] Art. 2 (see Ch. X, S. 4 below).

[95] For a general discussion, see W. Hoffman-Riem, 'Defending Vulnerable Values: Regulatory Measures and Enforcement Dilemmas', in Blumler (ed.), *Television and the Public Interest*, 173.

programme standards, makes their breach hard to determine. This demands a lengthy and costly procedure. Minor penalties, such as reprimands and small fines, may not be adequate to deter companies making an appreciable profit, while more serious remedies are too draconian. The imposition of a large fine means there is less money to spend on quality programmes. Further, no regulatory authority or court can contemplate with equanimity the termination (or even suspension) of a broadcasting licence. The FCC, for instance, was extremely reluctant to refuse licence renewal on the ground (primarily or merely) of a failure to comply with the Fairness Doctrine or other programme standards.[96]

It is particularly difficult to apply sanctions to public broadcasters, which in view of their importance to the community could only in exceptional circumstances be ordered to discontinue transmission. Informal administrative or political control is easier to exercise. A serious breach of the impartiality or other programme standards might be a matter for the BBC Governors or in Germany the Broadcasting Council. In Britain control is also exercised in some limited respects by the Broadcasting Complaints Commission (BCC) and the BSC.[97] In France and Italy there is a significant measure now of independent control over public as well as private broadcasters. The position in France is particularly interesting. Under Article 13 of the broadcasting law (as amended in 1989) the CSA must ensure balance in the public programme companies' programmes. It is empowered to communicate its view in public to the company's administrative council whenever there is a grave violation of programme obligations; its president may be ordered to stop the violation.[98] But the CSA may not impose fines or suspend or withdraw permission to broadcast, a power it enjoys in the case of private broadcasters.

The IBA had been able to enforce standards informally by previewing particular programmes and overall schedules. As the broadcaster it even had the reserve power to commission balancing programmes itself.[99] The Authority could also exercise the normal remedies for breach of contract, if the regional companies broke its terms. Finally, it had statutory power to suspend or determine its obligation to transmit their programmes after notice had been given of three breaches of contract.[100] With the end of its

[96] See B. F. Chamberlain, 'Lessons in Regulating Information Flow: The FCC's Weak Track Record in Interpreting the Public Interest Standard' (1982) 60 *N. Carolina L. Rev.* 1057. In one famous case a FCC renewal was reversed, because there had clearly been violation of the Fairness Doctrine: *Office of Communication of the United Church of Christ* v. *FCC* 425 F. 2d. 543 (DC Cir. 1969). The FCC refused to renew, partly on grounds of breach of the Doctrine, in *Brandywine Main Line Radio* 24 FCC 18 (1970).

[97] See Ch. VII, S. 4 below for the Complaints Commission.

[98] The discretion of the CSA to determine the gravity of infringement has been approved by the Conseil constitutionnel: Dec. 88-248 of 17 Jan. 1989, Debbasch, 319.

[99] Broadcasting Act 1981, s. 3(2).

[100] Ibid., s. 21.

scheduling powers in 1993, the ITC may apply a range of sanctions for breaches of licence conditions (requiring licensees to conform to the standards set out in the legislation and the ITC Code and to honour their programme promises). They range in severity from a power to direct the broadcast of a correction or apology to a power to revoke a licence.[101] Whatever the sanction, the ITC must give the company concerned a reasonable chance to state its case.

Some features of these powers should be emphasized. First, the ITC may direct a broadcaster not to repeat a broadcast if its transmission involved a breach of its licence. This is the only circumstance in which the ITC now has censorship powers over Channel 3 (or Channel 4 or 5) programmes.[102] Secondly, there are limits on the financial penalties which may be imposed: for a first offence during the licence period, it is 3 per cent of advertising revenue received during the relevant accounting period, and for a second or further offence it is 5 per cent of such revenue. A licence period may be shortened for up to two years, but the licensee may subsequently apply to have that sanction lifted. These penalties are clearly more severe than a direction to apologize or not to repeat a programme, but the statute does not indicate when their imposition would be appropriate. The ITC appears to have a broad discretion. With regard to revocation, it is implied that the failure must be a continuing one and it is expressly provided that it must be such as to justify that severe penalty.[103] The Commission must serve a notice specifying the respects in which the licence-holder is in breach and indicating its intention to revoke unless it is remedied. Judging from the experience of other legal systems, it is unlikely that this draconian power will be exercised frequently.[104] The ITC has no power to terminate Channel 4's licence, although the other disciplinary powers apply to it.

The French law of 1989 appreciably strengthens enforcement powers over private broadcasters. The CNCL was able to issue an order requiring them to comply with their programme obligations, and in the event of a failure to comply could suspend the licence for a month or withdraw it. Alternatively it could apply to the President of the Section du contentieux of the Conseil d'État. He was, and is, entitled to issue an immediate injunction and impose an *astreinte*.[105] This is a fine levied cumulatively for

[101] Broadcasting Act 1990, ss. 40–2.

[102] The ITC does, however, have power to preview any advertisement or class of advertisement: cl. 15(4) of the Standard Form Regional Channel 3 Licence.

[103] Ibid., s. 42(1).

[104] For the reluctance of the FCC to revoke, or even fail to renew, broadcasting licences on grounds of breach of programme standards, see R. B. Horwitz, *The Irony of Regulatory Reform* (New York, 1988), 159–65.

[105] Law of 30 Sept. 1986, Art. 42-10, inserted by law of 17 Jan. 1989.

every day in which there is a failure to comply with a court order.[106] It is clearly a powerful remedy. Every day, for example, that a broadcasting company shows an excessive number of advertisements or fails to transmit a mandatory news bulletin, it is exposed to an increasing penalty.[107]

Without affecting this avenue of address, the new law gives the CSA power itself to suspend a licence or a particular programme for a month, to reduce the licence period for up to a year, to impose a fine (coupled eventually with a suspension), or to withdraw a licence altogether.[108] As with the British provisions, perhaps influenced in this respect by French law, the maximum financial penalty is 3 per cent of income assessed over a year, with a 5 per cent ceiling for further offences. The CSA may also exercise contractual remedies. Professional associations and trade unions representing people involved in broadcasting (but not viewers' associations) may formally request the CSA to exercise its penal powers. These aspects of the 1989 statute survived a vigorous constitutional challenge, partly based on the potential interference with freedom of speech which would be occasioned by an interruption of transmission.[109] The Conseil constitutionnel emphasized that the power to impose sanctions flowed naturally from the licensing authority; further, the law required penalties to be proportionate to the seriousness of the breach, a principle which should have been incorporated more clearly in the British statute.

The Italian broadcasting law of 1990 confers significant penal powers on the Garante (the Guarantor of Broadcasting and Publishing) whose responsibility it is, *inter alia*, to ensure observance of programme standards.[110] He has power to order a broadcaster to remedy any breach of these (or advertising) restrictions. In the event of a failure to comply (or an inadequate compliance with the duty to afford rights of reply) he may impose a fine up to 100 million lire or in serious cases suspend transmission for a period up to ten days. If there are repeated violations within the following year, transmission for a period from eleven to thirty days may be suspended, or in more serious cases withdrawal of the concession may be recommended. But only the Minister of Posts and Telecommunications may take this ultimate step.[111]

Clearly broadcasting laws give regulatory authorities considerable dis-

[106] See L. N. Brown and J. F. Garner, *French Administrative Law*, 3rd edn. (London, 1983), 71.

[107] See the use of this device by the Conseil d'État to enforce advertising limits against TF1, Debbasch, 300.

[108] Law of 30 Sept. 1986, Art. 42, inserted by law of 17 Jan. 1989, Art. 19.

[109] Decision 88-248 of 17 Jan. 1989, paras. 23–42, Debbasch, 319, discussed by B. Genevois, 'Le Conseil constitutionnel et la définition des pouvoirs du Conseil supérieur de l'audiovisuel' [1989] *Rev. fr. droit adm.* 215.

[110] For the Garante's powers, see the law 223 of 6 Aug. 1990, Art. 6.

[111] Ibid., Art. 31.

cretion whether to enforce programme standards and which sanctions to apply. But they may be induced to act if viewers' and listeners' associations put pressure on them, perhaps through litigation. The administrative law rules of standing are important. While associations, and *a fortiori* individuals, lack legal rights to compel the showing of programmes of a particular type or the deletion of an 'offensive' item from a television schedule,[112] they may have standing to bring an application for judicial review. A successful application may indirectly achieve the applicant's objects, since it compels the authority to reconsider its initial decision not to intervene. This has happened in both Britain and the United States. In the former the Court of Appeal and the Court of Session have granted individuals standing to compel the IBA to exercise its statutory powers to control allegedly 'indecent' items and to ensure the balance of views before a referendum.[113] More radically the DC Circuit Court of Appeals has recognized the standing of a listeners' group to challenge an FCC decision which had denied it a right to participate in licence renewal proceedings.[114] This support for citizens' participation rights at licence renewal applications was significant; it compelled the FCC to take more seriously its powers of control over programme standards.[115]

But citizens' groups can only participate effectively if they have adequate information. One method of equipping them with this is to compel broadcasters to keep lists and recordings of programmes which in certain circumstances must be supplied to complainants. The FCC has, however, significantly reduced the duties of licensees in this respect, while the DC Circuit Court of Appeals has held that a duty imposed on public stations to keep a record of every broadcast in which an important issue was discussed was an unconstitutional burden on their First Amendment rights.[116] In contrast the British Broadcasting Act 1990 compels broadcasters as a condition of their licence to keep a recording of every programme for ninety days and to produce this (and any transcript or script) for examination by the ITC.[117] They must also supply the BSC and the Broadcasting Complaints Commission with recordings to enable them to discharge their statutory responsibilities. (The BCC has jurisdiction to investigate complaints about unfair or inaccurate treatment in programmes or infringements of privacy.[118]) If the BCC requires, complainants must be supplied

[112] For viewers' rights, see Ch. II, S. 4 above.

[113] *Attorney-General ex rel. McWhirter* v. *IBA* [1973] 1 QB 629 (see S. 4 above) and *Wilson* v. *IBA* 1979 SLT 279 (see Ch. VIII, S. 2 below).

[114] *Office of Communication of the United Church of Christ* v. *FCC* 359 F. 2d. 994 (1966).

[115] Chamberlain, 'Lessons in Regulating Information Flow', 1074–5.

[116] *Community Service Broadcasting of Mid-America* v. *FCC* 593 F. 2d. 1102 (1978).

[117] S. 11. S. 145(5) requires broadcasters to keep recordings for 90 days (or 42 days in the case of sound recordings) for the BCC or BSC to consider complaints.

[118] For discussion of the Complaints Commission, see Ch. VII, S. 4 below.

with transcripts and given an opportunity to see or hear the programme about which the complaint has been made.[119] These rules would probably be inappropriate in the case of viewers' general complaints to the ITC about, say, bias or a lack of quality programmes. But they give some indication how enforcement procedures can on occasion be quite rigorous.

[119] Broadcasting Act 1990, s. 145(4).

VI
Competition Law

1. INTRODUCTION

The significance of competition law in the context of broadcasting regulation has been widely recognized. For example, the Italian Constitutional Court refused to permit private broadcasting (beyond the local level) until adequate anti-trust legislation had been introduced.[1] In France the Conseil constitutionnel required a significant strengthening of the anti-concentration provisions in the Chirac Bill of 1986.[2] Otherwise the constitutional value of pluralism would not have been adequately protected. The role of competition law has become more widely appreciated in the last twenty years. The first reason is that in many countries there has been a marked tendency for the broadcasting (and other) media to fall under the control of fewer companies. Secondly, with the deregulation of programme standards and (in some countries) the relaxation of the impartiality rules, the owners of broadcasting channels have more opportunity to influence public taste and opinion, albeit not to the same extent as the press barons.

The need for competition regulation is, therefore, much greater now than it was thirty or forty years ago. Broadcasting was then almost everywhere (except in the United States) a public monopoly. The position of the public companies was relatively rarely challenged on competition grounds, because it was usually considered that they could provide a wide variety of programmes and opinions. Indeed their monopoly was sometimes defended with the argument that plurality of opinion was best guaranteed within the public companies. If the system were opened to private entrepreneurs, a few powerful voices would dominate the media.[3] It may be said there is now adequate competition through the rivalry of the public and private broadcasting companies, but this case is not really sustainable. Public broadcasting, as we saw in the previous chapter, is often subject to more onerous programme standards than its private competitors. As it is not itself allowed to editorialize, it cannot balance any partial views expressed on private channels. Nor can a public channel always offer effective economic competition in view of the requirement to provide a

[1] Decision 148/1981 [1981] *Giur. cost.* 1379 and Decision 826/1988 [1988] *Giur. cost.* 3893.
[2] Decision 86–217 of 18 Dec. 1986, discussed in Ss. 2 and 3 below.
[3] See Decision 225/1974 of the Italian Constitutional Court [1974] *Giur. cost.* 1775.

range of serious programmes, attractive only to a minority of viewers or listeners.

Economic pressures have increasingly brought about concentrations within the broadcasting industry and the mass media generally. Newspaper companies, for example, hold significant shareholdings in broadcasting companies in order to participate in the profits of the latter and to safeguard their own financial position. The advertising industry has played an important role in reducing the number of competitors in both the newspaper and broadcasting sectors; the grant of favours to one outlet often renders impossible the survival of its rivals, even though they enjoy a relatively large circulation or audience.[4] The concentration of the broadcasting media in a few large companies does have advantages: they are able to afford expensive drama and other lavish programmes, and are in a better position than small independent companies to engage in investigative journalism. Further, it is arguable that only large companies in Europe can now compete with the United States networks, whether terrestrial or cable, in the provision of a comprehensive news service and for the purchase of films. These are powerful arguments. But they do not necessarily outweigh the obvious dangers posed by private concentrations to that variety of sources of information which is necessary for an effective democracy. At most they suggest that in some circumstances concentrations should be permitted, notwithstanding these dangers.

There is a paradox at the heart of this subject. Open economic competition, which anti-trust law is designed to promote, generally has the effect of reducing the number of competitors. Concentrations of media ownership, in both the newspaper and broadcasting industries, have resulted from the fierce rivalry for audiences and advertisers. This is, however, not an argument against the utility of monopolies and mergers legislation and other competition rules. Rather, it suggests that existing laws should be strengthened and rigorously enforced. Further, there is a strong argument for new forms of structural regulation, such as divestiture orders, and for the provision of public subsidies to encourage new entrants into the market.[5] The fundamental point is perhaps that it is not enough to promote *economic* competition. There is competition, for example, in the British newspaper industry and it used to exist in Italian broadcasting. But in both cases it has resulted in the dominance of the market by a handful of groups. What is crucial is that the law promotes a healthy rivalry of opinion and viewpoints—referred to by the German Consti-

[4] For a critical discussion of the impact of advertising on the mass media in the United States, see B. H. Bagdikian, *The Media Monopoly*, 3rd edn. (Boston, 1990).

[5] There is power to order divestiture after a monopoly or merger investigation: Fair Trading Act 1973, Sch. 8. Some countries, particularly in Scandinavia, give selective subsidies to newspapers, as well as providing general support through immunity from VAT.

tutional Court as journalistic (*publizistische*) rivalry.[6] Conventional competition regulation preventing, for instance, new combinations without disturbing existing patterns of ownership may not be enough to achieve this goal.

Concentrations in the mass media assume a number of forms. One case is that of *vertical integration*, where there is a link, for example, between a broadcasting company and advertising agencies. The risk to effective competition posed by this connection has long been appreciated in Britain. Advertising agents, and companies with control of them, are disqualified from holding a television or radio licence, as is now a body in which an advertising agent has an interest greater than 5 per cent.[7] A private broadcasting entrepreneur can use his links with the advertising industry to prevent his rivals from effectively competing with him by depriving them of access to advertising revenue. Advertising can be offered at a discount on associated television channels, a technique used in Italy by Publitalia, the group linked to Silvio Berlusconi's Fininvest company. This helped him to gain a dominant position by seriously weakening his competitors, unable to attract advertising.[8] Another type of concentration is *horizontal integration*, where there are links between companies in the same business. These are now particularly common in the press, where one company may control several daily and Sunday newspapers, but they also occur in the broadcasting media. Examples are the links between the national networks and local stations affiliated to them in the United States and those between the three national networks controlled in Italy by Berlusconi.

Other types of integration involve connections between the broadcasting media and the press and between the media and other industrial sectors. The phenomenon of *multi-media integration* has attracted recent attention, as press groups have increased their shareholdings in private broadcasting companies or have controlled them through subsidiary or linked companies. In Britain the best-known example of this is the connection between News International and its subsidiary, Sky Television, now British Sky Broadcasting (BSkyB) after the merger of Sky and British Satellite Broadcasting in November 1990. Other newspaper groups have significant shareholdings in some of the Channel 3 licensees. In Germany the giant multi-media Bertelsmann and Kirsch groups and the Springer press group have very sizeable interests in the new private television companies.[9]

[6] See the *Fifth Television* case, 74 BVerfGE 297 (1987).
[7] See Broadcasting Act 1990, Sch. 2, Part I, para. 6.
[8] See A. Pilati, 'Pubblicità: è finita l'espansione?' (1990) 15 *Problemi dell'informazione* 561, and G. Rao, *The Italian Broadcasting System: Legal (and Political) Aspects*, European University Institute Working Paper 88/369, 40–1.
[9] For a discussion of cross-ownership in Germany, see Humphreys, 280–92.

Despite the restrictions imposed on the freedom of broadcasters to editorialize and the impartiality requirements, cross-media ownership of television and the press poses some danger to the values of pluralism. Newspapers may be used to promote particular private television channels through favourable coverage of their programmes, while they ignore their rivals' channels.[10] Equally television can reflect the values of particular newspapers through their selection of news items and the prominence given to press editors and columnists.

Of equal concern, though less often discussed in British literature, is the phenomenon of *multi-sectoral integration*, where broadcasting companies are controlled by, for example, parts of the defence industry or property companies. This is well-known in the United States, where, for instance, the control of the NBC network by General Electric, a major defence contractor, may inhibit the presentation of news and the making of documentaries.[11] There are now a large number of international media groups and consortia. For example, the consortium awarded the licence for the fifth French television channel in 1987 was an alliance dominated by the French Hersant group and the Italian Berlusconi companies. The Luxembourg broadcasting company CLT is controlled by French, German, Belgian, and Luxembourg companies. In its turn it is a principal participant, together with the German international publishing company Bertelsmann, in one of the largest German satellite companies, RTL Plus.

Media concentrations may be regulated in a number of ways. Broadly there are two types of control: regulation by general competition law and control by rules tailor-made for the media. Both techniques may be used, though it seems more common now to place greater reliance on specific rules in the broadcasting legislation. One difficulty peculiar to Germany is that competition regulation there is a matter for federal law, while broadcasting is regulated by the *Länder*. There is thus a potential jurisdictional conflict. It seems to have been resolved with the Constitutional Court's ruling in the *Fourth Television* case that the federal unfair competition statute (*Gesetz gegen Wettbewerbsbeschränkungen* (*GWB*)) applies to broadcasting companies and (less clearly) that the federal cartel authority has jurisdiction. The state licensing authorities should take cross-media concentrations into account, when allocating broadcasting permits, in so far as these groups endanger the value of plurality of opinion.[12] The

[10] See the Sadler Report, *Enquiry into Standards of Cross-Media Promotion* (1991) Cm. 1436, discussed further in S. 4 below.

[11] See Bagdikian, *The Media Monopoly*, 208–10.

[12] 73 BVerfGE 118, 172–4 (1986).

competition statute and federal cartel jurisdiction equally apply to the public broadcasting bodies.[13]

In the second section of this chapter, two major constitutional questions concerning competition rules are discussed. Then the principal types of control are examined, though only the British rules are set out in detail. The rules on cross-media ownership are treated in the fourth section, while the fifth deals with the particular problem of the restraints on contracts for exclusive rights to show sports and other events. The chapter concludes with a short discussion of the relevant principles of European Community competition law.

2. CONSTITUTIONAL ARGUMENTS

There are two principal constitutional questions concerning the application of competition law principles to the broadcasting media. The first is whether the rules, in particular those imposing limits on cross-media ownership, are permissible under the freedom of speech and of the press clauses. The second is whether such rules might indeed be required in order to safeguard freedom of speech. The first issue has rarely been raised in European countries, but it has been litigated frequently in the United States. In its first major pronouncement on broadcasting regulation, the Supreme Court upheld the constitutionality of the Chain Broadcasting Regulations, under which certain network practices tying local stations exclusively to one network were outlawed.[14] It was argued that the regulations interfered with the local stations' freedom of speech by precluding them from entering into exclusive affiliation arrangements. The argument was weak, for the regulations were in fact designed to enhance the local stations' freedom to choose which programmes to transmit and to loosen network control over this choice. The decision was followed in a later case upholding the legality of the FCC rules restricting control of more than a limited number of radio and television stations.[15] The fullest discussion of the constitutional issues arose in the cross-media ownership case *FCC* v. *National Citizens' Committee for Broadcasting*.[16]

[13] Decision of the Berlin Kammergericht upholding the application of the *GWB* to the North Rhine–Westphalia public broadcasting authority: [1991] *Archiv für Presserecht* 745.

[14] *National Broadcasting Company* v. *United States* 319 US 190 (1943).

[15] *United States* v. *Storer Broadcasting Company* 351 US 192 (1956). At that time the FCC rules provided that no person or group could control more than 7 AM, 7 FM, and 7 TV stations, but it has now been relaxed to introduce a 12–12–12 rule: see Franklin and Anderson, 763–4.

[16] 436 US 775 (1978).

In the Court's unanimous judgment, Marshall J. held that FCC rules prohibiting the formation of combinations between newspapers and broadcasting licensees (and also requiring divestiture of either press or broadcasting interests in communities where there is only one newspaper and one broadcasting station) were compatible with the First Amendment. In the Court's view the regulations were a reasonable way of promoting the diversity of mass communications. They were intended to foster speech and did not discriminate against it on the basis of its content.

These decisions are surely correct. When broadcasting licensees or newspaper owners argue that anti-trust and other rules of competition law violate their freedom, their real complaint is that their property and economic rights have been interfered with. There can be no freedom of speech objection in principle to the application of these rules (though of course there may be reasonable objections to particular proscriptions). Their purpose is to multiply the number of voices which can use the mass media, and so they are clearly justifiable under constitutional freedom of speech clauses.[17]

There has been a similar debate in Germany concerning the constitutionality of the application of the federal unfair competition statute, the *GWB*, to the public broadcasting corporations. It has been argued that their responsibilities under Article 5 of the Basic Law to provide the basic broadcasting service, complementary to that offered by their private competitors, gives them immunity from the *GWB* and the jurisdiction of the federal cartel authority.[18] Further, it is said, it is wrong for federal law to intrude in broadcasting, a matter which the Basic Law has reserved for the *Länder*. The Monopolies Commission and Cartel Office have consistently taken the opposite view, and this has been approved by a Berlin court.[19] The *GWB* could be applied to prohibit the 30 per cent interest which the WDR public broadcasting company enjoyed in a private radio station, enabling the former to acquire a dominant position as the supplier of advertising. State laws could only exclude application of the federal competition law, if they were necessary to achieve the requirements of broadcasting freedom. Yet the Constitutional Court has refused to invalidate in principle joint arrangements between public and private

[17] For an excellent statement of this argument, see J. Lichtenberg, 'Foundations and Limits of Freedom of the Press', in J. Lichtenberg (ed.), *Democracy and the Mass Media* (Cambridge, 1990), 102.

[18] For a general discussion, see V. Porter and S. Hasselbach, *Pluralism, Politics and the Marketplace: The Regulation of German Broadcasting* (London, 1991), 136–41. A fuller treatment is to be found in essays in W. Hoffman-Riem (ed.), *Rundfunk im Wettbewerbsrecht* (Baden-Baden, 1988), esp. by S. Klaue, 'Zur Anwendung des Kartellgesetzes auf die öffentlich-rechtlichen Rundfunkanstalten', 84.

[19] Decision of the Berlin Kammergericht of 26 June 1991 (1991) 22 *Archiv für Presserecht* 745.

broadcasters, explicitly permitted by the North Rhine–Westphalia broadcasting statute.[20]

It is more difficult to decide whether effective competition regulation is mandatory under freedom of speech clauses. Arguably the decision whether to use anti-trust rules in this context should be one for the legislature; constitutional courts are ill-equipped to assess the adequacy of provisions of this character. Yet courts in Italy, France, and Germany have all ruled that commercial broadcasting must be regulated by anti-trust rules sufficiently stringent to safeguard plurality of opinion. The most forthright pronouncements have come from the Italian Constitutional Court. In 1981 it considered a reference from a Rome magistrate on the legality of the public broadcasting monopoly. RAI challenged the legality of some *de facto* national networks after they had started a national news service. The Court upheld the public monopoly, while leaving open the possibility that the constitutionality of private networks would be upheld, if adequate anti-trust legislation were enacted.[21] Such rules were necessary to stop the development of private monopolies and oligopolies. They had to prevent all links between broadcasters, the press, and other information sectors, as well as with advertising agencies, which threatened the plurality of opinion. These views were emphatically affirmed by the Court in 1988,[22] where it added that the interests of genuine local broadcasters should also be safeguarded. Transparency rules should be drafted to compel media companies to reveal their true ownership and financial assets. (Whether the rules in the 1990 law comply with these requirements will be considered later in this chapter.)

Similar principles influenced the Conseil constitutionnel when it considered the 1986 Broadcasting Bill.[23] It gave constitutional status to the principle of plurality of sources of information. Parliament was obliged to take it into account when formulating anti-concentration rules. These were found wanting in a number of respects. In particular, they omitted to provide a limit on the number of shares an individual or company could hold in different national television stations, nor were there any limits on the accumulations of cable licences or of radio and television licences. Perhaps most fundamentally the Bill failed to take account of cross-media ownership. These deficiencies were put right when the Bill went back to Parliament.

The German position is more complicated, because of the different roles of the federal and state authorities under competition and broad-

[20] *Sixth Television* case, 83 BVerfGE 238 (1991).
[21] Decision 148/81 [1981] *Giur. cost.* 1379.
[22] Decision 826/1988 [1988] *Giur. cost.* 3893, 3939.
[23] Decision 86-217 of 18 Dec. 1986, Debbasch, 245. For commentary, see D. Truchet (1987) 3 *Rev. fr. droit adm.* 343 and J. Chevallier [1987] *AJDA* 59.

casting law respectively. Competition law is a matter for the Bund; anti-competitive practices and mergers are controlled by the Berlin Cartel Office (Bundeskartellamt). But private broadcasting is regulated by state authorities.[24] In the *Fourth Television* case the Constitutional Court left open the question whether the federal Parliament should require an investigation by the competition law authorities before the grant of broadcasting licences.[25] But at that stage state authorities come under a constitutional obligation to consider the dangers posed by multi-media concentrations. There is, therefore, the same constitutional hostility to media concentrations as in France and Italy.

3. ACCUMULATION AND OTHER RULES

There were relatively few specific competition rules in Britain before the enactment of the Broadcasting Act 1990. Earlier legislation required the IBA (formerly the ITA) to do all it could to secure adequate competition to supply programmes between a number of independent programme contractors.[26] It was also required to ensure the independence of television licensees from control by companies with a radio licence and vice versa. As (owing to the shortage of frequencies) there is only one licensee for each region, competition in effect means competition to supply programmes for the national network. In fact there was little real competition, as the five major companies shared the vast bulk of the time between themselves, leaving few opportunities for the smaller regional companies to contribute programmes for the network.[27]

The Broadcasting Act 1990 contains new provisions for networking arrangements and introduces a number of very detailed rules to prevent the accumulation of licences and hence the dominance of a handful of companies. The rules for networking are set out in section 39. The Channel 3 regional franchise-holders are required by their licences to make network arrangements which must be approved by the ITC. If these are not made by the date specified by the Commission, it may draw up the arrangements itself. In both circumstances the arrangements must be referred to the Director-General of Fair Trading. His responsibilities, set out in Schedule 4, are to report on whether the arrangements satisfy the 'competition test', and, if they do not, to specify appropriate modi-

[24] See Ch. IV, S. 3 above.

[25] 73 BVerfGE 118, 172–4 (1986).

[26] See e.g. the Independent Television Act 1954, s. 5(2), and the Broadcasting Act 1981, s. 20(2)(b).

[27] For a full discussion of the origin of the networking arrangements and the difficulties they gave rise to, see B. Sendall, *Independent Television in Britain*, i: *Origin and Foundation, 1946–62* (London, 1982), 55–7, 335–9, 387–90.

fications. In effect the networking arrangements must not restrict, distort, or prevent competition within the United Kingdom, though even if they have that effect they would still satisfy the test, provided they satisfy the criteria set out in Article 85(3) of the EC Treaty. The object of these rules is to prevent the large regional companies from stifling the opportunities of the smaller licensees to gain access to the network. The Director-General's report is binding on the licensees, but either they or the ITC may refer the matter to the Monopolies and Mergers Commission.[28]

Take-overs of licensees are now permitted after a one-year moratorium.[29] It follows that without specific rules prohibiting licence accumulation, there would be nothing to stop the more successful companies buying up their rivals' franchises. Schedule 2 contains such rules, another innovation of the 1990 Act. The detailed provisions are supplemented by regulations.[30] Among the principal restrictions are those prohibiting a person from holding more than two regional television licences, one national radio licence, or twenty local radio licences. The regulations provide in addition that he may not hold more than one licence for a large region, e.g. London or Yorkshire, or be awarded licences for two specified contiguous regions, e.g. the Borders *and* Central Scotland, North-East or North-West England.[31] The regulations also add some complicated rules for radio, designed to prevent the accumulation of local licences covering in total large areas of population.

Other provisions prohibit the accumulation of licences in different categories. For example, a regional television franchise-holder cannot hold more than a 20 per cent interest in a company with a licence for Channel 5, a domestic satellite service, or national radio. As in earlier legislation, there are rules against the accumulation of licences for both regional television and local cable or radio services: these apply only when each of the services is provided in an area which is to a significant extent the same as that of the other services.[32]

The stringency of the rules has been criticized, at least so far as they concern regional television licensees. One or two of the successful applicants may be vulnerable to take-over bids, largely because of the size of their cash bids. Companies from other EC countries will be able to

[28] The functions of the Director-General and of the MMC under the Broadcasting Act 1990 are without precedent in UK competition law. (I am indebted to Professor Richard Whish for this point.)

[29] Broadcasting Act 1990, s. 21.

[30] Ibid., Sch. 2, Part III, supplemented by SI 1991/1176.

[31] The latter restriction on licences in contiguous areas only applies until their grant, i.e. until a few weeks after the award of the licence by the ITC: SI 1991/1176, Art. 1(4). It did not, therefore, prevent the merger of the Yorkshire and Tyne Tees franchise-holders in the spring of 1992.

[32] Broadcasting Act 1990, Sch. 2, Part III, para. 6(7).

take them over after the one-year moratorium, but the more profitable UK television companies will not. The accumulation rules are designed to prevent the concentration of terrestrial television broadcasting into a few hands, in theory a desirable goal. But viewers in, say, Yorkshire may find it hard to understand why their Channel 3 broadcaster could be taken over by, say, Berlusconi, but not by Granada or LWT.

There are equivalent rules in the 1986 French statute, significantly amended in this respect after the ruling of the Conseil constitutionnel. Article 39 contains restrictions on holdings in broadcasting companies: for example, no person may control more than 25 per cent of the capital in a national licensee, nor more than 15 per cent in each of two. It is further forbidden by Article 41 to accumulate licences for two national television services, or one national service and one local or regional service. On the other hand, it is possible to accumulate regional television licences, provided the population covered by these franchises does not in combination exceed 6 million, and the same is true for cable, provided the population covered does not exceed 8 million. Article 41-1, inserted after the Conseil ruling, contains complex rules designed to prevent multimedia holdings. For example, no licence for television or radio can be issued if the holder would then find that he had interests in more than two kinds of media (radio, television, cable, and the press) with more than a prescribed coverage. Comparisons are difficult, but it seems that these rules are a little laxer than the English equivalents, with the exception of the provisions in Article 39 prohibiting large capital holdings in one franchise-holder.

The German rules, like the French, prohibit large capital holdings and place limits on the accumulation of licences. With regard to the former, the new state treaty provides that licences for nationally available television channels with news programmes should not be allocated to companies where one partner enjoys 50 per cent or more of the capital or voting shares.[33] A company may only be allocated a licence for two nationally available channels, of which only one may be a general or news service.[34] There are comparable provisions in the *Länder* broadcasting laws to prevent accumulation of licences for both national and regional services.[35]

In contrast the Italian rules on the accumulation of national licences in the 1990 legislation are extraordinarily lenient. One person may control up to 25 per cent of the national television or radio licences (of the total

[33] State treaty of 31 Aug. 1991, s. 21(2). A participant who holds between 25 and 49 per cent of the capital or voting shares in one company may only have a comparable interest in two others of less than 25 per cent: ibid., s. 21(3).

[34] Ibid., s. 21(1).

[35] See e.g. North Rhine–Westphalia law of 11 Jan. 1988, s. 6(3), Rhineland-Pfalz law of 24 June 1986, s. 5(3), and Saarland law of 11 Aug. 1987, s. 40(3).

available on the national plan) or three such licences, provided the 25 per cent limit is not exceeded.[36] As Italian commentators have pointed out, this is a bizarre rule, intended, it would appear, to allow Berlusconi to keep all his three networks.[37] Its absurd character is highlighted by the contrastingly strict statutory prohibition of the accumulation of one national licence and one local licence, whether for radio and television.[38] The same article also forbids the holding of more than one local television or radio licence in any zone, or more than three local television or seven radio licences altogether (serving a population of not more than 10 million inhabitants altogether). There must clearly be some doubts about the constitutionality of the provision permitting three national licences, for it would seem to violate the requirement of plurality of expression, formulated so trenchantly by the Constitutional Court in its *sentenza* of 1988. But the Italian law of 1990 is more rigorous in its cross-media ownership rules.

4. CROSS-MEDIA OWNERSHIP RULES

There was no provision restricting cross-media ownership of newspapers and broadcasting licences when commercial television was introduced in Britain in 1954. Indeed, it was not always thought in the early days to be a problem requiring legislation; the ITA appeared to encourage newspapers to participate in the companies which applied for franchises,[39] though there were reservations on the part of the Labour opposition owing to the Conservative sympathies of most newspapers. In response to anxiety about the influence of the press, the 1963 Act gave the ITA broad power to stop or suspend transmission of a company's programmes if newspaper shareholdings produced results against the public interest.[40] Subsequently the Annan Committee found no evidence that the press had attempted to influence the programmes of companies in which they had an interest and did not recommend any amendment to the law. But it was, in its view, undesirable for total press holdings in any company to amount to more than 25 per cent.

The 1990 Act contains a number of specific rules, with one controversial omission from their coverage. The proprietor of a national or local

[36] Law 223 of 6 Aug. 1990, Art. 15(4).

[37] *Il sistema radiotelevisivo*, 293–312.

[38] Art. 19.

[39] Sendall, *Independent Television in Britain*, i, 71; Annan Committee Report, *The Future of Broadcasting* (1977) Cmnd. 6753, paras. 13.31–13.33.

[40] Television Act 1963, s. 8. The provision was repeated in the Broadcasting Act 1981, s. 23.

newspaper may not hold more than a 20 per cent interest in a body which holds a licence for a Channel 3 regional television service, Channel 5, or national radio. The limit also applies to the converse situation, where the broadcasting licensee has more than a 20 per cent holding in a national or local paper.[41] There are similar rules to control cross-ownership of cable services or local radio *and* local newspapers. Regulations introduce other limitations on the cross-ownership of national papers and local radio or domestic satellite services.[42]

The controversial omission is the deliberate failure on the part of the government to extend these rules to the cross-ownership of newspapers and non-domestic satellite services. As intended, the effect is to allow News International to keep its shareholding in Sky Television, now BSkyB after the merger of the two satellite services. The government defended the omission against fierce opposition criticism with two arguments.[43] The first was that space on the Astra satellite (from which the non-domestic satellite service is broadcast) is not a scarce resource, so the usual arguments for cross-media ownership rules do not apply. The implication is that it is open to other bodies to institute channels on Astra, which in any case is not itself broadcasting on frequencies allocated to Britain. But this assumes that cross-media ownership rules are only necessary because of the physical scarcity of broadcasting frequencies.[44] It is surely arguable that they are necessary because otherwise one company will acquire a dominant influence, whether that is attributable to physical scarcity or not. The other contention was brutal, but perhaps more persuasive; if cross-media ownership restrictions had been extended to cover Sky Television, its owner Rupert Murdoch would simply have moved its studios and personnel to the mainland of Europe and continued to broadcast from a satellite which would then have been entirely outside British jurisdiction. This last point shows the need for the development of more effective European rules in this area.

Cross-media rules were introduced in the French law of 1986 after the intervention of the Conseil constitutionnel. There is no simple prohibition of ownership of a national newspaper and a significant holding in a

[41] Broadcasting Act 1990, Sch. 2, Part IV, paras. 2 and 3. These rules do not prohibit cross-ownership of a local paper and a regional television licence, unless they cover the same geographical area.

[42] SI 1991/1176, regs. 14 and 15.

[43] See Standing Committee Debates on the Broadcasting Bill, cols. 380–8, and the debate on the Report stage, 172 HC Deb. (6th ser.), col. 253 (D. Mellor, MP, Under-Secretary for State, Home Office).

[44] The United States Supreme Court has defended the constitutionality of the cross-media ownership rules in relation to the First Amendment by reference to the physical scarcity argument: see *FCC* v. *National Citizens' Committee for Broadcasting* 436 US 775, 798 (1978).

broadcasting company, as in Britain. Instead, in the interests of pluralism at the national level, it is forbidden to acquire a television, radio, or cable permit, if the result of the grant would be that the holder accumulated more than two of the following: one or more television licences covering in total a population of 4 million, one or more radio licences covering in total 30 million people, one or more cable licences covering 6 million inhabitants, and the control of one or more newspapers which enjoyed more than 20 per cent of the total national circulation of comparable daily papers.[45] There are similar provisions with regard to local and regional concentrations.[46]

The rules introduced by Article 15 of the Italian law of 1990 were presumably designed to meet the requirements of the Constitutional Court rulings in 1981 and 1988. Nobody may now hold a national television licence, if he controls a company which publishes daily newspapers the circulation of which exceeds 16 per cent of the total daily circulation in Italy, or two licences if his newspapers' circulation exceeds 8 per cent. Finally, nobody may hold three licences, if he also owns a national newspaper, irrespective of its circulation.[47] Berlusconi is in effect compelled to divest himself of the Milanese daily paper *Il Giornale*. Oddly the provisions do not apply to the cross-ownership of radio and daily newspapers nor of the broadcasting media and weekly periodicals (a very influential branch of the media in Italy). Nor is there a rule restricting ownership of local television stations and newspapers. But there is a complex provision annulling all future transactions which would lead to a media company acquiring more than 20 per cent of all media resources, or to a multi-sector conglomerate (a body with two-thirds of its resources deriving from the mass media) acquiring more than 25 per cent of such resources. This provision can be criticized: the definition of 'media resources' for the purposes of the concentration rules omits the resources obtained from book-publishing, the production and distribution of films and television programmes, and the sale of music.[48]

There was a complex and tortuous history to the enactment of these strange rules. Broadly the Italian legislature was concerned to safeguard Berlusconi's position, while satisfying the constitutional need for adequate anti-trust and cross-ownership rules. At one time the government considered an *opzione zero*, under which it would have been illegal to own both a national newspaper and a national television channel. This was considered too crude, and doubts arose after the Court's ruling of 1988

[45] Law of 30 Sept. 1986, Art. 41-1.
[46] Ibid., Art. 41-2.
[47] Law 223 of 6 Aug. 1990, Art. 15, para. 1.
[48] See the commentary by R. Lanzillo in *Il sistema radiotelevisivo*, 312–26.

whether it would pass constitutional muster. It was then replaced by a variant of the formula now set out in Article 15 of the 1990 law.[49] Although Berlusconi will have to surrender control of a daily paper (or to consider giving up one of his national channels), the impact of the measure is much harder on the Fiat group. This controls daily newspapers such as *La Stampa* and *Corriere della Sera*, and it will probably be illegal for it to own a national network. As commentators have pointed out, the new law is intended to preserve things as they are, rather than bring into effect a radical anti-concentration and cross-ownership reform. There must be doubts whether the provision would survive a fresh constitutional challenge.[50]

Another difficulty concerns the relationship between the specific provisions in the broadcasting law and the rules in the general competition statute enacted later in 1990.[51] The latter provides that its provisions are not to derogate from the specific ones in the earlier legislation. Further, it is for the Garante per la radiodiffusione e l'editoria, the official charged with supervising the private broadcasters under the broadcasting law, to apply the rules of the competition statute to the television companies (and to the press).[52] This clearly implies that the general competition rules concerning abuse of a dominant position, as well as the detailed provisions of Article 15 of the broadcasting law, apply to the media. Moreover, both the rules about mergers in that statute and those in Article 5 of the general law may apply.[53] This would appear to be a recipe for jurisdictional conflict.[54] It is surely important to be clear which rules apply and which authority is competent to apply them. The British Broadcasting Act may have given rise to similar difficulties when it states that the responsibilities of the ITC to ensure fair and effective competition in broadcasting services is not to affect the functions of the Director-General of Fair Trading, the Monopolies and Mergers Commission, or the Secretary of State.[55]

Although there has been as much anxiety in Germany as in other

[49] For a history of the various drafts, see D. Giacalone, *Antenna libera: la RAI, i privati, i partiti* (Milan, 1990), ch. IX.

[50] See the comments 'Opinioni a prima lettura sulla legge 6 agosto 1990, n. 223: disciplina del sistema radiotelevisivo privato' (1990) *Il diritto dell'informazione e dell'informatica* 779, esp. 803 (P. Caretti) and 829 (E. Zanelli).

[51] Law 287 of 10 Oct. 1990, esp. Arts. 2–6.

[52] Ibid., Art. 20, paras. 1 and 9.

[53] Competence to apply the rules about mergers in the general law is not left to the Garante, but reserved for the general competition authority: see ibid., Art. 20, para. 1. The Garante, however, has jurisdiction to enforce the anti-concentration rules in Art. 15 of the broadcasting law: see Art. 31 of the law of 6 Aug. 1990.

[54] See the comments of R. Lanzillo in *Il sistema radiotelevisivo*, 326–7.

[55] Broadcasting Act 1990, s. 2(3).

countries about the dangers of cross-media ownership, the law there is relatively less developed.[56] There are no provisions in either the state broadcasting treaty or in the state press laws. But most of the *Länder* broadcasting statutes do contain restrictions, which vary a little in their strictness. For example, both Hamburg and Hesse forbid grant of a broadcasting permit to an applicant who dominates the state press market.[57] The Hesse law also excludes from commercial broadcasting publishers who dominate a local press market in part of the state, and even forbids their participation in an applicant company. An applicant must in addition show that there are no concentration law objections to his application, and, if requested by the state regulatory authority, must inform the Cartel Office of his application.[58]

One aspect of the phenomenon of cross-media ownership is whether rules should be formulated to prevent one part of the media from promoting the interests of an associated company engaged in another media service. The matter has recently been considered by John Sadler in a report to the Secretary of State for Trade and Industry.[59] He was commissioned to study the extent to which branches of the media unfairly promote the interests of associated companies, with particular reference to the links between News International newspapers (*The Times*, *The Sunday Times*, *Today*, the *Sun*, and the *News of the World*) and Sky Television, an associated company. There were also allegations of discrimination by the IBA against Sky and in favour of its competitor, BSB, in its handling of advertisements for the two satellite services on Channel 3. The report did not consider that the possibly lower costs of Sky advertising in the News International papers was a significant factor in its eventual success. Nevertheless, Sadler concluded that it was desirable to prevent promotion of associated media both by discriminatory advertising rates and policies and by editorial matter.[60] He recommended, perhaps rather more controversially, that this should be a matter for self-regulation rather than for a change in the law. Self-regulation of the press in other areas, for example, in controlling infringements of privacy, has not proved particularly successful. In principle this is a subject which should be covered by competition law.

[56] For a general discussion, see Porter and Hasselbach, *Pluralism, Politics and the Marketplace*, 121–7.

[57] Hamburg law of 3 Dec. 1985, s. 19(2); Hesse law of 30 Nov. 1988, s. 15(1).

[58] Ibid., s. 15(3).

[59] *Enquiry into Standards of Cross Media Promotion* (1991) Cm. 1436.

[60] Subsequent to the Sadler Report, the Monopolies and Mergers Commission held that the BBC's use of free air-time to promote magazines published by an associated company distorted competition in sections of the consumer magazines market: *Television Broadcasting Services* (1992) Cm. 2035.

5. EXCLUSIVE BROADCASTING AGREEMENTS

Broadcasting companies increasingly compete with each other to acquire exclusive rights to transmit prominent events, particularly football games and other sports events. It was Sky's exclusive coverage of a cricket series in the West Indies in 1990 which firmly established it in the public eye and gained it an unassailable competitive advantage over BSB. A number of legal questions arise in this context. The most important is how far agreements of this kind should be controlled by competition law. It is also arguable that, although these agreements are not necessarily wrong, their impact should be moderated by allowing other broadcasting companies a right to transmit a short report or highlights of the event. Otherwise there might be an unjustified infringement of broadcasting freedom, whether that is looked at from the perspective of broadcasters or of viewers, some of whom might not have access to the satellite service which had acquired exclusive rights.

The legal position in Britain changed in the Broadcasting Act 1990. Before that the BBC and the IBA had enjoyed an opportunity to secure broadcasting rights to show certain 'listed events' on the same terms as those on which a cable or satellite broadcaster proposed to acquire them.[61] These events, entirely of a sporting character, include the Cup Final, Wimbledon, and the Derby and Grand National horse-races. When commercial television had been introduced in 1954, a ban on agreements for their exclusive coverage had been contemplated by the government, but it was decided merely to give the Minister (then the Postmaster-General) a reserve power to outlaw them if necessary.[62] In fact the power was never used, probably because the voluntary arrangements between the broadcasting bodies and the organizers of sports events were generally regarded as satisfactory. To have prohibited such agreements would have been to interfere with the rights of the organizers to maximize their profits and publicity, a point repeatedly made by the government during the debates on the Broadcasting Bill in 1990.[63]

The new Act only precludes exclusive arrangements for the showing of the listed events on a pay-per-view basis.[64] There is nothing to stop a satellite or cable company acquiring exclusive rights, provided no special charge is imposed on viewers to watch the transmission. There was, therefore, fierce competition in 1992 to secure an exclusive right to show the new Premier League football matches, a battle won by BSkyB (with

[61] Cable and Broadcasting Act 1984, s. 14.

[62] Television Act 1954, s. 7. The provision was repeated in the Broadcasting Act 1981, s. 30.

[63] See 521 HC Deb. (5th ser.), cols. 1694 ff. and 533 HL Deb. (6th ser.), cols. 728 ff.

[64] Broadcasting Act 1990, s. 182.

the help of the BBC) over the ITV companies. These games are not listed events, so BSkyB will be able to impose pay-per-view arrangements for their coverage on television. Nor is this possibility confined to sports events. The same arrangements could conceivably be made in respect of House of Commons debates, the Coronation, or other public events. In that situation it is perhaps easier to see that there would be an interference with the fundamental interests of viewers not enjoying access to the channel with the exclusive rights.

But courts are reluctant, as we saw in Chapter II, to uphold enforceable rights for viewers to see particular programmes. In one pertinent case, an Italian court refused to recognize that people living in Rome and its vicinity had a constitutional right to watch a football international between Italy and England, which RAI had agreed not to show in that area (in the interests of crowd attendance at the match).[65] But that does not rule out the intervention of competition law if an agreement has the effect of seriously distorting or restricting competition. The Bundesgerichtshof, the highest civil court in Germany, has held that an exclusive agreement between the two public broadcasting channels and the Deutsche Sportbund contravened the unfair competition law. What was particularly objectionable was that the agreement (*Globalvertrag*) totally excluded private broadcasters from transmitting a wide range of sports events for a period of five years. The public broadcasters were not obliged to cover any of the events, but had to choose which ones to cover within six weeks of it taking place. Only if they opted not to transmit would other broadcasters have an opportunity to acquire non-exclusive transmission rights. The Court held that the agreement unduly restricted the entry into the market of private competitors.[66]

An important development in German law was the amendment of the 1987 *Staatsvertrag* to mandate provision by the states of a short reporting right. The amendment was made at the instigation of the public broadcasting authorities, which had become anxious at the ease with which some of their commercial rivals managed to secure exclusive rights, including the right to transmit Wimbledon in the year in which the tournament was won by Boris Becker and Steffi Graf.[67] Broadcasters now enjoy a right of free access to all public events for the purpose of making a short report (*Kurzberichterstattung*), limited generally to ninety seconds. The organizer of the events may still exclude coverage altogether, and is

[65] Decision of Rome Court of 12 Nov. 1976, summarized in Pace, 278.

[66] See [1990] *NJW* 2815. Among the important points established by the Court is that the federal unfair competition statute applies to the procurement contracts of public broadcasters and that to apply competition law did not infringe their constitutional broadcasting freedom.

[67] For a vigorous argument for the amendment, see E. W. Fuhr, Legal Adviser to ZDF, in *ZDF Jahrbuch 1988*, 31–8.

entitled to demand reimbursement of any costs incurred through exercise of the access right. There are some doubts about the constitutionality of state legislation implementing the amendment now incorporated as section 4 of the 1991 state broadcasting treaty. Organizers of sports events argue that the broadcasters' access and reporting rights interfere improperly with their constitutional rights to contractual freedom (an implication from Article 2 of the Basic Law guaranteeing the right to development of personality) and to property (Article 14).[68]

The same problems have arisen in Italy. The courts have recognized a reporting right (*diritto di cronaca*) on the part of broadcasting organizations, while denying them a right of access to show the whole event.[69] There is a right to show news of the event, not the event itself as news (*la notizia dello spettacolo, non lo spettacolo come notizia*). What is conceded is a right to transmit a report of no more than three minutes. It is based on Article 21 of the Constitution. As in Germany the character of the organizers' competing right is far from clear. In the view of one court it is a property right, akin to the rights of authors.[70]

An amendment was moved to the British Broadcasting Bill to institute a limited reporting right of the kind recognized in Italy and Germany. It was intended to supplement the 'fair dealing' defence in the copyright legislation and to establish a public right to information. The government successfully resisted it partly on the ground that its introduction would be incompatible with the deregulatory character of the 1990 measure; in any case the existing fair dealing defences to actions for breach of copyright met the difficulty.[71] The second point was substantiated when Scott J. held that BSB was able to avail itself of the defence of fair dealing 'for the purpose of reporting current events', when it broadcast on its sports news programme extracts from the BBC's World Cup transmissions.[72] The defence to an action for breach of copyright is, however, quite different from the institution of a right of access for the purposes of reporting, which would of course render the freedom to copy upheld by Scott J. unnecessary. Under the German rules, for example, it is permissible for the broadcasting organization exercising the access right to introduce its own commentator and camera crew into the ground for

[68] For an analysis concluding that the reporting right is constitutional, see T. Brandner, 'Kurzberichterstattung und Verfassungsrecht' (1990) 21 *Archiv für Presserecht* 277.

[69] See the decisions of the Rome Courts reported in [1981] 1 *Il foro italiano* 520–2, and in [1988] *Diritto dell'informazione e dell'informatica*, 132.

[70] See the judgment of the Rome Court reported in [1988] *Diritto dell'informazione e dell'informatica* 132, criticized in the note by F. Morese following the report, 'Manifestazione sportiva: diritto dell'organizzatore e diritto di cronaca'.

[71] See 521 HL Deb. (5th ser.), cols. 1740–5.

[72] *BBC* v. *British Sky Broadcasting Ltd. (formerly BSB)* [1992] Ch. 141.

the purpose of reporting. It does not have to rely on the film of the company enjoying exclusive transmission rights.

A Council of Europe Recommendation has called for member states to recognize a broadcaster's short reporting right.[73] It covers all 'major events', defined as 'any event in which a broadcaster holds the exclusivity for the television broadcast and which is considered by one or more broadcasters from other countries as being of particular interest for its (their) public'. There is no absolute time limit on the length of a short report; it must be adequate to allow the public to appreciate the essential aspects of the event. The Council has explicitly recognized that to some extent property rights should give way to freedom of information. The same principle is also affirmed by the Transfrontier Television Convention.[74]

Competition law should ensure that exclusive contracts do not totally shut out competitors from covering a range of events over a long period of time, and it should allow for the limited reporting rights recognized in some continental countries. The law should in particular scrutinize agreements made by satellite and cable companies, at any rate while they remain minority services. Otherwise there is a real danger that the interests of those without access to the newer media will be significantly prejudiced.[75]

6. EUROPEAN COMMUNITY LAW

The phenomena of international media integration and transnational broadcasting have encouraged the development of European competition law to ensure the plurality of information at the continental level. The third Ministerial conference of the Council of Europe on media policy was devoted to this subject. Its first Resolution called on member states to exchange information on their experiences in this area, with a view to developing suitable policies. It invited the Committee of Ministers to set up a consultation procedure for periodic reporting by states on the extent of their media concentration.[76] The terms of the Resolution are too general to inspire confidence that any decisive action need result. European Community law is more likely to be the source of measures to meet the dangers resulting from concentrations of media power.

A number of articles of the Treaty of Rome are relevant to competition

[73] Recommendation R (91) 5 adopted on 11 Apr. 1991.

[74] Art. 9, discussed in Ch. X, S. 3 below.

[75] See E. M. Barendt, 'Press and Broadcasting Freedom: Does Anyone have any Rights to Free Speech?' [1991] *Current Legal Problems* 63, 75–9.

[76] Experts have prepared a valuable study of the Council of Europe states' concentration laws for the Steering Committee on the Mass Media: CDMM (92) 8.

regulation.[77] Among them is Article 37, intended to prevent state monopolies of a commercial character from discriminating with regard to the marketing of goods between nationals of member states. It would appear, for example, to prevent a monopoly broadcaster from purchasing films from only national producers or from discriminating in their favour with regard to the terms of purchase. But much more important are Articles 85 and 86. The former prohibits agreements between undertakings and concerted practices which

> may affect trade between Member States and which have as their object or effect the prevention restriction or distortion of competition within the common market . . .

Article 85(3), in conjunction with Article 89, enables the Commission in effect to exempt any agreement from these rules, if it contributes to improving the production or distribution of goods or if it promotes technical or economic progress. Article 86 prohibits abuse by one or more undertakings of a dominant position within the Common Market or a substantial part of it. There is a non-exhaustive list of practices which may constitute such abuse.

Article 90 is also relevant to the legal position of broadcasting. Its first paragraph prohibits the enactment or maintenance of any measures concerning public undertakings or undertakings with special rights which are contrary to the non-discrimination and competition provisions of the Treaty of Rome. But that is qualified by Article 90(2):

> Undertakings entrusted with the operation of services of general economic interest or having the character of a revenue-producing monopoly shall be subject to the rules contained in this Treaty, in particular to the rules on competition, in so far as the application of such rules does not obstruct the performance, in law or in fact, of the particular tasks assigned to them.

One question is how far broadcasting bodies, in particular public broadcasters, are subject to competition law under the Treaty. This was particularly pertinent when European broadcasters commonly enjoyed a monopoly under their state's law, but is now of declining significance.

A number of decisions of the European Court of Justice have examined these provisions in the broadcasting context. The first, the famous *Sacchi* case,[78] raised the question whether the (then) broadcasting monopoly of RAI was contrary to Article 86. The Court held that a state monopoly,

[77] For a full commentary on the relevant European Community law provisions, see R. Whish, *Competition Law*, 2nd edn. (London, 1989), chs. 7 and 8. Also see M. Coleman, 'European Competition Law in the Telecommunications and Broadcasting Sectors' (1990) 11 *Europ. Comp. Law* 202.

[78] [1974] ECR 409: also discussed in Ch. X, S. 4.

including one covering cable, was not illegal as such, but that the conduct of the monopoly was subject to competition law, in so far as it did not obstruct performance of the tasks assigned to the broadcaster. Further, the monopoly's conduct could amount to an abuse of a dominant position, though that was a matter for the national court to decide in the circumstances. Thus, it would be contrary to the Treaty for a public broadcaster to discriminate in the prices it charged advertisers on the basis of their nationality or to enter into agreements with film companies to show their films and not those from other studios. It might also be a breach for the broadcaster to enter into exclusive agreements for showing films or to cover sports events; it could not argue that these contracts are essential to its role as a public broadcaster offering a comprehensive service and that, therefore, it would be wrong under Article 90 to apply competition law principles.[79]

A later case concerned the agreement of RTL, the Luxembourg monopoly broadcasting company, and its subsidiary Information publicité for the latter to enjoy an exclusive right to conduct telemarketing advertising on the former's channels. This meant that the broadcasting company would no longer accept advertisements carrying an invitation to telephone an agent, unless the telephone number given was that of Information publicité. A key issue was whether Article 86 applied, where the Luxembourg monopoly was established by law. The Court held that it did.[80] Article 90 did not confer immunity from the competition rules, unless their application prevented the monopoly from discharging its essential tasks. It did not matter whether the dominant position was created by the conduct of the company or by the law itself. Further, it was an abuse of that dominant position, for RTL to reserve the separate, but related, activity of telemarketing to a company with which it was linked, when that activity could equally have been discharged by competitors. Clearly the consequences of vertical integration between broadcasters and advertising agents is now subject to Community law, at any rate when they have an effect on inter-state trade.[81]

The compatibility of a broadcasting monopoly with Community law has been raised most recently in a reference from a Thessaloniki court.[82] The European Court of Justice reaffirmed the principles stated in *Sacchi* that a (Greek) public broadcasting monopoly was not as such contrary to Community law, but that it must be conducted in conformity with the EC

[79] See the Commission decision in *Re German TV Films: The Community* v. *Degeto Film GmbH* [1990] 4 CMLR 841.

[80] *Centre belge d'études de marché* v. *Compagnie luxembourgeoise de télédiffusion* and *Information publicité* [1985] ECR 3261.

[81] For this concept, see Whish, *Competition Law*, 242–50.

[82] *Elliniki Radiophonia Tileorassi* [1991] ECR 2925.

principles of free movement of goods and services and its competition law. It was for the national court to determine whether the Greek broadcasting monopoly's practices constituted an abuse of a dominant position, and, if so, whether they could be justified under Article 90(2) by its particular responsibilities. Further, the grant of exclusive transmission and retransmission rights was contrary to Article 90(1), in so far as those rights could be exercised under a discriminatory policy in favour of the monopoly's own programmes (unless the application of the competition rules interfered with the particular responsibilities of the public broadcaster). The effect of these complex pronouncements is that member states must consider how far a broadcaster's monopoly powers are really essential to its public service responsibilities.

The Brussels Commission has intervened twice in the case of European Broadcasting Union (EBU) agreements. It forced members of the EBU, in effect all the public broadcasters in Europe, to drop plans to fix agreed common rates and conditions for supplying news items to non-members.[83] Its members were, therefore, compelled to negotiate separately about such rights. But the Commission has subsequently indicated that it is prepared to approve under Article 85(3) the EBU sublicence agreement.[84] Sublicences are granted for deferred transmission of, and news access to, sports events covered by the Eurovision exchange arrangements (under which members of the EBU acquire rights to transmit events in other members' countries).

The Commission's most significant ruling, however, was its decision in the *Screensport* case.[85] A consortium of EBU members (the Eurosport Consortium) entered into a number of agreements with Sky Television for the exclusive showing by the latter on its satellite sports channel, Eurosport, of sports programmes produced or acquired by consortium members. The arrangement was challenged by Screensport, another company offering a sports channel satellite service transmitted from the Astra satellite. The Commission found two restrictions on competition. First, the agreement prevented competition between Sky and the Eurosport Consortium, while, secondly, it denied Screensport's opportunities to compete with Sky for the transmission of the events. The Commission refused to exempt the agreement under Article 85(3), finding no improvement in the distribution of goods or services in this disproportionate fetter on competition. It also ruled Article 90(2) inapplicable. Even if the national broadcasting organizations (members of the Eurosport Consortium) could be regarded as undertakings falling under that article,

[83] *Re EBU* [1987] 1 CMLR 390.
[84] *Re the Application of the European Broadcasting Union* [1991] 4 CMLR 228.
[85] Commission decision of 19 Feb. 1991, OJ L 63/32.

it would be wrong to apply it to cover transnational activities of this commercial character.

Community competition law will undoubtedly have a greater impact in the future. For example, the Community Merger Regulation may apply when the control of broadcasting companies changes hands.[86] Mergers which meet the Regulation's turnover thresholds must be referred to the Brussels Commission for it to determine whether they create or strengthen a dominant position impeding effective competition.[87] The merger between Sky and BSB was subject to a preliminary investigation by the Commission to see whether it contravened the Regulation. The Commission accepted the argument that the merger was exempt from control, as each party had more than two-thirds of its turnover in one state, and that, therefore, there was no Community dimension.

Member states may not apply their own national competition legislation to mergers with a Community dimension.[88] But they may take appropriate measures to protect certain legitimate interests, other than those taken into account by the Regulation, provided the measures are compatible with Community law.[89] 'Plurality of the media' is one of these interests. This is the first time Community law has explicitly recognized the importance of this value to competition law.

[86] Reg. 4064/89, OJ L 395/1; [1990] 4 CMLR 285.

[87] The co-ordination, including the institution of a joint venture, of the competitive behaviour of independent undertakings, falls outside the Regulation: see *Sunrise* (breakfast-time television licence-holder) agreement, Commission Decision of 13 Jan. 1992.

[88] Merger Regulation, Art. 21(2).

[89] Ibid., Art. 21(3).

VII
Access to Broadcasting

I. INTRODUCTION

Many commentators, particularly on the political left, have argued that broadcasting freedom entails the recognition of rights of access. The freedom, it is said, should not only be enjoyed by channel owners, professional broadcasters, and those public figures given the opportunity to appear on the media. It should also include rights for minorities and ordinary individuals to speak on television and radio.[1] Sometimes it is argued that there is a constitutional right of access to the broadcasting media. More usually, as in Britain, the case is made for statutory provision for the right.

One context in which the claim is frequently made is that of political and election broadcasts. Political parties contend, sometimes before the courts, that they are entitled to broadcast or to have their press and regular annual conferences covered by radio and television. This topic is sufficiently important to be treated in a separate chapter, which follows this one. Another related issue is whether political parties, social groups, Churches, and charities should have a right to advertise on the media. The distinction between political advertisements and conventional political broadcasts is that the former are paid for by the party. Advertisements for social and religious causes are really a special type of access broadcast; the question how far there are constitutional and legal rights to show them is discussed in this chapter.[2] Rights of reply are also discussed, because to some extent the arguments for recognizing them are similar to those put forward for access rights. Moreover, it is not always easy to distinguish between them.

The first argument for access rights is that the public is entitled to hear the range of opinions held by different groups, so that it can make sensible choices on political and social issues; in particular these views should be exposed on television, the most important contemporary medium. We have seen that the audience's interest does justify some restraints on broadcasters' freedom: for example, impartiality rules and positive pro-

[1] See the Annan Committee Report, Cmnd. 6753 (1977), paras. 3.14–15 and 18.4–6, and the view of Tony Benn, MP, reported in S. Hood and G. O'Leary, *Questions of Broadcasting* (London, 1990), 42–3.

[2] See Ss. 2 and 3.

gramme standards.[3] But it does not follow that access rights should be recognized. A regulatory authority, such as the ITC or the CSA, can formulate programme standards without upholding such rights. Indeed, their recognition might make it more difficult for a regulatory authority to secure a balanced range of programmes. Too many groups with a particular point of view, say, environmental and conservation societies, might exercise rights of access. This would lead to a lack of balance or necessitate the provision of rights of reply by other organizations to ensure that the audience hears both sides of the question.

It is more common now to focus instead on the interests of those claiming the right to broadcast. They contend that access to radio and television should not be the exclusive preserve of licensees and professional broadcasters. Broadcasting in its present organizational form does not, it is said, provide a good market-place for ideas; it is dominated by commercial considerations.[4] Arguments of equality may also be deployed to support access rights for minority groups to balance the generous opportunities afforded established political parties, Churches, and other establishment bodies. A theoretical argument is that freedom of speech means the freedom to communicate effectively to a mass audience, and nowadays that entails access to the mass media. Finally, it is said (in some Italian literature) that rights of access provide some compensation for the 'expropriation' by the public monopoly of the freedom to broadcast.[5] The assumption is that, in the absence of a justification for that monopoly (provided in Italy by Article 43 of the Constitution),[6] there would be a right to broadcast in the same way that everyone has a right to say or write what he likes in his own home. This last argument cannot be used to support access rights in the context of private broadcasting. But the other points canvassed in this paragraph, if acceptable, would justify the recognition of access to both public and private channels.[7]

Despite a superficial attractiveness, these arguments are unacceptable. Freedom of speech does not entail any right to communicate effectively. No legal system provides its citizens with the means and opportunities to address the public in the way each considers most appropriate.[8] More-

[3] Ch. II, S. 1.

[4] A classic exposition of this and other arguments for access is made by J. A. Barron, 'Access to the Press: A New First Amendment Right' (1967) 80 *Harv. L. Rev.* 1641.

[5] See F. Gabriele, 'L'accesso tra corte costituzionale e legislatore: una parabola discendente giustificata?' in *Il servizio pubblico radiotelevisivo* (Naples, 1983), 253, 256–8, and S. A. Romano, 'Diritto d'accesso e riforma della RAI' [1976] *Giur. merito* 90.

[6] See Ch. I, S. 3 above.

[7] G. Gamaleri, 'Radiotelevisione e accesso con particolare riferimento all' emittenza locale', in P. Barile, E. Cheli, and R. Zaccaria (eds.), *Radiotelevisione pubblica e privata in Italia* (Bologna, 1980), 349, 351–3.

[8] For a general discussion of positive or claim-rights to free speech, see E. Barendt, *Freedom of Speech* (Oxford, 1987), ch. III.

over, as the Annan Committee pointed out, to grant everyone a right to use an access channel, even one available all the time, would be to give every adult a worthless right to use it for a second a year.[9] Limited access rights, enjoyed only by important political and social groups (as in Italy) may be more valuable.[10] But even their recognition would involve some interference with the editorial freedom of channel controllers and programme schedulers, and it may be more difficult as a consequence to achieve a balanced range of programmes. Further, a channel might find it hard to create any clear identity for itself, if it had to devote a substantial amount of time to relaying the programmes made by pressure groups.

There are also practical objections to access rights. It may be very difficult to decide, for example, which groups are to be given access, and when and how often such programmes are shown. There is a danger some groups will be unduly privileged, an argument which has been made frequently about the opportunities given the Churches in Germany.[11] These points weigh particularly heavily against the recognition of constitutional rights, for courts are not competent to formulate them with any precision. They are perhaps less persuasive in the context of legislation. Statutes can lay down detailed rules for the allocation of access opportunities. The next two sections of the chapter deal respectively with the constitutional arguments and some legislative rules. The fourth section contains a detailed discussion of the right of reply and the United States Fairness Doctrine, under which channels were compelled on occasion to transmit the replies of pressure groups to programmes already broadcast. Whatever the weaknesses of the general arguments for access rights, there is a relatively strong case for their recognition in the context of cable, a topic which is treated in the last section of this chapter.

2. CONSTITUTIONAL ACCESS RIGHTS

The question whether there are constitutional access rights has been canvassed in a number of countries. The fullest discussion may be found in the decision of the United States Supreme Court in *Columbia Broadcasting System* v. *Democratic National Committee* (subsequently referred to as the *CBS* case).[12] The broadcasting company refused the Democrats

[9] Annan Committee Report, para. 3.14.

[10] See S. 3 below.

[11] C. Link and A. Fahlke, 'Kirkliche Sendezeiten in Rundfunk und Fernsehen' (1983) 108 *AöR* 248, 262, and D. Dehnen, 'Zur Verfassungsmässigkeit des sogenannten Drittsendungsrechtes der Kirchen im öffentlichen-rechtlichen und privatrechtlichen Rundfunk' [1986] *DVBl.* 17.

[12] 412 US 94 (1973).

and a business group campaigning for peace in Vietnam advertising time to comment on contemporary political issues. Its refusal was upheld by the FCC, but the DC Circuit Court of Appeals ruled that an absolute ban on short pre-paid editorial advertisements infringed the First Amendment, especially as CBS and all other broadcasters took commercial advertisements.[13] That constituted impermissible discrimination.

The campaigners' constitutional arguments gained some strength from the earlier decision of the Supreme Court in the *Red Lion* case (fully discussed later in this chapter) upholding aspects of the FCC Fairness Doctrine.[14] Under this doctrine (now repealed) the Commission used to require licensees to devote a reasonable proportion of broadcasting time to coverage of public issues and to treat each side of a controversy fairly. The Court had emphasized in *Red Lion* that in view of the special characteristics of broadcasting, licensees did not enjoy absolute freedom of speech under the First Amendment. Their rights should be considered in conjunction with the interests of listeners and viewers and of people who would like to broadcast. It followed that the FCC could compel a licensee 'to share his frequency with others' and require the provision of a right of reply to a personal attack. But the Supreme Court in the *CBS* case, allowing the broadcasters' appeal by a majority of 7–2, refused to take the further step of upholding a *constitutional* right of access.

There were significant differences between the members of the Court majority. All of them saw difficulties in upholding constitutional access rights, largely on the ground that they would interfere with the broadcasters' freedom to draw up their schedule. Further, wealthy individuals and pressure groups would have greater opportunities to purchase advertising time. But Burger CJ., in the leading judgment, joined on this point by four other members of the Court, said it was unnecessary to decide whether the First Amendment (or the Communications Act 1934) would render unconstitutional a Commission decision to compel some access rights. Indeed, the Chief Justice was clearly influenced by the facts that the FCC had hitherto considered the Fairness Doctrine adequate to ensure the presentation of a wide variety of views, and that it was reviewing it in the light of the access issue. But two other members of the majority, Stewart and Douglas JJ., took the more radical view that any right of access, even if instituted by the Commission or by Congress, would violate the broadcasters' First Amendment rights. They held that broadcasters are entitled to the same freedom of speech as newspapers, with the implication that the Fairness Doctrine itself should be reconsidered.

The dissenting judgment of Brennan and Marshall JJ. emphasized the

[13] *Business Executive Move for Vietnam Peace* v. *FCC* 450 F. 2d. 642 (1971).

[14] 395 US 367 (1969), and see S. 4 below for further discussion.

inadequate time devoted by broadcasters to the discussion of controversial issues, even under the Fairness Doctrine. Quite apart from the audience's interest in such discussion, the freedom of groups and individuals to effective expression justified recognition of some access rights to radio and television.[15] The proper balancing of all free speech interests precluded the absolute right of licensees to exclude the Democrats' claim. Moreover, access would not interfere with the freedom of CBS to speak, only with its freedom to decide who else should use its network. The dissenters' last point was that the broadcasters' refusal to take issue advertisements was contrary to normal First Amendment principles, in that commercial advertising was treated more favourably than political speech.

The principal arguments are evenly balanced. Some of the majority's points are unpersuasive. The grant of some access rights would not interfere with the overall freedom of broadcasters to pursue their own editorial line (an aspect of their First Amendment rights), though there would be some (perhaps minor) restriction on their freedom to draw up their own programme schedule. It is unclear whether a properly regulated access scheme need give significant advantages to wealthy individuals and corporations.[16] Indeed, serious access programmes (as opposed to political spot advertising) might give greater exposure to the views of the poor and minorities. Attempts by wealthy associations to purchase all the available time could be countered by regulating the price at which it is sold.

However, merely to make these points shows the difficulties in supporting a *constitutional* right. Legislative or administrative rules must formulate, among other matters, how much time should be allocated overall to access programmes, how long they may be, which groups and individuals are entitled to make them, and how balance is to be achieved. In the absence of such rules, courts are right to deny individual access rights. In this context it is interesting to note the dissenters' emphasis that the question was not whether there was an absolute right of access for the complainants, but whether the absolute denial of access could be sustained. Brennan J. would have remanded the case to the Commission for it to formulate appropriate rules. That course would have been compatible with broadcasting freedom.[17] The freedom is guaranteed in the interests of the public as well as those of professional broadcasters; as a constitutional value it justifies the institution of some access entitlements, particularly where minority voices would otherwise not be heard. But these rights should be legislative, rather than constitutional.

[15] For access to public forums to hold meetings, see Barendt, *Freedom of Speech*, ch. III, s. 3.

[16] See N. Johnson and T. A. Westen, 'A Twentieth Century Soapbox: The Right to Purchase Radio and Television Time' (1971) 57 *Va. L. Rev.* 574.

[17] See Ch. II, S. 1 above.

The approach described in the previous paragraph is similar to that adopted in other contexts by the German Constitutional Court. It interprets broadcasting freedom as a constitutional value, requiring in some circumstances positive provision by the legislature.[18] The access issue has been extensively discussed in German literature, particularly with regard to election broadcasts and the transmission of church services and other religious programmes.[19] But the Constitutional Court has never recognized a right of individual or group access, and at least two rulings of the Federal Administrative Court would appear to reject it.[20] As will be seen in the next chapter, the Constitutional Court has laid down principles for the allocation of election broadcasts, but even in that context there is no suggestion of constitutional rights. A party has only a right to be treated fairly in relation to other parties if the broadcasting companies arrange for the transmission of some broadcasts.[21] It has been suggested that the Churches enjoy a privileged right to access under Article 4 of the Basic Law guaranteeing freedom of religion. That includes *Bekenntnisfreiheit*, the freedom to profess religious belief, but that does not include a right to have broadcast services or other religious programmes.[22]

In fact the argument whether the German Churches enjoy constitutional rights in this context is now largely academic. First, they have been given generous statutory rights under broadcasting laws. (Doubts about the constitutionality of such access rights are considered in the next section.) Secondly, the Catholic and Protestant Churches, and the Jewish community, are represented on the public broadcasting councils and the private broadcasting regulatory authorities.[23] The access debate in this context (as in others) has been replaced by the argument whether the Churches and other religious organizations should be free to apply for broadcasting licences.[24]

The character of access rights has been vigorously discussed in Italy, following the ruling of the Constitutional Court in 1974.[25] It held the RAI public monopoly could only be justified on certain conditions. One was that access must be allowed so far as possible to the political, religious, and social groups, representing the various strands of opinion in society.

[18] See the discussion in Ch. II above, and the *Third Television* case, 57 BVerfGE 295, 319–21 (1981).

[19] See the articles referred to in n. 11 above, and J. Lücke, 'Die Rundfunkfreiheit als individuelles Zugangsrecht' (1977) *JZ* 41.

[20] See 39 BVerwGE 159 (1971) and 1985 *DÖV* 1014 (Decision of 16 Aug. 85).

[21] See Ch. VIII, S. 2.

[22] Dehnen, 'Zur Verfassungsmässigkeit des sogenannten Drittsendungsrechtes der Kirchen', 22.

[23] See Ch. III, S. 4 and Ch. IV, S. 3.

[24] See Ch. IV, S. 4 above.

[25] Decision 225/1974 [1974] *Giur. cost.* 1775.

The Court made it clear that statutory provision for access was required by Article 21 of the Constitution guaranteeing freedom of expression; elsewhere in the judgment it referred to the need for legislation to render effective and to guarantee *il diritto di accesso*. The implication might be that the Court was protecting a constitutional right, though the legislature was required to make detailed provision for its application (as it in fact did in Article 6 of the 1975 law). According to one approach, based on paragraph 5 of the Court's judgment, access rights are the price paid by the public monopoly for its expropriation of the constitutional right to express opinions freely.

A Rome court has twice taken the view that the 1974 decision formulated an individual right, guaranteed at the constitutional level.[26] On each occasion it referred the constitutionality of the access provisions of the 1975 law to the Constitutional Court, because it considered they did not adequately protect the applicants' rights. As they concern aspects of the 1975 statute, the detailed discussion of these cases is left to the next section. In principle, the arguments for upholding constitutional access rights in Italy are no more persuasive than they are in the United States or Germany. It is in any case doubtful whether the Italian Constitutional Court envisaged them. It referred to the obligation of public broadcasters to ensure that the maximum level of access is made available, 'if not to individual citizens, but at least to all the most relevant groups for expressing the variety of views in society'.[27] Access was viewed as a goal or a policy, rather than a matter of fundamental right. It was for Parliament to determine which groups should enjoy access and to lay down other appropriate rules. In contrast the Court expressly required protection by law of the individual's *right* of reply (my emphasis).

Individuals and groups, therefore, do not have constitutional rights of access to the broadcasting media. Access rights can only be framed effectively by a legislature or by a specialist administrative agency, such as the FCC. This does not, however, mean that statutory (or other) access rights do not have a constitutional dimension. A supreme court may hold, as the Corte costituzionale did in 1974, that some provision should be made for access as a matter of constitutional policy. That is also in effect what the dissenters said in the *CBS* case. On this approach, the constitutionality of specific access provisions may be challenged by those denied access. Such challenges have been brought in Italy, albeit without success.[28] The approach does not mean, however, that there are individual constitutional rights to access.

[26] See the references of the Pretura di Roma to the Constitutional Court made on 3 Jan. 1976 and on 9 Nov. 1982, reprinted in Pace, 340 and 371 respectively.

[27] [1974] *Giur. cost.* 1775, 1789 (the translation is the author's).

[28] See below, S. 3.

There is a clear similarity here with the question (discussed in Chapter IV) whether there is a constitutional right to institute private broadcasting stations. We concluded that there is no such individual right, but that the courts in Italy and Germany have held (to varying degrees) their public broadcasting monopolies unconstitutional. In both contexts (access rights and the right to private broadcasting) the constitution may be of importance in requiring the legislature to act; but this does not entail recognition of individual constitutional rights. There is another constitutional issue in this context. Courts may be required to decide whether specific legislative provision for access infringes the broadcasting companies' free speech (or programming) rights. It has already been noted that Douglas and Stewart JJ. in the *CBS* case took the view that it would. We come to that question in the next section after some statutory provisions have been outlined.

3. LEGISLATIVE RULES

In a number of countries some groups enjoy statutory access rights. The most important questions are whether the rules create rights which are enforceable in the courts and whether access opportunities, or rights, are a permissible limit on the broadcaster's own constitutional freedoms. There are also important issues about which groups enjoy access, and how often and for how long such broadcasts may be made. Party political broadcasts are perhaps the most important context for these questions. In this chapter we are concerned with the access opportunities of other social and cultural groups, especially the Churches, which frequently enjoy a privileged position.

In Britain the Churches have traditionally enjoyed informal opportunities, for example, to have religious services broadcast. But from the 1970s other groups, such as trade unions and community groups, have from time to time been given access both to the BBC and to the independent channels. The Annan Committee welcomed this development. However, it did not think that a general right of access should be recognized, largely for the reasons already discussed. Further, there were doubts whether these programmes really benefited or informed the viewers: '[to] let everybody say anything that they like produces Babel'.[29] The Committee was firmly of the view that it should be for the professional broadcasters to determine who should be given access, although that course entailed some hard choices. Its position perhaps reflects an élitist, almost patrician stance.

A marked change in climate became apparent in the 1980s. First,

[29] Annan Committee Report, para. 18.11.

Channel 4 was required to commission 'a substantial proportion' of its programmes from independent producers. The channel from the outset encouraged access programmes, seeing its role as that of a publisher rather than a producer of its own programmes. As a result independent production companies mushroomed. A second development was the government's decision in 1987 to require both the BBC and the ITV companies to commission 25 per cent of their programmes from independent producers. The Peacock Committee had recommended that for reasons of cost and efficiency the proportion of such programmes be increased to 40 per cent over a ten-year period; its evidence suggested that independent producers were more cost-conscious than the 'comfortable duopoly' of the BBC and the ITV companies.[30] Indeed, it has largely been for economic reasons that the Conservative government has pursued this path, free speech considerations playing relatively little part.

The Broadcasting Act 1990 now places a legal obligation on the ITC to ensure that a Channel 3 licensee's service will allocate not less than 25 per cent of total programme time to independent productions.[31] An equivalent obligation is also imposed on the BBC.[32] The Director-General of Fair Trading is empowered to prepare annual reports to the Home Secretary on the extent to which the BBC meets this requirement. The ITC can enforce it through the imposition of licence conditions, sanctioned by fines or a shortening of the licence period. Although these requirements now have legal significance, they can only be enforced by administrative procedures, largely at the discretion of the regulatory authorities. There is no suggestion that independent producers have an enforceable title to have a particular programme shown. In any case few of these items are the 'personal view' programmes of the kind advocated by supporters of access entitlements. Independent producers admittedly provide some incentive for the television companies to control their own costs and in that way they promote efficiency. Whether they increase the variety and quality of programmes shown on television is, however, a moot point.

Another recent change in British law has been the relative liberalization of 'issue advertising'. Under the earlier broadcasting legislation, political and religious advertising was forbidden.[33] More surprisingly, items relating to the needs or objects of charities could not be broadcast without the permission of the IBA, which extended the ban to advertising.[34] This latter rule was frequently reconsidered by the Authority, and its removal was recommended by the Annan Committee.[35] The ban was eventually

[30] Peacock Committee Report (1986) Cmnd. 9824, paras. 645–7.

[31] Broadcasting Act 1990, s. 16(2)(h). The same requirement is imposed on Channels 4 and 5, and domestic (but not non-domestic) satellite channels.

[32] Ibid., s. 186.

[33] Broadcasting Act 1981, Sch. 2, para. 8.

[34] Ibid., s. 4(5).

[35] Annan Committee Report, para. 12.18.

lifted in 1989. The Broadcasting Act 1990 retains the prohibition on political advertising,[36] but has removed that imposed on religious commercials. The ITC Advertising Code, however, lays down strict limits on the latter: they must not attempt to expound doctrine or generally solicit funds, but are acceptable in so far as they describe the organization's activities or publicize its services and meetings.[37]

The continued ban on political advertising is hard to sustain in principle. It is widely framed, for it applies not only to the commercials of political parties, but to 'any advertisement which is directed towards any political end', or any advertisement related in any way to an industrial dispute (unless it is a public service announcement of the government).[38] Its maintenance is probably favoured by the established political parties, who enjoy privileged access under the rules set out in the next chapter. Unfortunately it prevents pressure groups from campaigning on television for a change in policy, for example, for a higher subsidy for British Rail or against nuclear power stations, because these objects would be regarded as political. On the other hand, the government is free to promote its privatization policies and make other public announcements, a freedom extensively used when the national utilities were sold in the 1980s. The justification usually given for the rules is that they stop the purchase of air-time by richer pressure groups.[39] It is unconvincing. That goal could be achieved by sensible restrictions on advertising expenditure or by overall limits on the number of advertisements any group (or individual) is able to show over a particular period. It is also hard to see why commercial advertising to promote a product is acceptable, but not advertising designed to show that the purchase or use (of particular cosmetic products, for example) might for moral or political reasons be undesirable.

German law sometimes recognizes an entitlement to broadcasting time (*Anspruch auf Sendezeiten*). Although this is not constitutionally required, the laws governing public, and to a lesser extent private, broadcasting channels confer rights on the Churches and some other denominations to appropriate time for the transmission of their services and other religious programmes.[40] Similar arrangements must be made for the Jewish communities. The drafting of the rules in, for example, the ZDF *Staatsvertrag*

[36] Broadcasting Act 1990, s. 8(2).

[37] ITC Code of Advertising Standards and Practice (Jan. 1991), App. 5.

[38] Broadcasting Act 1990, s. 8(2)(a)(ii)–(iii).

[39] See Annan Committee Report, para. 12.18 for the traditional argument applied to charities, and 3515/70, *X & Assoc. of Z* v. *UK* 38 Coll. Dec. 86, for its adoption by the UK government in a political advertising case before the European Commission of Human Rights.

[40] See e.g. Saarland law of 11 Aug. 1987, s. 9 (applying both to public and to private broadcasters) and Lower Saxony law of 16 Mar. 1987, s. 21 (private broadcasters). A full list of the relevant provisions of the public broadcasting statutes is to be found in E. W. Fuhr, *ZDF-Staatsvertrag*, 2nd edn. (Mainz, 1985), 165.

raises a number of problems typical of access provisions: Which organizations are entitled to access and what is 'appropriate broadcasting time'?[41] The ZDF rules give access to the established Protestant and Catholic Churches, and to other religious associations active throughout the whole country, a rule which excludes minor sects and new cults with a local following.[42] It is right that the privilege was extended to Jewish communities, but now the question would arise in many countries whether the same facilities should be afforded the Muslim community. The Churches and ZDF have reached agreement on the appropriate time for these programmes, but in the absence of an understanding it would be hard for a court to impose a limit. The religious communities are responsible for these programmes themselves, as distinct from general discussion programmes, where the broadcasters retain full control. Transmission time is provided free, whereas a charge may be imposed by private broadcasters.

In France too the Churches now enjoy a right to transmission of their Sunday morning religious services on Antenne 2, the principal public channel. (Oddly this entitlement, unlike similar rights in Germany, does not cover feast days.) This obligation previously imposed by *cahiers des charges* is now contained in Article 56 of the 1986 law. Transmission costs are paid by the channel, subject to an annual limit. Under the preceding article broadcast time on the public channels is also given to trade unions and professional bodies; the detailed rules are made by the CSA.[43] In the view of the Conseil constitutionnel such access rules guarantee pluralism of opinion.[44] In 1990 the CSA gave nine organizations access rights for what in effect are short announcements of a maximum length each of ten minutes. The total time allocated for such programmes is only six hours a year divided between the two public channels.

A number of general questions may be posed about these requirements. The first is whether the obligation to transmit access programmes should, as in France, only be imposed on the public channels, or whether they should also extend to private channels, as in the case of some German *Länder*, for example, Saarland and Lower Saxony. Since these programmes are widely considered rather dull fare by viewers, private channels not obliged to carry them are given a valuable competitive advantage. They can also argue, perhaps with more conviction than the public channels, that to impose an obligation to transmit the programmes would interfere with their own (constitutional) broadcasting freedom. This is one aspect of the second question: whether now that there are more

41 Fuhr, *ZDF-Staatsvertrag*, 146–66.

42 ZDF *Staatsvertrag* of 31 Aug. 1991, s. 11(3).

43 For a detailed treatment, see C. Debbasch, *Droit de l'audiovisuel*, 2nd edn. (Paris, 1991), 517–19.

44 Decision 86-217 of 18 Sept. 1986, Debbasch, 245.

opportunities for private groups, including religious associations, to operate their own radio and television stations, there is any case for granting them legal rights of access to other private channels. One German commentator has doubted the constitutionality of the Church access rights, particularly to have programmes transmitted on private channels.[45] But the standard view appears to be that the special constitutional position of the Churches justifies their broadcasting privileges.[46]

More generally, limited provision for access should on balance be regarded as compatible with broadcasting freedom, despite the view of Douglas and Stewart JJ. in the *CBS* case.[47] The contribution such items make to informing the public outweighs the relatively slight interference with the broadcasters' programming freedom. It is quite clear that inclusion of access programmes does not interfere with the broadcaster's ability to present his own views or to take his own editorial line, a freedom which in any case is not recognized in most legal systems.[48] Statutory access provisions can normally be regarded as promoting, rather than restricting, broadcasting freedom. That would not be the case, however, if these items dominated the schedule, allowing the broadcasting companies only limited time for their own programmes and depriving them of any opportunity to create their own identity. Such an eventuality is, however, very remote.

The Italian law of 1975 contains comprehensive access rules.[49] One provision, discussed in the next chapter, concerns round-table political and electoral discussion programmes. The other rules are contained in Article 6 of the statute. It requires RAI to reserve a certain amount of transmission time for the parties and groups represented in Parliament, trade unions and political and cultural associations, ethnic, linguistic, and religious organizations, and other socially relevant groups which request access. At least 5 per cent of television time, and 3 per cent of radio time, must be reserved for access. A subcommission of the Parliamentary Commission determines access requests in the light of the criteria set out in the article and a regulation of the Parliamentary Commission;[50] there is an appeal from its decisions to the full Commission. RAI is required to provide free technical assistance.

Some aspects of these rules should be emphasized. First, only groups, and not individuals, have legal access opportunities. Further, it is unclear

[45] Dehnen, 'Zur Verfassungsmässigkeit des sogenannten Drittsendungsrechtes der Kirchen', 22.

[46] See e.g. Fuhr, *ZDF-Staatsvertrag*, 149–50.

[47] 412 US 94 (1973), discussed in S. 2 above.

[48] See Ch. V, S. 2 above.

[49] Law 103 of 14 Apr. 1975, implementing the requirements of Decision 225/1974 (discussed in S. 2 above).

[50] Regulation of 30 Apr. 1976 (published in *Gazetta ufficiale*, 15 May 1976).

whether there is any difference between the position of the groups explicitly referred to, albeit in general terms, by the article, and those other socially relevant bodies which request access. It has been suggested that the former enjoy enforceable rights, while the latter have only an interest which the Parliamentary bodies may recognize in their discretion.[51] This distinction seems now rather hollow in light of the cases discussed in the next paragraph. Thirdly, it is for the producers of these programmes to ensure that they do not infringe fundamental constitutional principles, and also that they are not used for commercial advertising.

However, the most important point is that access is regulated by the Parliamentary Commission. Its rejection of access claims has led to considerable litigation, and in two cases a court in Rome has referred questions to the Constitutional Court.[52] Broadly the issue was whether the rules satisfy the requirements laid down by that Court in 1974. Doubts about their constitutionality had arisen partly because the Subcommission (and the full Commission on appeal) do not exercise a merely technical control over the application for access, but sometimes review the programme's contents. More fundamentally reservations were expressed about the absence of any judicial control over the Commission's decisions. The courts had treated them as political, and so immune from review by either civil or administrative law judges. The Rome Court took the view that the 1974 ruling required an enforceable right of access (*un diritto soggettivo di accesso)* of constitutional significance, so it followed that Article 6 of the statute was invalid. The Constitutional Court has, however, twice refused to consider the merits of these references. In the first case, concerning claims by the Radical Party and promoters of the abortion referendum to participate in political discussion programmes, the reference was held irrelevant in that the applicants had not formally asked for access under Article 6.[53] In the later case, two groups had been allowed access in principle, but had been asked to make changes to their programmes before transmission.[54] The Court again held that it was inadmissible to refer a question about the constitutionality of Article 6, since the issue was really whether contents control by the Commission was legitimate.

While the Constitutional Court has avoided the question of substance, the Corte di cassazione in 1983 rejected an enforceable right of constitutional dimension, violated by the provisions of the 1975 law.[55] It did

[51] By R. Zaccaria, *Radiotelevisione e costituzione* (Milan, 1977), 378–9. His view is criticized by G. Corasaniti in *Diritto di accesso, diritto di rettifica, impresa di informazione* (Milan, 1986), 36, on the ground that it supports a violation of the principle of equality guaranteed by Art. 3 of the Constitution.

[52] See n. 26 above.

[53] Decision 139/1977 [1977] *Giur. cost.* 1822, reprinted in Pace, 355.

[54] Decision 194/1987 [1987] *Giur. cost.* 1437.

[55] Decision 1984/7072 [1984] *Giur. cost.* 175, with commentary by M. Manetti at 176.

not consider the Constitutional Court envisaged such a right in its 1974 judgment. Moreover, as a matter of principle it would be incompatible with the responsibility of the Parliamentary Commission to ensure the transmission of a comprehensive and balanced range of opinions. The Italian Court thus shared the doubts felt in other jurisdictions, particularly the United States, whether access can be reconciled with broadcasting freedom.

Whatever the merits of the theoretical arguments, in practice access programmes have not proved attractive. That may be partly attributable to an inherent lack of appeal, but RAI may also be responsible: they are scheduled early in the evening when there are relatively few viewers, and there is apparently no attempt to integrate them with news and current affairs programmes.[56] The 1975 reform must, therefore, in this respect be considered a failure. The access question has, moreover, become peripheral to the main debate in Italy about the status of the private networks and the need for adequate anti-concentration rules.

4. RIGHTS OF REPLY AND THE FAIRNESS DOCTRINE

Continental legal systems usually provide individuals and organizations with rights of reply to (factual) allegations in the press or on the broadcasting media. There is also such a right in United States broadcasting law, developed as an aspect of the Fairness Doctrine. Such rights afford, for instance, a remedy for defamatory attacks, which is speedier and far less costly than recourse to an action in the civil courts (or prosecution) for libel. Thus, from one perspective the primary importance of reply rights is remedial: to redress wrongs to the individual. But they also provide an opportunity for the person concerned to put information before the public, which can add to its knowledge about particular incidents. Hence these rights may be regarded as in some respects akin to access rights. The similarity is most striking when rights are claimed to reply to the messages in commercial or issue advertising, as used sometimes to be the case under the United States Fairness Doctrine. Pressure groups, such as Friends of the Earth, claimed rights to reply to advertising, for example, for cars and petrol, which, they argued, presented one side of a controversial issue. Such rights are different from access rights, in that they must be triggered by a broadcast or advertisement which takes one side on a particular question. But the exercise of reply rights in this context, like access programmes, are designed to present views which otherwise might not find a place in the broadcasting schedule.

[56] G. Corasaniti, 'Per un bilancio dell'accesso', in *Il servizio pubblico radiotelevisivo*, 291, 293–4.

In contrast, the rights of reply common in European jurisdictions are primarily exercised to answer allegations of *fact* about individuals, associations, or companies. Their personal character differentiates them from access programmes. British law does not provide a right of reply, but complaints of unfair treatment and invasion of privacy may be made to the Broadcasting Complaints Commission (BCC). The BCC may direct the broadcasting body to publish its findings, a sanction which bears some resemblance to the compelled publication of a reply. At all events it takes the view that the opportunity to complain to it satisfies the requirement now imposed on states by the Council of Europe Convention and Community Directive to provide a right of reply or equivalent remedy.[57]

The Fairness Doctrine was promulgated by the FCC in 1949 and repealed as part of its bonfire of controls in 1987. In the intervening years, it had been approved by the Supreme Court, and its application to issue advertising was upheld by other federal courts. It was always resented by broadcasters. The Doctrine's requirements were foreshadowed in a number of FCC rulings during the late 1930s and 1940s, but its authoritative, if wordy, exposition is to be found in the Commission's Report *In the Matter of Editorializing by Broadcast Licensees* (1949).[58] As its title indicates, the document was to a considerable extent concerned with the question whether station licensees were free to broadcast their own editorial policies. The Commission, reversing earlier rulings, concluded that they were.[59] More pertinently for the purposes of this chapter, it also upheld the 'affirmative responsibility on the part of broadcast licensees to provide a reasonable amount of time for the presentation . . . of programmes devoted to the discussion and consideration of public issues', and secondly, the requirement that a licensee must 'operate on a basis of overall fairness, making his facilities available for the expression of the contrasting views of all responsible elements in the community on the various issues which arise'.[60] These two general principles were known as the first and second prongs of the Doctrine. It is the second which is the relevant to the themes of this chapter, but the first was regarded as integrally linked to it, so much so that it was repealed when the second prong was held no longer sustainable.

It was, however, the right of reply aspect of the Doctrine which came before the Supreme Court in 1959. The Red Lion broadcasting station in

[57] Annual Report for 1989, HC 490, para. 14. For the European instruments, see Ch. X, Ss. 3 and 4.

[58] For the history of the doctrine, see F. W. Friendly, *The Good Guys, the Bad Guys and the First Amendment* (New York, 1976), chs. 1–5, and S. J. Simmons, *The Fairness Doctrine and the Media* (Berkeley, Calif., 1978), chs. 1–3.

[59] For this aspect of United States law, see Ch. V, S. 2.

[60] The quotations are from *In the Matter of Editorializing by Broadcast Licensees* 13 FCC 1246 (1949), para. 7.

Pennsylvania carried a strong attack on a left-wing journalist, Fred Cook, who had himself written a book critical of the extreme right-wing Republican Barry Goldwater. Cook claimed free reply time on the basis of various decisions of the FCC. At the same time the FCC promulgated regulations which clarified the personal attack rule: when an attack is broadcast on the honesty, integrity, or similar qualities of an individual or group, a free right of reply was to be afforded within a reasonable time and in any event no later than a week after the broadcast. There were exceptions, including attacks made by political candidates. In *Red Lion* itself, the DC Circuit Court of Appeals had upheld enforcement of the personal attack rule in favour of Cook, while the Seventh Circuit Court had sustained a challenge to the new regulations on the ground that they infringed broadcasters' First Amendment freedom of speech.[61]

The Supreme Court unanimously upheld the constitutionality of the personal attack rule, and by clear implication the Fairness Doctrine in its entirety.[62] White J. made the familiar point that broadcasting presents special problems for the application of freedom of speech principles, because there are fewer frequencies available than people who wish to use them. There could, therefore, be no objection to the FCC requirement that licensees share their broadcasting time by providing an opportunity for reply to personal attacks. The Court refused to accept the argument that this would chill speech by inducing licensees not to broadcast controversial programmes. If that were the case, the FCC would invoke the first prong of the Doctrine to compel their showing.

The scope of the Doctrine was then considered by the DC Circuit Court of Appeals in a number of cases. First, it held that the Commission could take the number of breaches by a station into account in determining whether to renew its licence. In *Brandywine* v. *FCC*[63] the Court emphasized it was not to be applied in a formalistic way, nor did it require more than a balanced presentation of opposing strands of opinion. Equality was not required.[64] The Doctrine had much in common with the standard programme obligations of public service broadcasters (considered in Chapter V), although it was also used to achieve limited access opportunities. Rights were granted to individuals or pressure groups to reply to commercial advertisements.

Initially the Court affirmed a FCC ruling which had required stations carrying cigarette adverts to devote a significant amount of time to presenting the case against smoking.[65] The FCC thought its ruling should be

[61] 381 F. 2d. 908 (DC Cir. 1967) and 400 F. 2d. 1002 (7th Cir. 1968).
[62] 395 US 367 (1969).
[63] 473 F. 2d. 16 (1972).
[64] *Public Media Center* v. *FCC* 587 F. 2d. 1332 (DC Cir. 1978).
[65] *Branzhaf III* v. *FCC* 405 F. 2d. 1082 (1968).

confined to this case, but that could not be justified in principle. Subsequently the Court of Appeals mandated counter-advertising by Friends of the Earth to commercials for large cars and leaded petrol,[66] and compelled the transmission of union advertisements advocating a boycott of a department store in response to its advertisements.[67] The second prong of the Doctrine applied because the advertisements adopted a position on a controversial matter. However, the Court declined to extend its coverage to advertisements which vaunted the qualities of a particular petrol.[68] In effect a line was drawn between editorial and standard product advertisements; the FCC subsequently ruled that commercials which made claims about the efficacy of particular products should be bracketed with standard advertisements and should not be subject to the Doctrine.[69]

Other difficulties arose outside the context of commercial advertising. Attempts were made to apply the second prong to documentaries and news items. For example, there was an unsuccessful complaint by a group, Accuracy in the Media, that an NBC documentary presented a partial view of the private pensions industry. The FCC had upheld this complaint and required the broadcaster to show a balancing programme, but the Court of Appeals allowed its appeal, partly on the rather dubious ground that the issue of pensions reform was so well established that it was not a matter of controversy.[70] To some extent the majority judges were influenced by fear that application of the Doctrine would inhibit First Amendment broadcasting freedom, an argument which had been taken less seriously in the commercial advertising cases. Another problem was which programmes should be taken into account when assessing the need for balance, always a major difficulty in applying impartiality and comparable requirements.[71] The question arose in a complaint by a right-wing pressure group that CBS news programmes presented an unfair picture of US defence needs. By a 6–3 majority the Court of Appeals upheld its dismissal by the FCC. Application of the Doctrine would have imposed a tremendous burden on the broadcasters, who would have been required to examine carefully every news item and current affairs programme to ensure balance.[72] One problem was whether this should be determined in the context of evening news bulletins, all news programmes, or all news and current affairs programmes.[73]

[66] *Friends of the Earth* v. *FCC* 449 F. 2d. 1164 (1971).

[67] *Retail Store Employees Union, Local 880* v. *FCC* 436 F. 2d. 248 (1970). These and other cases are fully discussed by Simmons, *The Fairness Doctrine and the Media*, ch. 5.

[68] *Neckritz* v. *FCC* 502 F. 2d. 411 (1974).

[69] The new policy was upheld by the DC Circuit Court of Appeals in *National Citizens Committee for Broadcasting & Friends of the Earth v. FCC* 567 F. 2d. 1095 (1977).

[70] *National Broadcasting Co.* v. *FCC* 516 F. 2d. 1101 (1975).

[71] See Ch. V, S. 2 above.

[72] *American Security Council, Education Foundation* v. *FCC* 607 F. 2d. 438 (1979).

[73] See the discussion of this case by Friendly, *The Good Guys, the Bad Guys and the First Amendment*, ch. 11.

The courts had been confident that application of the Doctrine to require replies to personal attacks or advertisements would not have a chilling effect on speech. This was an illusion in the context of cigarette advertising, where the effect of the *Branzhaf* ruling was the virtual disappearance of these commercials.[74] Doubts about the wisdom and constitutionality of the Doctrine became more widespread. In 1985 a Commission report concluded that it was no longer justified; it did not promote speech, but inhibited it. However, in view of the continued support it enjoyed in Congress, the FCC did not consider repeal appropriate. But in particular cases the Commission was increasingly prepared to leave things to the discretion of the broadcaster. Further reconsideration was then encouraged by two decisions of the Court of Appeals. In the first,[75] Bork CJ. urged the Supreme Court to review *Red Lion*. Subsequently the DC Circuit Court ordered the FCC to consider its constitutionality, when the Commission examined a complaint against a station in Syracuse, New York, which had shown advertisements promoting a nuclear plant without allowing a peace group the chance to reply.[76]

On this occasion the FCC found the Fairness Doctrine against the public interest, as it inhibited the showing of controversial programmes through stations' fear of requests for reply rights. It led to less rather than more vigorous public debate on the airwaves, a conclusion contrary to the Commission's own policy of 1949 and the opinion of the Supreme Court in *Red Lion*. The Doctrine's repeal was upheld by the DC Circuit Court.[77] According to two judges the ruling could be upheld as a reasonable interpretation of FCC statutory powers, but Judge Starr considered the policy and constitutional arguments interwoven. In his view the FCC was free to conclude that the Doctrine was now incompatible with the First Amendment, in light of the increase in the number of terrestrial radio and television stations and the growth of cable since the end of the 1960s. Also pertinent was the FCC's conclusion that its effect was to chill rather than foster speech. But even his judgment stopped short of a ruling of unconstitutionality; the FCC could reintroduce the Doctrine if the effects of deregulation warranted it. Two members of the Court (Chief Judge Wald dissenting on this point) held that the first prong, the requirement to cover important controversial issues, could also be dispensed with. It was no more than a support for the more important (and certainly more litigated) second prong, requiring balance in programme scheduling.

Shortly before its repeal, President Reagan had vetoed a Bill attempting

[74] Ibid., ch. 8.

[75] *Telecommunications Research and Action Center* v. *FCC* 801 F. 2d. 501 (1986), upholding with reluctance the FCC application of the Doctrine to teletext.

[76] *Meredith Corp.* v. *FCC* 809 F. 2d. 863 (1987).

[77] *Syracuse Peace Council* v. *FCC* 867 F. 2d. 654 (1988), cert. denied, 110 S. Ct. 117 (1989).

to enshrine the Doctrine in statutory form. The decision to repeal it has been criticized.[78] One anxiety is that there will be further dominance of the broadcasting media by conservative political action groups, which will be able to pay for access without fear of reply by political rivals. Certainly few episodes in United States media history have been more controversial. The case-law admittedly shows many of the difficulties in attempting to enforce reply rights outside the limited field of incorrect allegations about particular persons and associations. (The personal attack rule upheld in *Red Lion* survives the Doctrine's demise.) On the other hand, the arguments used to justify repeal are unpersuasive. It is hard to believe that broadcasters were really inhibited from showing controversial programmes, because they would be required to show a balancing item or run the risk of a complaint. Further, advocates of repeal, and indeed the leading judgment in the *Syracuse* case, assumed that a balancing programme is 'coerced speech', and therefore to be discounted when assessing whether the Doctrine really promoted, rather than inhibited, speech. That assumption is quite unwarranted. The balancing requirement at most restricted broadcasters' programming freedom, but it recognized the free speech interests of the public and of individuals and groups granted access.

European reply rights can be discussed more briefly. Well established in the case of the press, it would have been odd not to enforce them against the broadcasting media. In Germany they are regarded as protecting the constitutional rights of dignity and the free development of personality.[79] The contribution their exercise may make to the goal of public discussion is of secondary importance. Statutory provisions in France, Germany, and Italy, generally unlike those concerned with access, clearly confer legal rights. Indeed, in Italy the Constitutional Court's landmark ruling of 1974 required Parliament to formulate a right. Unlike the access interest of socially relevant groups, the entitlement is for the benefit of individuals as well as associations.[80]

The provision in the ZDF *Staatsvertrag* may be taken as typical of the German rules: a person or body directly affected by a factual allegation may claim a right of reply.[81] It must be asserted without delay, and at latest within two months of the broadcast. (The Bundesverfassungsgericht

[78] See the notes by R. S. Antao (1989) 63 *St. John's L. Rev.* 556 and by R. Samson (1990) 41 *Rutgers L. Rev.* 663.

[79] Fuhr, *ZDF-Staatsvertrag*, 122–3. Also see W. Seitz, G. Schmidt, and A. Schoener, *Der Gegendarstellungsanspruch in Presse, Film, Funk und Fernsehen*, 2nd edn. (Munich, 1990).

[80] Law 103 of 14 Apr. 1975, Art. 7. For a full discussion of the Italian law of reply rights, see P. Lax, *Il diritto di rettifica nell' editoria e nella radiotelevisione* (Padua, 1989), esp. 70–9. For the French law, see Debbasch, *Droit de l' audiovisuel*, 486–8.

[81] S. 9. For a commentary on the similar provision in the earlier state treaty, see Fuhr, *ZDF-Staatsvertrag*, 121–37.

had held that a limit of two weeks was unconstitutional.[82]) The reply must be broadcast without delay at a time of day similar to that when the offending broadcast was transmitted.

In Italy the right can only be successfully claimed against broadcasters when the allegation is in fact untrue.[83] In contrast, in France, and generally in Germany, it is enough for the complainant merely to allege that the broadcast was inaccurate, and a reply must be provided unless that is known to be untrue.[84] But in Germany the allegation must be one of fact which is capable of proof, and not one of opinion. On the other hand any alleged inaccuracy is enough to trigger the right in Germany, while in France the allegation must affect the aggrieved party's honour or reputation. If the broadcasting authority fails to transmit a reply, or imposes unjustifiable restrictions, the right can be enforced through the civil courts. There are, therefore, significant differences between the continental legal systems, and that is one reason why the European Commission proposed a measure of harmonization. The EC Broadcasting Directive requires all member states to provide a right of reply or equivalent remedies to any persons whose interests have been damaged 'by an assertion of incorrect facts'.[85] This formulation appears to follow the narrower right of Italian law; the right may only be exercised in reply to objective inaccuracies.

British law does not afford any right of reply of the continental character to attacks in the press or on the broadcasting media. The only comparable remedy in the latter context is the right of complaint to the Broadcasting Complaints Commission, a body first established on a statutory basis in 1981 and now regulated by the Broadcasting Act 1990.[86] It must have at least three members, who are appointed (now) by the Secretary of State for National Heritage; in practice the Commission has five members. Its function is to adjudicate on complaints of unjust or unfair treatment in programmes actually broadcast or of unwarranted infringement of privacy in, or in connection with obtaining material included in, these programmes. Like the Broadcasting Standards Council (BSC), the Commission enjoys jurisdiction over all BBC and private television and sound broadcasting, including licensed cable and satellite services. But in contrast to the BSC it is a quasi-judicial tribunal, and for that reason it was inappropriate to

[82] 63 BVerfGE 131 (1983). The Court intimated (at p. 143) that a right of reply exercised a long time after the offending broadcast might interfere with the broadcaster's rights under Art. 5 of the Basic Law.

[83] See now law 223 of 6 Aug. 1990, Art. 10, requiring both public and private broadcasters to provide a right of reply in appropriate cases.

[84] The Sudwestfunk state treaty and the Hesse public broadcasting statute are exceptions to this general rule.

[85] Art. 23. For further discussion, see Ch. X, S. 4.

[86] Ss. 142–50.

merge the two bodies as the government had contemplated at one stage.[87] The statute sets out detailed rules about the manner and time-limits for making complaints and the procedure for their consideration. The BCC may direct broadcasters to publish a summary of the complaint and its findings. In practice it generally orders publication in the *Radio Times* or *TV Times* and a broadcast of the summary, whether the finding was adverse to the broadcaster or not. The ITC and Radio Authority may be ordered by the BCC to issue directions for the publication and broadcast of the latter's decisions. Conditions in the independent broadcasters' licences must require them to comply with such directions, so BCC decisions are enforceable.[88]

The BCC produces annual reports with full summaries of its adjudications. These show that its jurisdiction is much wider than the field covered by continental rights of reply. Complaints are brought not only by individuals, but also by trade unions, commercial companies, charities, and pressure groups aggrieved by what they consider to be unfair treatment of their work, products, or services. 'Unfair treatment' is not confined to factual inaccuracies, but appears to include a failure to give the complainant advance notice of allegations against him or an opportunity to reply to points made in the programme.[89] More surprisingly, the unfairness may lie in the unflattering depiction of a group in a fictional programme,[90] the exclusion of a political party from a current affairs programme,[91] or in defects in the treatment of a particular subject.[92]

In comparison with continental reply rights, a complainant to the BCC does not have the right to frame his own answer. Moreover, it is unable to entertain a complaint if the treatment (or privacy infringement) is the subject of legal proceedings. It has discretion not to consider it if the complainant has a legal remedy and it is inappropriate for the Commission also to consider the matter, or if it appears for any other reason inappropriate to consider it.[93] These features of the law are incompatible with a *right* of reply, particularly one which under the Directive must be provided '[w]ithout prejudice to other provisions adopted by the Member States under civil, administrative or criminal law'.[94] The BCC may, therefore,

[87] For the BSC, see Ch. V, S. 4 above. Merger was contemplated in the White Paper *Broadcasting in the '90s: Competition, Choice and Quality* (1988) Cm. 517, para. 7.10. But the BCC itself considered the course inappropriate: Annual Report for 1989, HC 490, paras. 5–10.

[88] Broadcasting Act 1990, s. 146.

[89] For a critique of the BCC's decisions, see G. Robertson and A. Nicol, *Media Law*, 3rd edn. (London, 1992), 545–59.

[90] The *Brownies* case, Annual Report for 1990, HC 507, 93.

[91] *Falmouth and Camborne SLDP* case, Annual Report for 1991, HC 533, 81, also discussed in Ch. VIII, S. 4 below.

[92] *Terrence Higgins Trust* case, Annual Report 1992, HC 83, 19.

[93] Broadcasting Act 1990, s. 144(4).

[94] Directive of 6 Oct. 1989, Art. 23(1).

not be justified in its confidence that recourse to it satisfies the Directive's requirements.

5. ACCESS TO CABLE

The development of cable poses new access problems.[95] The relatively large number of cable channels, many of them surplus to the needs of the operator, attracts access claims by community and educational groups, Churches, and local government. Cable is primarily a local service, less expensive to use than national or regional television. On the other hand, the operator itself may have rights of free speech which would be infringed by a requirement to honour access claims; the scarcity and economic arguments which are employed to justify broadcasting regulation, and, therefore, access provision, may be less applicable in this context. Indeed, some United States courts have suggested that the position of cable for First Amendment purposes should be assimilated to the press.[96] A cable operator would be immune from any regulation of its channels. Quite apart from the question of principle, there is the practical question whether access programmes on cable are likely to be any more attractive to the viewer than they have been on the terrestrial channels. On the other hand the potential of cable for circulating local information and for interactive banking and shopping services suggests that access opportunities are potentially of enormous importance. As yet they have not materialized, at any rate in Britain.

The Broadcasting Act 1990, like the repealed Cable and Broadcasting Act 1984, makes no provision for access to cable. Indeed, the White Paper prefacing the 1984 measure rejected any rules of this character.[97] Its argument was that to compel access would require the operator to make invidious choices between groups seeking it; it was much better to give cable services a completely free hand. The 1984 Act did, however, require the Cable Authority to take into account at the franchise stage the extent to which applicants proposed to transmit programmes other than those made by them or their associates.[98] It was also to consider the

[95] For general discussion of this issue in Britain and other countries, see T. Hollins, *Beyond Broadcasting: Into the Cable Age* (London, 1984), esp. 283–4 and 325–8, and in the USA, see I. de Sola Pool, *Technologies of Freedom* (Cambridge, Mass., 1983), ch. 7, and P. Parsons, *Cable Television and the First Amendment* (Lexington, Mass., 1987).

[96] See *Midwest Video Corp.* v. *FCC* 571 F. 2d. 1025, 1056 (8th Cir. 1978), *Quincy Cable Television* v. *FCC* 768 F. 2d. 1434, 1450 (DC Cir. 1985), and *City of Los Angeles* v. *Preferred Communications* 476 US 488, 494 (1986).

[97] *The Development of Cable Systems and Services* (1983) Cmnd. 8855, para. 131.

[98] Cable and Broadcasting Act 1984, s. 7(2)(e) and (f). The subsection also required the Authority to take into account the extent to which the applicant proposed to include programmes provided by local voluntary associations and to assist them in their production.

range and diversity of programmes offered by applicants. These rules were designed to achieve one of the objectives of access provision, a variety of programmes for the viewers, without the complications of recognizing individual rights. But they were not repeated in the 'lighter touch' dispensation of the 1990 Act.

In contrast, cable access rules in the United States have been frequently discussed. FCC rules issued in 1976 required all cable operators with more than 3,500 subscribers to designate four access channels: one each for free public access, educational access, local government access, and leased access. The Eighth Circuit Court of Appeals upheld the challenge of the Midwest Video Corporation to these requirements on the ground that they exceeded the FCC's statutory powers, and this decision was affirmed by the Supreme Court.[99] Both Courts entertained doubts about the rules' constitutionality. The Circuit Court would almost certainly have been prepared to hold them unconstitutional if necessary. Access rules in its opinion interfered with the cable operators' First Amendment rights. But there were indications that the Courts might have been more sympathetic to a clear grant by Congress of access rights.

The courts have not adopted a uniform approach. A District Court judge has held that cable should not be assimilated to the press for First Amendment purposes.[100] Economic factors and the franchising system created a natural monopoly in the case of cable, and justified its regulation to ensure access for those not rich enough to operate their own system. The Court stressed that access rules did not discriminate between types of speech, let alone points of view, and did not interfere with the editorial control of operators over other channels. According to this approach one could conclude either that there is no infringement of the operators' First Amendment rights, or that the interference was necessary to achieve the legitimate goal of ensuring community participation in cable. Arguably what the operator is really complaining about is an interference with his commercial freedom to exploit his franchise in the most profitable way. Few cable operators exercise substantial control over the contents of the programmes they distribute, almost universally supplied by satellite companies and separate programme providers.[101]

The federal Cable Communications Policy Act 1984 now mandates some leased access channels and enables the cities on the award of franchises to require others as conditions for their allocation. Systems with more than 36 channels must offer 10 per cent of them for leased

[99] *Midwest Video Corp.* v. *FCC* 571 F. 2d. 1025 (1978), affirmed on appeal, 440 US 689 (1979).

[100] *Berkshire Cablevision* v. *Burke* 571 F. Supp. 976 (D. R.I. 1983).

[101] D. Brenner, 'Cable Television and the Freedom of Expression' [1988] *Duke LJ* 329, 333–41.

commercial use by persons unconnected with the operator, and for systems with more than 55 channels the proportion increases to 15 per cent. Cities may require the provision of channels for free public, educational, and governmental use. But their number is a matter for negotiation with the cable operator, and there is provision for it to reclaim them if they are unused. A leading commentator has argued for the constitutionality of these rules.[102] There is in his view no significant interference with the operators' own First Amendment freedom. The access user does not associate the operator with his message, and his speech, unlike the exercise of rights of reply under the Fairness Doctrine, could not be said to chill the operator's. Nor is there any interruption of the operator's own programme schedule, as there is when access is claimed on a terrestrial channel. The argument is persuasive. These points would not, however, carry conviction if there were any evidence that access channels deprived operators of opportunities to broadcast their own material.

Many German private broadcasting laws make provision for an open channel (*Offener Kanal*) which can be used by anyone wishing to broadcast.[103] But broadcasting institutions, the state and local authorities, and political parties are excluded from this entitlement. Advertising is prohibited, but use of the channel is in some states free. Allocation of time is left to the *Land* broadcasting authority, which in Saarland, for instance, is directed to afford opportunities for as many applicants as possible.[104] These provisions seem admirable in principle. On freedom of speech grounds there is an overwhelming case for requiring some cable channels to be devoted to access programmes.

[102] Ibid. 375–81.

[103] See e.g. Saarland law of 11 Aug. 1987, s. 52c, Hamburg law of 3 Dec. 1985, s. 30, Rhineland-Pfalz law of 24 June 1986, s. 18, and North Rhine–Westphalia law of 11 Jan. 1988, ss. 34–6.

[104] Saarland law, s. 52c (6).

VIII
Election and Political Broadcasting

1. INTRODUCTION

The regulation of election and political broadcasting poses a number of problems. They arise to some extent because the media authorities are subject to considerable pressure from political parties. This phenomenon has become more marked over the last thirty years or so, as television has taken the place of the public meeting in providing voters with political information and impressions.[1] The conduct of election campaigns is now substantially influenced by the parties' conception of what will make a good story for the main evening news on television, and party leaders in particular are packaged as if they were a commercial product to be sold to viewers. Moreover, political parties through their election and other broadcasts enjoy a privileged access to the media, which is much wider than the opportunities afforded other social and cultural groups. In some of the jurisdictions we are considering, such as France and Italy, this is a matter of legal right, while in Britain access has been entirely a matter of constitutional convention.[2] Only in Germany have the courts played a significant role in laying down basic principles to regulate the allocation of party broadcasts, obviously a contentious issue in a multi-party democracy.

From one perspective political broadcasts can be seen as a type of access programme, albeit one made by particularly important social groups.[3] Indeed, in Italy claims by minority parties that they have been excluded from political discussion programmes have been based on the general access provisions of the 1975 broadcasting statute, as well as on its provision specifically regulating political party discussion programmes (*tribune politiche*).[4] Therefore, some of the arguments of prin-

[1] For a general discussion of developments in Britain, see G. W. Goldie, *Facing the Nation* (London, 1977), A. Smith, *Television and Political Life* (London, 1979), and M. Cockerell, *Live from Number 10* (London, 1988).

[2] The Broadcasting Act 1990, ss. 36 and 107 now require the independent terrestrial television and national radio services to transmit party political broadcasts: see S. 2 below.

[3] Report of the Committee on the Future of Broadcasting (the Annan Committee) (1977) Cmnd. 6753, para. 18.15.

[4] See e.g. the decisions of the Pretura di Roma and of the Corte costituzionale reprinted in Pace, 340 and 355, and Decision 1984/7072 of the Corte di cassazione [1984] *Giur. cost.* 175.

ciple canvassed in the preceding chapter are relevant in this context.[5] For example, the points which may be made against recognition of individual access rights (whether constitutional or statutory) also apply to political broadcasts. It is difficult to formulate such rights for political parties, when they will inevitably conflict with the rights or interests of other parties and groups and those of the broadcasting companies. How far, for instance, should minority parties enjoy a right to make political broadcasts or to participate in a televised electoral debate, when the major party leaders and the broadcasting body think a discussion between the Prime Minister and the leader of the principal opposition party would be of more interest to the public? Questions of this kind are not easily answered by courts. It is not surprising that in this sensitive area they prefer to state broad principles, such as the duties of broadcasters to be fair and impartial, rather than attempt to formulate enforceable access rights.

It is also possible to see political and election broadcasts as a form of political advertising. Indeed a party may pay the broadcasting company or network for time to transmit its message, as has been the usual practice in the United States and more recently in Italy. In Britain political advertising is statutorily forbidden.[6] The usual justification for the restriction is that otherwise rich, well-established parties would be able to afford much more advertising time than new or minority parties.[7] This is unconvincing. It is perfectly possible to impose limits on the duration and frequency of, and on the charges for, such advertisements, so that some time could be afforded by less well-off groups. That seems to have been the view of the Conseil constitutionnel, when it rejected a challenge to the constitutionality of the original version of Article 14 of the 1986 *loi* permitting advertising by political parties outside election campaigns: the provision did not in its view violate the constitutional principle of equality, because the CNCL (now replaced by the CSA) could draw up rules which would prevent richer parties from taking advantage of the dispensation.[8] Rules of this kind would, however, be unconstitutional in the United States. The Supreme Court, following its decision in *Buckley* v. *Valeo*,[9] would hold expenditure limits on broadcast advertising by political parties and election committees incompatible with the First Amendment.

[5] See Ch. VII, Ss. 1 and 2.

[6] Broadcasting Act 1990, s. 8(2)(a).

[7] See the United Kingdom argument in 4515/70, *X & Assoc. of Z.* v. *U.K.* 38 Coll. Dec. 86.

[8] Decision 86-217 of 18 Sept. 1986, Rec. 1986, 141, Debbasch, 245. Political advertising has subsequently been prohibited by the law of 15 Jan. 1990, amending in this respect Art. 14(2) of the law of 30 Sept. 1986.

[9] 424 US 1 (1976). For discussion of this case and the limits on election expenditure generally, see E. M. Barendt, *Freedom of Speech* (Oxford, 1987), 49–52.

It is indeed arguable that a total prohibition on political advertising, as imposed in Britain, is contrary to freedom of speech and broadcasting. Generally political speech is more fully protected than commercial speech, so if broadcasters are legally free to show advertisements for goods and services, it is hard to see why they should not be able to show advertisements for political parties and pressure groups.

However, some degree of regulation in the interests of equality of opportunity of political parties is desirable, and in some jurisdictions constitutionally required. Political broadcasting is significantly different from commercial advertising, and even perhaps from general access programmes. It now plays a crucial part in the efficient working of an informed democracy. That role justifies regulation to ensure fairness and balance between political parties. It is perfectly legitimate for a broadcasting authority to take ordinary commercials on a 'first come, first served' basis, and it may be tolerable for it to discriminate between various access programmes. But balance and impartiality, if not absolute equality, are rightly required in the case of political and election broadcasts. This is primarily a matter of (constitutional) principle. It is also relatively easy in practice to devise rules to ensure fairness between the parties. In the case of referendums this can be done by requiring equal time for proponents of the 'Yes' and 'No' votes. Admittedly overall fairness and balance is harder to achieve in the case of multi-party political broadcasts (as will be discussed later), but even here the task is not as complex as the administration of general access rules for pressure groups.[10]

This chapter explores the regulation of political broadcasting in the interests of overall fairness and balance. The next section is concerned with the principles governing election broadcasts, while Section 3 deals more briefly with other types of party political programmes and government statements. The common characteristic of all these broadcasts is that they are largely under the control of a political party. The last section of the chapter is concerned with the application of the fairness and balance principles to news and other programmes for which the broadcasting companies are themselves responsible.

A threshold question is how and by whom these principles are determined. A constitutional court, as in West Germany, may lay down the basic principles. Subject to them and to the requirements of the *Parteiengesetz*, broadcasting time is determined by the state broadcasting authority. In Britain and Italy, on the other hand, the politicians themselves have generally exercised direct control over the allocation of election and other party broadcasts. A Party Political Broadcasting Committee

[10] See Ch. VII, S. 1 above.

(PPBC) has effectively regulated political and election broadcasting in Britain (though not Northern Ireland) since 1947, and has allocated broadcasting times between the parties on the basis of various criteria to be discussed later in this chapter.[11] But in the absence of agreement between the parties before the 1987 General Election, the broadcasting authorities themselves (the BBC and the IBA) allotted the times. The 1975 Italian statute provides for the televised round-table political discussions (*tribune politiche, tribune elettorale*) to be governed by the Parliamentary Commission. Its decisions are not reviewable in the courts, an immunity which enables it to exclude minor parties and independents and which has naturally been the subject of considerable criticism.[12] As has, however, already been intimated, this is an area where courts are reluctant to intervene, even though they must be aware of the risk of bias on the part of political and parliamentary bodies.

Two other general issues should be discussed. The first is whether the principles should differ for public and private broadcasting. Originally they were of course formulated in the context of the former, except in the United States. In Britain the arrangements for political and electoral broadcasts made after the last world war with the BBC now apply to all national and regional terrestrial broadcasting, but not to cable and satellite. The Broadcasting Act 1990 requires licensees (for Channels 3 and 5, as well as Channel 4) to show political broadcasts as a condition of their licence; the ITC may for this purpose tell them which parties are to be given broadcasting opportunities, and regulate how long these broadcasts may last.[13] On the other hand, in Italy the private sector has been entirely unregulated in this context, as it has been until recently in virtually all others. This has been exploited in recent elections, particularly by the Socialist Party, long a supporter of Berlusconi, which paid less than other parties for its spots in the 1987 election.[14] An attempt to regulate the practice in the 1990 broadcasting law failed; a provision which would have required private broadcasters to charge the same rates and apply the same conditions to all parties and candidates was deleted when the measure reached the Chamber of Deputies.

The German Constitutional Court does not, it seems, require any positive rules to guarantee equality of advertising rights on the private broadcasting media. In its landmark ruling of 1962,[15] which laid down the fundamental principles of election broadcasting, the Court intimated that,

[11] See Ss. 2 and 3 below.

[12] See M. Manetti, 'L'accesso al mezzo radiotelevisivo pubblico come situazione giuridicamente protetta' [1984] *Giur. cost.* 176, 201–6.

[13] S. 36.

[14] P. Mancini, 'La "prima volta" degli *Spots* politici' (1984) 9 *Problemi dell' informazione* 7.

[15] 14 BVerfGE 121 (1962).

when private radio and television were permitted, broadcasting time could be freely purchased by the parties according to their financial resources. The fundamental principle of equality of opportunity only required that the legal order did not discriminate between the parties in an arbitrary way.[16] In contrast the French Conseil constitutionnel required the legislature to frame rules to prevent the wealthier parties from taking advantage of the opportunities for political advertising created by the 1986 law in its original version (but now removed by an amendment to its terms in 1990).[17]

In principle the same rules should apply to political and election broadcasts on public and private channels. Allowing parties to buy time according to their means would entail treating the private broadcasting media in the same way as the press, as the German Constitutional Court explicitly recognized. Now whether parity of treatment is generally appropriate, it is certainly not in this context. The principles of broadcasting freedom should be weighed with, and interpreted by reference to, other (constitutional) principles of equality of opportunity for political parties and of non-discrimination.[18] It would make nonsense, it is suggested, of the fairness rules applying to the public broadcasting sector, if parties were free to purchase more time for election broadcasts on private channels. (This argument might not apply in a society such as the United States of America, where there is no well-established public system with a firm tradition of political neutrality.) In principle it seems as unacceptable for a private broadcaster to exclude a political party from access to his station by charging high advertising rates, as it would be for access to be denied altogether on the ground of its political beliefs.

A second general question is how far broadcasting companies retain a residual right to veto or control the contents of these programmes. A distinction should be drawn between party political and election broadcasts on the one hand, and the coverage of press conferences and election debates on the other. The latter are subject to the editorial control of the broadcasters; indeed it is for them to decide whether to transmit them at all, and what are the appropriate times and other arrangements for their transmission. Thus it is for the networks in the United States to decide whether to televise a Presidential press conference and whether to allow a rival candidate (from the same party) the same opportunity.[19]

[16] 14 BVerfGE 121 (1962) 134.

[17] Decision 86-217 of 18 Sept. 1986, Rec. 1986, 141; Debbasch, 245. The law of 15 Jan. 1990, Art. 22 forbids all political advertising.

[18] See e.g. the German Basic Law, Arts. 3 (equality before the law) and 21 (free establishment of political parties), and the Italian Constitution, Arts. 3 (equality before the law) and 49 (freedom of association for political parties).

[19] *Kennedy for President Committee* v. *FCC (Kennedy I)* 636 F. 2d. 417 (DC Cir. 1980). Also see below, p. 187.

Equally they are free to exclude minority party Presidential candidates from televised debates between the Republican and Democratic Party candidates.[20] The courts denied the applicant candidates constitutional and statutory rights in these cases. This was not necessarily because such rights would infringe the First Amendment freedom of broadcasters. The explanation for the decisions is that the Federal Communications Act only recognizes a limited right of access for political candidates to purchase time from licensees.[21]

In Britain and Germany it is also accepted that it is for the broadcasters to choose who appears on current affairs programmes, though editorial discretion is subject to the general obligations to be fair and impartial.[22] It would not be permissible for a broadcaster, whether public or private, to present a discussion programme or series of such programmes, where one party's voice predominated over the others or where one party was totally excluded. A German case indicates how editorial discretion may be limited in the case of programmes shown shortly before elections.[23] The Constitutional Court upheld an order restraining a public broadcasting channel from transmitting three days before an election a discussion programme which excluded the Greens. The application of fairness and impartiality standards requires great sensitivity in this context, especially in the area of news broadcasts. What is clear, however, is that broadcasters have some, if limited, discretion.

In contrast it is for the political parties to determine the content and style of their own broadcasts, and of course they are free to misrepresent their own (and their opponents') intentions. In Britain at any rate, the parties provide and pay for their own film, though they may get technical advice from broadcasting staff.[24] Difficulties may arise if the broadcasting institution considers that the election or other party political programme violates the law. For example, an extreme right-wing party broadcast might contravene the law on incitement to racial hatred. The German Constitutional Court has held that the Intendant is entitled to examine the programme before its transmission to see whether it violates the criminal law, and in a clear case to prohibit it.[25] But allowing the party's appeal in this case from the Administrative Appeal Court of Münster,[26] the Constitutional Court ruled that it was wrong to stop the broadcast on

[20] *Johnson & Walton* v. *FCC* 829 F. 2d. 157 (DC Cir. 1987).

[21] *CBS* v. *FCC* 453 US 367 (1981).

[22] For a general discussion of broadcasters' discretion in the content of news broadcasts etc. during election campaigns, see A. Grupp, 'Redaktionell gestalte Rundfunksendungen vor Wahlen' (1983) 16 *Zeitschrift für Rechtspolitik* 28. See S. 4 below.

[23] 82 BVerfGE 54 (1990).

[24] See Goldie, *Facing the Nation*, 134–5, and Cockerell, *Live from Number 10*, 71–4.

[25] 47 BVerfGE 198 (1978).

[26] [1976] *DVBl.* 585.

the ground that its tone was hostile to the spirit of the Constitution (*verfassungsfeindliche*). The Intendant's power to exercise some degree of preliminary control did not violate the prohibition of censorship contained in Article 5(3) of the Basic Law. In the Court's view the control was not exercised over the contents of the party broadcast, but was designed to ensure that it was a genuine election broadcast.

The German Constitutional Court also pointed out that political parties have no constitutional right to broadcast on radio and television; their only constitutional right is to equality of opportunity. A limited degree of administrative control to ensure that their broadcasts were genuine contributions to electoral debate did not, therefore, infringe their rights. The United States Supreme Court would not agree with that. It has unanimously held that broadcasting companies have no power to control the remarks of candidates exercising their statutory right to equal broadcasting opportunities under the 1934 legislation.[27] There is a case for allowing the broadcasting authorities some residual control, but it should be exercised only in exceptional circumstances.[28]

2. ELECTION BROADCASTS

It is strange now to remember that the first election broadcasts in Britain were transmitted only in 1951, and that at the election the previous year the parties had actually declined the BBC's invitation to address the electorate in this way.[29] Forty years later a politician's ability to charm viewers at home is regarded as a highly significant attribute, and sometimes is even considered decisive to the election result. In principle there is an argument for recognizing some right of access of political parties to make use of television and radio during election campaigns, or at least a legally enforceable right to equal or fair treatment. Yet in this area there is relatively little law, and only in Germany have the courts formulated constitutional principles. The explanation lies in the understandable, if regrettable, desire of the political parties to reserve to themselves as much effective control as possible, reinforced by a reluctance on the courts' part to interfere in such delicate matters.

In some countries the basic framework is set out in legislation. This is, for example, the position in France, where the 1986 law, like its predecessor of 1982, requires the public broadcasting stations to transmit election broadcasts; the precise obligations are laid down in the *cahiers des*

[27] *Farmers Educational & Cooperative Union* v. *WDAY* 360 US 525 (1959).

[28] A German case has emphasized the limited scope of the Intendant's powers: Decision of Administrative Court of Berlin of 18 Jan. 1989 [1990] *NJW* 402.

[29] Goldie, *Facing the Nation*, 92.

charges and by administrative rules of the CSA.[30] Election broadcasts on the private channels in France are also regulated by its recommendations.[31] The United States Communications Act was amended in 1971, in effect to allow all candidates for federal office the right to reasonable free access or (if the broadcasters prefer) to purchase it from broadcasting stations.[32] The right is compatible with the First Amendment;[33] in practice access is enforced by the FCC, which may withdraw a licence if it finds that the licensee has wilfully or repeatedly failed to grant it. The Court said that broadcasters were required to accommodate the candidate's needs so far as possible, though they were also entitled to take into consideration the amount of air-time previously sold to the candidate and the disruptive effect on the station's schedule. But candidates have no right to free air-time, even to balance the advertisements paid for by their wealthier rivals.[34]

A legal system may refuse to recognize any right of access, whether paid for or free, but recognize a right of political parties to equal or fair access, once television and radio channels have freely decided to transmit election broadcasts. But there may be some difficulty in determining exactly what a right to fair treatment entails in this context. In particular it is not clear whether fairness and equality of opportunity require the equal treatment of political parties and groups, no matter what their size or importance may be. If not, what does fairness require, and are there any workable standards to help decide hard cases? There is also the question, already touched on, whether fairness should be applied equally to both public and private broadcasters.

The fullest consideration of these questions is to be found in the jurisprudence of the German Constitutional Court, particularly in its key ruling in 1962.[35] Public broadcasting authorities, it stated, should be neutral during election campaigns and respect the equal opportunities of political parties. But this does not entail any right to absolute equality of access to the airwaves. Elections should lead to the formation of a government; the work of the legislature would be rendered difficult if a

[30] Law of 30 Sept. 1986, Art. 16(1), replacing Art. 14 of the law of 29 July 1982. Also see Art. 15 of the *cahiers* of Antenne 2 and of FR3.

[31] Law of 30 Sept. 1986, Art. 16(2).

[32] See *Kennedy for President Committee* v. *FCC (Kennedy II)* 636 F. 2d. 432 (1980), where it was held that the amendment was not intended to institute a right to free air-time to reply to the broadcasts of opponents; the licensee could satisfy his obligations by providing free time or by selling it.

[33] *CBS* v. *FCC* 453 US 367 (1981).

[34] *Morrisson* v. *Mt. Mansfield Television* 580 F. Supp. 512 (DC Vt. 1974). Some commentators argue for the introduction of free access rights, as one way of reducing the escalating costs of elections: C. Kendrick, 'The Case for Re-regulation of Campaign Broadcasting' (1992) 21 *Southwestern Univ. L. Rev.* 185.

[35] 14 BVerfGE 121 (1962).

large number of small parties were represented there. Therefore, the political parties capable of forming a government should be given more opportunity to present their case on radio and television. This argument was buttressed by reference to the responsibilities of the broadcasting authorities under Article 5 of the Basic Law: they are entitled to take account of the respective strengths of the political parties in allocating broadcasting opportunities.

An important factor in this allocation is the strength of the parties at the previous election, but this cannot be the only consideration, for otherwise more recent political developments would be ignored. Other relevant factors are the length and continuity of the parties' existence, their membership, the extent and strength of their organization, and their representation in Parliament and government (at the level of both Bund and *Länder*). In contrast, the Court thought irrelevant the number of candidates a party fielded. It is too easy for it to put up a candidate for each seat, and it is not, therefore, a reliable indicator of its strength. As will shortly be discussed, British practice seems to take a different view on this last point. In the 1962 case the Bundesverfassungsgericht rejected a constitutional complaint by the Free Democratic Party, the third force in German politics, that Westdeutscher Rundfunk had refused it the share of broadcasting time to which it was entitled: although it had won only 7.5 per cent of the seats after the last *Land* election in North Rhine–Westphalia, for the current election it was allocated 17 per cent of the total time allocated the three major parties on television and 23 per cent of such time on radio. The Intendant had, therefore, exercised his discretion in a constitutionally proper manner.

While emphasizing the entitlement of the three large parties (CDP, SPD, FDP) to most of the available broadcasting time, the Court also made it clear that smaller parties should not be totally excluded from access.[36] Their treatment has given rise to difficulties in other cases. For example, claims by the Greens and other newer parties to equal treatment with the traditional parties have been rejected.[37] But the *Parteiengesetz* requires that (minority) parties with representation in the Bundestag must be given 50 per cent of the opportunities, including access to the media, afforded the larger parties,[38] and even new groups participating in elections for the first time are entitled to some access.[39] Overall the approach of the German courts strikes a nice balance between the demands of fairness and equality of opportunity on the one hand, and a sensible

[36] 14 BVerfGE 121 (1962) 138.

[37] See 34 BVerfGE 160 (1973), 48 BVerfGE 271 (1978), and (1981) 34 *DÖV* 186 (decision of Administrative Appeal Court for Rhineland-Pfalz).

[38] 1984 *BGBl.* 1, S. 243.

[39] 48 BVerfGE 271 (1978).

appreciation of the functions of elections on the other. From the parties' perspective, it may be hard to see any justification for disparate treatment; it is easier to explain in terms of the interests of the electorate in greater exposure to the arguments of the groups which might form a government.

Similar issues have arisen in litigation in Northern Ireland and Scotland. In the *Lynch* case[40] representatives of the Workers' Party complained that they had been excluded from an 'Election Forum' and a 'phone-in' programme. (These are admittedly not election broadcasts in the strict sense, but they have more in common with the latter than they do with news and current affairs programmes.) The party was excluded because it did not satisfy both of the two BBC requirements that they had candidates in at least five constituencies and also had polled at least 5 per cent of the vote in the Northern Ireland Assembly Election of 1982. Although it easily satisfied the former criterion, the party had polled only 2.7 per cent in the previous year's election. Hutton J. expressed serious doubts whether the BBC had an enforceable duty to be impartial, but even if it were under such a duty, no clear breach had been established. Impartiality did not require equality of treatment, and the twofold requirement for access was not unreasonable. German courts would presumably agree with the judge's rejection of the argument that the number of candidates was decisive, but might be less happy to accept the party's total exclusion from access programmes. Nor is Hutton J.'s point that its views were presented in regular news programmes persuasive. The distinctive feature of election and other similar broadcasts is that they are under the control of the party. The ruling denied the Worker's Party any opportunity to put across its ideas in its own way.

Even more difficult problems were raised in a Scottish case.[41] The Scottish National Party (SNP) challenged the allocation of party election broadcasts for the General Election of 1987, which had been made by the broadcasting authorities in the absence of agreement between the parties. The three major parties (Conservatives, Labour, and the Liberal–SDP Alliance) were given five broadcasts each, the SNP two, and Plaid Cymru one. (Of the five broadcasts for the major parties, transmitted in Scotland, two were specifically 'Scottish broadcasts', while the other three were transmitted throughout Britain.) The applicants' argument was that the IBA was in breach of its duties to be impartial and to show balance in the subject-matter of programmes, since it had not given enough weight to the Scottish dimension; in Scotland the SNP was entitled to equal treatment with the major British parties on the basis of the number of

[40] *Lynch* v. *BBC* [1983] 6 NIJB 1.
[41] *Wilson* v. *IBA (No. 2)* 1988 SLT 276.

candidates and the votes it had received recently in local by-elections. Lord Prosser agreed that there is a duty on the IBA to ensure a proper balance between the parties in the allocation of election broadcasts, but found that it had been discharged through the equal allocation of the specifically 'Scottish broadcasts'.[42] For the IBA to have imposed absolute equality would have been to ignore the United Kingdom dimension put forward by the three major British parties. The Court would intervene only if the authorities had acted unreasonably in discharging their statutory duties.

In contrast it is easier to lay down clear duties for referendums, where the electorate is invited simply to vote 'Yes' or 'No' to a particular proposition. The British broadcasting authorities allotted equal broadcasting time to the two umbrella organizations campaigning on the two sides in the 1975 Common Market Referendum.[43] This did not cause any legal difficulties. But the referendum on Scottish devolution led to litigation. The IBA proposed to divide direct broadcasting time equally between the major political parties, three of whom supported a 'Yes' vote and only one 'No'. The opponents of devolution successfully applied for an interdict to stop this series of broadcasts. The distribution violated the duty to show balance, which in this context required the equal treatment of proponents and opponents of devolution, not of the political parties.[44]

It is a nice question whether this interpretation of balance could sometimes be satisfactorily applied to general (or other) elections.[45] In some circumstances, where the political parties are divided on a single important issue which is the focus of the election, it might be right to allocate broadcasting time on the basis of equal treatment for the different views on that issue, rather than on the basis of the parties' respective strengths. But this will be very exceptional. In modern democracies, for better or worse, the rival claims of the parties to govern (or to take seats in the legislature) are more significant than the merits of particular issues, which in any case frequently change in importance during the course of the campaign. Further, in multi-party politics there are more than two views on most issues, so the solution adopted in the Scottish case would rarely be appropriate for election broadcasts. What is clear is that courts required to interpret fairness and balance requirements (whether constitutional or statutory) may be compelled to reflect on some fundamental principles:

[42] It was also held that the obligation to ensure that 'due impartiality is preserved on the part of the persons providing the programmes' only concerned the programmes of the programme companies and did not apply to the inherently partial party political broadcasts.

[43] D. Butler and U. Kitzinger, *The 1975 Referendum* (London, 1976), 195–201.

[44] *Wilson* v. *IBA* 1979 SLT 279.

[45] See A. E. Boyle, 'Political Broadcasting, Fairness and Administrative Law' [1986] *Pub. Law* 562, 581. (The discussion in this chapter of United Kingdom law is much indebted to this article.)

these include the purpose of elections or referendums, the status and rights of political parties (given constitutional recognition in some countries), and the role of broadcasting in relation to the political process and to the press.

Given these difficulties, judicial reluctance to intervene is not surprising. Further, political parties wish to keep control. This has been most marked in Britain and Italy. As has already been mentioned, under what is tantamount to a constitutional convention, election broadcasts in Britain are allocated by a Party Political Broadcasting Committee (PPBC) composed of representatives of the political parties and of the two broadcasting authorities.[46] When it was established after the last world war, only the Labour and Conservative Parties were represented, but the Liberals were admitted in 1960 and the two Nationalist parties in 1974. These changes reflected the improved performance of the smaller parties, as did the allocation of broadcasts. For example, in 1959 the Liberals had two election broadcasts, compared to five for the two major parties, but after their better results then and in subsequent by-elections, they were allowed three broadcasts in elections up to February 1974 and four in the October election that year. In the 1987 election, when the parties could not agree, the broadcasting authorities themselves granted the Liberal–SDP Alliance parity with the two old parties, while in 1992 the merged SLD was given four broadcasts, the major parties having five each. Since 1950 minor parties which put up at least fifty candidates have each been allowed one broadcast. It is not clear what criteria are applied when these decisions are taken. One Director-General of the BBC has testified that broadcasts are allocated according to the strengths of the parties in the House of Commons before dissolution,[47] but it seems now that the number of candidates and the votes of the parties at the previous election are also relevant. It cannot be right to allocate purely on the basis of previous electoral performance, for otherwise the claims of a new party, like the SDP, would be ignored until after it had contested one election.

There are considerable obstacles to mounting any legal challenge to allocation decisions. There are first the problems already mentioned of determining what fairness and balance require in the circumstances of an election campaign. Judges prefer to leave these questions to the discretion of broadcasting authorities and intervene only if it has been exercised arbitrarily. Additionally there are some doubts whether the BBC, a non-statutory body, is subject to judicial review, though these do

[46] See ibid. 575–80 for a full discussion of this Committee. Also see H. F. Rawlings, *Law and the Electoral Process* (London, 1988), 152–5.

[47] *Grieve* v. *Douglas-Home* 1965 SC, 315, 326 (Election Court).

not arise in the case of the IBA or ITC.[48] In so far as the authorities effectively leave the allocation to the PPBC (in effect the political parties) it has been argued that they have improperly delegated their discretion to a body, which is judge in its own cause.[49] However, a Scottish court in the first British case to discuss election broadcasts was wholly unwilling to entertain a challenge to the arrangements for national election broadcasts.[50] In contrast, when the broadcasting authorities under pressure from the major parties on the PPBC threatened to change the time of a Plaid Cymru election broadcast, the leader of that party was secured a mandatory injunction to compel them to show it at the agreed time. The Court of Appeal was very critical of the authorities' apparent deference to the PPBC.[51]

Comparable problems have arisen in Italy. Access to political and election broadcasts on public television is regulated by the Parliamentary Commission (Commissione parlamentare per l'indirizzo generale e la vigilanza dei servizi radiotelevisivi). The Commission itself allocates the times of party broadcasts during election and referendum campaigns, and, it seems, exercises effective control over the director of these programmes, although strictly he is responsible to the Director-General of RAI.[52] Attempts by minority parties and referendum proponents to challenge decisions of the Commission (either for excluding them from participation in the cycle of political and election programmes or for giving them too little time) have met with no success.[53] The courts have held that the Commission, as an organ of Parliament, is not subject to review, either in the ordinary or in the administrative courts. The political parties represented in Parliament do have rights to election broadcasts, but their allocation is a non-reviewable political question.[54] Thus there is no redress for the minority parties or independent deputies to whom the larger parties have denied equivalent opportunities.[55] It is surely unsatis-

[48] It is for this reason that the legal challenges in the two Scottish cases were brought against the IBA rather than the BBC.

[49] *Ecology Party* v. *BBC & IBA* (unreported, 1984), discussed by Rawlings, *Law and the Electoral Process*, 160.

[50] See Lord Migdale in *Grieve* v. *Douglas-Home* 1965 SC 315, 326.

[51] *Evans* v. *BBC & IBA*, *The Times*, 26 Feb. 1974. For a critical discussion of the case, see J. Potter, *Independent Television in Britain*, iii: *Politics and Control 1968–80* (London, 1989), 164–7.

[52] E. Cheli, 'Pubblicità e politica: il caso italiano' [1981] *Diritto radiodiffusione e telecommunicazione* 229, 235.

[53] In particular see the rulings of the Corte costituzionale in case 139/77, reprinted in Pace, 355, and of the Corte di cassazione in Decision 1984/7072 [1984] *Giur. cost.* 175.

[54] Ibid. 200–4.

[55] E. Grassi, 'Elezioni locali e propaganda radiotelevisive tra pubblico e privato', in P. Barile, E. Cheli, and R. Zaccaria (eds.), *Radiotelevisione pubblica e privata in Italia* (Bologna, 1980), 365.

factory in principle for control to be vested in a Parliamentary body dominated by the established parties.

3. OTHER POLITICAL BROADCASTS

Political parties make considerable use of the media outside election campaigns. They do this to some extent through regular political broadcasts made under their own control and partly through the broadcasters' coverage of their conferences and other activities. In this second type of programme editorial control remains with the channel and its staff, though politicians consistently try, often successfully, to exercise influence over its presentation.[56] Arrangements for regular party political broadcasts in Britain follow the pattern for election broadcasts. Their allocation is determined by the PPBC, largely on the basis of the parties' performance in votes at the previous general election, although by-election results after the first two years of a parliament are also taken into account.[57] Sometimes the broadcasting authorities may take the initiative, particularly in order to secure better opportunities for minor parties unrepresented on the Committee. It is no longer necessary for the broadcasts to be shown at the same time on all channels.

There is of course no question in Britain of an entitlement to make such programmes. A party excluded from the arrangements would have no recourse in the courts, unless it could argue that the authorities had violated their duties of fairness and balance. Nor would an application to the European Commission of Human Rights be successful, for it has been decided that there is no right of access under the Convention for a political group wishing to advertise its arguments on television.[58] (Interestingly, the Commission stated that there might be a violation of the Convention if a political party were denied broadcasting opportunities at election time when other parties were afforded them.)

Other countries are more generous in this respect. For example, the French law of 1986 confers access rights on political parties represented by a group in either the Assembly or the Senate.[59] Detailed rules have been issued by the CSA.[60] Nine groups share the time allotted for television broadcasts, five hours thirty minutes annually divided between the

[56] See Cockerell, *Live from Number 10*, 128, 163–4, 181–3, 201.

[57] Boyle, 'Political Broadcasting, Fairness and Administrative Law', 575–8. The allocation of party political broadcasts is set out in the annual BBC Handbooks.

[58] 4515/70, *X and Assoc. of Z.* v. *UK* 38 Coll. Dec. 86.

[59] Law of 30 Sept. 1986, Art. 55(2).

[60] Decision 90-11 of 9 Jan. 1990, discussed by C. Debbasch, *Droit de l'audiovisuel*, 2nd edn. (Paris, 1991), 521–2.

two public channels, and one hour thirty minutes allotted on Radio France. But unlike in Britain there is no free access to private television and radio channels. (The French law of 1986 did give parties the freedom to advertise on all channels at their own expense, but the provision was never implemented; in 1990 the law was amended and all political advertising is forbidden.[61]) In Italy political parties may advertise on the private channels and have the same right to participate in the regular round-table political discussion programmes (*tribune politiche*) on RAI that they enjoy for election discussion programmes.[62] The allocation of such opportunities is, however, a matter for the Parliamentary Commission, and the right, therefore, cannot be enforced in the courts.

Another type of broadcast is the ministerial or governmental announcement. Sometimes it might be made on a wholly non-controversial matter, for example, to discourage drinking and driving, to announce an anti-drug campaign, or to outline measures taken to meet a natural catastrophe. In Germany the federal and state governments, and sometimes other public authorities, have legal rights to make announcements of this kind on both public and private channels.[63] These announcements have no political content and do not present problems. This is not the case with politically controversial broadcasts, where the opposition might well claim that it should enjoy an opportunity to reply. In Britain these questions are governed by an *aide-mémoire* representing an agreement between the parties and the BBC. It was revised in 1969, to provide for an automatic right of reply to broadcasts on matters of prime national or international importance.[64] Previously it had been for the BBC itself to decide whether to allow the opposition an opportunity to broadcast in reply to the Prime Minister (or other government member), a task which had sometimes put it in great difficulty, as, for example, during the Suez crisis. Gaitskell, the Leader of the Labour Opposition, successfully claimed a right of reply, as he did a few years later when Macmillan broadcast on the application of the United Kingdom to join the Common Market.[65] Not only is an automatic right of reply fairer as between the government and main opposition party, but its recognition may have led to a decline in the use (and abuse) of the ministerial broadcast.[66]

[61] Law of 15 Jan. 1990, Art. 22, amending Art. 14 of the law of 30 Sept. 1986.

[62] Law 103 of 1975, Art. 4.

[63] See e.g. Rhineland-Pfalz law of 24 June 1986, Art. 14, North Rhine–Westphalia law of 11 Jan. 1988, Art. 19, and Saarland law of 11 Aug. 1987, Art. 9.

[64] The text is printed in an appendix to the annual BBC Handbook. Also see Boyle, 'Political Broadcasting, Fairness and Administrative Law', 582–3.

[65] For discussion of these episodes, see Cockerell, *Live from Number 10*, 49–52, 84–5.

[66] The institution of the automatic right of reply followed what some considered the excessive use of the ministerial broadcast by Harold Wilson: Cockerell, *Live from Number 10*, 115–17.

In practice government ministers, in particular the Prime Minister, find it more profitable to secure publicity for their activities in other ways. A television press conference or an interview on a widely watched current affairs programme is more likely to achieve their ends than the austere format of a ministerial broadcast. Moreover, press conferences and interviews do not attract any right of reply by the opposition. Admittedly statutory balance and fairness requirements apply, so it is incumbent on the broadcaster to grant similar facilities at some stage to opposition parties.[67] However, a subsequent opportunity to participate in a similar programme is not as valuable as an immediate right of reply; public interest in the subject may have evaporated and the circumstances and timing of the later programme may be significantly different from those of the earlier one. This distinction is nicely illustrated by a French case.[68] Under the 1982 law (as now under the 1986 statute), there was a right of reply (*droit de réplique*) to government broadcasts made at its own initiative.[69] But no right of reply was granted when a television channel invited the Prime Minister to answer questions at a press conference. The Conseil d'État upheld the High Authority's view that in these circumstances only the general requirements of equality and respect for the balance of opinion applied.

Events like press conferences and annual party conferences fall into a category situated between formal party broadcasts on the one hand and regular news coverage and current affairs programmes on the other. As will be discussed in Section 4, news broadcasts are subject to the loose and generally unenforceable duties of balance and impartiality, rather than immediate rights of reply. Press and annual conferences, however, are convened by the parties themselves, and the former at least are covered by the broadcasting media at the parties' request. There is, therefore, something to be said for treating them in the same way as formal political and election broadcasts. That would mean that where a governing party convenes a press or special conference, a right of reply should be granted the principal opposition party, followed by a discussion between all the major parties, as now happens automatically in the case of controversial ministerial broadcasts in Britain.[70] Alternatively, if the Prime Minister holds a press conference on a controversial topic covered live on television (whether public or private), the broadcasting authorities

[67] This was the view of the BBC when party press conferences were first televised in the 1950s: Goldie, *Facing the Nation*, 116–17.

[68] *Labbé & Gaudin*, C.E. 20 May 1985, Rec. 157, noted by N. Griesbeck, 1986 DS. J. 12, and by R. Errara [1986] *Pub. Law* 155.

[69] Law of 29 July 1982, Art. 33; law of 30 Sept. 1986, Art. 54. The *droit de réplique* is to be distinguished from the *droit de réponse* of persons who have been defamed: see Ch. VII, S. 4.

[70] Boyle, 'Political Broadcasting, Fairness and Administrative Law', 582–3.

should be under a legal duty to give the same treatment to a press conference convened by the main opposition party. The comparative rarity and identifiability of these events make it relatively easy to enforce reply rights or general duties of balance. However, as will be discussed in the next section, in the United States press conferences are treated in the same way as conventional news stories and escape the 'equal opportunity' rules.

4. NEWS AND CURRENT AFFAIRS PROGRAMMES

Unlike party broadcasts these programmes are controlled by the broadcasting authority and its staff. It is for the editor to determine what should be included in news bulletins and which topics discussed in current affairs programmes. Clearly they should not be subject to government or party political control, although politicians are as free as other people to impose conditions on the circumstances in which they are interviewed.[71] As in other contexts, broadcasters must not pursue a particular editorial line, must produce balanced programme schedules, and must be impartial.[72] In Britain, for example, the ITC must do what it can to ensure that news—bulletins and programmes—(on all channels) 'is presented with due accuracy and impartiality'.[73] Further, complaints may be made to the Broadcasting Complaints Commission (BCC) in respect (*inter alia*) of 'unjust or unfair treatment' in television or radio programmes (public or private).[74] This procedure applies to news and current affairs programmes, allowing political parties in some circumstances to complain that they have been improperly treated. Broadcasters charged with implementing these provisions may come under pressure from the government and other politicians. Supervisory agencies, such as the ITC, FCC, or the CSA, can assist broadcasting bodies to resist improper pressure by defending their decisions. Of course they should intervene when the broadcasters have not treated a politician or his party fairly.

The difficulties of this area of broadcasting law are well illustrated by the English case *R.* v. *Broadcasting Complaints Commission, ex parte Owen*.[75] The leader of the Social Democratic Party, with the support of the Liberal Party leader, complained to the BCC that over a period of more than two months the views of the two Alliance parties had received

[71] During election campaigns a candidate has the right to stop the broadcast of any item, such as an interview, in which he is actively taking part, but not to stop the broadcast of a film showing him campaigning: see *Marshall* v. *BBC* [1979] 1 WLR 1071.

[72] For a full discussion of these duties, see Ch. V, S. 2.

[73] Broadcasting Act 1990, s. 6(1)(c).

[74] Broadcasting Act 1990, s. 143(1)(a).

[75] [1985] QB 1153.

very little coverage on news and current affairs programmes in comparison with the Labour Party, although at the general election the previous year (1983) it had received almost as large a share of the vote (not, of course, under the first-past-the-post electoral system reflected in the number of seats). The BCC held it had no jurisdiction to consider this type of political complaint about inadequate coverage in a range of programmes, and also ruled that even if it had jurisdiction it would not be appropriate to exercise it in these circumstances. While deciding with some hesitation that the Commission did have jurisdiction, the Divisional Court accepted that it had lawfully exercised its discretion not to investigate the complaint. In particular the Court thought it was impossible for the BCC to rule without interfering with the broadcasters' editorial policy on a political issue. In essence the complainant was arguing that the Alliance should have more or less the same coverage as the official opposition party because it had obtained nearly as many votes at the last election. The broadcasters were entitled to take a different view. The Court was less impressed with the practical argument that it would be burdensome to analyse the news broadcasts and other programmes over a long period in order to adjudicate.

The Divisional Court adopted the same cautious approach as other British courts do when asked to enforce impartiality in election broadcasts;[76] the standards leave considerable discretion to the broadcasting bodies and their judgement should only be questioned if it is grossly unreasonable or arbitrary. In fact the challenge in the *Owen* case was to the BCC's refusal to investigate the complaint, rather than a direct review of the broadcasters' discretion. The Commission had felt unable to decide what standards should govern news and current affairs broadcasts in a multi-party democracy, though it is arguable that this is a matter which a regulatory authority (though perhaps not the BCC, a complaints body) might be expected to consider.

A reluctance to intervene is also evidenced in a number of Italian cases, where the Radical Party and other minority groups, or the promoters of a referendum, complained that RAI had not given them adequate coverage.[77] The public broadcasting service must be objective and impartial, but the courts rejected the argument that the duty entailed an enforceable right for political parties to be given fair or comprehensive news treatment. Nor was the Rome Court of Appeal impressed by an argument that inadequate news coverage violated Article 21 of the Constitution guaranteeing freedom of speech.[78] There was no evidence

[76] See in particular *Wilson* v. *IBA (No.2)* 1988 SLT 276 discussed in S. 2 above.

[77] See the decisions of the Pretura di Roma of 10 June 1976 and of 15 June 1977, and of the Tribunale di Roma of 8 July 1978, reprinted in Pace, 273, 281, 284.

[78] Ibid. 303, reprinting decision of 19 July 1982.

that there had been any interference with the freedom of programme-makers. The basic principles of the 1975 law were to be safeguarded by the Parliamentary Commission rather than the courts. This conclusion was hardly satisfactory from the perspective of minority parties or extra-Parliamentary groups. The remedy is to leave enforcement of the principles of balance and fairness with an agency, independent as far as possible from political control, rather than attempt to fashion individual rights enforceable in the courts.

On the other hand, courts and complaints bodies may intervene in extreme cases. The German Constitutional Court upheld the order granted the Green Party to restrain the showing on Westdeutscher Rundfunk Köln (WDR) of a discussion programme shown three days before the state elections.[79] The discussion would have included leading candidates of three main parties (CDP, SPD, and FDP), but not the Greens. In these circumstances it was more important to avert the serious injury to their right to fair electoral opportunity, than to respect WDR's editorial freedom under Article 5 of the Basic Law. The Court was able to intervene, because of the protection afforded by the Constitution to the rights of political parties to fair treatment; it should also be remembered that the application was for a restraining order in an emergency, and the judgment did not, therefore, conclusively resolve how the constitutional rights should be balanced. In Britain the Broadcasting Complaints Commission has held that a television current affairs programme treated a local Social and Liberal Democrat constituency party unfairly by more or less omitting it from a feature about the constituency; this concentrated on the prospects of the Labour and Conservative candidates, despite the fact that at the previous election the candidate for the Alliance (the predecessor of the SLD) finished second.[80] The salient point is that this was a complaint by an individual constituency party about unfair treatment in a particular feature, rather than (as in the *Owen* case) a grievance about overall injustice over a range of programmes.

The United States Communications Act 1934 has generally been interpreted to give maximum discretion to broadcasters and to recognize only limited rights for candidates and political parties. Under amendments to the legislation made in 1959, a number of exemptions were introduced from the requirement imposed on station owners that they afford equal opportunities to all candidates for public office. This requirement had begun to hinder broadcasters in their presentation of news; if one candidate received publicity, then equal time would have to be provided for others.[81] From 1959 the equal opportunities rule did not apply to bona fide newscasts, news interviews and documentaries, and live coverage of

[79] 82 BVerfGE 54 (1990).
[80] Annual Report of the BCC 1991, HC 533, 81.
[81] The origins of the exemptions from the equal time rule are briefly discussed in S. J. Simmons, *The Fairness Doctrine and the Media* (Berkeley, Calif., 1978), 47–50.

bona fide events, such as the political conventions. Even in these cases stations remained subject to the looser constraints of the Fairness Doctrine discussed in Chapter VII. At first the FCC considered that these exemptions did not preclude application of the equal opportunities rule to press conferences convened by candidates, but this opinion was revised after ten years and the change approved by the DC Circuit Court of Appeals.[82] It held that there is no statutory right to equal coverage of press conferences, a matter over which broadcasters are allowed substantial discretion. The networks were therefore free to give air-time to the press conferences of President Carter when he was seeking re-election and to deny coverage of the apparently less newsworthy conferences held by his rival, Senator Ted Kennedy.[83] The Court pointed out that the Senator did have a right to purchase television time under section 312(A)(7) of the Communications Act. But that was not really equivalent to the facilities enjoyed by the President.[84] The Court of Appeals has also rejected the argument that there is a First Amendment right to equal coverage of a candidate's press conference.[85] Subsequently it denied a minor party Presidential candidate a right either under the Constitution or under the equal opportunities rule to participate in a televised debate between Republican and Democrat Party candidates.[86]

The cavalier treatment in the United States of the arguments (both statutory and constitutional) for equal opportunities is not surprising. With the retreat from the *Red Lion* principle discussed in the previous chapter,[87] both courts and FCC have generally stressed the First Amendment rights of broadcasters. Legally they are treated in much the same way as newspaper owners. There has been no tradition in the USA of equal free access of government and opposition to a public broadcasting system; instead parties have been free to advertise on the commercial networks without financial limits. Moreover, the amendments of 1959 clearly permit, though they do not require, the exemption of press conferences and election debates from the equal opportunities rule. I have suggested, however, that in principle press conferences ought to be subject to right of reply or equal time rules in the same way as ministerial (and party political) broadcasts. Otherwise it is too easy for governing political parties to evade the strict rules (prevailing in most European jurisdictions) designed to ensure the fair treatment of government and opposition. The interpretation placed on the amendments to the Communications Act benefits incumbents, because their activities and conferences are more newsworthy than are those of their challengers.[88]

[82] *Chisholm* v. *FCC* 538 F. 2d. 349 (1976).

[83] *Kennedy for President Committee* v. *FCC (Kennedy I)* 636 F. 2d. 417 (DC Cir. 1980).

[84] The right to purchase time has been held constitutional with regard to the First Amendment in *CBS* v. *FCC* 453 US 367 (1981): see S. 1 above.

[85] *Kennedy for President Committee* v. *FCC (Kennedy I)* 636 F. 2d. 417.

[86] *Johnson & Walton* v. *FCC* 829 F. 2d. 157 (DC Cir. 1987).

[87] Ch. VII, S. 4.

[88] See Powe, ch. 9.

IX
Advertising

1. THE ROLE OF ADVERTISING

Private radio and television are largely financed by revenue from advertising and sponsorship. The other source of support for commercial broadcasting comes from subscription income, though at present that is much more significant for cable and satellite than it is for terrestrial services. In many countries advertising also provides finance for public broadcasting, additional to the licence fee or equivalent charge (discussed in Chapter III). Only in Britain, of the jurisdictions considered in this book, is the public broadcasting system entirely forbidden to support itself in this way. Prohibitions on commercials in Italy and France were lifted in 1957 and 1968 respectively, well before the advent of private broadcasting, while it has always been an important source of support for ARD and ZDF. Advertising is a feature of all European broadcasting systems, with the exception of Norway; it has only recently been introduced in Sweden on one of the three terrestrial television channels.[1]

In the case of public broadcasting, advertising was only regarded at first as a subsidiary source of income to supplement the licence fee. Strict limits were imposed on the frequency of commercials; in France and Italy there have also been ceilings on the amount of revenue a public broadcasting authority could raise from advertising.[2] The primary purpose of these restraints is to preserve the quality of programmes against the pressure of advertisers to remove serious items from the schedule. Secondly, advertising limits are imposed to safeguard the income of the daily and periodical press, which has often feared a loss of advertising revenue to the broadcasting media.

With the advent of private broadcasting in all major European countries (save for Austria) and the increasing tolerance of commercials on public channels, advertising has become a prominent feature of the broadcasting landscape. With the reluctance of governments to raise the licence fee, public broadcasters are increasingly compelled to turn to advertising and sponsorship for financial support. In France Antenne 2,

[1] Advertising was only permitted in Belgium by the law of 6 Feb. 1987: *Moniteur belge*, 3 Apr. 1987.

[2] For details of these rules, see S. 4 below.

the major public channel after the privatization of TF1 in 1986, receives well over half its revenue in this way.[3] Advertising agents have been prominent in pressing for relaxation of programme standards and the restraints imposed on commercials. Naturally they are also eager to exploit the opportunities created by the development of satellite and cable, though these openings may mean that terrestrial broadcasters, private and public, will find it harder to attract advertising revenue in the next few years.[4]

Indeed, the danger now is that broadcasting, particularly television, will be governed by commercial pressures. Broadcasters will become solely concerned with audience ratings and not with their programmes' intrinsic quality. As an American advertising agent has explained: 'The networks are in the business not of delivering programmes, that's not their business. The networks' business is to deliver audiences.'[5] Increasing competition between terrestrial, cable, and satellite channels reinforces the tendency to draw up schedules dominated by mass entertainment material.

This development may be accompanied by changes in the relationship between programme companies and advertisers. While advertising agents are usually ineligible to apply for broadcasting licences,[6] they may supply large chunks of a daily programme, mostly films and soap operas, to private channels. This used to be common in the United States until the 1950s.[7] Under another practice, known as 'barter syndication', networks and large broadcasting companies provide local channels with programmes at discount prices or even without charge. The latter are, however, contractually required to take their advertisements from the agencies which pay the programme provider. While the practice may enable smaller broadcasting companies to show films they could not otherwise afford, it has disturbing implications for their programming freedom.[8] Similar arrangements have enabled Berlusconi to increase his dominance

[3] In the late 1980s it received about 60–65 per cent of its income from advertising, compared to about 35 per cent for RAI in Italy and for ZDF in Germany: see *Europe 2000: What Kind of Television?* (Report of the European Television Task Force, Manchester, 1988), table 3.1.

[4] For a sympathetic view of the demands of advertisers, see C. Veljanovski, 'The Role of Advertising in Broadcasting Policy', in C. Veljanovski (ed.), *Freedom in Broadcasting* (London, 1989), 99. Also see H. Merkle, 'Europafernsehen aus der Sicht der Werbungtreibenden', in *Europafernsehen und Werbung* (Baden-Baden, 1986), 61–9.

[5] Quoted in J. G. Blumler, 'Television in the United States: Funding Sources and Programme Consequences', in *Research on the Range and Quality of Broadcasting Services* (report prepared for the Peacock Committee), 108.

[6] See Ch. IV, S. 4 for the rules on eligibility to apply for private broadcasting licences.

[7] D. Kellner, *Television and the Crisis of Democracy* (Oxford, 1990), 43–6; B. H. Bagdikian, *The Media Monopoly* (Boston, 1990), 140–1.

[8] Blumler, 'Television in the United States', 100. Also see the *Guardian*, 9 May 1988, 23.

of the broadcasting market in Italy. It had been the aggressive innovative practices of his advertising company Publitalia which made it possible for him to acquire a leading position in that market during the 1980s.[9]

The importance of advertising in the European broadcasting context was highlighted in 1989 by the enactment of the EC Broadcasting Directive and by the agreement of the Council of Europe Transfrontier Television Convention. The background to, and general content of, these measures is discussed in Chapter X. What may be emphasized here is the part played by advertising considerations in shaping these measures. Advertising agents want to communicate their messages freely across national boundaries in order to attract the attention of viewers in a number of countries.[10] This is difficult, if not impossible, when states are free to prohibit the retransmission of commercials which violate their own advertising codes, although they comply with the requirements of the transmitting state. The answer is to provide for the free reception and retransmission of broadcasts which satisfy the advertising (and other basic) rules of the state where they originate—the principal object of the two European measures. These rules must, however, comply with the standards set out in the Directive or the Convention.

Neither the Convention nor the Directive adopts the view that advertising should be wholly unregulated. Both measures require restraints on its frequency and contents. Such restrictions are also a standard feature of national laws, now of course influenced by the requirements of the two European documents. It is, however, worth exploring at the outset whether these restraints can be justified in the light of freedom of expression and other constitutional arguments. This topic is examined in the next section. The third section looks at the status of advertising under the European Convention on Human Rights and Fundamental Freedoms: how far is it covered by 'the right to freedom of expression', and, in so far as it is, what arguments can be made under Article 10(2) to justify the imposition of limits on the frequency of commercials or their particular content? The fourth section contains a comparative survey of some standard restrictions in the legal systems discussed in this book. The chapter concludes with a detailed examination of the provisions concerning advertising in the Directive and Television Convention.

In this chapter we are primarily concerned with commercial advertising, that is, advertising designed to promote the sale of goods or services. But it also deals with the different, if related, phenomenon of sponsorship. Under this practice, companies (other than the broadcasting company) finance programmes with a view to promoting their name, image, or

[9] A. Pilati, 'Pubblicità: è finita l'espansione?' (1990) 15 *Problemi dell'informazione* 561.

[10] To some extent a pan-European advertising market is developing; see *Television without Frontiers* (1985), HL 43, 189 and 192.

products.[11] In some ways sponsorship is less intrusive and, therefore, less objectionable from the viewers' perspective. But it poses similar, perhaps greater, dangers to the ability of broadcasters to draw up their own schedules, free from commercial pressure.

Advertisers and their clients constantly try to find ways round the legal restraints on the number, frequency, and content of commercials. One technique is the phenomenon known as 'product placement', in which a film features, say, a well-known model of car in such a way as to enable viewers to identify it. This is generally explicitly prohibited by regulation or by advertising code. It is even harder to control indirect advertising, that is, the publicity displayed at a sports or other event covered on television. The phenomena of product placement and related practices are discussed in Section 4.[12]

A final introductory point is that commercial advertising should be distinguished from political and religious advertising. In this chapter we are concerned with the former. Political advertising was covered in Chapter VII. It is a special type of access programme, as are programmes made by Churches and cultural and social groups. That chapter also dealt with the rights of reply to 'issue advertising', that is, commercial advertising which implicitly takes one side on an important political question, for example, whether large cars are bad for the environment. Although the line between pure commercial and issue advertising may be hard to draw, it is possible for courts to do it.[13] In any case, whatever the significance of the distinction was for the United States Fairness Doctrine, it is unimportant for the purposes of this chapter. Issue advertising promotes the goods or services of a particular company, and should, therefore, be regarded as commercial. It does not matter whether there is also an accompanying social message.

2. THE CONSTITUTIONAL POSITION OF ADVERTISING

In many countries (but not Britain) there is a vigorous debate about the constitutional position of broadcast advertising. Some lawyers argue that it is covered by freedom of expression.[14] Advertising on radio and television, it is said, is a form of commercial speech and, therefore, is entitled to a degree of protection. There is also an argument, supported

[11] See the definition in the ITC Code of Programme Sponsorship (1991), 3.

[12] See pp. 207–8 below.

[13] See the decisions of the DC Circuit Court of Appeals discussed in Ch. VII, S. 4.

[14] See e.g. A. Lester and D. Pannick, *Advertising and Freedom of Expression in Europe* (Paris, 1984), and A. Hesse, 'Werbung und Rundfunkfreiheit' (1987) *ZUM* 548. But contrast the view of H. Bethge, 'Der Verfassungsrechtliche Stellenwert der Werbung im öffentlichen-rechtlichen Rundfunk' [1983] *Media Perspektiven* 690.

by authority in Italy (discussed below), that broadcast commercials should be covered by the constitutional clause on freedom of economic initiative. The implication of both these arguments is that government is not free totally to prohibit advertisements on the media. It is clearly not entitled to outlaw them from the pages of newspapers and magazines, and the same might be true for radio and television. Moreover, some restrictions on the content of particular commercials would be constitutionally suspect.

On the first argument the issue is to some extent an aspect of larger questions concerning the status of commercial speech. Should commercial speech generally be afforded the same degree of protection under a freedom of expression clause as political and social speech? Should all forms of commercial speech be treated in the same way? The tendency recently has been for constitutional courts, in particular the United States Supreme Court and the Bundesverfassungsgericht, to treat commercial speech, including promotional advertising, as covered by freedom of expression.[15] There are powerful arguments of principle against this development.[16] But it has probably been inevitable, given the crucial role of advertising in free market economies and the difficulties in drawing sharp lines between political and commercial speech. But courts have equally been reluctant to afford the latter the same degree of protection as political or moral discourse. This is most marked in the cases concerning promotional advertising of goods and services.[17] Courts in the United States are willing, for example, to uphold state regulations requiring advertisers to supply information to prospective purchasers.[18] They have even countenanced the outright prohibition of personal canvassing of clients, where there is a well-substantiated risk that they may be misled or oppressed.[19]

On this line of authority broadcast commercials should probably enjoy only a low level of protection under a free speech clause. Their dramatic immediacy renders viewers extremely vulnerable; it is not always easy for them to avoid exposure to television advertising, particularly when it punctuates exciting moments in a film or drama. Further, commercials are so short that it is impracticable to require them to contain much information about the product or service they are promoting. For these

[15] *Virginia State Board of Pharmacy* v. *Virginia Citizens Consumer Council* 425 US 748 (1976); 71 BVerfGE 172 (1985).

[16] See in particular C. E. Baker, *Human Liberty and Freedom of Speech* (New York, 1989), ch. 9.

[17] For a short discussion of some leading cases, see E. M. Barendt, *Freedom of Speech* (Oxford, 1987), 58–62 and 310–11.

[18] *Zauderer* v. *Office of Disciplinary Counsel of Supreme Court of Ohio* 105 S. Ct. 2265 (1985).

[19] *Ohralik* v. *Ohio State Bar* 436 US 447 (1978).

reasons advertising regulation is easier to justify in this context than it is in that of newspapers, magazines, or hoardings.

Questions about the legitimacy (and constitutionality) of advertising regulation can be approached from another angle. It can be asked what the object is of the government prohibition or regulation: Is the control intended to prevent a particular type of commercial message from reaching the public, or is it instead intended to limit the number and frequency of commercials on radio and television in order to protect the coherence of programmes in the interests of listeners and viewers? A total ban on broadcast advertising or a restraint on the amount of revenue the media receives from this source may, depending on the circumstances, serve diverse objects. These restraints may be intended to preserve the character of a public service or community channel, or alternatively (or additionally) to safeguard the flow of advertising revenue to the press or private channels. But equally advertising controls may be designed to stifle a private broadcasting channel unable to raise revenue in any other way.

Some of these justifications would clearly be suspect on free speech grounds. For example, prohibitions on tobacco or alcohol advertising are content-based restrictions, which would have to be justified as serving a substantial public interest, such as the preservation of public health. On the other hand, restrictions on the practice of advertising, for example, limits on the frequency of commercials, are imposed to serve the viewers' interests in the appreciation of serious, high-quality programmes. They are designed to promote, and not to interfere with, broadcasting freedom.[20] It is difficult, for example, to regard a total ban on advertising during the coverage of a religious service or state occasion as an interference with freedom of expression. The same might be said of limits on the time it can occupy. Admittedly restraints of this kind limit the commercial freedom of the station owner to maximize his revenue, but that is not the same as an infringement of free speech.

This analysis is also relevant to counter any argument that commercial companies and their advertising agents have a fundamental right to buy broadcasting space. We saw in Chapter VII that courts have refused to recognize constitutional rights of access. In light of the general status of commercial speech, the case for a right to show advertisements is even weaker than that made for access programmes generally. Quite apart from that point, restraints on advertising are imposed to protect the free speech interests of the viewing public. They are surely entitled to more weight than the interest of advertisers in achieving access to the media to promote their wares.

The argument is, however, quite different if the object or effect of the

[20] For this concept, see Ch. II above.

government regulation is to starve private broadcasting of its revenue. In the German *Fourth Television* case the Constitutional Court held that there was no constitutional objection to the reliance of private broadcasters on advertising revenue.[21] That might lead to commercialization of these channels, but there was nothing unconstitutional about that result, as long as the public channels continued to provide a broad range of programmes.[22] The Court added that private broadcasting should not be so hedged around with restrictions as to make it unattractive to advertisers and so unviable.[23] Draconian programme standards and restraints on advertising would, therefore, be constitutionally suspect.

These remarks were clarified in the *Fifth Television* case, where the Court upheld a provision in the Baden-Württemberg statute outlawing all advertising on public local and regional television.[24] Its object was to safeguard the press and the private channels. The Court deliberately refrained from deciding how far advertising is constitutionally guaranteed as an aspect of *Rundfunkfreiheit*, in the same way that the advertising pages in a newspaper are covered by freedom of the press. What it did say was that the Basic Law required public broadcasting to be adequately financed in some way or other. If other sources of income, such as the licence fee, were unavailable, the exclusion of advertising revenue would be constitutionally suspect. This reasoning would seem even more applicable to private broadcasting, where advertising income is the main source of revenue. In principle, laws and codes may regulate the frequency of advertisements, but the regulation would become unconstitutional if it endangered the survival of a broadcasting company, whether public or private.

This conclusion may be based either on a freedom of expression clause or on a constitutional provision guaranteeing freedom of economic initiative. The Italian Constitutional Court has preferred the latter alternative. It has in general refused to extend the freedom of expression clause (Article 21) to promotional, as distinct from informational, advertising.[25] According to the Court this type of advertising is an aspect of economic activity which can be regulated in the public interest.

[21] 73 BVerfGE 118 (1986).

[22] For this aspect of broadcasting law, see Ch. III, S. 3 above.

[23] 73 BVerfGE 118, 157 (1986).

[24] 74 BVerfGE 297 (1987). In its decision of 6 Oct. 1992 the Court upheld the ban on advertising on the third public channel, as there was no evidence that without revenue from this source the plaintiff, Hesse Rundfunk, would be unable to survive.

[25] Decision 68/1965 [1965] *Giur. cost.* 838. For a general commentary on this aspect of Italian law, see A. Pace, *Problematica delle libertà costituzionali, Parte speciale*, 2nd edn. (Padua, 1992), 393–4. Also see A. Vignudelli, 'Alcune note sulla communicazione pubblicitaria nelle radiotelevisione' [1983] *Giur. it.* 421, and E. Roppo, 'Pubblicità televisiva ed emittenti private' [1983] *Foro italiano* 1143.

But a requirement to eliminate all advertising from foreign broadcasts retransmitted in Italy was held an unconstitutional violation of Article 41, guaranteeing the freedom of private economic initiative.[26] The Court considered this a more appropriate basis for its intervention than Article 21: there was no interference in its view with the free circulation of ideas. But a regulation of commercials so draconian as to imperil the existence of private broadcasting is surely an indirect fetter on freedom of expression. It is as constitutionally suspect as, say, a discriminatory tax on the advertising receipts of a newspaper.[27]

In contrast to the German and Italian courts, the French Conseil constitutionnel has been unsympathetic to constitutional arguments, whether based on the freedom of communication or the right to commercial freedom (*liberté d'enterprise*). Despite these arguments, it twice upheld a ban on advertising on local radio. Nor was it impressed by the further point that the ban discriminated against *private* radio channels, since *public* radio was free to finance itself in this way.[28] The total ban was lifted in 1984, but the Conseil rejected a complaint against a rule that private (unlike public) broadcasters could not accumulate both advertising revenue and a public grant.[29] The Council took the view that neither free speech nor freedom of private enterprise was absolute, and that the legislature was entitled to impose reasonable limits in the public interest. It could treat public and private broadcasters differently in view of their different functions and responsibilities.

Only in the United States is the view taken that the regulation of advertisements on the broadcast media is almost always incompatible with freedom of speech. In 1984 the FCC even repealed its restrictions on advertising during children's programmes, on the assumption that the quality of these programmes was best guaranteed by the market.[30] Recently Congress has enacted the Children's Television Act 1990 imposing a duty on the FCC to formulate minimal advertising rules in this context.[31] But this provision is unusual in the USA. There are no other restrictions on the frequency of commercials, though advertisements for tobacco products, as in many other countries, are forbidden.[32] This approach is in line with the favourable attitude generally taken in the

[26] Decision 231/1985 [1985] *Giur. cost.* 1185.

[27] See the United States case striking down such a tax under the First Amendment: *Grosjean* v. *American Press* 297 US 233 (1936).

[28] Decision 81–129, Rec. 1981, 35, Debbasch, 186, and Decision 82–141, Rec. 1982, 48, Debbasch, 198.

[29] Decision 84–176, Rec. 1984, 55.

[30] See A. L. Thorburn, 'Regulating Television for the Sake of Children' (1989) 67 *University of Detroit L. Rev.* 413.

[31] The provisions are incorporated in the Communications Act 1934, ss. 303A–B.

[32] See S. 4 below.

United States to commercial speech. As in other contexts it puts a premium on the interests of commercial broadcasters and appears, at any rate from a European perspective, to ignore those of viewers.

There is, therefore, no simple answer to the question how far, if at all, broadcast advertisements are covered by constitutional free speech or economic freedom clauses. Much depends on whether a constitutional court is concerned with regulation of the general practice of advertising or with the control of a specific advertisement on the basis of its content. The second alternative clearly raises freedom of speech issues, as such a ban outlaws an advertisement because it advocates a particular message. On the other hand, regulation of the overall practice by limits on the frequency of commercials in the interests of viewers and listeners does not seem to raise serious free speech issues. There is no real infringement of broadcasting freedom in this case, since that concept takes account of the audience interest as well as that of the broadcaster. Equally it might be concluded that the infringement of the latter's freedom of speech may be justified by the strong public interest in programme quality.[33] But a strict limit on advertising may be open to constitutional scrutiny if it threatens to dry up this source of revenue entirely and so endanger the survival of private broadcasting. That case can be argued either on the basis of an excessive regulation of economic freedom or as an indirect infringement of freedom of expression.

3. ADVERTISING AND THE EUROPEAN CONVENTION ON HUMAN RIGHTS

The freedom of European states to impose restraints on broadcast advertising would be significantly reduced, if it were protected under the European Convention on Human Rights. Article 10(1) guarantees the right to freedom of expression, including the right 'to receive and impart information and ideas without interference by public authority and regardless of frontiers'. There is, however, no provision in the Convention, or in any of the Protocols, equivalent to the articles in the German and Italian Constitutions guaranteeing a right to economic enterprise.[34] As yet the European Court and the Commission of Human Rights have not ruled on the status of media advertising. We must await

[33] There is also another argument that it is necessary to safeguard the rights of authors and directors not to have their work distorted through the excessive interruptions of advertising: see S. 4 below.

[34] Arguments might conceivably be based on Art. 1 of the First Protocol, guaranteeing the right to the peaceful enjoyment of property. It is very doubtful whether this right is pertinent, since private broadcasters do not 'possess' their channels. But even if applicable, the Protocol authorizes states to control the use of property in the general interest.

the decision on the application by a Swedish local radio station that its rights under the Convention were infringed when it was closed down for defying the national ban on radio advertising.

The most relevant authority is the decision of the Court in the *Barthold* case that a newspaper article drawing attention to the poor state of veterinary services in Hamburg and indirectly publicizing the applicant's own clinic was covered by Article 10.[35] The concurring opinion of Judge Pettiti argued for recognition of a right of private broadcasters to rely on advertisements as a source of finance.[36] Otherwise they could not survive. This is a tenable argument. But it is only relevant to total prohibitions or draconian restrictions on advertising. In contrast reasonable restrictions on the frequency of breaks do not imperil commercial broadcasting.

A later decision of the Strasbourg Court has emphasized the discretion of member states in regulating commercial speech.[37] It may be inferred that standard limits on the amount of advertising would easily survive scrutiny under the Human Rights Convention. Further, the later Transfrontier Television Convention requires states to impose such limits in the case of programmes which may be received and retransmitted in other countries. There is, therefore, a strong presumption that they do not necessarily violate freedom of expression.[38]

A decision of the Austrian Constitutional Court in 1986 held that in some circumstances media advertising is covered by Article 10. The Austrian public broadcasting authority had infringed the article, when it refused without reasons to accept advertisements for a weekly newspaper.[39] The decision itself is unexceptionable. Unreasonable discrimination in the acceptance of advertisements does raise free speech issues, and is, for instance, explicitly proscribed in the British legislation.[40] The Austrian case does not, however, afford any support for the view that the practice of advertising is covered by the Convention, so that rules on the length of advertising breaks would be incompatible with it.

A decision that Article 10(1) covers a broadcaster's right to schedule as many advertisements as he wishes would have serious implications. States would then have to justify under Article 10(2) imposition of limits on the frequency and duration of advertisements, or financial ceilings on the amounts of money which may be raised in this way. The difficulty is that none of the aims set out in the article is obviously relevant to these limits, save possibly the general goal 'the rights of others'. There is no authority

[35] *Barthold* v. *Germany* [1985] 7 EHRR 383, discussed in Barendt, *Freedom of Speech*, 60–1 and 310.
[36] [1985] 7 EHRR 383, 407.
[37] *Markt Intern* v. *Germany* [1990] 12 EHRR 161.
[38] For the Transfrontier Convention rules, see S. 5 below.
[39] Decision of 27 June 1986 (1986) *EuGRZ* 481.
[40] Broadcasting Act 1990, s. 8(2)(b).

for holding that this phrase is elastic enough to cover the interests of viewers and listeners in relatively uninterrupted films and other programmes, let alone a general public interest in a media free from the dominance of commercial groups. A more promising argument might be that the restrictions are necessary to safeguard the rights of the press and other media to receive some advertising revenue.[41]

A content-based restriction on the acceptance of particular advertisements is another matter, as it is in the case of national constitutions. A state should be required to justify under Article 10(2) a total ban or serious restrictions on, say, the acceptance of advertisements by matrimonial agencies or undertakers, since this outlaws or limits the communication of particular messages on the basis of their content. It may in fact be easy to support some restrictions as necessary to protect health or morality or the reputation or rights of others. That is almost certainly true of the now common prohibitions on tobacco and alcohol commercials.

4. RESTRICTIONS ON ADVERTISING

Advertising on radio and television is regulated in many ways. Only in the United States is this for the most part a matter of self-regulation under the Codes of the National Association of Broadcasters. In European countries there are significant limits on the time permitted for commercials, on their frequency, and on their content. These are sometimes imposed by statute or regulation; then they are clearly legally binding. But often they are contained in the codes of the regulatory authorities. Codes comprise a mixture of precise rules and vaguer guide-lines, the former being enforceable as conditions of the broadcaster's licence or terms of its agreement with the authority. Other restrictions may be imposed by the general law, in particular by regulations prohibiting misleading advertising.[42]

This section begins with an overall survey of the rules specific to the broadcasting media, and continues with a discussion of time and frequency limits. There is a short treatment of the principal content controls and subsections on the control of sponsorship and product placement. I discuss finally the moral rights of authors and directors of films to control what they consider to be the excessive interruption of their works on television—one of the few aspects of private law examined in this book.

[41] This was accepted by the German Constitutional Court in the *Fifth Television* case, 74 BVerfGE 297 (1987).

[42] e.g. the British Control of Misleading Advertisements Regulations, SI 1988/915, implementing the EC Directive of 10 Sept. 1984, 84/450/EEC OJ L 250/17.

(i) General rules

Usually a number of general rules are set out either in the primary legislation itself or in the regulations and codes made under it. There is very little in the Broadcasting Act 1990, in contrast to earlier British statutes; most of the rules are contained in Codes issued by the ITC in January 1991. The Act requires the Commission to do all it can to secure the exclusion of political advertising, to prohibit unreasonable discrimination in the acceptance of advertisements, and to exclude the sponsorship of programmes by bodies the goods or services of which may not be advertised.[43] Otherwise it is for the ITC to determine the content of the Codes it is required to draw up, though it must consult the Secretary of State with regard to prohibited classes of commercials and, more controversially, carry out any directions he gives it.[44] The Commission may in particular give directions with regard to the maximum amount of time permitted for advertisements, their frequency, and their exclusion from specific programmes.[45]

The most important standards in the Code are that 'advertisements must be clearly distinguishable as such and recognisably separate from the programmes', and that they must be legal, decent, honest, and truthful.[46] (Similar requirements are found in other systems, for example, in the Italian broadcasting statute[47] and in the decrees and *cahiers des charges* governing the French broadcasting companies.[48]) Subliminal advertising, and commercials which gratuitously play on fear or which exploit superstition, are also prohibited. Advertisements from charities may now be accepted, though only subject to conditions regarding both the character of the charity and the tone of the advertisement.[49] The absolute ban on advertising by religious bodies or for religious purposes has been removed, but these commercials will only be accepted in certain types of case and subject to a number of restrictions.[50] Broadly they may provide information about religious services and other activities, but not fund-raise.

Under the French statutes of 1986 and 1989, the government lays down the basic advertising rules by decree. An attempt to confer some regulatory power on the CSA was judged unconstitutional, as exceeding

[43] Broadcasting Act 1990, s. 8.

[44] Ibid., s. 9.

[45] Ibid., s. 9(8).

[46] ITC Code of Advertising Standards and Practice, 3.

[47] Law 223 of 6 Aug. 1990, Art. 8.

[48] Decree 87-37 of 26 Jan. 1987 governing all the private channels, Arts. 2–3 and 8–10, and Decree 87-717 of 28 Aug. 1987, containing the *cahiers* of Antenne 2, Arts. 51–6.

[49] The rules are set out in Appendix 4 of the Code.

[50] ITC Code, Appendix 5; also see Radio Authority Code of Advertising Standards and Practice and Programme Sponsorship (Jan. 1991), Appendix 7.

the scope of authority which could legitimately be delegated to an administrative agency.[51] The law itself contains two provisions of interest. First, Article 73 imposes limits on the interruption of films; there may only be one advertising break, unless the CSA is prepared to authorize others in the case of very long films, while there can be no interruption to films shown on public or subscription television channels. The explanation for this difference is that these latter channels are primarily supported by other sources of revenue and are less dependent on advertising. Secondly, the 1986 statute provides that Parliament determines the total amount the public broadcasting companies may receive from advertising revenue, though its allocation between the channels is a matter for their decision.[52] The legislature can, therefore, safeguard the interests of the press and private broadcasters, which rely even more than public companies on this source of finance.

The Italian legislation makes provision for the imposition of a ceiling on RAI's advertising revenue. The Parliamentary Commission used to establish a ceiling annually in the light of the receipts of RAI and the press.[53] The broadcasting law of 1990 transfers this responsibility to the Prime Minister.[54] It is for the Minister of Posts to suggest the ceiling and then the Prime Minister must consult the Garante and the Cabinet. The limit must be fixed with regard to the projected difference in the expenditure on broadcast advertising in the current year, compared to that established in the previous year. What is interesting about this rule, compared to that in the earlier Italian legislation, is that the ceiling is designed to protect the advertising revenue of private broadcasters, rather than that of the press.

The Parliamentary Commission has also had authority to lay down general rules for the control of the content of advertisements to protect consumers and to ensure that they do not unduly detract from RAI's public service responsibilities. In fact it has left regulation to the Società per azioni commerciale iniziative spettacolo, an associate of RAI. In effect, therefore, there was self-regulation, as far as the public broadcasting body is concerned, until the enactment of the 1990 law. There was, of course, for a long time no regulation at all of the private

[51] See Ch. III, S. 4 above for further discussion.

[52] Art. 53. The government rejected an amendment to give Parliament power to allocate this revenue between the broadcasting companies. For a discussion of the growing dependence of the public companies, particularly Antenne 2, on advertising revenue, see G. Drouot, 'Le Secteur public de l'audiovisuel dans la loi de 30 septembre 1986' [1987] *Rev. fr. droit adm.* 399, 405–7.

[53] Art. 21 of the law 103 of 14 Apr. 1975. For commentary on the Commission's powers in this respect, see R. Zaccaria, *Radiotelevisione e costituzione* (Milan, 1977), 430–6.

[54] Law 223 of 6 Aug. 1990, Art. 8(16). For commentary on the background to this revision and on the text of the law, see R. Zaccaria, in *Il sistema radiotelevisivo*, 194–210.

networks, though the so-called temporary Berlusconi law of February 1985 did introduce limits on the time allowed for advertisements.[55] The Broadcasting Act of 1990 has introduced rules for both public and private sectors, some of which are discussed later in this section.

In contrast to the chequered history in Italy, there have always been clear rules in Germany. The *Rundfunkstaatsvertrag* of 1991 contains a number of general provisions applicable to both public and private broadcasting, most of which are similar to the English and French rules mentioned earlier. But cultural and religious, as well as political, advertising is forbidden.[56] The treaty also contains detailed rules for public and for private broadcasting, the former being somewhat more restrictive than the latter. While for both sectors advertisements are forbidden during the coverage of religious services and during children's programmes, it is only in the public system that they are prohibited on Sundays and on holidays. Further, they may not be shown on the ARD and ZDF channels after 8.00 p.m. The *Länder* may, however, agree to change these restrictions.[57] The state laws reproduce these rules, though they may contain additional restrictions. In practice the restrictions on advertising on the private channels are more or less uniform; the rules in the *Staatsvertrag* are supplemented by more specific directives agreed by the Landesmedienanstalten (state broadcasting authorities).

(ii) Time and frequency restrictions

Regulation of the frequency of television advertising, as with regard to the control of its content, is now relatively uniform throughout European countries, as their laws must conform to the requirements of the Council of Europe Transfrontier Television Convention and (for member states of the Community) the EC Broadcasting Directive. But they are free to impose tougher limits, and the Directive permits them to devise more lenient rules for broadcasts which may not be received in other Community states.[58] In fact the major European jurisdictions considered in this book often impose stricter limits on television advertising, particularly for public broadcasting, while applying comparable rules for radio (to which the European instruments do not apply).

As already mentioned the ITC may impose directions on the amount of television advertising. Interestingly the Radio Authority has no comparable power, so the matter is left to the judgement of licensees. The Commission distinguishes between the rules applicable to Channels 3, 4, and 5, and those governing cable and satellite channels. With regard to

[55] Law 10 of 4 Feb. 1985, Art. 3-*bis*. For this law, see Ch. I, S. 4 above.
[56] *Rundfunkstaatsvertrag* of 31 Aug. 1991, s. 6.
[57] Ibid., ss. 13–16 and 26–7.
[58] The terms of these two European measures are considered in S. 5 of this chapter.

the latter, where it has never exercised control over the broadcasters' schedules, it is content merely to apply the minimum rules required by the two European measures: no more than 15 per cent of daily transmission time may be devoted to spot advertising, and in any given hour it can occupy no more than 20 per cent (12 minutes). However, for Channels 3 and 4 (and it is anticipated Channel 5) more stringent limits are imposed to safeguard viewers' interests. The total amount of advertising in any day must not exceed an average of 7 minutes per hour, while in peak hours (7.00 to 9.00 a.m. and 6.00 to 11.00 p.m.) there must on average be no more than $7\frac{1}{2}$ minutes per hour.[59] It is interesting to note that initially a limit was imposed of 6 minutes' advertising an hour on average. Both that limit and the limit on peak-time advertising were raised in 1986, but the advertisers' pressure to raise the general limit to an average of 8 minutes an hour has so far been resisted.[60]

These rules are supplemented by a number of others. Some preclude the insertion of advertisements during the course of certain broadcasts: those, for example, covering a religious service or a formal Royal occasion, schools programmes, and news, documentaries, or children's programmes of less than a half an hour in length. The ITC may specify other programmes, for example, those of a particularly sensitive nature, which are not to be interrupted. These rules apply to all types of television service, while Channel 3 and 4 programmes are subject to slightly more stringent limits: for example, a play of less than half an hour may not be interrupted.

Other important rules govern the timing of advertising breaks within particular types of programme. It is a general principle that they may only be made at points where some interruption in continuity would otherwise occur, and, further, they must not damage the integrity or value of the programme. Breaks may only be taken in the intervals of sports programmes and other similarly structured events—though American football shows how the rules of a game may be manipulated to create frequent commercial breaks. In the case of other programmes there should normally be a period of at least 20 minutes between breaks. In order to comply with the Directive, the rules for the interruption of films have been altered: films, whether made for the cinema or television (but excluding serials and light entertainment), may not be interrupted with a centre break if their duration is less than 45 minutes, while longer films may be interrupted once for each complete period of 45 minutes, with a further break if the scheduled duration is at least 20 minutes longer than two or more complete periods of 45 minutes, i.e. at least 110 minutes.

[59] These rules are set out in detail in the ITC Rules on Advertising Breaks (Jan. 1991).
[60] Information obtained from the Annual Reports of the IBA.

There are other rules for Channels 3 and 4 concerning the length of advertising breaks: 3 or 3½ minutes depending on the length of the scheduled programme. Finally, there will be careful scrutiny of individual advertisements lasting more than 1 minute.

The equivalent provisions in other European jurisdictions are almost as complex, but may be stated relatively briefly. The basic rules governing private broadcasting in the German *Rundfunkstaatsvertrag* have been revised to implement the EC Directive.[61] In the 1981 treaty advertising breaks were only permitted in programmes of 60 minutes' length, but under the 1991 revision the rules are very similar to the British rules outlined in the previous paragraph. On the other hand, the stricter rules for public broadcasting have been retained.[62] Not only is advertising still forbidden on Sundays and holidays, but it is not to exceed on average 20 minutes a day assessed over the year. For radio the states may impose a limit up to 90 minutes a day.

The French and Italian advertising rules also differentiate between public and private broadcasting. In France Antenne 2 and FR3 are limited to 6 and 5 minutes' advertising respectively per hour averaged over the year, and no more than 12 or 10 minutes in any given hour (*heure donnée*). The premier private channel, TF1, is obliged not to transmit more than 6 minutes' advertising on a daily average and no more than 12 minutes in any hour. It has also undertaken not to show commercials during the news and not to show them for more than 4 minutes during the one break permitted for films and other long fictional works.[63] There are overall time-limits for the other private channels, but they may show commercials during news or drama programmes and there is a more generous limit of 4½ minutes for the interruption of films. Nice questions have arisen in enforcement proceedings before the Conseil d'État.[64] It confirmed that broadcasting companies are bound by the decisions granting them permission to broadcast, as well as the statute and regulations.[65] More particularly, it ruled that the limits were to be applied by reference to any period of 60 minutes (*heure glissante*) rather than a clock hour, a rule now incorporated in the Council of Europe Convention and the EC Directive.[66]

The Italian Broadcasting Act 1990 discriminates between public and private broadcasters. The former are only allowed to transmit adverts for

[61] *Rundfunkstaatsvertrag*, s. 26.
[62] Ibid., s. 15.
[63] Decision 87-26 of 4 Apr. 1987 (awarding the concession of TF1), Art. 18.
[64] For the enforcement of programme and advertising standards in France, see Ch. V, S. 6 above.
[65] Decision of 16 Mar. 1988, 1988 Rec. Leb. 124.
[66] Convention, Art. 12(2); Directive, Art. 18(2).

4 per cent of total weekly broadcasting time and 12 per cent of every hour, while national private licensees (for both television and radio) are permitted to show them for up to 15 per cent of total daily broadcasting time, with a ceiling of 18 per cent for each hour. There is a slightly more generous limit (20 per cent per hour) for local commercial broadcasting, and a much more restrictive one (5 per cent per hour) for community radio.[67] This is in conformity with the EC Directive. What is more difficult to reconcile with that instrument is a provision in Article 8 of the law. It appears to allow an advertising break (of unspecified length) in the showing of theatrical and operatic performances and cinema films during the natural intervals between acts or screening periods, but for works longer than 45 minutes further interruptions for every act or screening period are permitted. Another break is permitted for films or other performances which exceed by more than 20 minutes two or more such periods of 45 minutes each, i.e. which are at least 110 minutes long.[68] Films in Italy are normally shown in two parts, so the provision would seem to allow the television presentation of a film of more than 45 minutes' length to be interrupted three times, with another break if it is a long film. Under the Directive only one interruption is permitted for each period of 45 minutes,[69] so there must be doubts about the legality of the Italian rules in this respect.

The Garante has discretion to decide which programmes of cultural significance and which educational and religious programmes must not be interrupted.[70] This also seems an unsatisfactory implementation of the Directive; that requires states completely to exclude advertising during the broadcast of religious services and to forbid such breaks during news bulletins, documentaries, and religious and children's programmes of less than half an hour.[71]

(iii) Restrictions on content

Although in principle content-based restrictions may be subject to challenge on freedom of speech grounds, in practice there is relatively little controversy about them. The rules in European countries must now conform to the requirements (which are relatively similar) set out in the EC Directive and the Council of Europe Convention.[72] Thus member states must prohibit all tobacco advertising (not just cigarette advertising)

[67] The detailed rules are set out in law 223 of 6 Aug. 1990, Art. 8(6–9).
[68] Ibid., Art. 8(3). For commentary on this difficult provision, see P. Caretti, in *Il sistema radiotelevisivo*, 165–9.
[69] Directive, Art. 11(3).
[70] Ibid., Art. 8(4). For the Garante, see Ch. IV, S. 3.
[71] See P. Caretti, in *Il sistema radiotelevisivo*, 168.
[72] Directive, Arts. 12–16, and Convention, Art. 15.

and advertisements for drugs only available on prescription in the transmitting state. Advertisements for alcoholic drinks must comply with a number of rules, e.g. that they should not link consumption to enhanced physical performance, driving, or social or sexual success. The Directive requires states to draw up rules to prevent harm to children; in particular advertisements must not directly exhort minors to buy a product or service or encourage them to persuade their parents or others to do this.[73]

Generally national rules go further than these minimal requirements. For example, the ITC Code of Advertising Standards and Practice contains a list of products and services for which commercials will not be acceptable: they include betting and gaming, guns and gun clubs, private investigation agencies, and pornography. There are a number of detailed restrictions on advertisements for introduction agencies and alcohol and on commercials shown when children are particularly likely to be watching. The Radio Authority's Code contains comparable rules.

As far as other European countries are concerned, French law specifically forbids advertisements for alcoholic drinks (defined as those of more than 1 per cent alcohol), films, and the press.[74] These prohibitions are not found in the Directive or the Convention. The Italian law itself implements the Community ban on advertising medicines available only on prescription, but leaves the incorporation of other Directive rules to Ministerial decree.

There is widespread agreement that these regulations can be justified in the interests of health and morality. Even in the United States, where commercial speech is usually entitled to a high degree of constitutional protection, a ban on the broadcast of cigarette advertising has been upheld.[75] The outlaw of tobacco and probably alcohol advertisements in Europe would almost certainly be sustained under the European Convention on Human Rights, as 'necessary in a democratic society . . . for the protection of health or morals'.[76]

(iv) Sponsorship

Sponsorship was originally banned (with limited exceptions) in Britain, because it was thought inevitable that commercial sponsors would control programme content. The Television Act 1954, in a provision repeated in

[73] Directive, Art. 16.

[74] Decree 87-37 of 26 Jan. 1987, Art 6. The total prohibition of advertising alcohol dates from the law of 30 July 1987. Also see the *cahiers des charges* in Decree 87-717 of 28 Aug. 1987, of Antenne 2, Art. 59, and of FR3, Art. 61.

[75] *Capital Broadcasting* v. *Mitchell* 333 F. Supp. 582 (1971).

[76] Art. 10(2). The European Court allows member states a wide margin of discretion in applying these restraints: *Handyside* v. *U.K.* [1976] 1 EHRR 737.

legislation until the reform of 1990, forbade the broadcast of any material stating, suggesting, or implying that any part of the programme had been supplied or suggested by an advertiser. That did not, however, preclude the inclusion of sponsored items, such as the broadcast of opera or sports events, which the IBA considered proper for inclusion because of their intrinsic interest.[77] The BBC remains totally prohibited by clause 12 of its Licence and Agreement from transmitting sponsored programmes.

Sponsorship is not prohibited by the new broadcasting legislation, but the ITC has drawn up a code to regulate it.[78] As with advertising rules, it must comply with the requirements of the EC Directive and the Transfrontier Television Convention.[79] These are in substance identical. The sponsor must be clearly identified at the beginning and/or end of the programme. The content and scheduling of programmes must not be influenced by the sponsor in such a way as to endanger broadcasting freedom, nor must such programmes encourage the purchase or rental of his goods or services. Sponsorship of news and current affairs programmes is forbidden, as it is by companies which cannot advertise their products, namely tobacco and medicines. In the former case there is a significant danger to the accuracy and impartiality of information, while the latter prohibition is framed to prevent evasion of the advertising rules. The ITC Code follows these rules, supplementing them with some details, for example, concerning the content and length of sponsor credits.

The French rules for private broadcasting broadly follow the same lines as those imposed by the ITC Code.[80] There are somewhat stricter rules for the public broadcasting companies. Under the 1986 statute, as amended in 1989, they may only accept sponsorship for programmes falling within their educational, cultural, and social responsibilities.[81] There are strict limits on the mention which may be made of the sponsor's name or products. The latter themselves may not generally be shown, though they may be awarded to competitors in a televised game show, provided this is done in a strictly neutral fashion.[82]

German law now has common rules for the sponsorship of public and private broadcasting.[83] They follow the requirements of the Television Convention and liberalize German law considerably. Under the 1981 State Treaty and state legislation, sponsorship was only allowed in public broadcasting when it was purely disinterested, while sponsors were

[77] S. 4(6), and proviso (c). The comparable provisions in the Broadcasting Act 1981 were ss. 8(6) and (7)(c).
[78] ITC Code of Programme Sponsorship, Mar. 1991.
[79] Directive, Art. 17, Convention, Arts. 17–18.
[80] Decree 87-37 of 26 Jan. 1987, Art. 11.
[81] Law of 17 Jan. 1989, Art. 20, replacing Art. 48(2) and (3) of the law of 30 Sept. 1986.
[82] Decision 87-327 of 7 Dec. 1987, Arts. 5–6.
[83] *Rundfunkstaatsvertrag* of 31 Aug. 1991, s. 7.

permitted to finance a programme on private television on condition that there was no connection between its content and their interests.

There are some interesting features in the Italian rules contained in the 1990 legislation. Two of them show a failure to implement the EC Directive. First, the law contains no ban on sponsorship of news and current affairs programmes; private broadcasters may need to finance these programmes by this means.[84] A second point is the omission of the Community rule prohibiting sponsored programmes from encouraging the purchase or rental of the sponsor's products or services. Finally, sponsored programmes are to be taken to include advertising for at least 2 per cent of their total length for the purpose of assessing daily advertising limits for television.

(v) Product placement

Mention was made in the first section of this chapter of the growing use of 'product placement' to evade advertising restrictions. The practice is now outlawed by Article 10(4) of the EC Directive: 'Surreptitious advertising shall be prohibited.'[85] It also violates the principle that advertising should be recognizable as separate from the rest of the programme. In Britain the practice is forbidden by the ITC Sponsorship Code. It is defined there as 'the inclusion of, or reference to, a product or service within a programme' for money.[86]

However, it is hard to regulate comprehensively every conceivable practice by which goods or services may be promoted within the context of television programmes. The Code provides that a programme-maker may acquire a product or service at less than its full cost, provided its use in the programme is essential and it is not given 'undue prominence'.[87] The enforcement of such a broad rule inevitably involves the exercise of some judgement.[88] What matters is that there is no understanding, explicit or implicit, under which an identifiable product is mentioned or given extensive coverage, when this treatment is not warranted. The same principle applies when television covers, say, a sports events, where advertising is prominently displayed. The ITC Code makes it clear that coverage of the advertising or reference to the sponsors of the event is acceptable, provided it is justified by the editorial needs of the programme.[89]

[84] Law 223 of 6 Aug. 1990, Art. 8(12–15). For commentary, see G. V. Briante and G. Savorani, in *Il sistema radiotelevisivo*, 172–89.

[85] Also see the Convention, Art. 13(3).

[86] ITC Sponsorship Code, rule 14(a).

[87] Ibid., rule 14(b).

[88] See the *Guardian*, 6 July 1992, 25.

[89] ITC Code of Programme Sponsorship, rule 16.

In Germany the phenomenon may give rise to breaches of unfair competition law. The surreptitious advertising of one product by, say, the compère of a quiz show may damage the business of the company marketing rival goods. The Munich Court of Appeals (Oberlandesgericht) has held that the advertisement on ZDF of a video cassette showing the Wimbledon men's final in 1985 (won by Boris Becker) might violate the competition statute, at least if an intent to infringe its rules could be imputed to the presenter of the programme. As the broadcast was made some months after the final, the presenter could not argue that his real intention was to inform the public.[90] The same approach has been taken more recently by the Bundesgerichtshof.[91] It held that the second channel had violated both the state treaty and the unfair competition statute when it advertised a book linked to a crime thriller film it was showing. The Court considered that this promotional practice, like product placement, violated the requirement to keep advertising separate from programmes and may mislead consumers. (Recently the Monopolies and Mergers Commission has held that the BBC's promotion of some magazines produced by an associated company distorted competition.[92])

(vi) Moral rights of authors

Excessive advertising on television may be controlled by actions to protect the moral rights of authors. The rights of film directors are particularly important in this context. European legal systems, implementing the Berne Copyright Convention,[93] typically provide that an author has the right, *inter alia*, to object to derogatory action in respect to his work, which would be prejudicial to his honour or reputation. The question is whether the insertion of advertising breaks in the televised transmission of a film (or drama or opera), against the director's consent, violates his moral rights. There is a lot of case-law on this topic in Italy. In some early decisions, the courts accepted the argument that there might be a violation if there were an excessive number of lengthy commercial breaks.[94] Everything turned on the facts. But in a major reconsideration of this jurisprudence the Rome Appeal Court has held

[90] (1988) 19 *Int. Rev. of Industrial and Intellectual Ppty. Law* 263, with note by F. Henning-Bodewig. For a general analysis of product placement in German law, see the same author, 'Product Placement und Sponsoring' [1988] *Gewerblicher Rechtsschutz und Urheberrecht* 867.

[91] Decision of 22 Feb. 1990 [1990] *Gewerblicher Rechtsschutz und Urheberrecht* 611.

[92] *Television Broadcasting Services* (1992), Cm. 2035.

[93] Art. 6 *bis*.

[94] See Decisions of Rome Court of 30 Dec. 1982, *Foro italiano* 1983, i, 1143, and of 30 May 1984 [1985] *Giur. civile* 2054, and of the Milan Court of 13 Dec. 1984 [1985] *Diritto dell'informazione e dell'informatica* 231 (Zeffirelli case).

that an advertising break as such infringes a director's moral rights.[95] In the case itself there was clearly excessive advertising, for out of two hours scheduled for the film almost half an hour was taken up by commercials. But the Court rejected the earlier pragmatic approach. It was inconsistent with the principle of legal certainty, giving too much discretion to the judges. Further, the Court rejected the argument that the right of economic activity recognized by Article 41 of the Constitution precluded authors from objecting to advertising breaks; that right cannot be exercised incompatibly with social utility, which includes the interest of viewers in seeing films without (excessive) interruption.

The issue has also arisen in France.[96] A Paris tribunal has held that it was a breach of the directors' rights for TF1 to show without their agreement a film in two parts, with advertising spots interrupting each half.[97] The Court rejected the arguments that the *droit moral* of authors should be interpreted in the light of the expectation of television viewers, and that an inhibition on advertising would affect the broadcaster's financial position. The latter argument could only be supported if TF1 had shown that the loss of advertising revenue could imperil its survival. The fact that Article 73 of the 1986 broadcasting legislation permitted one break during a television showing of films was irrelevant to the enforcement of authors' rights.

Moral rights have been introduced into British law by the Copyright, Designs and Patents Act 1988.[98] In principle the author's right not to have his work subjected to derogatory treatment, recognized by section 80, would appear to protect film directors against excessive advertising, though it seems unlikely that an English court would adopt the rigorous approach of the Rome Appeal Court. Moreover, unauthorized cuts in the script of a television play have been held to be in breach of the agreement between author and broadcaster, so there is perhaps also the possibility of a contractual remedy for excessive advertising.[99] In the United States case *Gilliam* v. *American Broadcasting Companies*,[100] an injunction to restrain breach of copyright was granted to restrain the broadcast of a

[95] Decision of 16 Oct. 1989 [1990] *Giur. cost.* 490, with note by O. Grandinetti, 'Diretto all'integrità dell'opera cinematographica e *spots* pubblicatari', 499. Also see T. Collova, 'Commercial Breaks during Films on Television' (1990) 146 *RIDA* 124.

[96] For a discussion of moral rights in the context of the broadcasting media in France, see C. Debbasch, *Droit de l'audiovisuel*, 2nd edn. (Paris, 1991), 546–647.

[97] Decision of 24 May 1989, (1989) 143 *RIDA* 353. Also see the decision of the same Tribunal of 29 June 1988, *Marchand et autres v. 'La Cinq'*, holding that the showing of a film with the logo of La Cinq superimposed (without the director's consent) violated his moral rights: Debbasch, 289.

[98] For a commentary on the provisions, ss. 77–85, see G. Dworkin and R. D. Taylor, *Blackstone's Guide to the Copyright, Designs and Patents Act 1988* (London, 1990), ch. 8.

[99] *Frisby* v. *BBC* [1967] Ch. 932.

[100] 538 F. 2d. 14 (2nd Cir. 1976).

Monty Python comedy, which had been cut (in contravention of the limited editing rights granted by the plaintiffs) to insert advertising breaks. The Court held that copyright law could protect artists against mutilation of their work and consequent damage to their reputation. The same result on these facts could be reached by an English court.

The significance of moral rights in this context has been recognized in the Television Convention and the EC Directive. Under both measures advertising breaks may only be inserted in such a way that 'the rights of rights holders are not prejudiced'.[101] However, reliance on these rights (whether moral, copyright, or contractual) is an ineffective method for regulating excessive advertising. One point is that they are only relevant to creative works, in practice (it seems) cinema films. Moral rights cannot be claimed to limit the interruption of news, current affairs programmes, and quiz shows or other light entertainment. Further, copyright and moral rights litigation only resolves one case at a time, rather than laying down general rules. The most important point is that film directors and other authors come under enormous pressure to waive their moral rights, or at any rate to grant broadcasting companies the right to insert advertisements or to make other modifications considered necessary for reproduction of the work on television. The alternative is a total lack of exposure on the most popular entertainment medium. The rules concerning permissible breaks contained in advertising codes are a much better way of safeguarding the interests of viewers and listeners. The author's interest in protecting his artistic integrity may coincide with those interests, but it is fundamentally different. In a few instances moral rights may justify a more severe restriction on advertising than that imposed by the general law. But generally they play a very subordinate part in its control.[102]

5. THE HARMONIZATION OF ADVERTISING RULES

We saw in the first section of this chapter that there has been considerable pressure to co-ordinate the advertising rules for broadcasting in Europe. It influenced substantially the preparation of the European Commission's Green Paper *Television without Frontiers*, which in its turn led to the Broadcasting Directive of October 1989. Cultural factors perhaps played a more important part in the origins of the Council of Europe Transfrontier Television Convention agreed a few months before the

[101] Convention, Art. 14(1); Directive, Art. 11(1).

[102] For some reflections on this argument in the context of Italian law, see Grandinetti, 'Diritto all'integrità dell'opera cinematographica e *spots* pubblicitari', 499–506.

enactment of the Directive. The political and legal background to these measures is fully considered in Chapter X (Sections 3 and 4). The object of these pages is to outline the advertising standards set out in the two instruments.[103]

In the Commission's Green Paper a minimum degree of harmonization was contemplated. All broadcasting organizations which were not financed by a licence fee would be free to take commercial advertising, subject only to a ceiling of 20 per cent of daily broadcasting time.[104] States would be free to impose more severe restrictions on their broadcasting channels, but not more generous limits on the frequency and length of commercials. These suggestions were significantly modified in the Directive. Like the Transfrontier Television Convention, it is essentially a co-ordinating measure. Both measures provide that states must allow the reception and retransmission of broadcasts emanating from other member states, provided they comply with the standards set out in the instrument.

The principal advertising provisions in the two documents are very similar. Both contain the fundamental principle that advertising must be recognizable and separate from other parts of the programme; both prohibit subliminal and surreptitious advertising.[105] The limits on the duration of advertising are imposed in almost identical terms: no more than 15 per cent of daily transmission time, with a limit of 20 per cent within any given one-hour period (Article 12 of the Convention and Article 18 of the Directive). The principle that normally advertising should be transmitted in blocks and that spot advertising is the exception is formulated in both documents, albeit in different ways.[106]

Perhaps most striking is the similarity of the rules about the frequency of advertising breaks. Normally they are to be inserted between programmes, but they may also be inserted during them, provided there is no prejudice to the integrity of the programme and to the (moral and other) rights of authors.[107] A programme consisting of autonomous parts or covering a sports or other similarly structured event may only be interrupted between the parts or in the intervals of the event. For programmes other than these, there should be an interval of at least 20 minutes between advertising breaks.[108] There may be one break in the transmission of audiovisual works (a term referring to cinema films and films made for television, but not serials, light entertainment, and documentaries) for

[103] For an account of the part played by the advertisers' lobby in shaping the measures, see J. Tunstall and M. Palmer, *Media Moguls* (London, 1991), 93–9.

[104] *Television without Frontiers*, COM(84) 300 final, 262–74.

[105] Convention, Art. 13; Directive, Art. 10.

[106] Convention, Art. 13(1); Directive, Art. 10(2).

[107] Convention, Art. 14; Directive, Art. 11.

[108] In an earlier draft of the Convention, this interval was mandatory.

each period of 45 minutes; a further interruption is permitted if they last at least 20 minutes longer than two or more periods of 45 minutes, i.e. at least 110 minutes. We have seen that the British, French, and German rules comply with these requirements, but there is a doubt about the compatibility with them of the Italian rules.[109] Finally, advertising is not permitted during the broadcast of a religious service, nor in the course of certain other programmes of less than 30 minutes' duration. These are religious and children's programmes, news, and documentaries.

The content restrictions and sponsorship rules in the two measures, outlined in Section 4 of the chapter, are also extremely similar. One major difference, however, is that the Directive allows states to impose stricter limits (than those contained in Article 18) on the time allocated for advertising. This discretion enables them to protect 'pluralism of information and the media'.[110] In other words, restrictions may be imposed to protect the flow of advertising revenue to the press. States are also free not to apply the Directive's common advertising rules to purely internal broadcasts, that is, those which may not be received in other states.[111] This qualification safeguards the position of local advertising channels, common in Italy.[112]

[109] See S. 4(ii) above.
[110] Directive, Art. 19.
[111] Ibid., Art. 20.
[112] See Ch. X, S. 3 below for discussion of Art. 16 of the Convention, which prohibits in certain circumstances the broadcast of advertisements directed at the audience in a particular state.

X
International and European Law

1. INTRODUCTION

Technological developments in the last two decades have transformed the character of broadcasting. The advent of cable and satellite television not only has repercussions for national legislation, but also has made more imperative the formulation of international and continental rules. Radio broadcasting across frontiers did not create many problems, though there was considerable controversy concerning the legality of the Soviet jamming of Western broadcasting aimed at audiences in the Eastern European bloc. The positioning of geostationary satellites around the world, enabling television broadcasts to be beamed from, say, the United States to Europe or Asia (and sometimes vice versa) creates difficulties of a different order. Television is a more powerful medium, less limited than radio by cultural and linguistic frontiers. *Dallas* and *Dynasty* have been successfully exported to the Old World. More importantly pictures of the peaceful revolutions of 1989 in Germany and Czechoslovakia encouraged the Rumanians to take to the streets at the end of the year. Viewers in other Eastern countries and in Western Europe were then able to watch the unfolding of that final revolution. Initially there were low-power satellites which could be received only by collective aerials and retransmitted through cable systems. But the programmes of direct broadcasting satellites (DBS) can be picked up by anyone prepared to put a dish on their roof. Satellite broadcasting has become, therefore, a real alternative to conventional terrestrial broadcasting. Its reception area is not confined by national boundaries.

These developments create a number of legal problems. There are questions about the control over, and access to, outer space, relevant for the stationing of broadcasting (and other) satellites. More important, however, is the conflict between the principles of the 'free flow of information' and 'prior consent'. The United States and most Western European countries, including the United Kingdom, argue that it is generally contrary to international law for the reception of (satellite) broadcasts to be jammed or in some other way inhibited by a recipient state. There may on this view even be an international law right to the free flow of information. On the other hand, lawyers in developing countries, and in the Soviet Union (at least in the 1960s to 1980s), have denied this right. They contend instead that the transmission of broadcasts across frontiers requires the prior consent of the recipient state. In its absence transfrontier satellite broadcasting would violate that state's sovereignty.[1] Other lawyers have argued for less extreme positions, in particular, that transfrontier broadcasting could only be restricted on the grounds that the *content* of a particular broadcast offended some vital interest of the recipient state such as public order or a rule of international law, for example, that outlawing racialist propaganda. The terms of the discussion have altered in recent years. Many states, including some in Western Europe, have imposed quotas with the object of preventing the domination of their television channels by cheap American films and soaps. For countries such as France what is at stake is not so much political sovereignty as cultural integrity. But the legality of these rules is also in doubt, although they are to be found in both the European Convention on Transfrontier Television and the European Communities (EC) Broadcasting Directive.

There is no general international convention on satellite broadcasting, nor for that matter any relevant case-law of the International Court of Justice. Claims to international law rights and freedoms in this context are based on customary international law, derived from other conventions and state practice. Admittedly there is an important Resolution of the General Assembly of the United Nations (December 1982), but this is not binding. Technical matters, however, are regulated by the International Telecommunication Union (ITU), a specialist United Nations agency with its headquarters in Geneva, which allocates frequencies to states and which has issued a number of detailed regulations to prevent interference. One of its best-known rules is Radio Regulation 428A, which proscribes the 'spill-over' of terrestrial broadcasts across national boundaries, unless it is technically unavoidable. The rule provides perhaps some legal basis for the 'prior consent' principle.[2] The terms of the Convention establishing the ITU and its Radio Regulations are legally binding.

The absence of clear international law rules regarding the content of transfrontier broadcasts provides some incentive for their development on a regional basis. In Europe the members of the Council of Europe agreed a Convention in May 1989, and then a few months later the EC issued a Directive. The two instruments formulate the same fundamental principle: the reception of broadcasts emanating from member states must be allowed

[1] The debate is chronicled in S. F. Luther, *The United States and the Direct Broadcasting Satellite* (New York, 1988), chs. 4 and 5.

[2] Ibid. 101–5. Also see J. Freeman, 'Toward the Free Flow of Information: Direct Television Broadcasting by Satellite' (1979) 13 *Jo. of Int. Law and Economics* 329, 336–47. There is a good discussion of the ITU in the Council of Europe paper *Television by Satellite and Cable*, Mass Media Files No. 8 (1985).

in other jurisdictions, provided they comply with common standards for programmes and advertising. The Directive creates enforceable rights which must be protected by the national courts of EC states. Its provisions are considered at the end of this chapter, after a brief discussion of the main international law arguments and the history and content of the Council of Europe Convention.

2. INTERNATIONAL LAW

The first attempt to formulate binding rules of international law in the broadcasting context was the 1936 Convention concerning the Use of Broadcasting in the Cause of Peace.[3] The agreement was reached under the auspices of the League of Nations, of which the USA was not a member; it was, therefore, not a party to the Convention. Twenty-eight states, including Britain, signed, but it never came into force. Its object was largely to prevent the use of radio for propaganda purposes, an aim also pursued after the Second World War by many states, particularly in the Soviet bloc. The principal forum for attempts after 1945 to achieve international agreement has of course been the United Nations. The Charter itself does not contain any relevant provision, but the Universal Declaration of Human Rights adopted by the General Assembly of the United Nations in 1948 lays down 'the right . . . to seek, receive and impart information and ideas through any media and regardless of frontiers'.[4] A similar right is provided by Article 19 of the International Covenant on Civil and Political Rights 1966, a convention sponsored by the United Nations, now ratified by enough states to be in force.[5] (It has not been ratified by the US Senate, so it is difficult for that country to base any argument on its terms.)

It is sometimes argued that these provisions, although not directly binding, support the existence of a customary international law right to broadcast across frontiers, the 'free flow of information' principle advocated by the United States.[6] But this is doubtful. Quite apart from the question

[3] See E. A. Downey, 'A Historical Survey of the International Regulation of Propaganda', in *Regulation of Transnational Communications*, Michigan Yearbook of International Legal Studies (New York, 1984), 341.

[4] Art. 19.

[5] For discussion of these provisions, see L. Gross, 'Some International Law Aspects of the Freedom of Information and the Right to Communicate', in K. Nordenstreng and H. I. Schiller (eds.), *National Sovereignty and International Communication* (Norwood, NJ, 1989), 195.

[6] See W. E. Spiegel, 'Prior Consent and the UN Human Rights Resolutions', in *Regulation of Transnational Communications*, 379, and S. Magiera, 'Direct Broadcasting by Satellite and a New International Information Order' (1981) 24 *German Yearbook of Int. Law* 288.

how far the Declaration and the International Covenant can be relied on by broadcasting companies (or for that matter the institutional press), the rights formulated in these documents are significantly qualified. Both measures, especially the International Covenant, make it plain that the rights are to be exercised subject to the limits imposed by law in the interests of others and for the protection of morality and public order.

These exceptions are broad enough to justify the banning of a foreign broadcast which the recipient state reasonably believes might create violence and disorder, or incite racial and other forms of hatred. More importantly they also provide a basis for the 'prior consent principle'. A state must be able to ensure foreign broadcasts do not conflict with these vital interests. On the other hand the policy of jamming Western broadcasts often employed by the Soviet Union in the post-war years probably went beyond permissible state control.[7] It was exercised indiscriminately to prevent the reception of 'objective news' and current affairs programmes, as well as items which the authorities might with some reason have considered subversive of their regimes. Jamming was frequently condemned by General Assembly Resolutions, but the Soviet Union continued to defend its legality. It successfully resisted the introduction of a specific prohibition of the practice in the Helsinki Accords of 1975.[8] In the absence of universal acceptance of an international freedom of the airwaves, it is hard to claim a customary right to broadcast across national frontiers; customary rights must be based on general state practice.[9] The truth is that neither this right nor the legality of indiscriminate jamming has been satisfactorily established in international law.

The growing phenomenon of satellite broadcasting has encouraged greater efforts to find an acceptable solution to the problem, though they have not been greeted with universal acclaim. The legal principles have been debated by the Committee on Peaceful Uses of Outer Space (COPUOS) instituted by the General Assembly in 1958. Its deliberations led to the signing in 1967 of the Outer Space Treaty.[10] It contains general principles concerning the use of outer space, including the siting and exploitation of broadcasting satellites. Broadly it establishes the principle

[7] R. B. Price, 'Jamming and the Law of International Communications', in *Regulation of Transnational Communications*, 391. A more sympathetic view of the Soviet position is taken by G. Gornig, 'Der grenzüberschreitende Informationsfluss durch Rundfunkwellen: zur Frage der Volkerrechtswidrigkeit von Jamming' (1988) 15 *EuGRZ* 1.

[8] Price, 'Jamming and the Law of International Communications'.

[9] See Gross, 'Some International Law Aspects of the Freedom of Information and the Right to Communicate', and I. Brownlie, *Principles of Public International Law*, 4th edn. (Oxford, 1990), 5–11.

[10] Luther, *The United States and the Direct Broadcasting Satellite*, ch. 4; J. E. S. Fawcett, *Outer Space: New Challenges to Law and Policy* (Oxford, 1984), ch. 4; Council of Europe, *Television by Satellite and Cable*, 20–1.

of the free use of outer space, so prohibiting claims of sovereignty in this area. On the other hand, states are responsible for all activities, including those of private bodies, and they must ensure that they are carried out in conformity with the principles of international law. Strangely there is no definition of 'outer space' to distinguish it from the air-space over which states may exercise sovereign powers. The ITU began to plan orbital positions for broadcasting and other satellites and to assign frequencies in the 1970s. Naturally most of the satellites were launched by the United States or the Soviet Union. In 1976 a number of equatorial countries, led by Columbia, issued the Bogota Declaration, asserting state sovereignty over that part of the geostationary orbit which lay above their countries. The claim was predictably resisted by the superpowers, and the issue has not yet been resolved. In principle, a 'first come, first served' rule seems crude, and some right of equitable access to space should be guaranteed.

The 1967 Treaty did not attempt to resolve the conflict between the 'free-flow' and 'prior consent' principles. Discussions in COPUOS were inconclusive for a long time. One indication of majority opinion was given by the Unesco Declaration of 1972, which stressed the necessity for states, taking into account the principle of freedom of information, to reach prior agreement with recipient states concerning satellite broadcasts.[11] This principle was opposed by the United States and most European countries, which continued to assert the 'free-flow' principle. The former argued that it would be incompatible with its First Amendment to subscribe to any international agreement or resolution which legitimized a veto by recipient states on foreign programmes. Even some United States scholars have found this argument unconvincing.[12] There is first the difficulty whether constitutional rules apply to international treaties. Secondly, the federal government itself imposes some controls on the import and export of mail, while the FCC regulates who may broadcast within the country. If there is no commitment to an absolute free flow of information into the USA, it is hard to see how any such right can be claimed for broadcasting outside it. But equally the Soviet case that the prior consent of the recipient state is justified by state sovereignty is unconvincing, for foreign broadcasting does not generally invade the essential attributes of that principle, control over the national territory and political independence.[13] Other states, in particular Canada and Sweden, formulated compromises which embodied recognition of both competing principles.

Eventually in December 1982 the General Assembly passed a Resolution

[11] Ibid. 23.

[12] See in particular M. E. Price, 'The First Amendment and Television Broadcasting by Satellite' (1976) 23 *UCLA L. Rev.* 875.

[13] H. C. Anawalt, 'Direct Television Broadcasting and the Quest for Communication Equality', in *Regulation of Transnational Communications*, 364, 368–71.

stating principles for international direct television broadcasting.[14] Consensus proved impossible. It was passed by a majority of 107–13, with 13 abstentions. The United States, the United Kingdom, Germany, and Italy were among the countries opposing the Resolution, while France, Canada, and Sweden abstained. Among the principles are the equal rights of states to engage in international satellite broadcasting and equal access to technology, state responsibility (already stated in the Outer Space Treaty), and the desirability of co-operation, both generally and in the field of copyright. The most important principle is that set out in paragraphs 13 and 14. It requires states intending to institute a DBS to notify the proposed receiving state and promptly to enter into consultations if asked by the latter. An international DBS may only be established after this requirement has been satisfied. This imposes in effect the 'prior consent' rule (albeit in a very diluted form). It is hardly surprising, therefore, that the Resolution was opposed by most Western states. A General Assembly Resolution is not binding in international law. Moreover, in view of the lack of unanimity, it can hardly be regarded as evidence for a customary law rule of prior consent.

There is more general support for a limited power on the part of states to restrict the reception and retransmission (by cable) of particular foreign broadcasts on the basis of their content.[15] Under the international covenants mentioned earlier states appear free to ban the reception, for example, of broadcasts from abroad which they consider likely to endanger national security, public order, public health, or morals.[16] Indeed, if widely used, this power would not fall far short of the 'prior consent' rule. It certainly goes beyond the limited powers to prevent the free reception of broadcasts emanating from other member states allowed by the two European measures considered later in this chapter.

With the collapse of the Soviet bloc in Eastern Europe the argument between the proponents of 'free flow of information' and of the 'prior consent' rule is heard less often. Instead the most contentious issue is the legality of the quotas commonly imposed by national broadcasting systems on the import of foreign programmes. Quotas inhibit the programming freedom of national terrestrial broadcasters as well as the freedom of cable companies to retransmit whatever foreign satellite programmes they choose. The justification for their imposition is the desirability of protecting national cultural identity.[17] British and Canadian viewers, for example,

[14] UN Resolution 37/92 of 10 Dec. 1982, UN Doc. A/37/5(1983). The text is published in (1983) 77 *Am. Jo. of Int. Law* 773.

[15] B. A. Hurwitz, 'The Labyrinth of International Telecommunications: Direct Broadcast Satellites' (1988) 35 *Netherlands Int. Law Rev.* 145.

[16] See International Covenant on Civil and Political Rights, Art. 19(2).

[17] There is a wealth of literature on the arguments for and against quotas. Sympathetic to restrictions to protect national cultures are Y. Littunen, 'Cultural Problems of Direct

who watch a continuous stream of *Dallas* and Hollywood films may lose the sense of what is to be British or Canadian. The motive for quotas may be to protect employment in the national film and television industries. These industries face decline because it is so much cheaper to import United States films than to produce a comparable product inside the country; television companies, particularly smaller independent ones, are tempted to swamp their schedules with American material.

But to the disgust of educated élites, films and soaps from the USA are very popular with viewers; it can be argued that quotas entail some restriction on their freedom. There are other arguments of principle against their imposition. Applied indiscriminately, they would enable totalitarian regimes to shut out foreign current affairs programmes and documentaries presenting a view of their country other than that favoured by the government.[18] International mass media contribute visions of society which may counter that provided by a state monopoly. Frequently the real argument for quotas is not so much that they enable broadcasters to show quality programmes, but that they protect home-produced trivia against the competition provided by American equivalents. This is an unattractive example of protectionism. But even if the motive is genuinely cultural, it may be questioned how far national culture should be protected. What would we think about a rule requiring the BBC Symphony Orchestra to include 50 per cent British music in its programmes? (This is much less than the quota for British (now EC) programming followed by the BBC and imposed on the independent sector.[19]) Finally it is difficult to define satisfactorily the criteria for meeting a quota: does the identity of a United Kingdom (or EC) programme depend on how it is financed, where it is made, the nationality of the producer, director, or principal actors, or some combination of all these factors? (It is usual to exclude some programmes from the quota rules, as they do not involve cultural enterprise. For example, news bulletins, advertising, sports events, and teletext are excluded under the EC Directive and the Transfrontier Television Convention.[20]) Often the distinction between programmes which satisfy a quota and those which do not will be hard to draw.

Despite these arguments, the imposition of quotas has become increasingly popular both in Europe and in some other countries. France

Satellite Broadcasting' (1980) 32 *Int. Social Science Jo.* 283 and A. J. Wiesand, 'Dämme gegen eine Flut von Billig-Programmen?' (1985) *Media Perspektiven* 191. A summary of the legal position in European countries is to be found in *Towards a European Common Market for Television*, European Media Institute Monograph No. 8 (Manchester, 1987).

[18] I. de Sola Pool, 'Direct Broadcasting Satellites and the Integrity of National Cultures', in Nordenstreng and Schiller (eds.), *National Sovereignty and International Communications*, 120, 122–9.

[19] For national quotas, see Ch. V, S. 3 above.

[20] Directive of 3 Oct. 1989, 89/552/EEC, OJ L 298/23; Council of Europe Convention on Transfrontier Television, 16 Mar. 1989, Art. 10.

has imposed them since 1975 in the schedule of conditions binding broadcasting companies.[21] The rules are set out in the *cahiers des charges* of the public companies and in decisions of the CNCL regulating the private chains.[22] Antenne 2 and FR3 are both required to show at least 50 per cent French programmes, and the former is also obliged to show at least 300 hours annually of original French programming. The 50 per cent quota is also imposed on the private channels; sometimes there have been disputes whether they are meeting this condition, and in particular whether the quota is to be assessed annually or daily.[23] The Italian law of August 1990 contains complex rules in this context.[24] Both public and private national channels must reserve for the first three years of their licence at least 40 per cent of the time devoted to films to EC productions; after that period the proportion is to rise to 51 per cent. These obligations are imposed to satisfy the EC Directive requirements discussed in Section 4 of this chapter. Half of this proportion must be Italian works, and then a fifth of these works must have been made within the last five years. Outside Europe, Canada has imposed quotas in an attempt to protect its national culture against take-over by its southern neighbour. The Canadian Broadcasting Corporation is required to provide programming which is 'predominantly and distinctively Canadian'.[25]

In contrast other countries regard quotas as unnecessary, impracticable, and sometimes undesirable in principle. They seem never to have been highly regarded in Germany. Public and private channels in Britain have each observed a quota of 86 per cent of British and EC works; as far as Channel 3 licensees are concerned, this is now imposed by the requirement to devote a 'proper proportion' of the schedule to Community-made programmes.[26] The BBC and the IBA, however, were opposed to the attempt by the Brussels Commission to impose a numerical quota in the Directive.[27] Their argument for the most part was that this would be cumbersome and legalistic. There was also some opposition on principle on the ground that quotas inhibit viewer choice and might prevent the growth of satellite film channels. Further, there has been no support for them in other countries, such as Switzerland and Luxembourg, where there has always been a mixture of languages and cultures; the latter

[21] For details, see C. Debbasch, *Droit de l'audiovisuel*, 2nd edn. (Paris, 1991), 433 and 440.

[22] See Decree 87-717 of 28 Aug. 1987, Arts. 26, 27, and 44 (*cahiers des charges* of Antenne 2), and Decision 87-2 of 15 Jan. 1987, Arts. 4–5 fixing the rules applicable to private terrestrial television.

[23] See the 2nd Annual Report of the CNCL, 1987–8, 195.

[24] Law 223 of 6 Aug. 1990, Art. 26.

[25] Broadcasting Act 1991, s. 3(1)(m).

[26] Broadcasting Act 1990, s. 16(2)(g).

[27] See the Report of the HL Select Committee on the European Communities, *European Broadcasting* (1986–7) HL 67, 11.

country has also profited economically from its role as the base of international broadcasting companies.

The arguments of principle are indeed evenly balanced. Clearly quotas infringe the interests of some channel owners and perhaps many viewers. It is less obvious that they are really contrary to broadcasting freedom. As we saw in Chapter II, that value requires the formulation of positive standards to guarantee a variety of programmes in the interests of viewers. On that perspective, it would be justifiable to impose quotas on some channels, particularly the public ones and perhaps the principal commercial terrestrial channels. Otherwise there is a danger that viewers might cease to enjoy access to drama, films, and other programmes made in their own country (or in the European Community). There is a less strong case for applying these rules to satellite or subscription channels.[28] Another point is that while their aims are laudable, quotas are a crude method of preserving national culture and a native film industry.

There are also doubts about the legality of quota rules. These first concern their compatibility with the General Agreement on Tariffs and Trade (GATT).[29] At present there is no difficulty, since GATT only applies to goods and not to services. But the USA has been pressing for its extension to the latter sector, and this has been one of the topics under consideration at the negotiations known as the Uruguay Round. Extension of the existing articles to cover services would cause difficulties for quota rules. However, exceptions could be provided, as in the case of the cinema (already covered by GATT). Further, special exemptions could be added to protect national cultural identity, although there is every reason to believe that these would be fiercely opposed by the USA. Pressure from the United States film industry and by the federal government on its behalf was one factor leading to the weakening of the quota provisions in the EC Broadcasting Directive. Arguably the existence of these provisions, however bland, in the Directive gives the EC countries a bargaining counter at the Uruguay Round.

Quotas may be incompatible with the European Convention on Human Rights. Article 10(1) protects the freedom to communicate information and ideas 'regardless of frontiers'. This certainly covers broadcasting.[30] The imposition of quotas does constitute an interference with the freedom of broadcasters to devise their own programme schedules. But, as we have just seen, these rules may well be compatible with broadcasting freedom and therefore with the right to freedom of expression applied to

[28] The British Broadcasting Act 1990 does not appear to impose the European quota obligation on the BSkyB non-domestic satellite service, although it should do so in order to meet the requirements of the EC Directive and the Council of Europe Convention.

[29] See *Towards a European Common Market for Television*, Annex A.

[30] See the cases discussed fully in the following section of this chapter.

television. If, however, the European Court of Human Rights were to hold that there is an infringement of Article 10(1), a state imposing quotas might be in difficulties. None of the aims stated in Article 10(2), in pursuance of which restrictions on freedom of expression may be justified, really covers the preservation of national identities or cultural values. A television company might, therefore, challenge a quota before the Commission of Human Rights with some chance of success. In its defence it would be argued that both the EC Directive and the Council of Europe's own Television Convention require states to introduce the restriction.

3. THE EUROPEAN CONVENTION ON TRANSFRONTIER TELEVISION

The phenomenon of cross-frontier broadcasting has long been familiar in Western Europe. The small size of the countries has made inevitable some spill-over of radio and later television broadcasts into neighbouring states. In a few cases culture and language are the same on both sides of a border, so making the export of broadcasts to another country attractive. Large international media groups have emerged, anxious to exploit new technological possibilities to create something like a genuine European broadcasting industry. For example, the powerful Fininvest company controlled by Silvio Berlusconi owns three national television channels in Italy (as well as indirectly controlling others), had a large shareholding in La Cinq in France before its collapse in 1991, and has important interests in Spain and more recently Eastern Europe, including Russia. Densely cabled countries, such as Belgium, Holland, and Switzerland, have long had access to broadcasts from many other states, relayed to them through their cable systems. Satellites, and DBS in particular, now make enjoyment of this facility even easier. Groups of public broadcasting companies from different countries have combined to transmit satellite programmes over a large area. 3-SAT, for example, is a satellite television channel mounted by ZDF and the Austrian and German Swiss public broadcasting corporations.

With these developments there is a good case for some common broadcasting regulation. Otherwise states would be able to impose their own controls on foreign broadcasts, with regard, say, to advertising or programme standards. The exercise of these powers might substantially inhibit the reception of satellite programmes or their retransmission by cable systems. Advertisers in particular have complained about the difficulties they face in having to meet divergent legal requirements.[31] On the other hand, a state would be unwilling to surrender its broadcasting powers

[31] For further discussion of this point, see Ch. IX, S. 1 above.

over foreign programmes with complete equanimity, unless it were satisfied that they met some minimal standards, for example, to prevent the excessive interruption of programmes by advertising or the showing of grossly indecent films.

European regulation attempts to resolve these difficulties. But there has been uncertainty about the appropriate forum for their resolution and to some extent whether a cultural or a commercial approach should predominate. The Council of Europe, instituted after the last world war to safeguard human rights and foster democracy, has for a long time been interested in media problems.[32] In 1976 a Steering Committee on the Mass Media was set up to examine them from the perspective of their impact on human rights and their cultural implications. This perspective has remained paramount and contrasts, as will be seen in the next section, with the emphasis placed by the European Community institutions on broadcasting as a commercial service.

A discussion of the legal background to the Council of Europe Television Convention must begin with the earlier Convention on Human Rights and Fundamental Freedoms of 1950. Article 10(1) provides:

> Everyone has the right to freedom of expression. This right shall include freedom to hold opinions and to receive and impart information and ideas, without interference by public authority and regardless of frontiers. This Article shall not prevent States from requiring the licensing of broadcasting, television or cinema enterprises.

The right to freedom of expression may be subject to restrictions and conditions which are prescribed by law and are necessary to achieve one of the aims set out in Article 10(2), for example, to protect the reputation or rights of others, or to prevent disorder. Some of the legal points arising from these provisions are discussed in other chapters; for example, the question whether there is a right to institute a private broadcasting station[33] and how far advertising limits may be upheld.[34] In this chapter we are concerned primarily with the Convention's application to transfrontier broadcasting.

The European Court has considered this issue in two cases decided in 1990. In *Groppera*[35] the application was brought by a Swiss radio company,

[32] See *Council of Europe Activities in the Mass Media Field*, a paper by its Human Rights Directorate (Strasbourg, 1983), and F. W. Hondius, 'Regulating Transfrontier Television: The Strasbourg Option' (1988) 8 *Yearbook of European Law* 141. This part of the chapter is much indebted to his article.

[33] See Ch. IV, S. 2.

[34] Ch. IX, S. 3. See C. Hauschka, 'Auswirkungen der Auslegung des Art. 10 der Europäischen Konvention für Menschenrechte auf Wettbewerbsrecht, Medienrecht und das Recht der Freien Berufe' (1987) 11 *ZUM* 559.

[35] *Groppera Radio* v. *Switzerland* (1990) 12 EHRR 321.

whose subsidiary broadcast from a station across the border in Italy. That station had not been licensed, and because of that the Swiss authorities refused to allow the reception and retransmission (by cable) of its pop music programmes. The Court ruled that Article 10 covered both over the air radio and retransmission by cable; it rejected the argument that a music station fell outside the provision because its transmissions did not contain information or ideas. Much more complicated were the questions raised about the scope of the third sentence of Article 10(1); does it entitle a state to prohibit broadcasts from stations which had not been licensed by another state, and could a licence be refused on other than technical grounds? The Court, unlike the Human Rights Commission, held that a state could rely on Article 10(1) to justify the imposition of conditions to prevent a cable company from retransmitting broadcasts from an unlicensed foreign station; however, the licensing power could only be used on technical grounds to prevent undue crowding of the wavelengths and in the circumstances set out in Article 10(2). The majority of the Court considered the Swiss government's aims were legitimate. The restrictions on the retransmission of Groppera's broadcasts were imposed to prevent telecommunications disorder and to protect the rights of other licensed radio stations. The measures taken were not a disproportionate means of preventing evasion of the Swiss licensing scheme; the Court also emphasized the absence of censorship of the applicant's programmes on the basis of their content.

The applicant was successful in the other case, *Autronic* v. *Switzerland*.[36] The Swiss government had denied it permission to use a dish aerial for the reception of uncoded television programmes from a Soviet telecommunications satellite in the absence of USSR consent. Among the key points in the Court's judgment was its ruling that Article 10 covers a freedom to choose the means of communication as well as its substance, and that, therefore, it encompasses a right to receive television programmes by a dish. It confirmed the earlier ruling in *Groppera* that the licensing of broadcasting facilities was permissible only on the grounds referred to in Article 10(2), but on this occasion held the Swiss rule was not necessary to prevent communications disorder. A crucial point was that it had become standard practice for states to allow the reception of uncoded broadcasts from telecommunications satellites without requiring the consent of the transmitting state.[37]

These decisions did not resolve every legal problem. In particular, it is unclear whether the Court would permit a recipient state to apply its rules

[36] (1990) 12 EHRR 485.

[37] The Court also rejected the argument that the ban was necessary to prevent the disclosure of confidential information, for there was no evidence that any was transmitted.

on programme content to broadcasts emanating from other countries which are parties to the European Convention. Answers to the most important questions of principle are now provided by the Transfrontier Television Convention: all participating states are generally obliged to allow the retransmission of broadcasting services which comply with the conditions set out in the Convention, whether or not they also comply with the standards set by the recipient state. But the principles set out in the earlier Human Rights Convention may still be relevant to the interpretation of the later agreement.

The first steps towards the formulation of the Television Convention were taken in the 1980s, with the preparation of a number of reports by the Steering Committee on the Mass Media and the subsequent passage of Recommendations of the Committee of Ministers. They covered topics such as the principles of television advertising, the use of satellite capacity, and copyright issues. As a leading commentator has put it, these recommendations became 'building blocks' for the Convention.[38] A further impetus was provided by the contemporary developments in the European Community after publication of the Brussels Commission's Green Paper (1984). Some countries thought the emphasis of the EC on the commercial aspects of broadcasting endangered its cultural role. Moreover, the Council of Europe has many more members and covers a much wider area than the Community. A common criticism of the latter's activity in this context is that it is artificial for it to regulate television, when its boundaries do not follow natural broadcasting zones.[39] For example, Austria and Switzerland are affected by German radio and television services. But as they are not EC states, they could not participate in the development of Community legislation. From this perspective the larger Council of Europe provides a more natural forum for continental regulation. At all events, following a conference of media ministers in Vienna, the Committee of Ministers in January 1987 instructed the Steering Committee to draft a Convention.

It was eventually decided to conclude the Council of Europe Convention before the EC Directive was agreed. That procedure enabled a wider range of states to participate in the drafting of the former; if the Directive had been issued first, its contents would have pre-empted resolution of many issues by the the Council of Europe. There were considerable difficulties in drafting the advertising limits and the quotas for European works, problems which also occurred in the negotiations leading to enactment of the EC Directive. The text was finally agreed in March 1989

[38] Hondius, 'Regulating Transfrontier Television', 152.

[39] Report of the HL Select Committee on the European Communities, *Television without Frontiers* (1985–6) HL 43, 16.

and the Convention left open for signature two months later. In addition to the member states of the Council of Europe, it may be signed by other states which are parties to the European Cultural Convention (at that time the Vatican and Yugoslavia) and by the European Community. The Convention entered into force in 1992, when seven states had ratified it.

The Convention covers the transmission and retransmission, whether by terrestrial transmitters, cable, or satellite, of television programme services which may be received in other states which are parties to the Convention. It does not apply to radio, nor is it of any relevance to purely internal programmes. The fundamental principle is set out in Article 4:

> The Parties shall ensure freedom of expression and information in accordance with Article 10 [of the Human Rights Convention] and they shall guarantee freedom of reception and shall not restrict the retransmission on their territories of programme services which comply with the terms of the Convention.

It is for the transmitting party under Article 5 to ensure that the programme services comply with the common standards set out in the Convention. For satellite transmissions, the responsible state is the state where the up-link is situated, or where that is situated in a state not a party to the Convention it is the state which grants the use of the frequency or satellite capacity.[40] Thus British Sky Broadcasting beams up programmes from its ground station in London to the Luxembourg satellite Astra; the United Kingdom is therefore responsible for these transmissions, but if Algeria, say, rented a channel on the Astra satellite, Luxembourg would be responsible for ensuring that the programmes satisfied the Convention requirements. Provided the programme services satisfy these requirements, other states may not inhibit reception nor prevent retransmission within their jurisdiction. That is the case even if the broadcast would not meet the standards imposed by the recipient state on its own television services. For example, the retransmission in Britain of an interview with an IRA supporter shown on French television could probably not be restricted, although the broadcast of such interviews by the BBC and independent licensed services has been banned.[41]

There is one controversial exception to this general rule. Under Article 16 a recipient state may apply its own advertising rules to commercials which are specifically and with some frequency directed at its audiences and not those in the transmitting state. This is so even if otherwise they comply with the rules in the Convention governing duration, frequency, and content.[42] The object is to prevent distortions in competition and to

[40] Art. 5(2).
[41] See Ch. II, S. 2 above.
[42] See Ch. IX, S. 5 above.

safeguard the broadcasting system in a country which imposes particularly draconian limits on the volume of advertising. The provision was inserted at the request of The Netherlands, which had felt that advertising directed at the Dutch market endangered the survival of its non-commercial broadcasting system. The exception does not apply if the protective rule discriminates against advertising from other states, for example, if only advertisements by Heineken and other Dutch brewers were allowed, but not British or German beer commercials. Despite this qualification, the exception remains controversial and may well be contrary to the Treaty of Rome, as interpreted in the *Dutch Advertisers* case (discussed later)[43] and to the Human Rights Convention. If advertising is covered by Article 10 of the latter, there would be considerable difficulty in supporting a prohibition on its reception and retransmission in a state other than the transmitting state; for there would clearly be a violation of the right to impart and receive information regardless of frontiers, and it is hard to see how the prohibition could be justified under Article 10(2).[44]

Broadly the substantive provisions fall into two parts. There are a number of rules, first about programme standards, and secondly about advertising and sponsorship. Two provisions are particularly noteworthy under the first heading. Article 9 requires each state to examine the legal measures required to ensure that the public's access to (or information about) major public events is not undermined by exclusive broadcasting agreements. The legal difficulties of these agreements have been considered elsewhere in this book.[45] The Convention provision is very weak, in that it only requires states to examine the problem. Moreover, it is unclear in that the text refers to the right of the public to information, while the title of the article is 'Access of the public to major events'. The right might be protected by, say, an entitlement to show a three-minute sound and picture report on all channels of a football match covered live by only one. But arguably public access to the event is denied if the match is shown solely on a subscription channel to which a minority subscribe. A recent Recommendation of the Committee of Ministers urges states to introduce short reporting rights for major events, that is, those where one broadcaster holds exclusive rights to show the event and broadcasters in other states consider it to be of particular public interest.[46]

Article 10 on cultural objectives is as vague. States must ensure 'where practicable' that broadcasters 'reserve for European works a majority

[43] See below, p. 231, and see the article by I. E. Schwartz, 'Fernsehen ohne Grenzen: zur Effektivität und zur Verhältnis von EG Richtlinie und Europarats-Konvention' (1989) 24 *Europarecht* 1.

[44] For discussion of the treatment of advertising under the Human Rights Convention, see Ch. IX, S. 3 above.

[45] Ch. VI, S. 5 above.

[46] Recommendation No. R(91) 5.

proportion of their transmission time', excluding time given to news, sports events, games, advertising, and teletext. A disagreement between states on the application of this rule is not, as is the usual procedure, to be referred to arbitration, but may at the request of one party be referred to the Standing Committee set up by the Convention (see Articles 20–2). States must also endeavour to prevent broadcasting having an adverse impact on the press and cinema. In an unusually precise rule, and one, moreover, incorporated in the Convention at a late stage, films are not to be shown on television within the first two years of initial showing in the cinema, unless the rights-holders in the film agree.[47]

Apart from these rules, interesting because they have no counterparts in the British legislation, there are general rules prohibiting programmes containing pornography, giving undue prominence to violence, or inciting racial hatred.[48] Programmes unsuitable for children must be shown at a time when they are unlikely to be watching. News must depict events fairly. States must provide for an effective right of reply or other equivalent remedies.[49] (In Britain this requirement is perhaps satisfied by the opportunity to complain to the Broadcasting Complaints Commission.[50]) Perhaps it is not surprising that these provisions are so thin. Content regulations vary considerably from state to state, and it would have been impossible to come to any agreement on more detailed rules. Moreover, states are not generally concerned whether foreign services contain, say, a suitable proportion of educational and religious programmes or meet other internal positive programme requirements.

In contrast the advertising rules are relatively detailed. The principal dispute about them was whether advertising should be confined to blocks between programmes, as in Germany, or whether interruptions of programmes should be allowed.[51] The compromise is that the former is the general rule, but 'natural breaks' are allowed, provided they are inserted so as not to prejudice the value of the programme or the author's moral rights.[52] There are also bans on advertising particular products.[53] The details of these provisions and the rules permitting sponsorship of programmes have been discussed in the previous chapter.[54]

Disputes between states must be resolved by one of the prescribed procedures: conciliation by the Standing Committee or arbitration.[55]

[47] Art. 10(4).
[48] Art. 7.
[49] Art. 8.
[50] See Ch. VII, S. 4, for discussion of this question.
[51] See J. Tunstall and M. Palmer, *Media Moguls* (London, 1991), 93–9.
[52] See Arts. 13(1) and 14.
[53] Art. 15.
[54] Ch. IX, S. 5.
[55] See Arts. 25 and 26.

However, if an alleged violation of the substantive rules is of a clear and serious character and it persists for two weeks after notice has been given to the transmitting state, the recipient state may exceptionally suspend provisionally the transmission of the offending programme service. If the alleged violation persists for eight months, there is a general power to suspend retransmission. These powers do not apply, however, in the case of breaches of the obligations to present news fairly, to provide a right of reply, or to honour the quota rules.[56] When exercising their powers of suspension, states should take account of the requirement under the Human Rights Convention that the freedom of broadcasting across frontiers should only be restricted if that is necessary to satisfy one of the aims set out in Article 10(2). A suspension should also be a proportionate remedy for the violation. In this respect the powers of recipient states are wider than they are under the Directive.

4. THE EUROPEAN COMMUNITIES DIRECTIVE

Developments in the European Communities have run parallel to those in the Council of Europe. Two years after a Resolution passed in 1982 by the European Parliament, the Brussels Commission published proposals for harmonizing aspects of the member states' broadcasting laws. Despite the expression of strong reservations concerning Community competence, the Commission proceeded with the issue of a draft Directive in June 1986. Eventually this was enacted by the Council of Ministers in October 1989, a few months after the opening of the Council of Europe Convention for signature. There are considerable similarities between the two instruments, though also one or two significant differences. One of these is that the Directive lays down some minimum standards for all television broadcasts, whether or not they are capable of reception in another state. Another distinction is that provisions of the EC Directive may create directly effective rights, that is, rights which must be enforced in national courts, while the Convention is not enforceable in British law nor in that of many other countries. Community states must apply EC rules, rather than the Convention; for them the latter is only relevant where there is no pertinent provision in the Directive.[57]

Broadcasting is not mentioned in the Treaty of Rome. Moreover, in so far as it is a cultural activity, its regulation in principle should be a matter for the member states. But it can also be regarded as a commercial

[56] Art. 24.

[57] European Convention on Transfrontier Television, Art. 29(1). The Directive, Art. 24 provides that in fields which are not co-ordinated by the Directive, rights and obligations resulting from broadcasting conventions are unaffected by it.

service, and to that extent it is a matter for Community competence. For Articles 59–66 provide for the freedom to provide (and receive) services across national boundaries. Other Articles of the Treaty may sometimes be relevant, in particular, those dealing with the free movement of goods.[58] The question was how far these rules could justify Community legislation. Answers have been provided by the European Court of Justice (ECJ). The first case was *Sacchi*,[59] where the owner of a cable relay undertaking had refused to pay RAI the mandatory licence fee. One of Sacchi's arguments was that RAI's monopoly inhibited the reception in Italy of foreign programmes and advertisements and, therefore, hindered the free movement of goods.[60] The Court dismissed this thin claim. The transmission of television signals, including advertisements, was normally to be treated as the provision of a 'service' for Community law. (Trade in physical material, such as cameras and film, would, however, be covered by the free movement of goods rules.)

But it was the companion cases, *Coditel* and *Debauve*,[61] which firmly established the legal position a few years later. The cases arose out of breaches of Belgian copyright and advertising rules by cable companies, retransmitting in the area of Liège programmes from Germany, where their transmission was of course not subject to Belgian law. In one case the breach occurred because the cable company transmitted German programmes, including advertisements, at a time when Belgian law still prohibited their insertion. In the other a film was shown in violation of the exclusive distribution rights assigned to a Belgian company. The cable companies argued that the application of the national restrictions to the retransmission of broadcasts emanating from other states infringed the freedom to provide services across frontiers guaranteed by Article 59.[62] The ECJ affirmed its ruling in *Sacchi*. It emphasized, however, that the Treaty only applied when services were provided across frontiers, and on one view the relevant service in these cases was the cable transmission in Belgium to the subscribers. In that event there would have been no Community element and Belgian law could have been applied without qualification. The ECJ seemed to regard the characterization of the

[58] See Arts. 30–7 of the Treaty of Rome on the elimination of quantitative restrictions on the free movement of goods, and Arts. 85–90, the competition rules, discussed in Ch. VI, S. 5 above.

[59] 155/73, *Italy* v. *Sacchi* [1974] ECR 409.

[60] For the competition aspects of the case, see Ch. VI, S. 5 above.

[61] 52/79, *Procureur du Roi* v. *Debauve* [1980] ECR 833 and 62/79, *Coditel* v. *Cine Vog Films* [1980] ECR 881.

[62] Art. 59 provides: 'restrictions on freedom to provide services within the Community shall be progressively abolished during the transitional period in respect of nationals of Member States who are established in a State of the Community other than that of the person for whom the services are intended'. For commentary, see D. A. Wyatt and A. Dashwood, *The Substantive Law of the EEC*, 2nd edn. (London, 1987), 217–22.

service as a matter for the national court; since the Belgian tribunal had already ruled that it was provided across frontiers, there was no further discussion of the point. But it might also have been argued that Article 59 was applicable, because advertisers in other states were prevented from reaching Belgian television viewers.

However, the Court held that as the Belgian rules on copyright and advertising were equally applicable to purely internal broadcasts, there was no discrimination on the basis of the nationality or the place of establishment (or residence) of the broadcasters. In the absence of harmonization of national laws, a state was free to ban advertising totally, provided it did not discriminate in applying the ban. Secondly, the freedom of services provisions did not prohibit the exercise of copyright (and assigned rights), as long as these rights did not create artificial barriers to trade between states. Community competence in this area was based on these ECJ rulings. The Commission's proposals in the Green Paper (discussed below) were designed to bring about the common market in broadcasting, which according to the Court in the Belgian cases had not been achieved by the Treaty itself.

Nevertheless, the Treaty principle of non-discrimination remains significant in this context, as shown in later cases. In the important *Dutch Advertisers* case,[63] a Netherlands law prohibited the retransmission by cable networks of foreign satellite (but not terrestrial) programme services containing advertisements specifically directed at Dutch viewers or with subtitles in Dutch. It was intended to preserve the non-commercial character of television in The Netherlands, which allowed only advertising arranged through a public monopoly agency. The ECJ held that the case did involve the Community rules on the freedom to provide services, since there were transfrontier services both in the provision of programmes by the satellite channels for the cable companies and in the advertising arranged by companies (mostly in Holland) with the former. The law was clearly discriminatory. The more difficult question was whether it could be upheld under Article 56 of the Treaty of Rome, which permits member states to maintain discriminatory rules on grounds of public policy. The ECJ ruled that this article could not be invoked for an economic end: to protect the monopoly position of the public advertising agency. Moreover, in so far as non-commercial aims were pursued, only proportionate measures could be upheld. While restrictions on the duration and frequency of advertisements might be justified, a complete prohibition on transfrontier satellite advertising was illegal.[64]

[63] 352/85, *Advertisers' Association* v. *The Netherlands* [1989] 3 CMLR 113.

[64] In two later cases the ECJ held other Dutch rules intended to restrict advertisements from abroad aimed at the Dutch market incompatible with the freedom of services rules in the Treaty of Rome: see Cases 288/89 and 353/89, decided by ECJ on 25 July 91.

In June 1984 the Commission issued its Green Paper *Television without Frontiers*, on the establishment of a common market in broadcasting.[65] (The description 'Green Paper' is misleading, since in its British edition at any rate it has a white cover.) Proceeding from the desirability of introducing a common market in broadcasting and advertising services, the Commission recommended the adoption of Community rules in four areas: advertising and sponsorship, copyright, rights of reply to personal attacks, and the protection of young persons. States should no longer be free to ban or impose restrictions on broadcasting services emanating from other EC countries which complied with these common rules. There was also a radical recommendation that member states be obliged to allow advertising not only on private channels, but also on their public channels if there were insufficient openings for advertisers on their commercial rivals. States would be permitted to impose more onerous restrictions concerning, say, the frequency of advertisements on their own internal channels. But they could not impose less stringent limits, for that would discriminate against foreign advertisers. The Commission's copyright proposals proved particularly controversial, and were eventually dropped from the Directive. Based on the view that national copyright laws inhibit the free flow of television programmes, the Commission recommended a statutory licensing system, under which broadcasters would have been free to retransmit programmes subject to copyright in another state, provided the rights-holder received some remuneration for the loss of copyright.

The Green Paper was not received with universal acclaim. The House of Lords Select Committee on the European Communities made a number of criticisms.[66] It doubted the legal competence of the Community in this cultural area. Even if these doubts were removed, the Green Paper was far too ambitious. The Committee thought it would be preferable to negotiate any necessary rules in other forums, such as the Council of Europe or the European Broadcasting Union. Doubts were also raised in other states, particularly Germany. There were difficulties in that country about the competence of the federal government to participate in the passage of EC legislation over an area which is the responsibility of the *Länder*. Bavaria indeed unsuccessfully challenged the federal government's competence before the Constitutional Court.[67]

On the other hand, there was enough approval in some states and in the European Parliament for the Commission to issue a draft Directive in

[65] COM(84) 300 final.

[66] *Television without Frontiers*.

[67] See 80 BVerfGE 74 (1989) for the refusal by the Constitutional Court to grant a temporary order restraining the federal government from signing the Directive.

1986.[68] Unlike the Green Paper it applied to radio as well as television, though subsequently coverage was limited to the latter. Its fundamental principle, enshrined in Article 1 of the draft, was that broadcasts in one state which comply with the common requirements of the Directive should be freely receivable and retransmissible in other member states. This has remained the central principle of the enacted Directive. The Commission introduced quota rules to promote the exchange of Community works between the member states and employment in the cultural field.[69] States would be required to ensure that at least 30 per cent (later rising to 60 per cent) of their programming time was reserved for 'Community works', a complex concept defined in Article 4 of the draft. The Commission decided to drop its Green Paper suggestion that advertising must be permitted on some channels in each member state: a state could continue to ban advertising on its own channels, though it would have to allow it on foreign broadcasting services, provided they complied with the common rules. There were also draft provisions for copyright and the protection of children and young persons, though not (at this stage) for the right of reply.

The quota provisions proved much the most contentious topic. The House of Lords Select Committee in a second report considered they interfered with the editorial freedom of broadcasters and that the need for them had not been shown.[70] A line of attack pursued by Germany was that to apply them to Community rather than European works created difficulties for states which shared a common language and culture with non-member states. In particular, films and documentaries from Switzerland, Austria, and (then) East Germany would not form part of the Community quota which each state must satisfy. There was continued resistance to the copyright proposals, but less so to the advertising and sponsorship rules. Amendments were made before its submission to the Council of Ministers in 1988.[71] At the instigation of the European Parliament, a provision for a mandatory right of reply was introduced. The term 'Community works' was defined so as to allow some films and other programmes from Council of Europe and EFTA states to fall within the quota. The requirement that advertising should normally be grouped in blocks was dropped. The decision to enact a Directive was taken at the European Council meeting at Rhodes in December 1988, when the heads of government agreed to expedite its passage in conformity with the principles in the Council of Europe Convention.[72]

[68] COM(86) 146 final/2.
[69] Art. 2.
[70] *European Broadcasting*, para. 66.
[71] COM(88) 154 final.
[72] Hondius, 'Regulating Transfrontier Television', 158.

In its final version the Directive is presented as a co-ordinating, rather than a harmonizing, instrument.[73] As already stated, the fundamental principle is that provided broadcasts satisfy its minimum standards, other member states must ensure freedom of reception and not restrict retransmission on their territory.[74] There is, however, a very limited right to suspend retransmission where there is clearly a serious and repeated breach by the transmitting state of its obligation to ensure that violent and pornographic programmes do not prejudice the development of minors. This represents a much narrower concession to the interests of recipient states than that allowed in the Council of Europe Convention.[75] Member states remain free to impose more stringent controls on their own internal broadcasts.[76] They are also free to apply less strict advertising limits in some respects.[77] More fundamentally the Preamble makes it plain that the Directive has no affect on the financing, organization, and content of broadcasting. The only provision about programme standards is Article 22, which requires member states to prohibit programmes which might seriously impair the development of minors, in particular pornographic or violent items. The same article also forbids broadcasts which incite hatred on grounds of race, sex, religion, or nationality. Unlike the Convention, the EC measures says nothing about the accuracy of news or the access of the public to major events. On the other hand, it was amended to require states to ensure that films are not shown on television for two years after their first release in the cinema, except with the consent of the rights-holders.[78]

The advertising and sponsorship rules closely follow those of the Convention; they have been discussed in detail in Chapter IX. Article 23 on the Right of Reply is, however, much fuller than the equivalent Convention rule.[79] Any person, regardless of nationality, whose interests, in particular to reputation and good name, have been damaged by an incorrect statement of facts on television must be given a right of reply or an equivalent remedy. The time span and procedures established by one state for the right's exercise must be appropriate for use by persons resident in another state. The right may be exercised without prejudice to other criminal, civil, or administrative remedies; British law is incompatible with this in so far as the Broadcasting Complaints Commission

[73] Directive 89/552, OJ 1989 L 298/23. For commentary, see R. Wallace and D. Goldberg, 'The EEC Directive on Television Broadcasting' (1990) 9 *Yearbook of European Law* 175.
[74] Art. 2(2).
[75] Directive, Art. 2(2) to be compared with Convention, Art. 24.
[76] Arts. 3 and 19. (The equivalent provision in the Convention is Art. 28.)
[77] Art. 20. For further discussion, see Ch. IX, S. 5 above.
[78] Art. 7.
[79] Convention, Art. 8.

may not entertain a complaint if the applicant has already started legal proceedings.[80]

Much the most interesting rules concern quotas, now imposed with regard to 'European works'. Under Article 4 member states must ensure 'where practicable and by appropriate means' that broadcasters reserve 'a majority proportion of their transmission time' for these works. That excludes the time devoted to news, sports events, games, and advertising. The proportion should be achieved progressively. After October 1991 states must provide the Commission every two years with a report on the application of the quota obligation (and also the duty under Article 5 to reserve 10 per cent of transmission time for European works made by independent producers). It is the Commission's responsibility to ensure these rules are properly applied.[81]

It is hard to believe that in normal circumstances such imprecise provisions could be the subject of legal enforcement. The term 'European works' is defined in detail to embrace work originating in EC countries, in other states which are parties to the Transfrontier Television Convention, or in some circumstances in other third countries.[82] The works must be 'mainly made with authors and workers residing in one or more' of these states, provided they are made or supervised by producers established in one of them, *or* alternatively 'the contribution of co-producers of those states to the total co-production costs is preponderant' and the co-production is not controlled by someone established outside those states. The definition shows the inevitable complexity of quota rules, and the endless room for argument whether they are satisfied. It is doubtful whether it is really worth while requiring states to compile statistical tables on these matters, and then compelling the Commission to assess whether they have honoured their obligations. A statement issued with the Directive made it clear that the Council of Ministers did not intend these provisions to be legally enforceable.[83] This was presumably designed to reassure the United States film industry, which had lobbied hard against them. In any event a violation could only be found in the plainest case, say, where a satellite channel showed virtually nothing but Hollywood films and soaps. It might then be a nice question whether the Commission could initiate proceedings under Article 169 of the Treaty of Rome against a member state which had made no effort to enforce the quota rules.

[80] See Ch. VII, S. 4.
[81] Art. 4(3).
[82] Art. 6.
[83] For doubts about the authority of this statement, see Wallace and Goldberg, 'The EEC Directive on Television Broadcasting', 192–3.

Although there are considerable similarities between the Convention and the Directive, they have emerged from different perspectives. The former was substantially inspired by cultural and human rights arguments, while the mainspring for the latter was the view that broadcasting is an economic service. But cultural considerations did influence the Directive. Its Preamble cites Article 10 of the Human Rights Convention. The quota provisions are designed to protect European culture, and the prohibition against showing films on television for two years after release is intended to protect the cinema, a goal which is both cultural and economic.

A leading EC lawyer has criticized the Convention for allowing parties relatively wide rights to suspend the retransmission of programmes emanating from other states.[84] He also doubts the legality under Community law of Article 16 of the Convention, prohibiting the transmission of advertising directed at audiences in a country (other than the transmitting state). That provision is intended to allow a state to preserve the character of its broadcasting system. But after its ruling in the *Dutch Advertisers* case[85] the ECJ would almost certainly hold such a prohibition contrary to the EC rules on freedom to provide services. This divergence affords a striking example of the clash between the economic and cultural perspectives on broadcasting. Perhaps regrettably the Community countries have decided that for them the former approach is preferable.

[84] Schwartz, 'Fernsehen ohne Grenzen', 4–8.
[85] [1989] 3 CMLR 113, discussed p. 231 above.

Select Bibliography

GENERAL WORKS

Great Britain

ANNAN COMMITTEE, *Report on the Future of Broadcasting* (1977) Cmnd. 6753.
GIBBONS, T., *Regulating the Media* (London, 1991).
MUNRO, C. R., *Television, Censorship and the Law* (Farnborough, 1979).
PEACOCK COMMITTEE, *Report on Financing the BBC* (1986) Cmnd. 9824.
REVILLE, N., *Broadcasting: The New Law* (London, 1991).
ROBERTSON, G., and NICOL, A., *Media Law*, 3rd edn. (London, 1992), ch. 15.

France

DEBBASCH, C., *Droit de l'audiovisuel*, 2nd edn. (Paris, 1991).
—— *Les Grand Arrêts du droit de l'audiovisuel* (Paris, 1991).
DROUOT, G., *Le Nouveau Droit de l'audiovisuel* (Paris, 1988).
GAVALDA, C., and BOIZARD, M. (eds.), *Droit de l'audiovisuel*, 2nd edn. (Paris, 1989).
THOMAS, R., *Broadcasting and Democracy in France* (Bradford, 1976).

Germany

BREMER, E., ESSER, M., and HOFFMANN, M., *Der Rundfunk in der Verfassungs- und Wirtschaftsordnung in Deutschland* (Baden-Baden, 1992).
BULLINGER, M., and KÜBLER, F. (eds.), *Rundfunkorganisation und Kommunikationsfreiheit* (Baden-Baden, 1980).
HUMPHREYS, P. J., *Media and Media Policy in West Germany* (Oxford, 1990), chs. 3–6.
PORTER, V., and HASSELBACH, S., *Pluralism, Politics and the Marketplace: The Regulation of German Broadcasting* (London, 1991).
Rundfunkrecht (Munich, 1990) (collection of texts of broadcasting treaties and laws).

Italy

BARILE, P., CHELI, E., and ZACCARIA, R. (eds.), *Radiotelevisione pubblica e privata in Italia* (Bologna, 1980).
GIACALONE, D., *Antenna libera: la RAI, i privati, i partiti* (Milan, 1990).
PACE, A., *Stampa, giornalismo, radiotelevisione* (Padua, 1983), chs. V–IX.
RAO, G., *The Italian Broadcasting System: Legal (and Political) Aspects*, European University Institute Working Paper 88/369.
ROPPO, E., *Il diritto delle communicazioni di massa: problemi e tendenze* (Padua, 1985).
—— and ZACCARIA, R. (eds.), *Il sistema radiotelevisivo pubblico e privato* (Milan, 1991).
ZACCARIA, R., *Radiotelevisione e costituzione* (Milan, 1977).

United States of America

Franklin, M. A., and Anderson, D. A., *Mass Media Law: Cases and Materials*, 4th edn. (New York, 1990), chs. XIII–XV.

Kellner, D., *Television and the Crisis of Democracy* (Oxford, 1990).

Parsons, P., *Cable Television and the First Amendment* (Lexington, Mass., 1987).

Pool, I. de Sola, *Technologies of Freedom* (Cambridge, Mass., 1983).

Powe, L. A., *American Broadcasting and the First Amendment* (Berkeley, Calif., 1987).

Comparative

Barendt, E. M., 'The Influence of the German and Italian Constitutional Courts on their National Broadcasting Systems' [1991] *Pub. Law* 93.

Blumler, J. G. (ed.), *Television and the Public Interest* (London, 1992).

—— and Nossiter, T. J. (eds.), *Broadcasting Finance in Transition* (Oxford, 1991).

Public Management and Control of Broadcasting, Report of the Colloquium held by the Swiss Institute of Comparative Law, Lausanne (Zurich, 1988).

WORKS ON SPECIFIC TOPICS

Public broadcasting

Briggs, A., *The History of Broadcasting in the United Kingdom*, 4 vols. (Oxford, 1961–79).

Burns, T., *The BBC: Public Institution and Private World* (London, 1977).

Coase, R. H., *British Broadcasting: A Study in Monopoly* (London, 1950).

Drouot, G., 'Le Secteur public de l'audiovisuel dans la loi de 30 septembre 1986' [1987] *Rev. fr. droit adm.* 399.

Morange, J., 'La Commission nationale de la communication et des libertés et le droit de la communication audiovisuelle' [1987] *Rev. fr. droit adm.* 372.

—— 'Le Conseil supérieur de l'audiovisuel' [1989] *Rev. fr. droit adm.* 235.

Fuhr, E. W., *ZDF-Staatsvertrag*, 2nd edn. (Mainz, 1985).

Lange, K., 'Über besondere verfassungsrechtliche Anforderungen an das Rundfunkprogramm', in *Presserecht und Pressefreiheit—Festscrift für Martin Löffler* (Munich, 1980).

Ossenbühl, F., 'Rundfunk Programm—Leistung in treühanderischer Freiheit' [1977] *DÖV* 381.

Starck, C., 'Rundfunkräte und Rundfunkfreiheit' [1970] *Zeitschrift für Rechtspolitik* 217.

Essays in *Il servizio pubblico radiotelevisivo* (Naples, 1983).

Private broadcasting

Fowler, M. S., and Brenner, D. L., 'A Marketplace Approach to Broadcast Regulation' (1981) 60 *Texas L. Rev.* 207.

STARCK, C., 'Rundfunkräte und Rundfunkfreiheit' [1970] *Zeitschrift für Rechtspolitik* 217.

Essays in *Il servizio pubblico radiotelevisivo* (Naples, 1983).

Private broadcasting

FOWLER, M. S., and BRENNER, D. L., 'A Marketplace Approach to Broadcast Regulation' (1981) 60 *Texas L. Rev.* 207.

KALVEN, H., 'Broadcasting, Public Policy and the First Amendment' (1967) 10 *Jo. of Law and Economics* 15.

VELJANOVSKI, C. (ed.), *Freedom in Broadcasting* (London, 1989).

BETHGE, H., *Rundfunkreiheit und Privater Rundfunk* (Frankfurt, 1985).

KLEIN, H. H., 'Rundfunkrecht und Rundfunkfreiheit' (1981) 20 *Der Staat* 177.

LÜCKE, J., 'Die Rundfunkreiheit als Gruppengrundrecht' [1977] *DVBl.* 977.

PACE, A., 'La radiotelevisione in Italia con particolare riguardo alla emittenza privata' [1987] *Riv. trim. di diritto pubb.* 615.

Competition law

COLEMAN, M., 'European Competition Law in the Telecommunications and Broadcasting Sectors' (1990) 11 *Europ. Comp. Law* 202.

EC COMMISSION, *Pluralism and Media Concentration in the Internal Market*, Green Paper, 1992.

HITCHENS, L. P., 'Media Ownership and Control: A European Approach' (1994) 57 *MLR* 585.

MONOPOLIES AND MERGERS COMMISSION, *Television Broadcasting Services* (1992) Cm. 2035.

SADLER, *Enquiry into Standards of Cross-Media Promotion* (1991) Cm. 1436.

TUNSTALL, J., and PALMER, M., *Media Moguls* (London, 1991).

HOFFMAN-RIEM, W. (ed.), *Rundfunk im Wettbewerbsrecht* (Baden-Baden, 1988).

—— (ed.), *Rundfunkrecht neben Wirtschaftsrecht* (Baden-Baden, 1991).

The Fairness Doctrine and Rights of Reply

BARRON, J. A., 'Access to the Press: A New First Amendment Right' (1967) 80 *Harv. L. Rev.* 1641.

BOLLINGER, L. C., 'Freedom of the Press and Public Access: Toward a Theory of Partial Regulation of the Mass Media' (1976) 75 *Mich. L. Rev.* 1.

BRENNER, D., 'Cable Television and the Freedom of Expression' [1988] *Duke LJ* 329.

FRIENDLY, F. W., *The Good Guys, the Bad Guys and the First Amendment* (New York, 1976).

SIMMONS, S. J., *The Fairness Doctrine and the Media* (Berkeley, Calif., 1978).

DEHNEN, D., 'Zur Verfassungsmässigkeit des sogennanten Drittsendungsrechtes der Kirchen im öffentlichen-rechtlichen und privatrechtlichen Rundfunk' [1986] *DVBl.* 17.

LÜCKE, J., 'Die Rundfunkfreiheit als individuelles Zugangsrecht' [1977] *JZ* 41.

SEITZ, W., SCHMIDT, G., and SCHOENER, A., *Der Gegendarstellungsanspruch in Presse, Film, Funk und Fernsehen*, 2nd edn. (Munich, 1990).

CORASANITI G., *Diretto di accesso, diritto di rettifica, impresa di informazione* (Milan, 1986).

LAX, P., *Il diritto di rettifica nell' editoria e nella radiotelevisione* (Padua, 1989).

MANETTI, M., 'L'accesso al mezzo radiotelevisivo pubblico come situazione giuridicamente protetta' [1984] *Giur. cost.* 176.

Election and Political Broadcasting

BOYLE, A. E., 'Political Broadcasting, Fairness and Administrative Law' [1986] *Pub. Law* 562.

COCKERELL, M., *Live from Number 10* (London, 1988).

GOLDIE, G. W., *Facing the Nation* (London, 1977).

KENDRICK, C., 'The Case for Re-regulation of Campaign Broadcasting' (1992) 21 *Southwestern Univ. L. Rev.* 185.

GRUPP, A., 'Redaktionell gestalte Rundfunksendungen vor Wahlen' (1983) 16 *Zeitschrift für Rechtspolitik* 28.

CHELI, E., 'Pubblicità e politica: il caso italiano' [1981] *Diritto di Radiodiffusione e Telecommunicazione* 229.

Advertising

COLLOVA, T., 'Commercial Breaks during Films on Television' (1990) 146 *RIDA* 124.

LESTER, A., and PANNICK, D., *Advertising and Freedom of Expression in Europe* (Paris, 1984).

VELJANOVSKI, C., 'The Role of Advertising in Broadcasting Policy' in C. Veljanovski (ed.), *Freedom in Broadcasting* (London, 1989).

BETHGE, H., 'Der Verfassungsrechtliche Stellenwert der Werbung in öffentlichen-rechtlichen Rundfunk' [1983] *Medien Perspektiven* 690.

HESSE, A., 'Werbung und Rundfunkfreiheit' [1987] *ZUM* 548.

BARILE, P., and CARETTI, P., *La pubblicità e il sistema dell' informazione* (Turin, 1984).

GRANDINETTI, O., 'Diritto all' integrità dell' opera cinematografica e *spots* publicatari' [1990] *Giur. cost.* 499.

VIGNUDELLI, A., 'Alcune note sulla communicazione pubblicitaria nella radiotelevisione' [1983] *Giur. italiana* 421.

International law

Essays in *Regulation of Transnational Communications*, Michigan Yearbook of International Legal Studies (New York, 1984).

HURWITZ, B. A., 'The Labyrinth of International Telecommunications: Direct Broadcasting Satellites' (1988) 35 *Netherlands Int. Law Rev.* 145.

LUTHER, S. F., *The United States and the Direct Broadcasting Satellite* (New York, 1988).

MAGLERA, S., 'Direct Broadcasting by Satellite and a New International Information Order' (1981) 24 *German Yearbook of Int. Law* 288.

NORDENSTRENG, K., and SCHILLER, H. I. (eds.), *National Sovereignty and International Communication* (Norwood, NJ, 1979).

PRICE, M. E., 'The First Amendment and Television Broadcasting by Satellite' (1976) 23 *UCLA Rev.* 875.

European law

CASSESE, A., and CLAPHAM, A., *Television in Europe: The Human Rights Dimension* (Baden-Baden, 1990).

EC COMMISSION, *Television without Frontiers*, Green Paper, 1984.

HONDIUS, F. W., 'Regulating Transfrontier Television: The Strasbourg Option' (1988) 8 *Yearbook of European Law* 141.

SALVATORE, V., 'Quotas on TV programmes and EEC law' (1992) 29 *CMLRev.* 967.

WALLACE, R., and GOLDBERG, D., 'The EEC Directive on Television Broadcasting' (1989) 9 *Yearbook of European Law* 175.

ASTHEIMER, S., *Rundfunkfreiheit—ein Europäisches Grundrecht* (Baden-Baden, 1990).

SCHWARTZ, I. E., 'Fernsehen ohne Grenzen: zur Effektivität und zur Verhältnis von EG Richtlinie und Europarats-Konvention' (1989) 24 *Europarecht* 1.

Postscript

I. BROADCASTING FREEDOM

The complex character of broadcasting freedom, and in particular its relationship to freedom of speech, was discussed in Chapter II. The German Constitutional Court in its recent major ruling on arrangements for assessment of the *Gebühren* (licence fees) has affirmed its view of the freedom. *Rundfunkfreiheit* is above all the freedom of broadcasters to choose their own programme schedule (*Programmfreiheit*). Most importantly, broadcasters have rights against the state to report events freely. But the freedom is not only a negative liberty protected against infringement by the state, but also requires the legislatures (of the *Länder*) to make positive provision to ensure pluralism of the subjects and opinions broadcast (*Vielfalt der Themen und Meinungen*). Provisions which give regulatory authorities wide discretion, for example, in their allocation of frequencies and licences to choose applicants with particular programme schedules are, therefore, contrary to broadcasting freedom.[1] In its licence fee ruling, the Court extended these principles to cover the financing of public broadcasting. They do not prescribe any particular form of financial support. But the arrangements must exclude the possibility of any political influence on public broadcasters' programme freedom. The detailed implications of these principles for the German licence fee are discussed in the following section.

The United Kingdom government does not always appear to share the same commitment to broadcasting freedom. In July 1994 it issued its proposals for renewal of the BBC Charter.[2] This is to be renewed for another ten years (compared to previous periods of 12 or, in 1981, 15 years). The government, like the National Heritage Committee of the House of Commons,[3] rejected the alternative of instituting the BBC by statute, a development which would have given it more security and which would have enabled MPs to contribute more fully to the terms of its constitution.[4] No reasons of substance were given for this preference

[1] See the *Sixth Television* case, 83 BVerfGE 238, 323 (1991).

[2] *The Future of the BBC: Serving the Nation: Competing worldwide*, Cm. 2621.

[3] *The Future of the BBC*, HC 77 (1993–4), paras. 46–52.

[4] *The Future of the BBC*, para. 6.5. The argument for setting up the BBC by statute is most fully developed in E. Barendt, 'Legal Aspects of Charter Renewal', 65 *Political Quarterly* 20 (1994).

for the Charter. Moreover, the White Paper did not contemplate any alteration to the arrangements for assessing the licence fee; it will continue to be assessed by the government, although for the foreseeable future it will be increased in line with inflation. The BBC would therefore be wholly unprotected by the law against any government threats to reduce the licence fee. On the other hand, the government accepted the Heritage Committee's suggestion that an affirmative resolution of the House should be passed to approve any exercise by the government of its unilateral power to order the BBC to stop broadcasting.[5] It is more than ever clear that the constitutional and financial arrangements for the BBC would be unacceptable in Germany.

Towards the end of 1993 the government of Ireland withdrew its ban on the broadcast of interviews with members of terrorist organizations and their supporters. The United Kingdom government took the same step a few weeks after the cease-fire announced by the IRA at the end of August 1994. Earlier challenges to the Irish and the UK bans had been held inadmissible by the European Human Rights Commission. This was perhaps not surprising in view of the substantial discretion (or 'margin of appreciation') allowed states in national security cases.[6] While accepting the argument that the ban did constitute an interference with broadcasters' freedom of expression, the Commission held in both cases that it could be justified as necessary to safeguard national security and to prevent disorder and crime.[7] The lifting of the ban ends a sad episode in the history of UK broadcasting law; it should not be forgotten that the government retains a wide power to prohibit the transmission of any programme or class of programme, a draconian power which would not pass constitutional muster in either the USA or Germany.

In contrast the ruling of the European Court of Human Rights in the Austrian public monopoly case (see pp. 75 and 81) carries considerable implications for the scope of broadcasting freedom. The Court ruled unanimously that the public broadcasting monopoly was incompatible with Article 10 of the European Convention (ECHR).[8] It could no longer be argued that there were only a very limited number of frequencies, so that there was no space at all for private broadcasters; moreover, other steps could be taken to prevent the development of private oligopolies. There is a striking statement of principle in paragraph 18 of the judgment:

[5] *The Future of the BBC*, para. 5. 34. See p. 36 above.

[6] See 11603/85, *CSSU* v. *UK* (1988) 10 EHRR 269, 277.

[7] See 15404/89, *Purcell* v. *Ireland*, 70 D & R 262, where the Commission accepted the argument that the broadcasting media had a greater impact than the press and that it was therefore legitimate to subject them to greater restrictions. The decision in 18714/91, *Brind* v. *UK* of 9 May 1994 holding the complaint inadmissible has not yet been reported.

[8] *Informations Verein and Others* v. *Lentia* [1994] 17 EHRR 93.

The Court has frequently stressed the fundamental role of freedom of expression in a democratic society, in particular where, through the press, it serves to impart information and ideas of general interest, which the public is moreover entitled to receive . . . Such an undertaking cannot be successfully accomplished unless it is grounded in the principle of pluralism, of which the State is the ultimate guarantor. This observation is especially valid in relation to audio-visual media, whose programmes are often broadcast very widely.

The Court would, it seems, require states to formulate positive rules to protect pluralism in the media. As a result Austria is now required to allow some private broadcasting. Perhaps the principle of pluralism could also be applied to compel states to introduce strong anti-trust laws or stricter programme standards. Such measures would combat the deleterious effects of those private broadcasting oligopolies, which fail to provide a balanced range of programmes. English readers may find this suggestion surprising. But such a development might be expected in France, Germany or Italy, where constitutional courts have required the enactment of (more effective) laws to foster the value of media pluralism (see the discussion at pp. 16–17, 21–2 and 27).

The pluralism principle marks a difference between the European and United States approaches to broadcasting regulation (and perhaps other aspects of freedom of speech law).[9] In the USA a common perspective now is that broadcasters should be accorded the same First Amendment rights as newspaper editors (or owners), and that the ruling of the Supreme Court in the *Red Lion* case[10] upholding the Fairness Doctrine should increasingly be regarded as aberrant.[11] Put shortly, according to the majority of US commentators, broadcasting freedom means that broadcasters are free to devise their own programme schedules, entirely immune from any public regulation.[12] In contrast the continental European approach is that the rights of broadcasters should be limited in the interests of pluralism, and further, that it is the duty of the legislature to take apppropriate steps to secure this end. Britain shares the European perspective, as shown by its strict impartiality rules.

2. The Organisation of Broadcasting

The Austrian case referred to in the previous section establishes that a public broadcasting monopoly is now incompatible with Article 10 of the

[9] This theme is explored by E. Barendt, 'Free Speech in Australia: A Comparative Perspective' 16 *Sydney Law Rev.* 149 (1994).

[10] *Red Lion Broadcasting Co.* v. *FCC* 395 US 367 (1969).

[11] See for example the view of R. Post, 'Meiklejohn's Mistake: Individual Autonomy and the Reform of Public Discourse' 64 *Univ. of Colorado L. Rev.* 1109, 1126–28 (1993).

[12] But see the decision of the Supreme Court in *Turner Broadcasting System* v. *FCC* 129 L. Ed. 2d. 497 (1994), discussed in S.3 below.

ECHR. The view that only a public broadcasting system can preserve the access of individuals and minority groups to the airwaves is no longer acceptable (see p. 57). On the other hand, the decision does not recognise any *right* of individuals or associations to set up a private channel: the argument deployed in s. 2 of Chapter IV is still sound.[13] Indeed, the European Court expressly indicated that some form of 'private participation in the activities of the national corporation' would satisfy the pluralism requirements of Article 10. This might be achieved, for example, by the provision of mandatory access rights for independent producers (as required by the European Broadcasting Directive).[14] The point is that member states must organize their broadcasting systems to allow for some degree of private participation; otherwise there would be a violation of the Convention. But no individual (or association) has a right under the ECHR to obtain a licence.

It is, in contrast, unclear whether the continued existence of public broadcasting is similarly guaranteed at the European level. The German Constitutional Court in the licence fee decision has re-affirmed the constitutional security of public broadcasting. Indeed, in that country the validity of the dual system is dependent on the continued ability of the long-established public companies to discharge their fundamental programme responsibilities; from that follows their right to adequate financial support.[15] It seems that in Germany this guarantee would only lapse if private broadcasters were by law required to provide the full range of programmes which characterises the principal feature of public service broadcasting. This would be an improbable development in view of the commercial pressures to which private channels are increasingly subject in very competitive markets. After its ruling in the Austrian case it is conceivable that the European Human Rights Court, like the *Bundesverfassungsgericht*, would protect the position of a public broadcasting system, at any rate in a member state where it was clear that the private channels did not provide that plurality of opinion and information guaranteed by Article 10.

At all events, the British government has decided that public broadcasting should survive, at least for the next decade, and that the BBC should continue to be 'the main public service broadcaster'.[16] The 1994 White Paper emphasizes the distinctive role of the BBC, in particular

[13] In support, see 17505/90, *Nydal* v. *Sweden* (1993) 16 EHRR CD 15 holding inadmissible a complaint that the Swedish community radio system denied individuals, in contrast to associations, a right to hold a licence.

[14] Directive 89/552, Art. 5: see S.6 below.

[15] The principle was first formulated in the *Fourth Television* case, 73 BVerfGE 118 (1986).

[16] *Future of the BBC*, para. 2.4. Presumably Channel 4 is the other public service broadcaster; since 1993, Channel 3 has been released from the obligation to inform, educate and entertain, the traditional public service remit (p. 106).

the priority it must give to the interests of audiences.[17] As far as its organization is concerned, the government recommends a number of quite significant changes. The new Charter should set out clearly the responsibilities of the Governors, in particular for the appointment of the Director-General, the Deputy Director-General and other members of the Board of Management. It should also spell out the Governors' financial duties and their accountability to the public. Their role is not to manage the BBC, as had sometimes appeared to be the case in the 1980s. The Charter is also to set out the functions of the National Broadcasting Councils for Scotland, Wales and Northern Ireland. On the other hand, there is no longer a requirement to constitute a General Advisory Council. This development is hard to square with the mood of public accountability which the government is anxious to encourage.

The Green Paper of 1992 rather coyly canvassed the possibility of changing the method for appointment of BBC Governors.[18] In principle the present system is hard to defend, for it allows the government of the day a monopoly appointment right.[19] But it is difficult to find a satisfactory alternative; other arrangements, in particular the German *Proporz* system (see pp. 61–2), may lead to open political controversy. Nevertheless, it is arguable that this would be more honest than the present system, which proceeds on the fiction that the government is indifferent to the political (and other) views of its appointees.

Another important feature of the White Paper is its treatment of BBC financing. It rejects, with persuasive arguments, the case for partial reliance on revenue from advertising or sponsorship, and appears to accept that a move to a subscription system would destroy the public service character of the BBC.[20] But the government is only prepared to continue the licence fee until 2,001; before then it should be reviewed to see whether any change would be desirable. In the meantime the BBC is encouraged to develop specialist subscription services. The White Paper does not contemplate any change in the procedure for assessing the fee, but the government will review whether it is right to continue revising it in line with movements in the Retail Prices Index. Any alteration to this system could have disturbing implications for the BBC's independence. There is nothing to stop a British government from threatening (or hinting at) a drop in the level of the licence fee if the Corporation's programmes displease it.

The German position affords a striking contrast. In 1988 the Bavarian Administrative Court referred the constitutionality of the licence fee

[17] Para. 2.6.

[18] *The Future of the BBC—A consultation document*, Cm. 2098, para. 7.20.

[19] See Barendt, 'Legal Aspects of Charter Renewal', 24–26.

[20] *Future of the BBC*, paras. 5.4–5.9.

system to the *Bundesverfassungsgericht*. The long delay before the latter's judgment in February 1994 shows the sensitivity and complexity of the issues. Under the state treaty the level of the licence fees is assessed by the Minister-Presidents of the *Länder*, who take the advice of a Commission (KEF) first established by the states in 1975. The KEF, since 1992 composed of state government representatives, members of the state Audit Offices and independent experts, considers the financial needs of the public broadcasting corporations every two years and makes recommendations for revision of the fees. But the final decision is taken by the states, subject to ratification by their Parliaments. The question was broadly whether these arrangements satisfied the constitutional requirement of *Programmfreiheit*, or whether alternatively the broadcasting corporations themselves should be free to assess the *Gebühren*.

The Constitutional Court first ruled, as already explained in section I of this Postscript, that the arrangements for financing public broadcasting must satisfy the constitutional principles of broadcasting freedom. Secondly, the licence fee is justifiable under these principles, as it enables the public broadcasting corporations to discharge their programme responsibilities free from the pressures of advertisers and irrespective of viewing figures.[21] The Court also held it was reasonable to charge the fee for mere possession of a receiving set, whatever the individual's viewing (or listening) habits. On the other hand, the interests of viewers and listeners must not be ignored, and for that reason it would be inappropriate to allow the broadcasters to assess the fees themselves.

The Court had more difficulty in determining the implications of its commitment to broadcasting freedom for the detailed licence fee rules. It was impossible to formulate and apply substantive standards, on the basis of which improper political and programme considerations could clearly be detected. Instead, the Court emphasized the need to set up a procedural framework, which would so far as possible preclude consideration being given to these irrelevant factors. The arrangements under the state treaty did not satisfy this requirement, so the states were required to revise it.[22]

Several defects were found in the current provisions. First, the treaty contained insufficiently precise standards and procedures for assessment of the fees. Secondly, the final decision was left to the states' governments and Parliaments, with only an advisory role for the KEF. This procedure did not guarantee assessment on the basis of constitutionally legitimate

[21] Decision of 22 Feb. 1994: extracts from the decision are reported in [1994] *JZ* 515 and (1994) 47 *NJW* 1942. The decision developed the principles stated in the Hesse Advertising case, now reported: 87 BVerfGE 181 (1992).

[22] Interestingly, the Court refrained from holding the existing provisions wholly invalid, since that would have entailed the illegality of the current licence fees.

considerations. The incentives for states to abuse their discretion were increased in the current competitive media landscape. A crucial point is that the fee level should be based on the financial needs of the broadcasting companies, that is, the resources required in order to discharge their programme responsibilities. The broadcasters' budgets should be controlled, but on technical, rather than political grounds. State laws should be introduced to lay down the composition and procedures of an independent control commission, free from political, as well as media, influence. The Court saw no constitutional objection to indexing some of the costs taken into account in determining broadcasters' needs. More importantly, it emphasized that reasons should be given for a decision not to revise the fees in line with changes in these costs. Such a decision can only be taken in the interests of viewers and listeners.

In contrast, in Britain the government has legally complete discretion over licence fee assessment. There is no independent commission to advise on the BBC's financial needs, let alone one with any power of decision. Most importantly, there is nothing to prevent the government using its powers to exercise influence over programme schedules, nor does it have any legal obligation to give reasons for not increasing the licence fee in line with rising costs.

It is perhaps appropriate to end this section with a few observations about the future organization of broadcasting. In all European jurisdictions the role of the public broadcasting corporations is increasingly questioned. This is not surprising, given that many of these countries have for most of the last ten years been governed by market-oriented governments, anxious to embrace the economic opportunities created by the communications revolution. The development of cable, satellite and other services (some inter-active, some multi-media) may well lead to a radical expansion in the number of readily available television channels. It may be difficult to sustain the position of public service channels in this environment, and it is perhaps largely for that reason that the UK government has only proposed a ten year renewal for the BBC Charter. Certainly it will be impossible to place any weight on the scarcity argument for broadcasting regulation (see pp. 4–6).

Nevertheless, there remain cultural and political arguments for the retention of public service broadcasting, though these may not justify the degree of regulation of private broadcasters found in some jurisdictions. First, public broadcasting is uniquely capable of reflecting a country's, or community's, cultural identity. This reflection may take the form of relaying sports and other events of national importance or ensuring that political debate is comprehensively and accurately represented. Secondly, the requirements of a balanced range of programmes and impartiality guarantee that one branch of the broadcasting medium is open to all strands of opinion. The market may find no place for minority tastes and unpopular views, but it is the unique responsibility of a public service broadcaster to ensure that the public has some access to them.

3. PROGRAMME STANDARDS

The White Paper on the BBC does not propose any substantive change to the Corporation's programme obligations. But is does sensibly propose that they should be clearly set out in the new Agreement, which is to be made between the government and the BBC.[23] It will state the BBC's independence on matters of scheduling and programme content, without, however, affecting the Secretary of State's power to ban a particular programme or class of programme. There will be explicit requirements to show a wide range of programmes of high standard and to treat controversial issues impartially. In principle, the obligations on the BBC should be at least as detailed and rigorous as those imposed under the 1990 legislation on Channel 3 licensees, but the White Paper does not appear to go as far as that.

There has been considerable concern about the willingness and ability of the new Channel 3 licensees to meet their programme obligations. With declining advertising revenue during the recession and their greater liability to the Treasury, it is hardly surprising that they have been tempted to schedule programmes of wide appeal, particularly at peak-time. This led to a relatively critical review by the ITC.[24] Religious programmes have, for example, been moved from their Sunday early-evening slot to the morning, while both drama and documentaries have tended to concentrate on crime. The attempt to move *News at Ten* to an earlier hour (with presumably a consequent change in name) was resisted by the ITC. On the other hand, current affairs programmes have continued to be scheduled during peak hours.

Chapter V of this book discussed the types of programme standards and the powers of the ITC and Radio Authority to enforce them for the private broadcasting sector. Some indication of the regulatory authorities' attitudes is provided by their quarterly Programme Complaints and Interventions Reports. As predicted in Chapter V (p. 113) the number of complaints to the ITC has increased significantly since the removal of its previewing powers. Many of them relate to the time at which particular programmes are scheduled and to matters of taste and decency. The ITC has expressed particular concern at the portrayal of violence, and indeed

[23] *The Future of the BBC*, paras. 3.13–3.15 and 6.29–6.34.
[24] *1993 Performance Reviews* (ITC, 26 May 1994).

issued a formal warning to Channel 4 concerning the display of a kitchen knife as a murder weapon at a time when children were likely to be viewing.[25] In one case a channel has been required to broadcast an apology (under s. 40 of the Broadcasting Act 1990) and the Commission has also drawn attention to its powers to fine or even withdraw the licence if a channel continues to break its licence conditions.

Breach of the impartiality principle has only been the subject of a small minority of complaints. In one well publicized dispute the ITC rejected a complaint by the Conservative Party that a Granada *World in Action* programme had been biassed in its treatment of tax increases; it was pointed out that spokesmen for the Party had declined invitations to appear on it.[26] In contrast, a programme dealing with employment policies in Northern Ireland was regarded as unbalanced. The ITC thought it should have been presented as a personal view programme.[27]

It is sometimes difficult to determine the boundaries between the functions of the ITC (and RA) to ensure compliance with the impartiality principle and the jurisdiction of the Broadcasting Complaints Commission (BCC) to review complaints of 'unjust or unfair treatment'.[28] In principle it seems a complaint that a programme lacked balance, and was therefore unfair to an individual, group, or for that matter political party, could be made to both the ITC and the BCC. The latter's investigation is more thorough, may entail an oral hearing, and is certainly more fully reported. In its most recent Annual Report[29] it suggested that complaints arising from political broadcasts are within the BCC's remit, where they are 'of a more personal nature'. It seems unsatisfactory that a broadcaster could be subject to the control of two very different bodies in respect of what is in substance the same complaint: unfairness in a programme. They might well take different approaches to the complaint. In any case, newspapers who commit analogous errors are not liable to review at all, since 'unfairness' is not as such a ground of complaint to the Press Complaints Commission.

The proliferation of quasi-regulatory bodies in the broadcasting context has been much criticized. Partly to meet this point, the government has decided to merge the BCC with the Broadcasting Standards Council (BSC).[30] The new BSC will have up to 15 members, drawn to some extent from existing members of the two bodies. It is to be responsible for revising the present Code.[31] Separate panels will consider complaints of

[25] See Programme Complaints Report, Oct.—Dec. 1993.
[26] Ibid., Jan.—March 1994.
[27] Ibid., July—Sept. 1993.
[28] Broadcasting Act, s. 143(1) (a). See pp. 184–6 above.
[29] Annual Report of the BCC 1994, HC 584, 5.
[30] *The Future of the BBC*, ch. 7.
[31] For a critique of the present BSC, see F. Coleman, 'All in the Best Possible Taste: The Broadcasting Standards Council 1989–92', [1993] *Pub. Law* 488.

unfair treatment and privacy invasion, and complaints concerning the portrayal of violence and sexual conduct. It is unclear whether the new Code will attempt to clarify the terms 'unfair treatment' and 'unwarranted infringement of privacy'. Although precise definition is impossible, some guidance on their meaning might be helpful to broadcasters, who sometimes complain of the unpredictability of BCC rulings.

The merger is to be welcomed, although it does entail the fusion of a regulatory body (with a research function) and a quasi-judicial tribunal, which has described itself as 'in part a poor man's libel court'.[32] But the reform proposed in the White Paper does not address the main issues. The first of these is the relationship between the ITC and Radio Authority on the one hand, and the new BSC on the other, Surely few people have been confused about whether to seek redress from the BCC or the (present) BSC; there is no conceivable overlap between a complaint about, say, bad language and one about an unfair programme. But the decision whether to complain to the ITC or the Complaints Commission has on occasion presented difficulties. Secondly, there is the fundamental question whether broadcasters should be subject to two (or more) regulatory (or quasi-judicial) bodies, when the press is immune from legal control in these areas.

In the United States difficulties have arisen with regard to the regulation of indecent programmes. Although some regulation of such programmes to protect young children is compatible with the First Amendment,[33] FCC rules have been repeatedly struck down by the DC Circuit Court. Following a ruling that there was insufficient evidence to justify confining indecent programmes to the 'safe harbour' of midnight to 6.00 a.m.,[34] Congress directed the FCC to ban the broadcast of such material at all times. The total ban was, however, held incompatible with the First Amendment, and the Commission was directed to issue reasonable 'safe harbour' rules.[35] Congress then enacted legislation requiring the FCC to ban the broadcast of indecent matter from 6.00 a.m. to midnight, but this fared no better than the Commission's earlier regulation.[36] The Court of Appeals held that the protection of young children provided a sufficiently compelling reason for restricting the transmission of indecent items, but the regulation must be narrowly tailored to achieve that end; precise evidence was required to show exactly when young children might be exposed to the risk of viewing such matter. It is doubtful whether the

[32] Annual Report of the BCC 1993, HC 806, 2. In this Report the BCC implicitly argued against its merger with other bodies.

[33] See *FCC* v. *Pacifica Foundation* 438 US 726 (1978).

[34] *Action for Children's TV* v. *FCC* 852 F. 2d. 1332 (DC Cir. 1988) (note 78 at p. 112 is inaccurate).

[35] *Action for Children's TV* v. *FCC* 932 F. 2d. 1504 (DC Cir. 1991).

[36] *Action for Children's TV* v. *FCC* 11 F. 3d. 170 (DC Cir. 1993), holding invalid the order made under the Public Telecommunications Act 1992, s. 16(a).

ITC's Family Viewing Policy, under which more adult material may be shown after 9.00 p.m. (see p. 113) would survive this strict judicial scrutiny.

In the recent *Turner Broadcasting* case the Supreme Court has considered the obligation of cable companies, imposed by Act of Congress,[37] to devote some channels for the transmission of local commercial and public broadcasting stations.[38] The majority of the Court held that these 'must carry' rules were content-neutral restrictions on the cable operators' freedom of speech. The Court unanimously considered it inappropriate to afford the operators only the degree of First Amendment protection conferred on terrestrial broadcasters.[39] But the majority equally held it would be wrong to subject the rules to strict scrutiny. They were designed to protect the interests of viewers without cable and so preserve the structure of the broadcasting system, rather than to interfere with the free decision of cable operators and programmers to show the programmes they wanted. The 'must carry' obligations applied, irrespective of the cable operators' schedules or the contents of the terrestrial programmes they were obliged to transmit. It is possible to see in the complex majority judgment of Kennedy J. a relatively sympathetic view of structural regulations which are intended to preserve the access of the public to a variety of sources of information.

4. COMPETITION LAW

The *Turner Broadcasting* decision is in line with earlier US rulings holding anti-trust rules compatible with the First Amendment. Although these rules may be inimical to the commercial freedom of established media operators, in principle they protect fair competition between broadcasting (and other media) companies and so promote the constitutional value of pluralism. European constitutional courts would have little difficulty in upholding their constitutionality; indeed, it is probably necessary for legislatures to enact such laws, if the values underlying media freedom are to be fully respected.

Nevertheless, there has been considerable pressure in the United Kingdom to relax some of these anti-concentration rules. At the end of 1993 the Secretary of State for National Heritage removed the restrictions

[37] Cable Television Consumer Protection and Competition Act 1992, ss. 4–5.

[38] *Turner Broadcasting System* v. *FCC* 129 L. Ed. 2d. 497 (1994). Earlier more limited FCC 'must carry' rules had been held unconstitutional: *Quincy Cable TV Inc.* v. *FCC* 768 F. 2d. 1434 (DC Cir. 1985), discussed at pp. 110–11.

[39] The scarcity rationale did not apply to cable, so there was no case for applying the principle in the *Red Lion* case (395 US 367 (1969), discussed at pp. 5, 158–9 above).

on the holding of two Channel 3 licences for large regions, though the ban on holding the two London licences remains (see p. 129 above).[40] As a result there have been mergers between Carlton and Central, Granada and LWT, Meridian and Anglia. The former company in each pair in effect took-over the latter, though the merged company must continue to honour the programme and other commitments entered into by the latter when they were granted their licences. There is, therefore, now much greater concentration in the Channel 3 network; the ITC estimates that the four largest groups now account between them for 82% of total Channel 3 advertising revenue.

At the beginning of 1994 the Secretary of State further announced that he would review the ownership restrictions affecting broadcasters, in particular the limits on cross-media ownership which had been introduced by the Broadcasting Act 1990 (see pp. 131–5). Several newspaper groups, such as Associated Newspaper and the Guardian Group, are keen to have these limits relaxed, so they can participate more fully in broadcasting. The ITC shares this perspective. Equally, it favours the application of the cross-media rules to satellite broadcasters, as they increase their share of the audience and total broadcasting revenue. The failure to bring Sky (now BSkyB) within these provisions was one of the most controversial aspects of the 1990 legislation (see p. 132). There is widespread agreement that the present licence accumulation rules are crude. The ITC has suggested a more flexible rule, under which any holding of regional Channel 3 licences should be restricted to, say, 25% of total advertising revenue for the network.[41] This has some appeal in theory, but might be difficult to enforce in practice.

The increasing competition between broadcasters to secure exclusive rights to cover sporting events has continued to excite controversy (see pp. 136–39). There is no doubt that the acquisition of such rights for live coverage of cricket (outside England) and Premier League football has played a large part in BSkyB's rapid development. Under the Broadcasting Act 1990 the acquisition of exclusive rights to show certain 'listed events' is precluded, if they are to be shown on 'pay-per-view' terms.[42] But the purchase of rights by subscription channels, such as the BSkyB sports channel, is not prohibited. The National Heritage Committee has recommended that the ban on exclusive transmission rights should be extended to subscription channels, while the list of events should be regularly reviewed. At the moment, for example, there is nothing to stop BSkyB or a cable company purchasing exclusive rights to show all of the Wimbledon

[40] SI 1993/3199, amending SI 1991/1976.
[41] ITC Memorandum to the Secretary of State on Media Ownership, 25 Feb. 1994.
[42] S. 182.

Tennis Tournament (save for the Finals), yet such a development would create a national outcry.

At the end of 1992 the EC Commission issued a Green Paper canvassing views on the need for specific Community legislation to control media concentrations.[43] It considered that national laws are adequate to protect pluralism. (In any case it is doubtful whether the Community is legally competent to promote freedom of expression, though it should take account of this value when enacting legislation it is entitled to introduce.)[44] But it concluded that some harmonization of mergers and anti-trust laws might be necessary to ensure the effective working of a single European market. For instance, a company with both media and non-media commercial interests might be induced to establish a broadcasting station in one state rather than another, because the laws in the latter preclude involvement in press or broadcasting by companies with non-media interests—although it would be more economically efficient for it to establish itself in that latter country. Under existing EC law a member state is free to apply its own anti-trust laws to non-national media companies, even if the effect of their application is to discourage those companies from establishing themselves in that state. This position is not affected by the Transfrontier Broadcasting Directive of 1989.[45]

The Green Paper was open to a number of criticisms.[46] The Commission might have been too optimistic about the capacity of member states effectively to tackle concentrations of media powers. Moreover, it is unclear that the Commission's policy of promoting competition, and thereby an effective internal market, would necessarily also safeguard pluralism. Economic competition tends to lead to concentration. What is important is that there should be journalistic competition, with a variety of broadcast programmes and representation of all strands of opinion. A harmonization Directive (or Regulation) enforcing to some extent common anti-trust rules might perhaps enhance economic efficiency, but there is little reason to believe it would also achieve the more important goal (in the media context) of plurality of information. At the time of writing it is unclear whether the European states will agree on the need for a Directive and there seems no immediate prospect of Community legislation.

[43] *Pluralism and Media Concentration in the Internal Market*, COM (92) 480 final. The general Merger Regulation 4064/89 does not contain any media specific rules (see p. 143).

[44] *Pluralism and Media Concentration in the Internal Market*, 59–61.

[45] Directive 89/552: see Ch. X, S. 4 above, and S. 6 below.

[46] For a full discussion, see L. P. Hitchens. 'Media Ownership and Control: A European Approach', (1994) 57 *MLR* 585–601.

5. ELECTION AND POLITICAL BROADCASTING

Two major developments emphasize the significance of this aspect of broadcasting law. The first is the landmark decision of the High Court of Australia in *Australian Capital Television Pty. Ltd.* v. *The Commonwealth*.[47] By a majority of 5–2 the Court held that amendments introduced in 1991 to the federal broadcasting legislation were invalid. These provisions prohibited paid political advertising on radio and television during election campaign periods, while providing parties and candidates with some free air time. 90% of this time was allocated under the 1991 statute to political parties already represented in the legislature on the basis of their share of first preference votes at the previous election, while the other 10% could be allocated to other parties and independent candidates at the discretion of the Australian Broadcasting Tribunal. The principal purposes of these rules were to prevent corruption and dominance of the air-waves by richer parties and candidates. Another object was to improve the quality of electoral debate on the media, since free-time television broadcasts had to be at least two minutes long and were to be unaccompanied by moving pictures; short sound-bite advertisements were in contrast prohibited.

Although the majority of the Court was sympathetic to these objectives, it concluded that they could be achieved by less restrictive means, such as limits on the amount of money which a party or candidate could spend, or on the time which could be purchased. The amendments were too sweeping in that they totally precluded access to the media at elections by pressure groups and by individuals who were not also candidates. Moreover, commercial advertisements were permitted, so the provisions discriminated against political election advertisements. The legislation was, therefore, held incompatible with the freedom of political speech which the High Court found implicit in the federal constitution.[48]

While it was surely right for the High Court carefully to scrutinize the total ban on political advertisements (see pp. 169–70 above), it is less clear that it did justice to the government's arguments in support of the legislation.[49] Political advertisements, particularly at election times, should be subject in the interests of fairness and balance to a degree of regulation which is unnecessary in the case of ordinary commercials. The decision in *Australian Capital Television* can be accepted if it is understood as holding

[47] (1992) CLR 106. For a full discussion of the complex constitutional issues in this case, see the articles in 16 *Sydney Law Rev.* 145 ff (1994).

[48] The existence and scope of this implied constitutional right are also discussed in the companion case, *Nationwide News Pty. Ltd.* v. *Wills* (1992) 177 CLR 1.

[49] See T. D. Campbell, 'Democracy, Human Rights and Positive Law', 16 *Sydney Law Rev.* 195 (1994).

only that the particular provisions were too crudely drafted and thus constituted impermissible means to achieve legitimate ends; it should not, however, be interpreted as outlawing all restrictions on political advertising on radio and television.

Recent events in Italy show that even relatively precise rules may fail to achieve their objective of fair and objective election broadcasting. The circumstances were, it is hoped, highly unusual. Silvio Berlusconi, the head of the Fininvest group which controls the three major private networks (see pp. 27–8), formed a new political movement, *Forza Italia*, during the summer of 1993. With the support of two other parties, the Northern League and the National Alliance (the ex-fascist party), it won the election held in March 1994. To a considerable extent this victory can be attributed to the favourable coverage received by Berlusconi and *Forza Italia* on his three channels and in the magazines and newspapers effectively under his control.[50]

The problem did not arise from legislative inactivity. At the end of 1993 Parliament in anticipation of the forthcoming election enacted a specific law.[51] It required the Parliamentary Commission to issue directives to RAI about equal opportunities for political parties to present election broadcasts, and their fair and impartial treatment in news broadcasts. Further, it laid down the same principles for the private broadcasting networks and stations; in the 30 day period before the elections, a channel intending to allow one party an opportunity to broadcast must give other parties the same opportunity under the same financial and other terms. But within this 30 day period other spot advertising on the broadcasting (and other media) is forbidden.[52] Candidates and members of political parties should only be portrayed in news and other regular broadcasts, when their presence was indispensable to a full treatment of the story.[53] These provisions were then supplemented by more detailed regulations issued by the *Garante per la radiodiffusione e per l'editoria* (see pp. 81–2), one of which defined 'spot *pubblicitari*' (advertising spots), the transmission of which was forbidden in the 30 days before the elections.[54] Other rules, for example, fixed the tariff for permitted election broadcasts and required them to be clearly separate from other programmes.[55]

Despite these apparently comprehensive rules, it seems clear that

[50] Under Law 223 of 6 Aug. 1990, Berlusconi is required to divest himself of all national newspapers, if he keeps three national television networks; in fact *Il Giornale* was sold to his brother, Paolo.

[51] Law 515 of 10 Dec. 1993 on electoral campaigns.

[52] Ibid., Art. 2.

[53] Ibid., Art. 1, para. 5.

[54] Regulation of 26 Jan. 1994, Art. 6.

[55] Ibid., Arts. 13–14.

Berlusconi was able to exploit his national television channels to his party's advantage.[56] The right-wing parties were consistently given more sympathetic treatment than their left and centre rivals, not only in the handling of news and current affairs, but also through skilfully placed statements and interviews in light entertainment programmes. One major defect in the rules was that some of them, in particular the prohibition on spot advertising, only applied for the 30 days before the poll, so the Fininvest channels were able to reveal their bias before then and give *Forza Italia* an early lead. There were no controls on statements of support for Berlusconi by the presenters of game and quiz shows (his employees), while the sanctions the *Garante* could employ for clear breaches proved ineffective. An operator with Berlusconi's resources could take the risk of the imposition of fines, while the ultimate penalty of a withdrawal of his licence to broadcast could safely be ignored (see p. 117).

The conclusion must be that in circumstances such as these it is very difficult, if not impossible, to control the abuse of television channels for political ends. The problem lies not so much in the weakness of the regulations for election broadcasting, but in the potential for political influence which is enjoyed by an individual with this degree of media power. It is hardly surprising that since the election Berlusconi's position as Prime Minister and controller of three national television networks has given rise to acute political difficulties. The Administrative Council of RAI is now dominated by government supporters,[57] while Berlusconi has shown no enthusiasm for surrendering any, let alone all, of his media interests. However, in August 1994 the *Garante*, much criticised for his apparent unwillingness to intervene during the election campaign, stopped the government exploiting its entitlement under the broadcasting legislation to compel RAI to broadcast government announcements.[58] Berlusconi had wanted it to transmit spots presenting a favourable image of government policies, a clear abuse of the power to compel broadcasts of public interest.

6. EUROPEAN LAW

In interpreting Articles 59–66 of the Treaty of Rome the European Court of Justice is required to balance the cultural aspects of national broad-

[56] See B. Rauen, '*Berlusconi: Wahlkampf mit den eigenen Medien*', [1994] *Media Perspektiven* 349.

[57] By Law 205 of 25 June 1993 the Administrative Council is now composed of 5 members, appointed by the Presidents of the Assembly and the Senate. The Council now appoints the Director-General of RAI (Cf. p. 64 above).

[58] Law 223 of 6 Aug. 1990, Art. 9(2).

casting systems against the Community rules on freedom of services (see pp. 229–31). The enactment of the Broadcasting Directive of 1989[59] does not resolve all the legal questions which can be raised in this context, for the Directive primarily co-ordinates national laws on a limited number of topics such as advertising restrictions and the control of pornography. In particular, it does not restrict the freedom of member states to outlaw the activities of their own broadcasting institutions conducted outside their territories. In the *Veronica* case[60] a Dutch broadcaster had been fined for financing the installation of a commercial station in Luxembourg (aimed at Dutch viewers), an activity contrary to a provision in the Netherlands media law. This rule was intended to preserve the pluralist character of the Dutch broadcasting system. That would be endangered by the use of funds to support a commercial broadcasting service, which would naturally attract viewers, and hence advertisers, away from their support for the Dutch system. The Court affirmed its earlier rulings that member states may act in derogation from the freedoms to provide services and to move capital across national frontiers, when the purpose of such action is to protect a national cultural policy, such as media pluralism.[61]

As far as the Directive is concerned, there has already been a reference to the ECJ by the English courts concerning the interpretation of Articles 2 and 22.[62] The Secretary of State for National Heritage exercised his powers under the Broadcasting Act 1990[63] to proscribe a foreign satellite service. He argued that he was entitled to ban the reception of the Red Hot Dutch channel, transmitted by satellite from Denmark, on the ground that its programme manifestly and seriously infringed Article 22, proscribing the broadcast of violent and pornographic matter. Two questions were referred to the ECJ. The first is whether the power provisionally to suspend 'retransmission' of pornographic broadcasts under Article 2 of the Directive applies to those received directly by satellite dish. Secondly, it is arguably unclear whether Article 22 totally prescribes pornographic and violent programmes which might *seriously* impair the development of minors, or whether they may be shown late at night when it may be assumed children will not normally view them. The former view is almost certainly correct, for the Article contains two distinct provisions; only programmes which might impair the development of minors, though not

[59] Directive 89/552. OJ 1989 L 298/23.

[60] 148/91, *Veronica* v. *Media Commission*, decided by ECJ on 3 Feb. 1993.

[61] See 288/89, *Gouda* v. *Media Commission* [1991] 1 ECR 4007, and 353/89, *Commission* v. *Netherlands* [1991] 1 ECR 4069, where, however, the ECJ found that the advertising and other restrictions were in fact imposed for illegitimate economic ends (see p. 231, n. 64).

[62] *R.* v. *Secretary of State for National Heritage,* ex parte *Continental Television* [1993] 2 CMLR 33 (DC) and [1993] 3 CMLR 387 (CA).

[63] S. 177.

in a serious way, may be shown after a 'watershed' or (to use the American term) during a 'safe harbour'.

A number of other legal difficulties have arisen under the Directive. One of them concerns the fundamental question which state has responsibility for ensuring that broadcasters comply with the Directive's standards. Article 2 imposes this duty on each Member State for all television broadcasts transmitted 'by broadcasters under its jurisdiction' or by broadcasters who make use of a frequency granted by, or a satellite up-link placed in, that country. The Commission takes the view that it is the state where the broadcaster is established, that is, where its head office is situated, which has jurisdiction over it, while the United Kingdom considers it is the state from the territory of which programmes are transmitted.[64] There is something to be said for both sides to this controversy. The Directive should certainly be clarified on this point; otherwise, it would be possible for two states to claim jurisdiction, if, for example, a broadcaster established in Italy were to take over a regional Channel 3 licence. Another difficulty concerns the legality of 24 hour shopping channels. It might seem that such channels contravene the advertising rules, which limit the amount of permissible advertising to 15% of daily transmission time (or 20% for direct offers to the public).[65] But arguably a 24 hour shopping channel does not fall within the advertising rules, since 'television advertising' means any form of announcement broadcast in return for payment or other consideration. Where a channel promotes its own products, the announcements are not broadcast in return for payment and so would appear to fall outside the definition. If that were the case, it would appear there would be nothing to stop a tobacco company promoting its own cigarettes on its own shopping channel; it is doubtful if that was the intention of the Directive.

These uncertainties should be clarified when the Directive is reviewed in October 1994. The Commission is required under the 1989 measure[66] to issue a report on its application and to make further proposals in this area. It has also published a report, submitted to the Council and Parliament, on the states' application of their quota obligations under Articles 4 and 5.[67] It found that about two-thirds of television channels satisfied the obligation to transmit a majority proportion of European works and that the general trend was for greater compliance. The Commission admitted,

[64] Thus the Broadcasting Act 1990, s. 43 defines a 'non-domestic satellite service' broadly as one in which programmes are transmitted from, or programmes are provided by a person in, the United Kingdom.

[65] Directive, Art. 18 (see p. 211).

[66] Art. 26.

[67] COM(94) 57 final. See V. Salvatore, 'Quotas on TV programmes and TV law', (1992) 29 *CMLRev*. 967.

however, that it was dependent on the cooperation of member states for it to monitor progress satisfactorily, and that some of the terms in the Directive provisions, such as 'where practicable' and 'progressively' (see p. 235), might need clarification. However, flexibility was necessary for the obligation to be applied sensitively to both terrestrial and specialist satellite channels.

Index